Lost Souls
The Forgotten Heroes of Eshowe

Book Three of the Anglo-Zulu War

James Mace

Legionary Books
Meridian, Idaho 83642, USA
http://www.legionarybooks.net

First Edition: 2018

Published in the United States of America
Legionary Books

Cover Images by Radoslav Javor, copyright © 2018 by Radoslav Javor and Legionary Books

All photography and maps are used with generous permission from the collection of Ian Knight

We had fearful hard times of it at Eshowe.

- Corporal Frederick License, Royal Engineers

Dedicated in memory of

Technical Sergeant Matthew Comiskey
U.S. Air Force
1975 – 2017

Though the span of life which we enjoy is short, may we make the memory of our lives as long as possible - Sallust

The Works of James Mace

Note: In each series or combination of series', all works are listed in chronological sequence

The Artorian Chronicles
Soldier of Rome: The Legionary
Soldier of Rome: The Sacrovir Revolt
Soldier of Rome: Heir to Rebellion
Soldier of Rome: The Centurion
*Empire Betrayed: The Fall of Sejanus
Soldier of Rome: Journey to Judea
Soldier of Rome: The Last Campaign

*Centurion Valens and the Empress of Death
*Slaves of Fear: A Land Unconquered

The Great Jewish Revolt and Year of the Four Emperors
Soldier of Rome: Rebellion in Judea
Soldier of Rome: Vespasian's Fury
Soldier of Rome: Reign of the Tyrants
Soldier of Rome: Rise of the Flavians
Soldier of Rome: The Fall of Jerusalem

*Die by the Blade

Napoleonic Era
Forlorn Hope: The Storming of Badajoz
I Stood with Wellington
Courage, Marshal Ney

The Anglo-Zulu War
Brutal Valour: The Tragedy of Isandlwana
Crucible of Honour: The Battle of Rorke's Drift
Lost Souls: The Forgotten Heroes of Eshowe
Cruelty of Fate: The Fight for Khambula
Tears of the Dead: Requiem of the Zulu Kingdom

*=Stand-alone novel or novella

Table of Contents

Preface

In January 1879, three columns of British soldiers under the command of Lord Chelmsford, commenced the invasion of the Zulu Kingdom. The southern No. 1 Column led by Colonel Charles Pearson advances on the old mission station at Eshowe. Their intent is to establish a fort and supply depot from which to support the centre No. 3 Column's advance on the Zulu royal kraal at Ulundi. As the vast column of British soldiers and their African allies slogs its way across the coastal hills, the incessant rain and threat of typhoid promise to be as fearful a nemesis as the lurking armies of Zulu warriors.

Unbeknownst to Pearson, calamity struck a hundred miles to the north when nearly half of No. 3 Column is destroyed during a catastrophic battle at a mountain called Isandlwana. Despite the garrison at Rorke's Drift subsequent repelling of the Zulu onslaught, the entire invasion is left in tatters. Over a thousand imperial soldiers now lie dead, in a war which the Crown never authorised or wanted.

Over the coming days, the Zulus surround the fort at Eshowe, cutting off all communications and resupply efforts. With the British Empire now reluctantly committed to war, reinforcements are dispatched from England. In a race against time, Lord Chelmsford rallies the arriving forces into a relief column. Should they fail to break through to Eshowe and relieve the garrison, Colonel Pearson and another thousand British soldiers will suffer the same fate as the poor souls whose bodies still lie unburied along the slopes of Isandlwana.

Cast of Characters

The British

Colonel Charles Knight Pearson – Commanding Officer, No. 1 Column
Brevet Colonel Forestier Walker – Deputy Commanding Officer
Lieutenant Colonel Henry Parnell – Commanding Officer, 2nd Battalion, 3rd Regiment of Foot (the Buffs)
Lieutenant Colonel Henry Welman – Commanding Officer, 99th Regiment of Foot
Commander Henry Campbell – Commanding Officer of the column's Naval Brigade
Major Shapland Graves – Detached from the 3rd Buffs to command the 2nd Regiment, Natal Native Contingent (NNC)
Captain Warren Wynne – Officer Commanding, No. 2 Field Company, Royal Engineers
Midshipman Lewis Coker – A young officer under Campbell's command, he is given charge of the column's Gatling gun crew.

Soldiers of H Company, 2/3rd Buffs

Lieutenant Robert Martin – Officer Commanding, he is an experienced officer having held his commission for eleven years.
Lieutenant Julius Backhouse – Company subaltern of similar age and experience as his officer commanding
Colour Sergeant Richard Bennet – The company's senior Non-Commissioned Officer (NCO). Thirty-three years of age, he's served in the Regiment for nineteen years since first joining as a 'Boy' at the age of fourteen.
Sergeant David Fredericks – A twenty-six-year-old section leader. Born extremely poor, he joined the Army as a means of escaping the workhouses. He now commands a section of twenty imperial redcoats.
Sergeants John Stirling, Arthur Davies – Section leaders
Corporal Robert Anderson – Assistant section leader under Sergeant Fredericks

Lance Corporal James Monroe – A member of Sergeant Frederick's section, also a company sharpshooter and marksmanship instructor.
Privates Charles Hymas, William Dunne, Howard Walters, Jonathan Peters, Harry Davies – Enlisted men

The Relief Column
Lieutenant Colonel Francis Northey – Commanding Officer, 3rd Battalion, 60th Rifles
Major Alexander Bruce – Acting Commanding Officer, 91st Highlanders
Captain Robert Lyttle – Officer Commanding, A Company, 91st Highlanders
Colour Sergeant Stanley Clinton – Senior NCO of A Company

The Zulus
King Cetshwayo kaMpande – King of the Zulus and former ally of the British
Prince Dabulamanzi kaMpande – Brother of King Cetshwayo who disobeyed his sovereign and attacked the British mission station at Rorke's Drift with a corps of 4,000 warriors. Humiliated by his defeat, he promises Cetshwayo he will restore honour to the royal house by expelling the British from his lands in the south of the Zulu Kingdom.
Godide kaNdlela – A seventy-year old *inkosi* and chief of the Nthuli clan whose lands encompass the Thukela regions of the Zulu Kingdom. With most of the *amabutho* rallying at the royal kraal of Ulundi, he has just 6,000 local warriors to face Pearson's onslaught
Mavumengwana kaNdlela – The younger brother of Godide and one of the architects of the Zulu victory at Isandlwana
Phalane kaMdinwa – A highly respected royal *induna*, tasked by King Cetshwayo with aiding Godide in the defence of the southern realm
Matshiya kaMshandu – Chief of the Nzuzu clan, near Eshowe
Somopho kaZikhala – An *inkosi* sent by Cetshwayo to lead the resistance against the invaders

11

Prologue: An Officer of Engineers

Shorncliffe Army Camp, coast of Kent, England
29 November 1878

Captain Warren Richard Colvin Wynne
Officer Commanding, No. 2 Field Company, Royal Engineers

One day's notice. That's all they gave me.

This mantra echoed through the mind of Captain Warren Wynne as he left his home in Eastbourne on the southern coast of England. It was a brisk and drizzly November morning with little time for goodbyes. His orders stated he must hasten to the military camp at Shorncliffe with all speed. There were few other details; only that he was being given command of a field company bound for Southern Africa. A soft kiss to his beloved wife, Lucy, while their sons fought back tears, pleading with their father to be home in time for Christmas, and he was gone.

Born to former Captain John Wynne, Royal Artillery, on 9 April 1843, Warren was the oldest of his surviving siblings. His elder brother and sister tragically died when they were seventeen. A superior student, particularly in the field of mathematics, Warren's

13

early education came at the Royal Naval School, New Cross, where he received numerous awards for academic achievement.

He grew into a modest and pious young man. Outwardly, he exhibited few of the adventurous and jingoistic traits usually found in those within the gentry class who sought a career in Her Majesty's Armed Forces. Indeed, it would have surprised no one had Warren decided to become a minister. He only rarely asked his father about his time with the Royal Artillery, and never spoke of any keen desire to venture off to some far-flung corner of the British Empire. It therefore came as a bit of a surprise, when Warren expressed his desire to follow his father's career path and seek out the Queen's Commission. James Wynne was pleased, though he stressed to his son, "Your talents would be wasted as an infantry officer!"

Given the family's influence, as well as young Warren's academic achievements at New Cross, he was accepted into the Royal Military Academy, Woolwich. Informally known as 'The Shop', the instructors at Woolwich prided themselves on *'nourishing the best brains in the Army'*. They trained cadets to become officers in the Technical Arms of the Forces, specifically the Royal Engineers and Royal Artillery. The curriculum was extremely challenging with emphasis on calculus, geometry, landscape drawing, and various other sciences, as well as experimental philosophy. Additionally, they were taught the standard officer courses on gunnery and military tactics. Due to their superior education, they bypassed the entry-level officer ranks of ensign / 2nd lieutenant and were gazetted as full lieutenants upon graduation.

Though for more reserved than most of his peers, Warren proved to be an astute student. His intent was to commission into the Royal Engineers, where his skills in mathematics might be best put to use. These positions were extremely competitive and offered only to the top ten in each class. Warren proved a quick learner at his military studies, while excelling during every course involving arithmetic and deductive reasoning. He graduated fourth in his class, passing out as an engineer lieutenant on 25 June 1862.

Like all who held the Queen's Commission during the Victorian Era, his promotions came painfully slow. Though the Army abolished the practice of purchasing commissions in 1871, most promotions came from seniority rather than merit. Matters were compounded by the issue of many senior officers holding onto their commissions long after age and infirmity rendered them unfit for active service. Thus, it was only after more than twelve years as a lieutenant that Wynne was finally gazetted to captain in February 1875. And now, after nearly four additional years of Home Service as an ordnance surveyor, he was hastened to assume command of one of the few companies of reinforcements being dispatched to Natal.

Shorncliffe Army Camp was located on the southeast coast of England in Kent. Established in 1794, it was best known for being the training ground of the famous Light Division during the Napoleonic Wars. Warren was quite familiar with the camp, as it was just a few hours by train from his home. He had taken part in numerous military exercises there and helped survey the ground for a new section of permanent barracks blocks. Situated on high ground north of Sandgate, with the open terrain leading towards the harbour at Dover, it was ideal to stage large numbers of troops and equipment bound for the Cape.

As he sat aboard the train, watching a cold mist whipping past the window of the car, Warren was puzzled. Why was he being posted to South Africa with such haste? After all, the war against the Xhosa had ended earlier in the year. He'd heard rumours about the land dispute between the Transvaal Boers, who now fell under British rule, and the powerful neighbouring Kingdom of the Zulus. However, that could not explain the need for hastening a field company of sappers to Natal. Besides, Her Majesty's government had stressed the need for a diplomatic solution between the Crown and the Zulu monarch, King Cetshwayo.

Wynne's thoughts were interrupted at the next station. The rain was now coming down in sheets, battering the windows of the car. The door was hurriedly opened and a lone passenger scrambled into the car, his head bowed. His face was partially hidden by a scarf, the upturned collar of his greatcoat, and a wide-brimmed hat.

The man's eyes lit up when he saw Warren. "Bless me, if it isn't Warren Wynne, Captain of Her Majesty's Royal Engineers!" He removed his hat and scarf, bringing a grin of recognition to Warren's face.

"It's good to see you, too, Walter." Warren stood, and the two clasped hands.

15

The new passenger, Captain Walter Parke Jones, threw off his thoroughly soaked greatcoat. "Well, if this isn't a pleasant surprise," he remarked, taking a seat across from Warren.

"I should have guessed you'd be volunteering for this little expedition," Wynne observed.

"And you didn't?" Jones asked incredulously. "Three years, seven months was more than enough time on Home Service for me, thank you very much! Of course, I have neither wife nor children, so it is up to the Army to keep me gainfully occupied and out of trouble."

The men shared a laugh, as the conductor blew his whistle and the train slowly lurched away from the platform.

Captain Walter Jones was a fellow engineer officer who graduated from Woolwich a year after Wynne. A bachelor with nothing to keep him at home in England, Walter volunteered for every Foreign Service posting he could muster. He served continuously abroad from 1868 to 1875, including three years in Southern Africa where he served under then-Major Anthony Durnford.

"And how is Lucy managing?" Jones asked.

"I am truly blessed to have a wife who understands the military life so well," Warren replied.

It was fortunate that Lucy Wynne was the daughter of a retired Royal Navy captain. Her innate sense of duty was only matched by her love for her husband and their three young sons. The eldest, Arthur, came from Warren's previous marriage. His first wife, Eleanor, having died of complications soon after Arthur was born. Lucy proved to be a loving and devoted mother, raising the young boy as her own. Leaving his family on such short notice, especially so close to the Christmas season, was difficult for the dedicated father and husband. Yet their shared sense of duty to Queen and Empire took precedence over any personal feelings.

"The pain of being apart only magnifies the joy when one returns home," Warren stated philosophically.

His friend shrugged. "The Army's been my mistress ever since I passed out of Woolwich," Jones remarked. "I guess you could say I traded love for adventure."

Wynne chuckled. "Still, nothing like being thrown together at the last possible moment and then rushed off to the Cape. Are they giving you a command?"

16

"Oh, yes!" Walter said, his voice and expression denoting his excitement. "No. 5 Field Company. I had hoped to serve with Durnford again but, from what I hear, he is now commanding native troops rather than acting as an engineer. A shame, really."

"I met him once," Warren recalled. "He was a guest speaker at my passing out ceremony. He was a captain then. I would think he'd be a colonel by now."

"I was with him when he attained lieutenant colonel, albeit that was five years ago. Thankfully, though, I missed that rather dreadful affair at Bushman's Pass. All the damned politicians and newspapers called it *Durnford's Disaster*. Bloody cheek of it all! I wasn't there but given that his natives stayed loyal to him says all I need to know about his character."

"From what I can remember, he's a good man," Wynne added. "I know he lost the use of his left arm, thanks to an enemy spear at Bushman's Pass."

"That he did," Walter affirmed. "And speaking of good men, I hear David Courtney is to be your senior subaltern."

"Yes, I know the name, though I don't think we've met."

"Your company is in good hands, my friend. It's been twelve years since he passed out from The Shop, and I know he was hoping to gain command of No. 2 Field Company. Lord knows, he's overdue for his captaincy."

"To be fair, I had to wait twelve years for my promotion," Warren recalled. "I'll have a word with him when next we see each other. I have two other subalterns, Harry Willock and Thomas Main. I know very little about them, except they each have a few years of experience. At least I'm not dealing with babes straight out of The Shop! I can only hope the Army has given me a good colour sergeant and corps of NCOs to lead our young sappers."

The two captains continued to banter away the time, watching the late autumn rains drizzling outside the rail car. While Jones read from a soggy newspaper, Warren pulled out a silver locket. Inside was a portrait of his beloved Lucy. He gently ran his thumb over it. In his baggage were small framed pictures of his sons and another of the entire family, taken around the previous New Year.

"I'm sorry to miss Christmas, my love," he whispered. "Hopefully I'll be home in time to celebrate next year."

Mercifully, the rains ceased about an hour before they arrived, albeit a fierce wind continued to blow in from the sea. With a loud whistle and the screeching of brakes, the train slowly ground to a halt at the station.

The door to the car was opened and an officer wearing a blue patrol jacket and cap bearing the Royal Engineers insignia climbed in. "Captain Jones," he said, with an appreciative grin. "By God, it's good to see you, sir."

"And you, Mister Courtney."

The officer then looked to Warren. "You must be Captain Wynne."

Warren nodded.

The officer came to attention briefly before extending his hand. "Lieutenant David Courtney, sir." Courtney appeared to be in his early thirties. Slightly taller than Warren, he was strongly built with an iron grip. Warren rightly reckoned his senior subaltern was not averse to getting his hands dirty with the enlisted sappers.

"I have a detail of twenty men to see to your baggage," the lieutenant continued. "I'm to escort you to the camp commandant."

"I may as well join you, as no one from my company has bothered turning up to greet me," Jones remarked.

"Your pardon, sir," Courtney added. "But you are the first from No. 5 Field Company to arrive. The commandant and staff will have all the details for you."

As they disembarked, the wind whipped their greatcoats about; each man clutching his hat close to his head. Lieutenant Courtney guided them over to the camp and to the officers' billets. "At least it will be warmer in South Africa, sir."

It would take a couple hours for his baggage to turn up, so Warren decided to visit the camp commandant—a colonel from the Coldstream Guards—in civilian dress. Doubtless, there was no shortage of work waiting for him. He'd awoken an hour before dawn that morning, and he knew this would be the first of many excruciatingly long days. It would not be until the day after his arrival that Captain Wynne would have the chance to parade his company. As he suspected, there was a slew of administrative tasks to sort out; not least of which was the assignment of a new paymaster-sergeant. He finally retired to his bed well after midnight.

Shorncliffe Army Camp, circa 1850s

The skies were grey, with a cold breeze blowing in from the English Channel as Warren woke around 4.00 the following morning. Fighting the urge to keep yawning, the bleary-eyed officer pulled on his trousers and blue patrol jacket. As he had no batman assigned to him yet, he set about making his own coffee. He used far too many grounds, and the black sludge made his face contort when he quaffed his first cup. Bitter as it was, it sufficed in waking him up.

There was a knock on his door, and as Warren called out, 'Come!' David Courtney stuck his head in.

"Beg your pardon, sir, but we're almost ready for you."

Warren nodded and forced down a second cup of the pungent brew, before donning his patrol cap and stepping out onto the open field nearest his billet.

No. 2 Field Company was formed into a large square, facing their colour sergeant, whose name escaped Wynne at the moment. His soldiers stood with their feet shoulder width apart, hands clasped behind their backs. They wore their heavy greatcoats, with their glengarry caps perched atop their heads. Warren recalled reading in the numerous reports that they had already turned in their blue Home Service helmets and were awaiting issue of the white Foreign Service variant. None of his men carried their rifles, as these had yet to arrive.

19

The sappers were mostly very young, even by standards of the time. Only a few had any sort of a proper moustache gracing the upper lip, and the captain reckoned most were still in their late teens. Thankfully, his NCOs appeared somewhat weathered with sufficient experience between them.

"Company, 'shun'!" the colour sergeant bellowed before doing a sharp about turn to face his officer commanding. The two then exchanged salutes. "The company is yours, sir."

Sapper, Royal Engineers in Home Service kit

The next few days were a near blur, as Captain Wynne dealt with the plethora of issues surrounding the mobilisation of an engineer company. There were not only personnel issues to address, including the late replacement of his paymaster-sergeant, but equipment and logistics transportation. It took three days before the camp quartermaster found the company's weapons and ammunition. Every day there were orders, counterorders, and ever-changing directives as to when the ship would arrive to take them to Southern Africa.

Engineer companies were substantially larger than their infantry counterparts with more than twice as many total soldiers in the ranks. Infantry companies were led by a captain, whereas engineers were commanded by a major, with a captain acting as his second. However, with no engineer majors available, Wynne assumed charge of the company, with the second-in-command position left vacant. Instead of the usual two subalterns, one colour sergeant, four sergeants, and four corporals, Wynne had three subalterns, one colour sergeant, seven sergeants, and seven corporals. Additionally, there were seven second corporals. These were similar in rank to infantry lance corporals, except second corporals were afforded the status of non-commissioned officers whereas lance corporals were not. And while 90 privates made up the bulk of other ranks in an infantry company, an engineer company at full strength numbered just over 200 sappers and drivers. Furthermore, there were billets within each engineer company normally only found at the battalion or regimental level. These included surgeon and paymaster sergeant. All that said, No. 2 Field Company was certainly not at full strength. Captain Wynne had just 125 total troops at his first parade to include officers, NCOs, sappers, and drivers, with no surgeon. However, a telegram from Aldershot reassured him that another thirty sappers and drivers would arrive at the camp before his departure.

During his first parade as officer commanding, Warren took a moment to introduce himself to his men, while stressing patience as they waited for equipment and supplies to arrive, not to mention the urgently-awaited orders that would tell them when they were departing and just where in the Cape Colony they were bound. He further implored his non-commissioned officers to keep their men employed and to ensure discipline was maintained to the highest standards expected of those wearing the uniform of Her Majesty's Forces.

After dismissing the formation, Warren met briefly with his subalterns, as well as the company's senior NCO, whose name the captain quickly recalled was Colour Sergeant Michael Smith. Smith was a tall man with a smooth, boyish face, contrasted sharply by the onset of much grey in his thick hair. This paradox made his age impossible to determine, though Warren could ascertain just from his demeanour and presence that he was a non-commissioned officer of much experience.

Logistics would become their greatest challenge. Field companies of the Royal Engineers were self-sustained, most often attached where needed rather than falling under one specific regiment or higher command. Hence, their logistical needs were particularly daunting. Expanding their transportation requirements was all of their engineer equipment; dozens of shovels and pickaxes,

21

as well as surveying equipment, block and tackle pulleys, and a plethora of other heavy tools needed for repairing roads, crossing rivers, and building forts. On top of it all, their baggage still had all the usual weapons, tents, camping equipment, rations, and ammunition.

Despite the unfamiliar and overwhelming new responsibilities heaped upon him, not to mention insufficient time and resources to get his company ready, Captain Warren Wynne made the best of the situation. For what felt like a single endless day and night, he toiled under the constant deluge of regulations and paperwork. During these stressful times, he was especially grateful for the company of Walter Jones. Though younger and having held his captaincy for less than two years, Jones was an old hand at preparing for overseas service. Something Walter forced on him repeatedly was the need to delegate.

"Make use of your subalterns and NCOs," he explained. "You take care of the paperwork and dealing with the depot staff. Let your immediate subordinates handle the sapper training, discipline, and sorting of your equipment. Honestly, the only time you should be dealing with the enlisted sappers in when some unruly fellow needs to be seriously sorted out, or should a man warrant a promotion or commendation."

While the entire camp looked like a disorganised gaggle—and in many ways it was—remarkably, just three days after Captain Wynne's arrival, No. 2 Field Company was ready for departure. It was with a touch of disbelief that Warren reviewed all of the checklists and saw that every sapper who was going to be assigned to his company had arrived, all weapons, kit, engineer tools, and baggage was issued and accounted for. Wagons and supplies had reached the docks and were ready to load onto transport. Rifles were issued and thoroughly inspected with any deficiencies brought to the attention of the armourer sergeant. Each man now wore his white Foreign Service helmet, adorned with the gleaming crest of the Royal Engineers.

"We're as ready as we're going to be," Lieutenant Courtney remarked on the evening of the First of December.

As he apprised his company, Captain Warren Wynne folded his arms and nodded approvingly.

One day's notice.

Chapter I: A Tedious Voyage

S.S. Walmer Castle
December 1878

The S.S. Walmer Castle

At dawn on Monday, 2 December 1878, No. 2 and No. 5 Field
Companies paraded on the grounds at Shorncliffe for the last time.
Every soldier wore his pack and white Foreign Service helmet, brass
plates gleaming in the early morning sun. Little did any of them
know that most soldiers in Southern Africa removed the brass plates
and stained their helmets a dingy brown soon after they arrived.

The two companies were joined on this damp, cool morning by
the Fife and Drums of the Coldstream Guards, along with the entire
band from the 45th 'Sherwood Foresters' Regiment.

"Company, 'shun'!" shouted Colour Sergeant Smith.

Captains Warren Wynne and Walter Jones, along with their
fellow officers, sat astride their horses. They would ride at a slow
trot in front of the company, leading them on the several-mile trek to
the harbour.

"By the left!" each of the colour sergeants boomed in turn.
"Quick march!"

With a preparatory rolling of the drums, the bands struck up with
The British Grenadiers; one of the official quick marches for the
Royal Engineers. Rifles slung over their right shoulders, over 300

sappers, drivers, and NCOs stepped off smartly, keeping in time with the music. The band continued to play until well after the companies were out of sight.

As they approached the docks where the S.S. Walmer Castle awaited them, Warren found himself shivering beneath his greatcoat. Though it wasn't unusually cold, the closer one came to the sea, the more the frigid air became. The docks were alive with activity as sailors and dockhands conducted the chaotic tasks of loading last-minute supplies and equipment aboard the ship. Near the passenger ramp, the Walmer Castle's captain and first mate, along with an Army quartermaster and adjutant went over the stacks of pages in the cargo and personnel manifest. The senior NCOs of each company halted their troops and told them to stand easy while the officers sorted out matters with the ship's crew.

"Captain Jones, Captain Wynne," the quartermaster said with a nod. "Good to see you."

"It's good to be here," Warren said, despite the sharp chill that ran up his spine.

"First thing we need your men to do is meet with my quartermaster sergeant. He'll issue them their sea service kit. Each man will have a bag with which to store his uniform."

"All supplies seem to be in order," the first mate spoke up. "If you two will kindly finish reviewing the personnel manifests, I'll take you to your quarters."

"Much obliged," Jones acknowledged.

Despite the appearance of utter disorder, both on the docks and aboard the ship, the crew was well-drilled; all knowing exactly where they were supposed to be and what they were doing. By 1.30 that afternoon, all soldiers, horses, and equipment were aboard ship. In addition to the military passengers were five women; the wives of officers and senior NCOs from the 99th Regiment, who were also being transported to the Cape. Four of them shared a pair of cabins. The only one getting her own quarters was Margaret Welman, the wife of the Regiment's commanding officer, Lieutenant Colonel Henry Welman.

According to Queen's Regulations, officers were authorised 195 of cubic feet of space in a private cabin when travelling by sea. Alternatively, they were given 270 cubic feet if two officers shared the space, as Captains Warren Wynne and Walter Jones were compelled to do, given the addition of the female passengers.

Conversely, in the open berths, private soldiers were given just 52 cubic feet of living space with NCOs only marginally more. There was a further 126 cubic feet of space required for each horse.

The sea service kit worn by the enlisted ranks consisted of a blue serge suit with worsted cap. These were thick and heavy with the purpose of saving their uniforms from unnecessary wear before they arrived in Southern Africa. An hour after the last soldier boarded, the Walmer Castle was ready for departure.

Instead of making immediately for the Cape, the ship's first day of travel took them around south-eastern England, docking at the town of Sheerness in the Thames estuary to take on coal. Much to Warren's joy, he was able to visit with his father and youngest brother, Charlie, during the day spent in port. His father-in-law, a retired Royal Navy captain, had learned of the Walmer Castle's unexpected stopover and arranged for John and Charlie Wynne to visit Warren one last time. John Wynne was an old Royal Artillery officer fast approaching his eightieth birthday. He'd slowed considerably since Warren last saw him, yet his eyes were still full of life.

"I wasn't sure if we'd see you before you left," John Wynne said, as his sons assisted him up the last few feet of the boarding plank.

The biting winds blew in from the sea, and the three hurried into Warren's cabin where Walter Jones lay on his bunk beneath several blankets, quietly reading a book. He stood and shook hands with John and Charlie as Warren made the introductions, before returning to the warmth of his bed and the escapism of his book.

"I'll never forget my first voyage across the Empire," John reminisced. "It was just as beastly cold that morning. I was much younger than you, then; little more than a boy. The Duke of York was still our Commander-in-Chief, though we knew Wellington would be his successor. Our voyage was even longer than yours, as we were bound for India. We traded the brisk cold for sweltering heat…" His voice trailed off as his mind wandered into the distant past.

Since they could remember, Warren and Charlie had heard their father tell numerous stories from his years spent with the Colours. Another brother, Arthur, had been so inspired by the elder Wynne's tales of adventure that he joined as soon as he came of age. Now a

26

captain with the 51st Regiment, he had departed for Afghanistan six months earlier.

"I should be glad to hear if he were brevetted to major," John remarked, when the subject of Arthur came up.

"Perhaps once they've given those filthy heathens a damned good thrashing," Charlie added.

"Perhaps." John smiled briefly, his eyes betraying concern for his son. After a moment, his expression became boisterous once more. He reached over and smacked Warren on the knee. "And it's about time Her Majesty's Forces got some use out of you."

"I have not lacked for work," Warren replied with a short laugh.

His father waved his hand dismissively. "Bah! Your talents are wasted building barracks blocks in Britain, my boy. The Empire needs more than men who can fight. She needs men with great minds." He tapped his finger against the side of his head. He then scowled as he spoke, in rather unflowering terms, about the British senior magistrate in the Cape. "Bartle-Frere is a pompous buffoon, and Lord Carnarvon was a fool for naming him High Commissioner. They are both convinced they can simply confederate Southern Africa. Yet, they know nothing about the troublesome Dutch and the various kaffir tribes. And how do the neighbouring Zulus fit into his little scheme?"

Warren winced at the mention of the Zulus. To most Britons, they were little more than one black-skinned tribe of savages among many. However, like his father, Warren had read extensively about the multitude of peoples in Southern Africa, particularly the Zulus. Culturally, the Zulus, Swazi, Xhosa, and other tribes were as varied as the English, Scots, Welsh, Irish, and numerous peoples of continental Europe. Few in Britain bothered to remember that it was King Shaka of the Zulus who gave the land that became Port Natal to the British in the first place.

"We've just finished one war in the Cape," Warren noted. "Let us hope cooler heads prevail before another one erupts."

"Yes," his father agreed. "Particularly with Arthur already fighting in Afghanistan. The British Empire is the largest the world has ever known, yet our armies can only manage so many conflicts at one time. Should Bartle-Frere drag Britain into another war, it will take minds like yours, as much as the rifle and bayonet, to see us through."

A few moments of silence followed before John abruptly changed the subject. "But enough about the troubles of Empire. It's a pity Lucy and the boys could not come see you off."

"Yes, well, it is difficult to travel with a new-born," Warren said. "Charles is just seven months old, and Harry barely a year older."

"Does Lucy plan on joining you in Natal?" Charlie asked.

"That all depends on how long I'll be away. I only had a day's notice before I was sent to Shorncliffe to assume command of my company. We've received no word yet regarding what our mission is or why we're being sent to the Cape in such haste."

"I think we can guess," John added.

His sons nodded in concurrence.

"I hope to only be gone a year," Warren continued. "However, should Her Majesty need my sappers in South Africa for longer, then yes, I would send for my family. Perhaps Arthur will be talking to me by then."

The three shared a smile at the mention of Warren's oldest son, named after his brother. A precocious boy of five, he could not understand why his father was leaving them so close to Christmas. At that age, he did not yet comprehend the concepts of duty and service to the Empire. On the morning of Warren's departure, young Arthur had buried his head in his mother's skirts and cried as the train pulled away from the platform.

There was a loud knock on the door, and a subaltern from Walter Jones' company stuck his head in. "Beg your pardon, sir, but we will be casting off soon."

"Never enough time," John Wynne sighed.

"We'll make the time when I return," Warren promised, as he helped him stand. He wrapped his greatcoat around himself before escorting his father and brother to the boarding ramp. Both John and Charlie promised to keep a close eye on Lucy and the boys.

Warren returned to the cabin and wrote a hasty letter to Lucy and gave it to the ship's pilot. In it, he promised to write again when they reached Madeira; the Portuguese-owned island several hundred miles to the west of Morocco. He also told his wife he would be keeping a detailed diary of his exploits in the far-flung corners of the Empire, which he intended to share with their sons someday.

On the morning of 3 December 1878, following a 10.00 parade of No. 2 and No. 5 Field Companies, along with the eight companies of infantry from the 99th Regiment, they at last departed for South Africa.

A shared officers' cabin aboard ship, from *The Graphic*

As expected, life aboard ship proved tediously dull for officer and enlisted soldier alike. Other than morning and evening parade on the top deck, there was little for the men to do. Card games were the most common way for soldiers to keep themselves occupied. Those who were literate read whatever books or magazines they could find. Some evenings the sappers would slide their bunks together, creating enough space in the open bay to stage skits or song-and-dance routines. These were often quite bawdy in nature.

With no work for the men, and only scant entertainment, Captain Wynne was concerned about the discipline of his extremely bored sappers. Surprisingly, during the first week, there were no issues to speak of. Whenever a soldier became a bit unruly, a quick cuff across the ear and a few profane words from his corporal sorted the matter. During his very first parade on deck, the officer commanding made it clear he wanted all disciplinary issues sorted at the lowest level possible. If a problem could be taken care of by a corporal or second corporal, so much the better. Only the most severe issues, such as gross insubordination or assault upon a superior, were to be brought to the attention of Captain Wynne and Colour Sergeant Smith. Thankfully, no such incidents were reported to the officer commanding.

To make the best use of his own time, Captain Wynne held meetings with his subordinate leaders in No. 2 Field Company during the early days of their voyage. While he worked closely each day with the subalterns and colour sergeant, he wished to know more about his non-commissioned officers. On the third day at sea, he held a two-hour meeting with the sergeants, and on the following day another with the corporals and second corporals. There was some variance, but most of the corporals and sergeants in No. 2 Company were in their mid to late twenties. All were knowledgeable in their craft, though only three sergeants, three corporals, and one second corporal had Foreign Service experience. Among these, Sergeant Richard Small had served in Southern Africa ten years earlier under then-Lieutenant Walter Jones. At thirty-six, he was the oldest and most experienced of the NCOs. Corporal Jason Peters was the youngest at just nineteen.

While Warren was confident in the technical and leadership skills of his non-commissioned officers, the man who inspired him the most was the company's senior NCO, Colour Sergeant Michael Smith. His voice carried far, yet he rarely raised it. Forty-one years of age, and the oldest member of No. 2 Field Company, Colour Sergeant Smith had just reached twenty-seven years with the Colours, the first four of which were as a 'Boy'. His previous service had seen him spend ten years in India and another four in Egypt. And while the senior NCO of a company was mostly concerned with training, discipline, and personnel issues, Michael Smith was an adept engineer in his own right. His understanding of field fortifications and the use of natural terrain were as good as any instructor at Woolwich.

"A pity you never became an officer," Warren said as the two leaned over the starboard rail on the mid deck. It was their fourth evening at sea, and the two were enjoying a splendid sunset over the ocean.

"Circumstances of my birth precluded that from ever happening, sir," Smith replied. "When one is the sixth child of a railway porter and a washerwoman, acquiring the Queen's Commission does not come up on the list of prospective careers."

"Still, you've done well for yourself."

"I left home at fourteen to join the Army as a Boy," the colour sergeant explained. "My parents were a bit sad when I left, though I think they were relieved to have one less mouth to feed."

The captain showed no surprise at this revelation. It was an all-too-common story among the enlisted soldiers; leaving home and joining the Army as a means of escaping the desperate poverty of Britain's lower working classes.

"I suspect this will be my last Foreign Service tour," the colour sergeant said, with a change of the subject.

"Why would you say that? Are you contemplating retirement?"

"I was," Smith admitted. "Then I was told the depot sergeant major at Aldershot is retiring in about a year, and my name is on the short-list to replace him. So, one more adventure abroad in Her Majesty's service. If I am not selected to be the next depot sergeant major, then yes, I will retire. Sergeant Small has been anxious for me to vacate this position for at least a couple years now. It would be rude to keep him waiting too much longer."

The first port call came on the fifth day of their voyage when the Walmer Castle reached the Portuguese island of Madeira. A thick mist clung to the ship throughout the morning, turning into torrential rain the closer they drew to the island. They reached the coal barge a little after noon. The engineer officers, along with those from the ship and the handful of ladies, braved the violent swells in rowboats as they headed ashore. Unfortunately for the enlisted soldiers, sappers, and ship's crew, there would be no shore leave. Even the officers would only have about three hours on land before they had to return to the Walmer Castle.

It was Sunday, and Warren had hoped to take in a church service. These were an extremely important part of his life back home. With no chaplain aboard the ship and so little time for such matters at Shorncliffe, he'd gone two weeks without partaking in religious services. Though a devout Anglican, even a Catholic Mass would have soothed his soul. His hopes were quickly dashed when he learned the local church had ended its weekly service two hours earlier. Despite this, and the incessant rain, he found the city of Funchal to be rather idyllic. He especially loved the Cathedral of Funchal, built in the late 1400s of cedar wood and surprisingly still well kept. The residents of the island were a fascinating mixture of Portuguese and various African peoples.

Besides being a stopover where steamships took on coal, Madeira housed the last telegraph station between Southern Africa and Europe. This meant that any communiqués from the Cape had to first be sent up by steamship from Cape Town; a journey that could take up to two weeks. This caused an oft-unnerving delay in message traffic between London and the colonies in South Africa.

Their short, wet sightseeing tour was over before it seemed like it had even begun, and by supper time the handful of officers and ladies were being ferried back to the Walmer Castle to continue the long voyage to the Cape.

Funchal Cathedral

On the 11th of December, with the Walmer Castle steaming its way along the western coast of Africa, Sir Henry Bartle-Frere issued his hateful ultimatum to the Zulu people. With conditions so damning and impossible for King Cetshwayo to comply with, the High Commissioner was setting the British Empire on an inevitable course for war with the Zulu Kingdom. Though everyone aboard the Walmer Castle, and indeed back home in Britain, was oblivious to this development, there was still much talk among the officers and sappers about the possibility of war with the Zulus. Officers talked incessantly about how this could lead to brevet promotions, while the enlisted men hoped for a 'Zulu War Medal' to adorn their uniforms.

"You have to admit, a campaign medal would be a nice addition to your uniform, especially if it comes with a brevet to major," Walter Jones remarked a couple weeks later, as he and Warren enjoyed their morning cup of coffee at the railing of the ship. Endless miles of ocean stretched out in every direction.

The brevet was a type of promotion offered to captains and above, who were either occupying a billet above their rank or for exceptional service. The brevetted officer would wear the insignia and be addressed as such; however, he would still be paid at his substantive rank. In an age where promotions were almost strictly by seniority, with officers often left languishing as lieutenants well into their thirties, campaign medals, mentions in despatches, and brevets for exceptional service were all ways to stand out amongst their peers and hasten the climb up the ladder.

"You might have the opportunity to win a brevet," Warren replied, before taking a sip of his piping-hot coffee. "I have no interest in such things."

"That is because you're modest to a fault, old friend. Field companies are supposed to be commanded by majors, so that already gives us an advantage. Besides, you have seniority between us."

"Seniority but not experience," Wynne corrected. "You, sir, have spent many years on Foreign Service, to include Southern Africa."

Jones chuckled and shrugged nonchalantly. "Well, last time I was in the Cape was nearly five years ago, and that was for a hunting trip to commemorate my tenth year with the Colours."

Walter took a long drink of his coffee, letting out a contented sigh before furrowing his brow in contemplation. "Say, today is Christmas Eve, is it not?"

"It is," Warren replied, with a note of melancholy. This would be his first Christmas away from Lucy and the boys.

The following morning, after talking with the ship's first mate who said they were still about three days from Cape Town, Warren sat at the tiny metal desk in his cabin and wrote another letter to his wife.

33

Christmas Day – I began the day by thanking God for that which we commemorate upon it, and then wished for you a 'Happy Christmas' in the truest sense of the words, and prayed that when it comes around next, we may spend it together with the dear children around us. I must say it has been very difficult to realise the fact of its being Christmas Day as far as external appearances go. I can but imagine your Christmas at home, with all the dear ones around you; the joyous church services, the congratulations, the Christmas cards, and above all the happy faces of the children.

We ought to be at Cape Town early on Saturday, i.e. three days hence, and glad indeed shall I be to be on terra firma again, and to learn particulars as to what is before us. I hope that by giving Cetshwayo and the Zulus a crushing blow now, they may be kept quiet for a long time to come.

I wonder whether the London papers will send out any correspondent to inform people at home of our doings. I hope so, for I shall find it difficult to communicate with you when in the field. I expect, however, that the Afghan affair will so eclipse ours that, but scanty notice will be taken of it, and yet to compare the two foes both in numbers and prowess, ours is the most formidable by all accounts, in cunning also, but their arms are inferior. I hope I shall hear something of their doings out there before we go up to the front. This time last year, Arthur was busy with his signalling operations in the expedition against the Jowakies. I wonder how he has succeeded this year in Afghanistan. I should like to train some signallers for our expedition, and may perhaps do so, for they would be very useful; but with so many other things on hand it is doubtful whether I could manage it.

Warren paused and set down his pen. While he was always very open with Lucy about his profession, did his Christmas letter really need to be so full of military speak? Then again, his letters were a compliment to his diary, which he hoped to share one day with his sons. He was a bit surprised by his wording of the potential conflict with King Cetshwayo and the Zulus. He knew nothing about the High Commissioner's ultimatum, but it was clear their two engineer companies being hastened so abruptly to the Cape portended the possibility of war.

His thoughts were interrupted by Walter Jones abruptly opening the door to their cabin. He was joined by the six subalterns from both companies. David Courtney carried a slew of tin mugs. One of Jones' officers held up a large bottle of brandy.

"No sense moping about when we have an entire bottle of Christmas cheer to share," the lieutenant remarked.

Though usually not one for the harsher of spirits, Warren gladly took a mug filled nearly half full of pungent drink. As soon as all the cups were distributed, the assembled officers stood in a circle and brought their mugs together.

"Happy Christmas, friends," Walter said.

"And a blessed New Year," Warren added.

Chapter II: Finally Here

Durban, Natal Colony, South Africa
28 December 1878

Table Mountain, just outside of Cape Town

By the time Captain Wynne and No. 2 Field Company arrived in
Cape Town on 28 December, Sir Henry Bartle-Frere's ultimatum
was two weeks from expiring with no peaceful resolution in sight.
Of course, no one aboard the Walmer Castle was yet aware of the
severity of the crisis with the Zulus. That morning, a Major Nixon
boarded the ship to inform Captains Wynne and Jones that the
women, children, and some of the baggage would be offloaded at
Cape Town within the day.

"Gentlemen," the major then said, "would you do me the honour
of joining my wife and I for lunch?"

"We'd be delighted, sir," Warren answered.

"Splendid! Also, Mrs. Frere is hosting a garden party this
afternoon in Wynberg. It's a short distance by rail, and I think it will
do you some good."

"We'll wear our best frocks, sir," Jones said reassuringly. He
called to one of his subalterns, "Mister Chard! Be a good man and
take charge of the offloading of our stores. I will return by evening."

"I'll see to it, sir," the lieutenant replied.

As the two captains walked down the loading plank, Warren felt
compelled to remove his hat and run his forearm across his already

sweaty brow. The drastic change in climate was a great shock for him. While frost clung to the ground in the English winter, the South African summer was stifling hot. Intensifying this was the dense humidity. Summer was also the rainy season in the Cape and the air felt thick to breathe.

"I say, we'll be nice and sweaty by the time we reach Wynberg," Warren observed.

"Ah, I keep forgetting this is your first trip to Southern Africa," Jones recalled.

"Sixteen years I've held the Queen's Commission," Warren noted. "And aside from a stint in Gibraltar, my entire career has been spent on Home Service. At least you're familiar with the Cape."

"It's been a few years," Walter reminded him.

"That fellow of yours, Chard's his name?" Wynne asked later, as they sat in a private car on the train bound for Wynberg. He noted the exacerbated expression on his friend's face at the mention of the lieutenant.

"He wasn't one of mine until recently. I didn't even have a vacancy, yet the fellows at Aldershot decided they needed to give him to me as an excess subaltern. He's a likeable enough fellow, even if he is completely hopeless."

"How so?" Warren asked.

"For starters, since when did 'The Shop' start offering engineer commissions to those who graduate towards the bottom of their class?" Jones grumbled. "I'll grant you, he's a capable enough builder and proved competent when assisting in the design of naval fortifications in Bermuda and Malta. That said, he lacks any sort of drive or ambition. He'll do what he's told and competently so, but he never takes the initiative. And unless one tells him to take charge of a project or task, he's quite content to allow others to sort it out. I swear I have never met an officer with less energy!"

Warren cracked an involuntary smirk at his friend's plight. He was grateful his own subalterns were men of both competence and ambition. Lieutenant Courtney was especially capable with more than a decade of experience, and Wynne hoped he was not long for his captaincy.

"Quite a beautiful country." Warren changed the subject, gazing out the open window of their car. With the rainy season in Southern

Africa came the foliage, green and lush. The prominent and aptly named Table Mountain stood majestically over Cape Town.

"From the top, one can see far across the ocean," Walter added.

"I've had my share of oceans for the time being," Wynne said, drawing a short laugh from his friend.

Wynberg was an old suburb of Cape Town dating back to the late 1600s. As the train pulled into the small platform, what surprised Warren the most was how much of the population consisted of white Europeans. Were it not for the heat and extreme humidity, he would have thought they were back in England, disembarking at Basingstoke or Reading. The black Africans he did see were all dressed in European clothing much like the working classes in Britain. He pointed this out to his friend as they disembarked and started the short walk to the Frere house.

"Class and social order exist as much in the colonies as they do back home," Walter observed. "I would say it is even more so here, as the kaffirs add another layer to the class structure. Most of the unskilled labourers and servants in Cape Town are natives. Not slaves, mind you, as the Empire had the decency to outlaw such barbarism nearly half-a-century ago. But like the poor classes in England, they know their place."

From Warren's initial observations, aside from skin colour, there was little to differentiate the black and white working-class peoples in Cape Town. Most of the whites spoke with familiar English and Scottish accents, which served as another reminder of home.

"Wherever we go, it is still England," Walter mused. He added with a short laugh, "Of course, I try not to use that phrase around my friends who happen to be Scottish, Irish, or Welsh! The further we go inland, the more you'll see the various European peoples who settled here. We tend to call all of them 'Boers', which is a Dutch term meaning 'farmer'. However, there are plenty of Germans, French, and even the occasional Italian or Spaniard among them. Once we leave Cape Town, which is really the heart of civilisation in this forgotten corner of the Empire, the less civilised the blacks tend to dress."

Major Nixon was waiting for them at the gates leading into the back garden at the Frere house. The two captains came to attention and saluted.

"Good to see you both made it," Nixon said, returning the courtesy. "I wanted to talk with you first. No doubt you're anxious for news from the front."

"Most definitely, sir," Walter asserted. "All we heard were rumours about possible trouble with the Zulus."

"It looks to be more than just a spot of trouble," the major explained. "The High Commissioner issued an ultimatum to King Cetshwayo on the 11th. It expires in two weeks."

"What were the terms?" Warren asked.

"I'll not bore you with the details for now. Suffice it to say, Sir Henry Bartle-Frere is demanding Cetshwayo disband his regiments and subject himself to the will of the Crown."

"No independent king will agree to that," Wynne conjectured.

"Which means our mission is to make the king no longer independent," Walter remarked.

"The General Officer Commanding, Lord Chelmsford, has already been preparing for this," Major Nixon continued. "Even now, three columns of imperial soldiers, local volunteers, and native auxiliaries are making their way to staging points along the frontier. His lordship has been asking Horse Guards to send reinforcements for months. And with the troubles in Afghanistan, your engineers are all we've received so far."

"Then I guess his lordship will have to make the most of us," Warren said.

The garden party proved uneventful, with just a handful of military officers, most of whom neither Warren Wynne nor Walter Jones were familiar with, along with a few local magistrates. Catherine Frere proved an amiable host, though she apologised that her husband was detained on urgent business in Pietermaritzburg. Warren could only speculate as to what said 'urgent business' was.

The following morning, Lieutenant David Courtney escorted the six women and five children off the ship and to their quarters; a large, single-room barracks. His wife was among the spouses, and she set about assisting the other families with making themselves comfortable. As much as he dearly missed Lucy and his sons, Warren was glad to not have the added concerns over his family's welfare, in addition to his daunting responsibilities as officer commanding of No. 2 Field Company.

They were soon compelled to say their goodbyes, as they boarded the ship once more for the five-day journey around the southern Cape to Durban. Warren spent his days chronicling the events of the past few days in his journal and completing a series of letters to his wife and family. He had heard about the notorious submerged sandbar which bisected the harbour at Durban and made disembarking a labour-intensive and hazardous task. He made mention of this in one letter to his brother, Charles, stating 'We should be in for a spot of adventure just getting off the ship!'

Storms and rough seas precluded their disembarking at Durban. The ship's captain elected to keep them further out to sea until the weather calmed. On the afternoon of 3 January, the harbour finally came into view. It would be another two days before any of the enlisted men, who had not left the ship since departing Britain, would finally go ashore.

The Walmer Castle sent a heliograph signal to the harbour, letting them know the two engineer companies and battalion of redcoats had arrived. That afternoon, a staff officer took a lighter out to meet with the engineer captains and Lieutenant Colonel Welman of the 99th Regiment.

"Gentlemen," the staff officer began, "as you know, Her Majesty's representative in the Cape has issued an ultimatum to King Cetshwayo. We do not anticipate him meeting the High Commissioner's demands, and so we must send all reinforcements to the columns post haste." He turned to Welman. "Colonel, sir. Your regiment will disembark at once and make its way east, to link up with Colonel Pearson and the No. 1 Column at Lower Drift."

Welman nodded. "I see from my maps that it is approximately 75 miles to the Thukela River. What can I expect for roads?"

"A muddy quagmire, I'm afraid, sir. There's been a drought the last few years in the Cape that ended abruptly a few weeks ago. Expect a day of rain for every one of sunshine for the next few months."

"We'll make due," the colonel asserted.

The staff officer then addressed Warren. "Captain Wynne, you will also be joining No. 1 Column. However, as combat troops take priority, we will not be able to send yours and Captain Jones' companies ashore until tomorrow."

"And if the infantry struggle on the muddy roads, I can only imagine how our heavy wagons will fare," Wynne observed.

"Where does his lordship need my sappers?" Walter Jones asked.

"Yours is an even longer trek," the staff officer answered. "You've been assigned to Colonel Glyn's No. 3 Column. They are mustering at Rorke's Drift about 160 miles north of here."

The remainder of the afternoon and well into the next day was spent preparing their personnel and equipment for disembarking. There were more than a few grumbles from the young sappers, who were nearly mad with tedium from having been at sea for nearly four weeks. The stopover in Cape Town was a cruel tease to them when only the officers had been allowed to disembark.

"The men are anxious," Colour Sergeant Smith explained that evening, as he met with Captain Wynne in his cabin. "However, they know that the sooner they complete their work, the sooner they can be off this ship."

"Meantime, I need to see about our provisions," the captain remarked. He had drawn up an extensive list of necessities he needed to sort out with the Commissary of Stores before his company could even think about beginning its trek towards Lower Drift. There were tents, camping equipment, tea kettles, cups, and other necessities that they had not brought with them from England. Furthermore, they needed to draw a month's allotment of rations. These consisted mainly of hard biscuits and tinned bully beef, though Warren intended to acquire as much grain and fresh vegetables as possible. Perhaps he might even be able to procure a few head of cattle to provide 'food on the hoof'.

The landing for the forces at Durban proved to be as chaotic as Warren feared it would be. Men, horses, and equipment alike had to be lowered in baskets onto the lighters and tugs waiting below. The rougher the rolling swells, the more awkward and precarious the transfer became. Fortunately, there were no losses of men or equipment, though many a soldier banged his knees, elbows, and other appendages as they were tossed about. The two captains went ashore with the first wave of equipment, tasking their senior subalterns and colour sergeants with overseeing the disembarking of their sappers and baggage. Regrettably, no provisions had been made by the critically understaffed commissariat to procure rations for their men. So, Warren took on the task of walking the streets of

Durban, locating grocers and venders to supply as much fresh produce as possible.

In addition to the acquisition of tents, camping equipment, and rations, Warren needed sufficient wagons and draught animals to haul their equipment. By comparison, an infantry company required just two wagons; one for tents and rations, the other for ammunition. Engineer field companies, on the other hand, needed at least ten wagons to haul their tools and engineer equipment, in addition to ammunition, rations, and tents. It was simply a matter of bad timing that the commissariat and quartermaster staff dispatched to the Cape had yet to arrive. The few who were on hand laboured diligently to ensure the engineers and redcoats from the 99th were properly equipped; however, the task was overwhelming. Of his own initiative, Captain Warren Wynne managed to procure seven mule wagons with sixty-two mules, fourteen horses, and four ox wagons.

By the evening of the 5th, both engineer companies were ashore with the young sappers all glad to be able to finally stretch their legs. A few remarked that when it came time to return home, they would sooner walk all the way back to Blighty. Their equipment was inventoried and stored in a large tin shed their officer commanding had acquired the use of. The newly-issued tents were erected and by midnight the company at last turned in for its first night on land. One could not exactly use the term 'dry land'. As the bugler sounded lights out, the heavens opened with a torrential rain soaking the entire camp.

"Welcome to South Africa, sir," Lieutenant David Courtney said.

He and the other subalterns joined their captain in his tent. The men had to speak loudly over the pummelling rain that echoed off the roof, while wind beat against the door flap.

"We've made a good start, gentlemen," Warren said, reviewing the notes he'd scribbled throughout the day. "Tomorrow will be labour-intensive, so I hope the men get some sleep tonight. In addition to our equipment and stores, it looks like we will be transporting ration and other resupplies for the main column. This means we will have an extremely large convoy of wagons to escort. I checked the local map, and it is sixty-six miles from here to Lower Drift."

"If this damnable country had decent roads, we could make that in about three days," Lieutenant Willock spoke up.

"Unfortunately, the only roads here are dirt tracks that are likely flooded quagmires," David Courtney remarked.

"Here are your tasks for tomorrow," Warren said, handing each subaltern a sheaf of papers. "My intent is to work our backsides off tomorrow and be ready to march on the 7th. The ultimatum to King Cetshwayo expires on the 11th, after which the British Empire will be at war with the Zulu Kingdom."

Nothing else needed to be said. Every man in No. 2 Field Company understood the sense of urgency facing them. Regardless of when the Zulus and the Crown went to war, Captain Wynne hoped that Colonel Pearson would refrain from beginning his advance until after the engineers arrived. He did not envy his friend, Walter Jones, whose journey to join No. 3 Column at Rorke's Drift was nearly three times as long. As Warren understood it, Lord Chelmsford was accompanying this particular column. He could only hope that the GOC did not act in haste.

The day had been long and gruelling, but Warren was satisfied with how he and his company had managed. The rain still beating down, he sat on the edge of his camp bed. With only the faint glow from an oil lamp, he wrote a brief letter to his wife. He then checked his pocket watch and saw that it was nearly 2.00. With wakeup scheduled for 4.30, Warren blew out the lamp and attempted to get a couple hours of sleep.

The previous night's rains left the entire camp a soupy mess. And yet, on the morning of 7 January, the sun shone brightly over the horizon. It promised to be a hot day, the air thick, as the scorching heat burned off the remnants of the night-time showers. While the subalterns set about the tasks Warren had assigned them, NCOs, sappers, and drivers laboured to sort out the numerous carts and wagons. Captain Wynne, meanwhile, rode his horse back into town to continue requisitioning the last of their stores. He also sought out the head commissary to see about the supplies they were escorting to No. 1 Column. He found Captain Walter Jones conducting similar tasks for his own company. The two had been nearly inseparable since the train ride to Shorncliffe, yet they'd scarcely seen each other since coming ashore at Durban. It was now nearly time for them to say goodbye.

"I see you've found a use for Lieutenant Chard," Wynne noted, nodding towards a light equipment wagon.

In addition to tents and some personal baggage, it held mostly shovels, pickaxes, and a few block and tackle pulleys. Six sappers loaded the wagon, under the supervision of a lone corporal. Chard, meanwhile, was content to observe while his batman sorted out his master's saddlebags and kit.

"Ah, yes. I told him if Her Majesty was going to pay him to be an officer, then he needed to act like one and start actually leading. It was nothing to find a few volunteer sappers plus his batman."

"Did you deliberately choose the youngest men in your company?" Warren asked, noting the youthful faces of Chard's sappers.

"Every soldier under the age of twenty is all-too-anxious to please," Jones conjectured. "It's only after a few shoddy details, consisting of back-breaking toil with little reward, that they wise up and never volunteer for anything again." They shared a knowing laugh.

Walter then remarked, "Driver Robson's a good lad. I told him to look after his officer like a batman should."

Wynne looked to his own convoy of wagons and sappers. Draught oxen and mules were being yoked, while NCOs got accountability of their soldiers and kit. All told, Captain Warren Wynne now had twenty-six wagons, nineteen horses, fifty-six mules, and three hundred and sixteen oxen under his charge. And while he had been unable to procure any wayward cattle, the commissariat had managed to help him scrounge up twenty-eight sheep as 'food on the hoof'. While these would only suffice to feed his men for a few days, just the idea of fresh meat would help raise his men's spirits.

"It looks like this is where I leave you, old friend." He turned and extended his hand to Walter, who firmly clasped it in return.

"Shall I race you to Ulundi?" Jones grinned.

Warren laughed and replied, "A case of brandy to the first man who reaches the king's kraal!"

No sooner had they departed Durban, Captain Warren Wynne and his company of engineers learned just how obstructed the roads in Southern Africa became when pummelled by a constant deluge from the heavens. It did not help matters any that most of No. 1 Column had already passed this way. They, along with the usual civilian merchant traffic between Durban and the town of Stanger had churned the muddy roads up terribly.

Every night their camp was subjected to torrential downpours and flooding tents, leaving soldiers and their kit soaked. The days were often rainy as well. Adding insult to injury, the men sank up to their calves in the sucking mud during much of the march. For every mile they trekked, the wagons laden with thousands of pounds of tools and baggage would have to be dug out several times. By the end of the first day, every man in No. 2 Field Company was a muddy, bedraggled mess. Their once bright crimson uniforms were streaked with filth. Still, they managed to keep a quicker pace than expected, travelling thirteen miles the first day and fifteen the second. Reveille sounded at 4.00 each morning, with the convoy ready to move out by 6.00. Each daily march lasted twelve hours, including the time needed for grazing oxen. This meant they averaged a mile to a mile-and-a-half every hour.

Though the road was meant to bisect the rivers at fording points, also known as *drifts*, it was a gamble as to whether anything could cross at all. Given the volatile weather and constant rains, it seemed to be mere chance whether the rivers would be in flood or passable. Even with viable drifts, it still took hours to get the entire convoy across each span of water.

"At least we know none of us will die of thirst," Colour Sergeant Smith said good-naturedly. He stood with his officer commanding, watching the wagons lumber away from their latest camp while the rain beat down on them.

"It does add a rather delicious smell to the air," Wynne observed, inhaling deeply through his nose. "You know, I keep hearing about the incessant heat of the Natal summer. So far, it has not been any worse than a June afternoon in England. I find the shrubs and wildflowers very striking. I've read about the cacti in drier climes of the Empire, yet here they grow twenty feet high!"

"Nothing troubles you, does it, sir?"

Warren shrugged. "Why should it? Wouldn't do me or the lads any use if it did. As long as I've got my health, there is nothing to complain about."

"Amen to that, sir."

The manner in which the colour sergeant said this last phrase gave Captain Wynne pause. He was uncertain if Smith was being sincere, or patronising. He seemed to recall hearing that whenever a chaplain was around, or if there was a church service being held, Colour Sergeant Michael Smith was conspicuous by his absence. He decided to pay it no mind for the time being. Whatever Smith's beliefs, they were his own business.

Health and hygiene was something the captain took with utmost seriousness. He daily stressed to his subalterns and NCOs the need for the men to take care of their kit, and that it in turn would take care of them. In particular they needed to maintain their greatcoats, which were the only things keeping many of them from catching pneumonia or typhoid in the unremitting rains.

The morning of the 11th, dawned bright. One of their wagons became upset in the mud near the Umhlati River the previous day and had to be unloaded, righted, and repaired. The company could not continue on until it caught up to them, and so Wynne gave his men time to wash both themselves, as well as their uniforms. He'd tasked Lieutenant Courtney with the wagon recovery detail and was glad to see his senior subaltern returning by horseback.

Courtney dismounted near the column of wagons and spoke to one of the other subalterns before walking over and saluting his captain.

"The wagons are ready to move out, sir. And we've repaired the broken axel from that unfortunate mishap yesterday. They should be joining us within the hour."

"Very good, Mister Courtney. It will be a late start today, but I'd rather the men be clean and the wagons in good repair."

The company had risen at 6.00, giving the tired soldiers a couple extra hours of sleep. At 10.45, with the sun high overhead, Captain Wynne gave the order to move out. He rode ahead with Courtney and a few escorts, soon reaching the Umvoti River. They all let out a resigned sigh at coming upon yet another river. This one was 100 yards in width with water waist deep. Thankfully, it was slow-flowing and the sappers would have little difficulty crossing. Having just cleaned their uniforms, Warren ordered them to strip down and carry their clothes and weapons overhead. The riverbed was mostly loose pebbles and small rocks which prevented the wagons from sinking too far. This made their latest crossing one of the least painful of the journey thus far. It was now only four miles to the column's supply depot at Stanger, and the company arrived around 3.30 that afternoon. Warren sought out the depot's commanding officer, an older major from the Army Service Corps. The two met in a rickety hotel being used as an officers' billet, as well as headquarters.

"What news from the column, sir?" Wynne asked.

"They began crossing the Thukela River yesterday," the major answered. "It was a nightmare for the lads from the Naval Brigade. One of their number got sucked under by the current. Poor lad. I was told that the first shots were fired yesterday; no other details. My guess is it was simply a few pot shots at their scouts, or else our own reconnaissance patrols getting a bit jittery and firing at shadows. Either way, it looks like the Zulus and the Crown are now at war."

"I see that it's seventeen miles to the drift from here." Warren pointed to a map on the table. "We've managed forty-five miles over the past four days. It will be a stretch to reach the Thukela by tomorrow."

The major concurred. "Yes, and there's two river crossings between here and there. The road leading out of Stanger is mostly clay. It's solider than what you've come through; however, the rains have rendered it very slippery. I imagine there will be a few bruised bottoms amongst your lads from falling onto their backsides."

"It's not them I worry about," Warren replied. "It's our damned draught animals. Several of our oxen have become sick, and one has died. Big, brutal beasts, yet they are surprisingly frail of health."

"And draught animals are something we cannot afford to lose," the major said candidly. "There is already a shortage in all the columns. As I understand it, Colonel Glyn's transportation officers with No. 3 Column are having to ferry their supplies and baggage forward in stages. There simply are not enough wagons and beasts to carry everything. Mind you, we are in scarcely better shape. Still, the sooner you reach the column the better. Given the nightmare of a time we had just reaching the Thukela, I imagine Colonel Pearson will need your sappers sooner rather than later."

47

The next morning, the company rose at 4.00, just before sunrise. Warren left Lieutenant Courtney in charge of the wagons again before riding ahead. The road was indeed mostly slick clay, and his horse's hooves nearly slid out from under it several times. As such, he kept to a modest trot. The company halted after crossing a small, deep stream near a sugar mill. A few miles further on, at a picturesque fording site along the Nonoti River, the men were allowed to bathe once more and have their lunch. Captain Wynne was pleasantly surprised at their rate of travel. They managed to cross the Sinkwazi River at around 3.15 that afternoon. With just a few more miles to go, and leaving Courtney in command, Warren rode the rest of the way to Lower Drift to seek out Colonel Pearson and see where he wanted the No. 2 Field Company.

It was a hectic scene at Lower Drift. Men and wagons alike were cueing to cross over on the ponts manned by sailors from the column's Naval Brigade. A rudimentary fort, which the men had named Fort Pearson, overlooked the crossing. Warren paused for a few moments and watched a company from the 99th Regiment cram onto the 30-foot long, 11-foot wide pont that would take them to the far side. It was now 4.30 in the afternoon, and the day growing late. He was informed that Colonel Pearson had already crossed the Thukela, and he should report to the column's Assistant Adjutant General, Brevet Colonel Walker, who was acting as Pearson's second-in-command. Warren found him not far from where the lone flat-bottomed pont was being dragged across the river along a span of rope anchored on either bank of the river.

"Ah, Captain Wynne," the colonel said. He smiled with relief, as Warren entered the headquarters tent. "Good to finally have you with us."

"Good to finally be here, sir. My lads should be in camp within the hour. Where would you like us?"

"Find yourself a spot near the fort," Walker directed. "There's plenty of open space for you and forage for your animals." He took a moment to catch the engineer captain up on where the column stood at that moment. "Infantry from the 3rd 'Buffs' Regiment and artillery have already crossed over. They've established camp on a site where Colonel Pearson wishes to establish a more permanent stone fort. That will be the first tasking for you and your sappers. The Volunteers, Pioneers, and NNC crossed over this afternoon.

And we're getting as many companies from the 99th across before it gets dark. You will accompany the remainder of their lot tomorrow." He dismissed the captain, who came to attention before taking his leave.

Warren walked his horse to a high point near the earthen ramparts of Fort Pearson, from where he could observe the crossing. Down below a large tree stood out. He later learned this was where the Zulu delegation had received the High Commissioner's ultimatum. Indeed, many now referred to it as *The Ultimatum Tree*.

Warren did not know the wide-open plain across the river, now teaming with redcoats and African auxiliaries, was the very place where Cetshwayo had won the amaZulu throne during a bloody civil war against his brother, Mbuyazi. That particularly brutal struggle had taken place twenty-two years before. One eyewitness was John Dunn, a white settler of Scottish ancestry who fought beside Mbuyazi, yet later befriended Cetshwayo. According to Dunn, more than twenty thousand were slaughtered during the final struggle between royal princes; two-thirds were women and children. The Zulus now called the place *Mathambo, the place of the bones*. Many of the slain Mbuyazi's followers, a faction known as the *iziGqoza*, were now fighting against their kinsmen as allies of the British.

The past week felt like a blur to Warren. It seemed only yesterday he was back home in Eastbourne, looking forward to the Christmas holidays with his family. Now, the British Empire was at war with the Zulus, and he was thousands of miles from home. Most people back in Britain knew little about the Zulus, and likely couldn't find places such as Durban, Stanger, or Lower Drift on a map. Nor could they pronounce most of the Zulu names for rivers and mountains in the region. Despite the chaos brought on by thousands of men and beasts, Captain Warren Wynne felt strangely alone.

"A lost corner of the world," he said quietly to himself. "Yet wherever we are, it is England."

Fort Pearson, overlooking Lower Drift, as seen from the Zulu side of the Thukela River

Chapter III: At Least It's Not the Workhouses

Lower Drift
13 January 1879

2nd Battalion, 3rd Regiment of Foot, 'The Buffs'
Taken in Ireland just prior to their departure for South Africa, April 1876

At least it's not the workhouses…

These words had echoed in the mind of Sergeant David Fredericks every morning since he joined the Army five years before. It was a phrase he used quite often on grumbling soldiers within his section, along with a plethora of harsher responses, depending on his mood. The temper of his men was particularly foul this morning. A night of hard rain had flooded their tent once again. This was, unfortunately, an occurrence that happened more often than not since 2nd Battalion of the 3rd 'Buffs' Regiment arrived at Lower Drift.

David was twenty-six years old and originally from the coastal English town of Whitstable, eight miles north of Canterbury. Born into terrible poverty, he grew up living in a cramped workhouse with several other families. Privacy was non-existent and living conditions were fetid and unsanitary. All but two of his eight brothers and sisters died from cholera or typhoid at very young ages. David, the oldest, did what he could to assist his parents, working in a machine shop as a labourer from the time he was six. The hours were long; the work both back-breaking and extremely dangerous.

His father was injured in a catastrophic accident at the factory, losing half his right arm. He struggled to find steady work afterwards. His mother, who toiled long hours in a textile mill, succumbed to severe haemorrhaging while giving birth to their last child, who also tragically perished. David was fourteen when these calamities struck the family in rapid succession. His father took to begging, though what little alms he managed to scrounge went to fuel his lust for the bottle.

David could not find it in him to hate his father, despite his essentially abandoning his three surviving children. The loss of an arm, which caused him to live each day in terrible pain, coupled with the death of his wife and youngest child, had left him seeking solace in drink. David's surviving brother and sister continued working in the factory under horrific conditions, scraping by with just enough to keep them from starving or being tossed out of the workhouse onto the street. He figured if the machines didn't kill them, they'd all die from consumption by the time they were twenty.

The great paradox of the Industrial Revolution was not lost on him. Rapid advances in technology had afforded vast opportunities for the British Empire with drastic improvements in science, medicine, and production. A burgeoning middle-class emerged in its wake; professional businessmen and entrepreneurs who could earn very comfortable livings for themselves and their families. Standards of education also drastically improved, with more children able to get at least some level of schooling. However, there was a terrible price demanded for this prosperity, and it was borne on the backs of society's poorest. For children of the less fortunate and destitute, there was little to no chance of schooling; just endless toil, disease, and poverty. All any of them had, outside of the filthy rags which passed for clothes, were their dreams.

Devoid of hope, David left home soon after his mother's death and sought work as a farmhand outside of Canterbury. Much to his dismay, the conditions for those who laboured under the plough were even worse than in the factories, and the pay substantially less. From well before sunrise until long after sunset, they sweated in the dirt. What made it especially difficult for the young lad as he grew into manhood, was just how mind-numbingly dull it was. The air was certainly cleaner, and he did have slightly more to each. Yet while farming strengthened his body, it rotted his mind.

The day after his twentieth birthday, he came to an epiphany; while the impoverished living in the cities at least had dreams of a better life—unrealistic and hopeless they may have been—the rural poor had no dreams at all. They simply did not bother with them. And yet he could not bring himself to return to Whitstable, despite his concern for his father and younger siblings. The only solace he found was in the company of a young woman named Lillian. An orphan, she had survived milking cows and shovelling horse stalls since she was eight. Lillian was a year older than David, and he found her both pretty and strong in equal measure. Even when filthy and dishevelled, her hair matted with sweat and grime, she could still enrapture him with her smile. The long and arduous hours of work left them little time to foster their growing relationship, yet they cherished every moment spent together. Their first night of passion was both awkward and clumsy as they made love under the light of the harvest moon, on a blanket behind a plough shed. Matters came to a head a few months later, when Lillian fell ill one morning. Upon learning that she was with child, David did the honourable thing and asked her to marry him.

It was soon after the birth of their son, also named David, that he approached his wife and told her, "I'll not have our child raised behind the plough or in a factory."

The only way out of poverty, that he could see, was by donning the red jacket and pledging his life to Queen Victoria and the British Empire. Lillian had her reservations; however, she soon consented.

The nearest depot belonged to the 3rd Regiment of Foot. Known as 'The Buffs' for the buff-coloured facings on their uniforms, they originated in Kent and had a history dating back 300 years. The 1st Battalion was, at the time, posted to India. The 2nd Battalion was on Home Service, with companies stationed at both Shorncliffe and Dover. With a newfound sense of determination and his wife and son accompanying him, David went to the depot and volunteered his services to Queen and Country.

The young man was taken aback when the recruiting sergeant berated him sternly upon seeing the young woman and baby. "This is not some bleeding charity!" the NCO snarled.

While the Army was not one to turn away healthy recruits, nor would they be so cruel as to tell a man to divorce his wife and abandon his family, the sergeant made it abundantly clear that only those with seven years of good conduct, or who achieved sufficient rank, could petition the regimental colonel to have his wife added onto what was called 'the married roll'. The specification of seven years was deliberate. Recent reforms allowed soldiers to enlist for six years rather than the previous obligation of twelve. Because most elected to leave the Army after their initial enlistment, this meant far fewer wives and children to provide for. This also explained why most soldiers in the ranks remained bachelors.

Even for those who met the criteria, vacancies on the married roll for a private's spouse were few. A man with a family could still enlist; however, his wife would receive no additional stipend from the Army until she was added onto the roll. David was further surprised to learn that the pay for a private was twelve shillings per week; two less than the meagre wage he received as a farm hand! What's more, stoppages were taken out for food, uniforms, etc. This certainly helped explain why so many young men, particularly those with wives and children, avoided military service. However, he was determined to join the Colours and, through the Army, provide a better life for Lillian and young David.

Lillian told him she could continue to work around the farm for the time being. Though compounded by having to simultaneously care for their child, she too saw the Army as a chance for the family to rise from the abject poverty which they had known their entire lives. And so, unable to sign his name, David marked an 'X' on the enlistment papers; taking the Queen's Shilling and pledging his life in service to the Crown.

Recruit training was extremely difficult, both physically and mentally. The instructors were brutal and the discipline fierce. While flogging was expressly prohibited on Home Service, this did not stop the instructors from using the sticks they carried to great effect whenever a recruit offended them. One morning with a light mist hanging in the air, and the sergeant-instructor screaming in his ear while slapping him about the face for having a button on his tunic undone, David Fredericks had to suppress the urge to smile. Despite the mental and physical pain, he'd never felt more alive! A part of him even wanted to thank the NCO for the severe chastising.

Most recruits dreaded the plethora of new tasks and drills they had to learn. David relished the challenge. For the first time in his life, his mind was allowed to grow and learn. He only wished he knew how to read!

Inspection parades were conducted twice a day. These were tedious, with recruits standing at attention while the corporals and sergeant-instructors thoroughly inspected their uniforms, weapons, and kit. Any infractions were met with unnaturally loud verbal chastisement, often coupled with a cuff across the ears and several hours of additional duty.

The rest of their time was spent training on marching, infantry tactics, and bayonet drill with classes on *Queen's Regulations and Orders for the Army*. The latest edition, dated from 1873, was a pocket-sized book, albeit extremely thick. It covered everything from enlistment and officer commissions to training standards, as well as pay, rations authorisations, leaves of absence, discipline, and uniform standards. Instruction on Queen's Regulations had to be conducted almost entirely verbally, as only a handful of recruits could read and write.

The one disappointment for the new soldiers was the glaring lack of actual time spent on the range with their Martini-Henry Rifles. The British Army prided itself on the marksmanship skill of her redcoats, yet only twice did they get to fire their weapons. And even then, they were given a mere twenty rounds each!

"Pass out of recruit training and Her Majesty might see fit to purchase you lot more cartridges," the sergeant-instructor had told them.

The time they did spend on the range was just enough to appreciate the rifle's fearsome kick. The Martini-Henry was a breach-loading, single-shot, lever actuated rifle. Among the first cartridge-utilising firearms issued to the British Army after the last muzzle-loading rifles were phased out, it fired a heavy .455-calibre bullet; enough to take down an elephant. David could only guess what it could do to the human body! It was also an extremely accurate weapon; a far cry from the muskets of the Napoleonic Era that had an effective range of less than a hundred yards. Even with only forty rounds to practice with over two training sessions, David became confident at striking targets out to 400 yards. The Martini-Henry could reach far beyond that; however, only a couple of the new soldiers could see well enough to attempt a shot at the 600 and 800-yard targets.

"Survive training, and I'll get more practice with the rifle," David reasoned.

He continued to persevere through every trial and graduated after eight weeks as a private assigned to H Company, 2nd Battalion of the 3rd Buffs. Lillian struggled to hold back her tears of pride the first time she saw her husband in his scarlet uniform with dark blue trousers, shako atop his head. Though he though the shako looked a bit odd with the pom on top, he preferred it over the glengarry cap, which had no brim and was pretty much useless as a form of headgear.

Though the Army gave him a few days of leave following his passing out ceremony, Lillian still had to work at the farm every day except Sunday. This did, however, allow David time to spend with his son, and he cherished every moment with the fast-growing lad. Knowing that he could be sent overseas and be parted from his family with little notice, he intended to make the most of whatever time he was given.

The farm where Lillian worked and lived was out in the country, ten miles from the regimental depot. Weeks of endless marching and military gymnastics had conditioned David and greatly improved his stamina. He found he did not mind the long walks. Though the weather had been fair and sunny, the sky turned dark the day before his leave ended, adding a pall of gloom to his return to the depot. As he kissed his wife goodbye, he promised Lillian this was the start of a new life for all three of them.

Duty days on Home Service were long and tedious. Yet, as reveille did not sound until just before dawn, David found himself getting far more sleep than he was used to on the farm. They were even given time in the evenings and on Sundays for leisure. Most soldiers attended church services on Sundays. David was not particularly religious and used his Sundays to spend time with his family; his walk to and from the farm taking about three hours each way.

The concept of leisure was completely foreign to him, and he was not sure what to do with himself after evening parade each day. His new-found mates taught him various card games, and he even took up sport, such as cricket. Despite the comradery and sense of belonging to something far greater, David knew he could not provide a better life for his family so long as he remained a private. Nor did he wish to wait seven years to petition to have Lillian added to the married roll. Promotions were extremely difficult to come by, as there simply were not that many billets available. An infantry company was made up of four sections with twenty to twenty-five soldiers apiece. Each section was led by a sergeant with a corporal to assist. There was also the rare lance corporal; a billet awarded to a private acting in a leadership position or with a special skillset. This explained why it was not uncommon among the few who decided to make the Army a career, to still be a private when they retired twenty years later. David Fredericks, however, was determined not to still be a private soldier when he was forty!

A few months after completion of recruit training, he began learning the one skill that could help him improve and eventually become eligible for promotion. That skill was literacy. Most soldiers came from the poor working class, and many could neither read nor write. Determined to teach himself to read, he sought the help of his assistant section leader, Corporal Frederick Milne. Milne, it turned out, was also from Whitstable. Two years older than David, he joined the ranks as soon as he came of age and by this time had served for five years.

During his first year with The Buffs, the battalion was posted to Ireland. Lillian and their son accompanied David, and she was fortunate enough to find work on a dairy farm. The conditions were cramped and uncomfortable, coupled by the incessant Irish rains. David, required to remain at barracks, saved all that he could from his wages to ensure his wife and child would not starve. He took his own meals at the mess, and the only 'luxuries' he allowed himself were a more comfortable pillow and extra blanket for his bunk, along with the occasional pair of socks.

While spending his evenings under the tutelage of Corporal Milne, the young private soon learned that in the Army, advancement was as much a matter of opportunity as it was ability. Barely a year after David enlisted, their section leader's enlistment expired. Milne was promoted to sergeant in his place. Because of the close working rapport the two had established, as well as the initiative and work ethics David demonstrated, Milne recommended Private Fredericks replace him as the section's corporal. It was on a drizzly Irish spring morning, with H Company on parade in their greatcoats, that Private David Fredericks was called before the company. He stood rigid at attention before his officer commanding, while the colour sergeant read aloud the order promoting him to corporal.

More than wearing the two white chevrons on his right shoulder, his responsibilities drastically changed. No longer was he just another rifleman. He was now responsible for assisting Sergeant Milne in running their section which, at that time, numbered eighteen soldiers. Among his duties was the enforcement of discipline; something he found distasteful when one of his former mates required a verbal or physical reprimanding. Milne also ordered him to join all section leader meetings and to disseminate both verbal and written orders to their men. This taxed his literacy skills, which were still very rudimentary. Milne, ever the mentor, coached David and often had him transcribe the notes and read them to the section. With seemingly endless repetition, his abilities to read and write improved dramatically.

Though a non-commissioned officer, he still could not petition to have Lillian added to the married roll until he either reached his seventh year in the ranks or achieved promotion to sergeant. However, the difference in pay was still considerable, and he felt he could take Lillian away from the farm. Before then, he only saw her perhaps once a week on Sundays, when his officer commanding gave him permission to spend the day with his wife and son. Wives who stayed with their husbands at barracks shared the same humble and cramped accommodations. If lucky, one managed to find a sheet to hang from the ceiling to partition off their bunk and have some measure of privacy. For those who grew up in the workhouses, this was nothing new. All David and Lillian Fredericks cared about was that their family was finally together. Their time in Ireland would soon prove short-lived.

In October 1876, 2nd Battalion of the 3rd 'Buffs' Regiment embarked for Cape Town, South Africa aboard a hired transport, the *St Lawrence*. Tragedy nearly struck when the ship collided with submerged rocks, 90 miles northwest of Cape Town. Three other vessels, including the HMS Active, came to their aid, saving the crew, soldiers, and their wives and children. During this crisis, David proved his mettle, keeping a cool head and assisting no less than six wives and five terrified young children off the foundering ship. He further took the initiative and formed a detail to save as much of their ammunition as possible. This was difficult given the weight of the boxes. Unfortunately, much of their ammunition and other stores were lost. Still, his efforts did not go unnoticed, and he received a personal commendation from their battalion commander, Lieutenant Colonel Parnell.

Two years later, during the Xhosa uprising, a sergeant in H Company was invalided home with severe rheumatism and discharged as no longer fit for service. David, who had been appointed to lance sergeant in the interim, was now promoted to full sergeant and given command of the previous NCO's section. While still required to make a formal petition to add Lillian to the married roll, this was little more than a formality. Lieutenant Colonel Parnell expressed his extreme pleasure at being able to, *'Assist the family of the man who proved his mettle in saving lives, as well as our stores'*.

The newly-promoted Sergeant Fredericks never knew he could have applied much sooner to add Lillian to the roll, having yet to learn that most rules and regulations could be waived with the right signatures. Still, the increase in his pay combined with the stipend now given to Lillian and little David greatly improved their station in life.

Lillian was especially fond of saying, *'We now eat as well as Her Majesty!'* It was a profound exaggeration, of course. But, given the squalor and state of near-starvation they endured for most of their lives, the quality of life brought by a sergeant's pay, humble as it was, with the additional married stipend, made Lillian Fredericks feel like a queen.

Cap Badge of the 3rd Regiment of Foot (The Buffs)

59

The incessant pummelling of rain on their tent brought David out of his reminiscing. As soldiers bickered incessantly about their soggy bedrolls and clothing, the sergeant let out a sigh and muttered once more, "At least it's not the workhouses."

In the cramped space of their tent, his men threw on their greatcoats and began rolling up their bed rolls. The assistant section leader, Corporal Robert Anderson, lit a small oil lamp which he hung from the centre pole. At least half the men were coughing up gouts of phlegm which they spat onto the saturated ground. This was worrying to David. No matter how well they kept their tent patched or how deep they dug drainage ditches around it every night, it seemed impossible for them to keep dry. Bedrolls that were soggy when strapped to packs were still wet when unrolled, making them susceptible to mould and rot. If the column was not departing the drift this day, and provided the weather cooperated, he would have his men hang their bed rolls, blankets, and greatcoats out to dry.

Soaked tunics and trousers hung from the support poles inside the tent. If the night proved cold and rainy, there was little they could do to dry their clothes. On the days it wasn't raining, the sun beat down, scorching the red-jacketed soldiers. The sweltering heat soaked their uniforms with sweat, leaving behind blotchy salt stains when they eventually dried. It was little wonder the extreme contrast between cold rain and blistering sun on a near-daily basis was playing havoc with the men's health and well-being.

Morale was high five days earlier when H Company was among those from The Buffs selected to be the first to cross into Zululand. Every man, from Lieutenant Colonel Parnell down to the youngest privates, expected to find swarms of enemy warriors waiting for them. A few had seen action during the Xhosa War, and they were anxious to test their mettle against the Zulus. Aside from scant sightings of enemy scouts, the crossing went unopposed. The Buffs established their camp and waited for the rest of the column to cross over. And they waited…and waited. Despite the best efforts of the sailors from the naval detachment, who established and worked the ponts tirelessly, the logistics involved in transporting so many men, draught animals, wagons, cannon, and other equipment was an agonisingly slow process. Slowest of all was the transporting of their stores. A rifle company of ninety to a hundred men could squeeze onto the flat-bottomed pont, but it could only support the weight of a single wagon.

"Goddamn it," a soldier snapped, as he pulled his greatcoat out of a puddle. "How in the bleeding fuck am I supposed to keep dry now?"

"Maybe next time you won't leave your greatcoat lying in a sodding puddle," Corporal Anderson rebuked sharply.

"We have enough risk of catching typhoid, dysentery, and God knows what, as it is," David added. "Let's not add negligence or stupidity."

"Hey, sergeant," another private said from the darkness, "at least it's not the workhouses."

This drew a few laughs from the otherwise disgruntled soldiers and even a grin from David. He was contemplating giving the soldier with the soggy greatcoat a couple hours of extra duty for his inattention but figured being soaked during the next rainstorm would be lesson enough. He ordered his section to finish packing their kit and be ready for morning parade in ten minutes.

As he donned his helmet and lifted the soaked tent flap, the sergeant was glad to see the rains had stopped for the moment. In contrast to the stench of filthy men in sweat-stained uniforms, the air outside smelled fresh. The sergeant took a deep breath in through his nose. As the sun began to crest over the hills to the east, he saw the sky was black with thick clouds. While he listened to Anderson berate another soldier whose kit had gotten wet, David was joined by Lance Corporal James Monroe.

In addition to Rob Anderson, David was fortunate enough to have the lance corporal to assist him. James served as a designated marksman with the company sharp-shooters and earned his 'lance jack stripe' when appointed as a musketry trainer for the company. His tasking as a skirmisher often took him away from the section; however, when he was with his mates, Lance Corporal Monroe always set the example as a calm, level-headed, detail oriented, and hardworking soldier. His outward level of maturity contrasted sharply with his nineteen years of age!

"Looks to be another beastly morning," James said, shaking out his greatcoat and slapping some dirt off his helmet before placing it back upon his head. "I hope the wind blows those clouds out of here."

"I hope so, too," the sergeant concurred. "To be honest, I'm a bit worried about some of the lads. If the weather keeps on like this, I fear half of them will be down with fever before we leave for Eshowe."

"Just imagine how it will be once the column begins its advance. Twelve hours on the march, fording rivers, digging wagons out of mud and shit, establishing camp at the end of it all with only scant amounts of time to eat our lovely ration of hard biscuits and tinned beef. If the lads are lucky they might get a few hours of sleep after *lights out*, though anyone who draws picquet duty is pretty well fucked."

"Still better than what I managed on the farm," David reasoned. He nodded back towards their tent. "Help Anderson get the lads in formation and conduct a quick kit inspection."

The lance corporal indicated agreement and went back into the tent. David grabbed his dirty tin cup from his pack and made his way to where Colour Sergeant Bennet waited by the command tent to brief the section leaders. Sergeant Fredericks had to constantly pull his feet out of the sinking mud as he strode over to the company's senior NCO. The mud coupled with the flattened tall grasses was very slick.

"Beautiful morning," Bennet said, taking a deep breath in through his nose and exhaling audibly. He held a tin mug full of steaming coffee. David reckoned it was the source of his good nature. Hot coffee, no matter how bitter, had a way of buoying the spirits of even the most disgruntled of Her Majesty's redcoats.

Colour Sergeant Robert Bennet was a career soldier. Thirty-three years of age and originally from Edinburgh, he'd joined the Army as a 'Boy' when he was fifteen. Despite his Scottish roots, there was only a slight trace of accent after spending much of his youth with the Army. His father, a private with 1st Battalion of The Buffs, died of cholera towards the end of the Second Opium War in 1860. Young Robert had just attested into the ranks as a Boy, and the Regiment subsequently became his sole family.

"It will be a fine morning if we can get the lads dried off," David remarked.

The other sergeants from the company were trudging through the muck toward them.

"Unfortunately, none of us can compel the Almighty to adjust the weather," Bennet remarked with a shrug. "Believe me, the chaplain has tried!"

The company's senior non-commissioned officer waved them over to the smouldering campfire. It was producing columns of thick smoke and very little flame. Hanging off a wire loop amid the billowing cloud was a tin kettle. Section leaders eagerly offered up their mugs, which the colour sergeant filled. Though the coffee was a thick sludge and scarcely lukewarm, to David and the other NCOs it was a taste of heaven.

"Any idea how long before we take the fight to the Zulus, colour sergeant?" section leader John Stirling asked. Stirling was also a Scot, originally from Dumfries. Twelve years he'd served with the Colours, six of those as a sergeant. He held seniority over David and the other section leaders.

"Probably not for a few more days," Bennet replied. "Colonel Pearson is as anxious to reach Eshowe as we are. However, the *Jack Tars* working the pont are still ferrying troops and supplies over. Had the years-long drought not suddenly ended and turned this place into a fucking swamp, we'd be well on our way. Thankfully, Captain Wynne and the engineers arrived yesterday. They've orders to build a supply fort on this side of the river. After which, they'll be doing their damnedest to make the roads passable for our wagons."

"I hope they plan on doing some repairs to the pont," Stirling added. "It wasn't exactly in the best condition when we crossed over."

"It'll become a priority once the bottom falls out while transporting the officers' baggage," David remarked snidely.

The company's senior NCO and his sergeants went over the duty roster for the day. Duty days after morning parade tended to be spent on guard duty, work details, or conducting maintenance on weapons and kit.

"There will be lots of digging and shovelling over the next few days," Bennet remarked. "The Royal Engineers were kind enough to send a company of sappers to guide us in building the supply fort Colonel Pearson wants established on this side of the river. I imagine everyone will be getting their hands dirty before long. In the meantime, it might make a suitable additional duty for any troublemakers in your sections."

David snorted. He'd just found an extra way to motivate his soldiers into keeping their kit dry.

Before dismissing the section leaders, Colour Sergeant Bennet had one last note for them. "Make certain your lads know that a postal courier should arrive sometime today. I recommend anyone with letters to send home do so now. Once we depart for Eshowe, it might be a month or more before we have the chance to send word to our families, either in the Cape or back in Blighty."

Chapter IV: Crossing the Thukela

Lower Drift
13 January 1879

Portrait of Charles Knight Pearson
He wears the Crimea Campaign Medal of 1854 with *Sevastopol* clasp

On the Natal side of the river, Colonel Pearson was taking stock of his column. Many of their wagons and most of the six companies from the 99th Regiment remained on the Natal side of the river. And while he was impressed by the work ethics and efficiency exuded by Commander Campbell and the naval detachment working the pont, progress was painfully slow. For the past two days, the Zulu Kingdom and British Empire had been at war. The sooner he could get his troops across the river and consolidated, the better. Priority this day, however, was getting Captain Wynne and No. 2 Field Company across, so they could begin work on the supply fort Pearson had ordered erected on the Zulu side.

At forty-four years of age, Colonel Charles Knight Pearson was a career officer first commissioned when he was eighteen. As a twenty-one-year-old lieutenant, he took part in the brutal Siege of Sevastopol during the Crimean War where he was *mentioned in despatches* for personal bravery. He was later awarded the Crimean Campaign Medal with *Sevastopol* clasp, along with the Turkish Crimea Medal. He spent the next twenty-one years with the 3rd 'Buffs' Regiment, rising up to lieutenant colonel and command of a battalion. Coming from a wealthy family, he was able to purchase most of his promotions before the army abolished the practice in 1871. In 1872, at just thirty-eight years of age, he was given a meritorious brevet to full colonel. Six years later, after his promotion was made substantive, he elected to retire from the army and was placed on half-pay. Scarcely a month later, Lord Chelmsford implored him to return to active service for the pending war with the Zulus. Pearson obliged after his lordship offered him command of one of the invasion columns. Though he maintained a stalwart deportment around his staff officers and men, the inclement weather and terrible conditions dampened his enthusiasm considerably.

"At this rate, it'll be July before we reach Ulundi," he muttered quietly under his breath.

"Last word we received from his lordship, they're having an even worse time of it than we are," his second, Colonel Walker, remarked. "The last message stated there are no roads to speak of for the centre No. 3 Column to utilise. The GOC mentioned nothing about Colonel Wood's column in the north, though I cannot imagine they are having it any easier."

"I'll be joining Captain Wynne across the river this morning," Pearson said. "The sooner his sappers start on the fort's construction, the sooner we can be on our way. Meanwhile, I'll leave you in charge of the crossing."

"Very good," Walker replied.

Lord Chelmsford's original intent was to launch a massive invasion force consisting of five columns, converging on the royal kraal at Ulundi and overwhelming the Zulus. However, there were serious manpower shortages brought on by Her Majesty's government's reluctance to pursue war with the Zulus. This was further exacerbated by the maddening lack of wagons, draught animals, and commissariat staff, which compelled him to revamp his strategy. There would still be five columns; however, only three would take part in the invasion.

The crux of the invasion fell on the centre No. 3 Column under Colonel Richard Glyn of the 24th Regiment. They were to cross the uMzinyathi River at Rorke's Drift and make straight for Ulundi, about fifty miles to the east. As Lord Chelmsford was accompanying Glyn, he had essentially usurped all control from him.

Colonel Sir Henry Evelyn Wood's No. 4 Column would harry the Zulus to the north, crossing near the town of Utrecht. He was to prevent numerous tribes, particularly the abaQulusi, from joining the main Zulu army. Wood's force was operating fairly close to Glyn's—about thirty or so miles to the north—and in theory could protect the centre column's left flank.

Colonel Pearson's southern No. 1 Column would advance northeast along the coast in the direction of a recently abandoned mission station called Eshowe. From there they would establish a supply and communications depot to both assist the centre column, as well as their own advance on Ulundi. As Lower Drift was more than a hundred miles from Rorke's Drift, Pearson was very much left on his own. Whereas communications between the GOC and Colonel Wood could be accomplished in a matter of hours, it could take days or even up to a week, depending on terrain and enemy activity, before Chelmsford and Pearson could relay any sort of messages to each other.

Lieutenant Colonel Anthony Durnford's No. 2 Column was much smaller than the others, consisting of a few hundred mounted black Africans and Natal warriors. They were a highly mobile force. Last Pearson knew, they were defending the crossing at a place called Middle Drift along the uMzinyathi River and being kept in reserve. The No. 5 Column under Colonel Hugh Rowlands was tasked with garrisoning Natal, preventing any unrest from the volatile natives and ever-troublesome Boers, as well as providing a reserve for the invasion forces.

With the ultimatum's expiration, Lord Chelmsford unleashed his three columns of imperial soldiers and their African allies. While the GOC personally accompanied Colonel Richard Glyn's No. 3 Column, the northern and southern columns were given free rein to use their initiative in fulfilling the commanding general's intent. Thus far, there had been little sign of the enemy aside from a few scouts. The terrain and weather had been a more formidable adversary than the Zulus. No. 3 Column crossed the uMzinyathi in only two days, albeit they had a pair of ponts, plus a useable fording site which their horses and draught animals could utilise. They had since advanced no further than the far bank. According to the despatch received by Colonel Walker, lack of roads and torrential rains rendered a continued advance impossible for the time being.

For Colonel Pearson, conquering the Thukela River was proving to be a far more daunting task. Having just a single pont, with no nearby fording points, created a maddening choke point as soldiers and wagons queued to cross over. The Thukela was wildly unpredictable and at flood stage nearly 300 yards in width. However, Pearson took solace in knowing that the southern approach went through the lands formerly belonging to the settler trader, John Dunn. This meant there was some semblance of a road to follow, even if the rains had turned it into a muddy quagmire.

Like the other two invasion forces, No. 1 Column was a mix of professional British infantry, settler volunteer horsemen, and battalions of indigenous warriors. The infantry consisted of the eight companies from 2nd Battalion of Pearson's own 3rd Regiment and an additional six companies from the 99th Lanarkshire Regiment. Supporting them were Royal Artillery, a contingent of sailors from the HMS Active, several troops of volunteer mounted rifles, the entire 2nd Regiment of the Natal Native Contingent (NNC), No. 2 Company Natal Native Pioneer Corps, and now the recently arrived No. 2 Field Company, Royal Engineers. All told, Pearson had 1,517 imperial redcoats, 312 cavalry volunteers, and 2,256 NNC warriors. Transporting this mass of men and material were 384 wagons and 24 carts, hauled by 3,128 oxen and 121 mules. These required an additional 622 conductors, drivers, and voorloopers. While the ample grasslands provided grazing for the oxen, copious amounts of mealie grains were transported on wagons to feed the mules.

The pont along the Thukela River, carrying a company from the 99th Regiment

Not long after Colonel Pearson took the pont across the river, another messenger from Lord Chelmsford arrived at the camp. The young 2nd lieutenant found Colonel Walker, who read the despatch before ordering the man to leave his horse on the Natal side of the river and cross with one of the companies from the 99th. It was a tight fit as nearly a hundred redcoats crammed onto the flat-bottomed boat. The first thing the officer noticed was how relatively clean and neat these soldiers appeared. Their tunics were still a bright scarlet and their helmets a pearly white with the brass plates gleaming in the sun. By contrast, the soldiers from the 24th Regiment up at the centre column, as well as those from the 3rd Buffs, were rather haggard in appearance. Their uniforms were faded and patched with helmets deliberately stained a dark brown and the brass plates removed.

"Newly arrived?" the messenger asked a boyish-faced private standing next to him.

"Yes, sir," the soldier replied. "We only landed at Durban on the 5th. Tis a far cry from the winter weather back home."

"That it is."

Scores of sailors heaved on the heavy ropes fixed to a pully system that would slowly drag the pont across the wide spans of the Thukela River. Once the pont lurched against the far bank, the messenger waited until the last of the redcoats disembarked before stepping off the boat. He soon found Colonel Pearson and his staff officers standing on the site of what would become known as Fort Tenedos; named after the ship where many of the sailors had been detached.

"Colonel, sir." The young man saluted.

Pearson returned the courtesy and took the message. As was typical of the GOC, the message was brief.

Colonel,

No. 3 Column has crossed at Rorke's Drift. Terrain is proving extremely difficult. Expect delays of a week or more. No. 4 Column crossed into Zululand on the 9th and is now harassing the enemy's northern territories. Keep me informed of your progress.

Chelmsford

Pearson resisted the urge to snort derisively at this despatch. The messenger had spent several days on horseback to deliver a note telling the colonel little he didn't already know. While he respected his lordship's abilities as a strategist and logistician, one of Chelmsford's more significant flaws was the lack of detail in his despatches to subordinates. The only fresh piece of information was that Colonel Wood had crossed into Zululand on the 9th of January, before the ultimatum had expired. Frustratingly, there was no intelligence about enemy movements. Then again, with the complete absence of professional cavalry in the Cape, Pearson reckoned that No. 3 Column's reconnaissance capabilities were in no better shape than his.

He was further concerned as to how the three columns were going to keep lines of communication open when they advanced into Zululand. Rorke's Drift was about 150 miles from the Thukela crossing with Utrecht another sixty or so further north. These distances would nominally shorten as they slowly converged on Ulundi in a giant pincer; however, the colonel worried that one of the columns might become overextended and cut off from possible support. The further they moved into enemy-held territory, the more hazardous it became for messengers. Hence why the GOC had directed they would now utilise local African runners, who might have a better chance at passing undetected by the Zulus.

Pearson's mission was to first establish a supply depot at an abandoned mission station known as Eshowe, approximately thirty-five miles from Lower Drift. They were to await further orders, either to continue to advance in the pincer towards Ulundi or act as a logistics hub in the event of a prolonged campaign. He understood Lord Chelmsford's intent was to draw the main Zulu *impi* into a decisive battle with No. 3 Column long before they reached Ulundi. But, the enemy had a say in the matter. From what Pearson could gather, no one in the entire British invasion force had any idea where the *impi* was.

"Has the column come into contact with the Zulus?" he finally asked, hoping to glean some viable information from this young officer, who was likely a glint in his father's eye when the colonel was first commissioned.

"Yes, sir, though not their main army. The NNC and a few companies from the 24th routed a small force at the stronghold of a local chieftain. They burned the kraal and killed a few dozen Zulus. *'First blood to us,'* as his lordship said. God willing, by the time I return, the path to Isandlwana will be useable."

"The path to where?" Pearson asked.

"It's about ten miles east of Rorke's Drift, sir," the messenger explained. "One can actually see it from the river crossing. Looks a bit like a sphinx in the distance. Fitting, since that is what adorns the collars of the 24th. The GOC intends to use it as a temporary staging area to bring supplies up then continue to advance on the Royal Kraal."

"And has his lordship received any intelligence on the whereabouts of the main *impi*?" the colonel asked.

The messenger shook his head, looking somewhat embarrassed. "No, sir. We know they are mustering at the Royal Kraal, but we have no eyes on them."

"Nor do any of us," Pearson muttered under his breath.

"Sir?"

The colonel quickly shook his head. He knew better than to voice his concerns in front of so junior a subordinate. He told him he would have a written response for Lord Chelmsford, complete with the status of his column's crossing and the arrival of No. 2 Field Company before the day was out.

71

Not far from where Colonel Pearson met with Lord Chelmsford's messenger, companies from 2/3rd Buffs were finishing morning parade.

Following their dismissal by their officer commanding, Lieutenant Robert Martin, and prior to briefing his section, David Fredericks pulled a battered envelope from his pack and handed it to Corporal Anderson. "Thank God at least one of our wives can read."

"Lucky for me Emma's father was a printer. It seemed only natural that she learned to read as a child."

Like his section leader, twenty-one-year-old Robert Anderson was married when he joined the Army. He, too, came from the poorest dregs of Victorian society, spending his formative years working in an ironworks. Emma taught him to read during their courtship, and she had always said he was not brought into this world to be a common labourer. When a fire destroyed the factory, killing a dozen workers and leaving the rest unemployed, Robert sought out the local recruiting sergeant and enlisted. A natural leader who was always calm, even under extreme duress, David was ever grateful to have him as his assistant section leader.

"You know I dread the day that I lose you," he remarked. "And not just because your wife reads my letters to Lillian for her! You're on the short-list for promotion, and I know Sergeant Davies' tenure is ending soon."

"I keep hearing that," Robert remarked. "Colour Sergeant Bennet told me the other day not to get too comfortable as your assistant. No doubt Monroe is anxious to earn his second stripe, even if it means being taken away from the sharp-shooters. Thing is, everyone thinks I'm ready for my own section except me."

"You're never truly ready," David conjectured. "It's kind of like being a parent, I suppose. I was not even remotely prepared when my son came into this world, but I managed. And as a sergeant, you have up to twenty-five 'sons' under your charge. If you're lucky, you'll have a competent corporal to assist you. If not, life will be a real bastard."

The NCOs shared a knowing grin. Though scarcely any older than most of their soldiers, the responsibilities brought on by their rank and experience made them feel much older. Of all the soldiers David had served with over the past five years, Robert Anderson was one of the most knowledgeable and competent he'd ever seen. He had no room for ego or pomposity and was one of the most natural leaders in the company. A daunting task awaited his replacement when the time finally came for him to leave the section.

Another growing challenge for the entire battalion was their constantly shrinking numbers. In addition to already being understrength, there were soldiers in H Company scheduled to return to Britain within the next few months, as their enlistments were set to expire. Three of these were in David's section. While the sergeant had spoken to each man about possibly staying with the Colours, the reality every regiment faced was that very few Victorian Era soldiers sought to make the Army a career. For every grizzled 'old sweat', there were a dozen fresh-faced youths in the ranks.

The recent Cardwell Reforms had also shifted the mandatory enlistment period from twelve years on active service to six, with the remaining six in the reserves. Consequently, the Army became even younger. David was reminded of this every day when he inspected his section. Even though Queen's Regulations said moustaches would be worn, and beards were authorised on Foreign Service, nine of the seventeen soldiers in the section were devoid of whiskers. David elected to shave his upper lip, as the few wisps of hair he managed to grow were so unsightly, he found it less embarrassing to simply shave. Conversely, Robert Anderson, who was five years younger than his sergeant, sported a thick 'manly' moustache with a full set of side whiskers. The only privates in the section with full beards were a pair of career soldiers who were both in their thirties.

Despite their collective lack of years, what the soldiers from H Company did possess was a measure of experience. During the Ninth Cape Frontier War against the Xhosa, most of the actual fighting was done by the 24th Regiment and the 88th Connaught Rangers. Most soldiers from 2/3rd Buffs were deployed to various locations along the frontier and saw little to no action. H Company, however, did take part in a pair of battles towards the end of the conflict. Though regarded as little more than a couple of skirmishes, for those who did the actual fighting, the chaos of blood-letting and the screams of the dying had shattered what little remained of their youthful innocence. In Queen Victoria's army, the concept of 'youth' was more a matter of a soldier's experience than his age.

A striking example of this was the recent arrival of four companies from the 99th Duke of Edinburgh's Regiment. Like most of the higher-numbered regiments, the 99th had one battalion instead of the usual two. Though most of the private soldiers were of similar age to their counterparts in The Buffs, these men were glaringly inexperienced. The last time the 99th saw action was twenty years before during the Second Opium War in China. They later served a three-year tour in South Africa from 1865 to 1868, but the colony had been relatively peaceful during this period. A subsequent ten years on Home Service, along with the discharge of most of the long-service veterans, meant the majority of those in the 99th were seeing active service for the first time; this included the officers and NCOs. As such, the veterans of The Buffs viewed the newly-arrived soldiers with a measure of scorn.

Down by the ponts, Lance Corporal James Monroe strolled along the riverbank. Across the swollen Thukela, a company from the newly-arrived 99th Regiment boarded the pont. With a loud cadence bellowed by the lead petty officer, scores of sailors heaved on the ropes, dragging the boat across the water. James rested the buttstock of his rifle against his foot, hands clasped around the barrel, as he watched the approaching mass of so many young and eager faces.

"Silly buggers still have their helmet plates on!" one private called out mockingly as he and his mates watched the company being ferried across the river.

The Foreign Service helmet was white, instead of the Home Service blue, with a brass regimental plate adorning the centre. Not wishing to make themselves any more conspicuous than necessary, soldiers serving in The Cape tended to remove the brass plates and soak their helmets in a brew of tea, dying them brown. Though they still wore the traditional red tunics, the bleaching of the sun and the salt stains brought on by constant sweating sapped the bright colour in a matter of weeks.

"Looks like a bunch of babies straight from the turnip patch." Monroe chuckled. His countenance then darkened. He found himself envious of the fresh-faced soldiers, so full of idealism and naivety. James was eighteen the first time he fired his weapon at an enemy

74

combatant. As a company sharp-shooter, he had far more opportunities to kill than his mates in the section. When he shot an enemy from several hundred yards, he could distance himself from what he'd done. Plunging his bayonet into a man's guts, as happened when the company stumbled into a band of Xhosa in a thick wood, had been a different matter entirely.

Unless a soldier stabbed an enemy through the heart, which brought with it the risk of one's bayonet becoming stuck in the ribs, death came slowly. It could take hours for a man stabbed through the guts to expire. From what the lance corporal had witnessed, it was an ungodly painful way to die. Most of the battalion had expressed envy that H Company had managed to get 'stuck in' with the enemy, even if only for a couple of minor engagements. To James Monroe, there had been nothing minor about watching the young warrior, who was likely scarcely older than he, die in agony after the lance corporal stabbed him through the bowels with the twenty-two-inch spike on the end of his rifle.

James shuddered.

"You feeling alright, corporal?" a soldier asked.

"Fine. Fine," he replied, before walking briskly away. He watched the sunrise for a few moments and gathered his thoughts. Privately, he wished it would never set.

Something he had never confessed to anyone was that he always dreaded the coming of night. The constant pummelling his hearing had suffered from firing his Martini-Henry rifle over the past year left a constant ringing in his ears, which was always more pronounced after 'lights out'. In the dead of night, his mind played tricks on him. He struggled to sleep. And if the wind blew just right, he swore he could hear the screams of the dying.

Captain Warren Wynne rose early, leaving morning parade to Lieutenant Courtney. He crossed the river to find their column commander. Colonel Pearson had ordered his engineer officer to join him for breakfast, so they could discuss the details of the fort. Though anxious to get his column to Eshowe, Pearson was not about to risk leaving Lower Drift undefended.

"This needs to be large enough to house our reserve stores," he explained, after his engineer officer arrived. "Can't leave our resupply operations at the mercy of this damned unpredictable river."

"Very good, sir," Warren concurred. "How large of a garrison will be posted here?"

"At least two hundred," the colonel answered. "Their task will be to guard the fort, as well as load wagons as they are sent ahead to the column."

The two officers walked towards the proposed site, about 600 yards north of the river. It was not ideal. There was an overlooking hill 300 yards away. Still, as it was commonly known that Zulu muskets were notoriously inaccurate, even at close range. Pearson felt there was little threat posed by the hill.

"Unless the Zulus somehow capture a thousand Martini-Henrys," the colonel stated. He then continued, "The storehouse itself will be sixty feet by fifty."

Warren took out his note pad and started making a few quick sketches of the terrain as Pearson explained, "I have tasked the quartermasters with requisitioning additional ammunition stores. This depot will mostly contain rations and fodder."

After taking a minute to make his notes, Wynne said, "I can have a detailed plan drawn up for you by tomorrow, sir. With your approval, we'll be able to begin construction straight away."

"Splendid," the colonel replied. "As you can see, there is no shortage of labour to draw from. I'll inform Colonel Parnell and Colonel Welman to have their infantrymen placed at your disposal."

After sixteen years with the Colours, Captain Wynne was being given a task that would allow him to utilise all the skills he'd first learned as a cadet at the Royal Military Academy, Woolwich. With great energy and fervour, he sketched out his detailed plans for Fort Tenedos. Measuring approximately 250 feet in length and 110 in width, it was roughly hexagonal in shape and more than just a set of rough earthworks. Similar to what The Buffs companies built on the south side of the Thukela, there would be an encircling ditch filled with sharp stakes and entanglement obstacles, a thick rampart sloping upward, parapet with firing positions for infantry, and several platforms at strategic points for cannon or rocket tubes.

Work on the fort began almost immediately after breakfast the following morning. As Sergeant David Fredericks and the other NCOs and officers within The Buffs suspected, their infantry would provide the bulk of the unskilled labour force. However, unlike David's previous life, where one could expect to be ploughing fields from sunrise to sunset, Captain Wynne broke the detail up into three-hour shifts called 'reliefs'. These varied in size depending on the immediate task. One of the initial reliefs involved twelve of Wynne's sappers digging sod for the revetments, five cutting wood for the profiles, and six establishing these along the perimeter. Another eight supervised the detail of 145 infantrymen acting as diggers.

The work was labour-intensive. The first couple feet beneath the surface consisted of soupy mud from all the recent rains. The surrounding ditch was supposed to be six feet in depth. However, in numerous places, the ground proved extremely rocky beneath the first few feet of mud and could only be dug down to four feet. By the morning of the 15th, the fort had taken shape. The outer ditch was mostly cleared and work on the ramparts, parapet, and infantry firing steps commenced. Warren kept meticulous records from each relief to include number of men used in what positions, along with exact measurements of what was dug away and built up. While certainly crude by European standards, the captain was confident that once completed, the defences could easily be held by a couple hundred men against whatever force the Zulus sent against them.

Fort Tenedos was completed on the 17th of January. Colonel Pearson was satisfied the fort would serve as a suitable depot for logistics stores coming across the Thukela. On the Natal side of the river, just two companies from the 99th remained to be ferried over. These would garrison the fort with a strong detachment from the Naval Brigade. With defensible forts established on both sides of the Thukela River, and his column mustered on the Zulu side, it was time for the invasion to commence in earnest. What troubled

Pearson now was something neither redcoat nor Zulu had any control over.

"We have enjoyed pleasant and cloudless weather these past two days. Yet, I fear this reprieve from the summer storms will not last. Captain Wynne, your sappers have done fine work since you've arrived, but I suspect your labours have only just begun."

"We didn't come all the way from Blighty to sit on our backsides, sir," the engineer officer asserted.

"I received a short despatch from his lordship this morning," Pearson continued. "It appears Colonel Glynn's boys have drawn 'first blood' in this war."

Though he was given this information by the GOC's messenger a few days before, he decided to wait until he received official word from Chelmsford before passing it on to the staff. Ironically, much of his lordship's despatch contained information Pearson already knew.

"Do we have any details, sir?" Lieutenant Colonel Welman of the 99th asked.

It was assumed that Richard Glyn's centre No. 3 Column would bear the brunt of any fighting. This caused much disappointment for Welman's young and inexperienced soldiers, who were anxious to prove their mettle in battle.

"Very little. Just that they destroyed the kraal of a local *inkosi* who happens to be one of the king's favourites, while killing around sixty Zulus. Like us, this damnable weather has slowed their advance to a crawl. In fact, according to this message, the centre column is still encamped along the uMzinyathi River across from Rorke's Drift. As difficult as it may seem, we have the best 'roads' in all of Zululand at our disposal."

These last words were not reassuring to the assembled officers. Least of all Captain Wynne, whose job was to make certain the old wagon trails were navigable by their heavy wagons.

Pearson went on to explain his plan for the upcoming march. "Given the volume of space required for the baggage wagons, the column is too large and ponderous to manage effectively. We will divide into two divisions during the march. I will personally take a 'flying column' and make for Eshowe with all speed. Colonel Welman, you will command the second division and follow us a day later. Hopefully, the weather will hold, and any damage we cause by driving through the soggy track will have dried out before you advance."

He then distributed his written directives stating where every infantry company, artillery piece, rocket tube, naval detachment, native auxiliaries, and engineers were supposed to stage the following morning. After answering a few more questions, the colonel dismissed his officers to disseminate his orders to their men. Only he and Walker remained.

His fellow colonel turned to him before leaving. "Tomorrow, we start hunting for Zulus."

The earthworks of Fort Tenedos, looking back at Fort Pearson on the hill

That evening, Warren took the time to pen a letter to Lucy. There was no telling when his letters would reach her. The column was, at last, taking the war to the Zulus, and personal correspondence was at the bottom of priorities for what few couriers were available. Still, he figured the letters to his beloved, coupled with his own journal, might make for a riveting read for his sons one day.

The column marches tomorrow. A detachment of Royal Engineers, with the Native Pioneers, heads the column, with

Mounted Infantry for escort, so as to make good the roads where necessary. It has just come on to rain, with thunder and lightning, and I fear the roads will be more troublesome than we had hoped.

He went on to discuss the issues regarding the size of the column and sheer number of wagons and beasts-of-burden before detailing some of the rumours he'd heard that day.

They say there has been a skirmish with Colonel Glyn's column of an insignificant nature; also, that the peace party in Zululand is on the increase. I should be sorry that the question should not be very permanently settled; at the same time, fighting or no fighting, or petty fighting, I shall be glad to have it finished. It is dreadful being so utterly without Sunday services, or anything to remind one of Heavenly things. I have been hoping and longing that I might get a letter before we march up country. However, in a day or two there will be a convoy coming up, so I hope it will bring a letter or two. I wish I could write more, but it is now 'lights out', so I have no chance. We start tomorrow at 3am.

Like every soldier in No. 1 Column, Warren longed for any sort of message from home, whether from his wife, his father, or any of his brothers. He wasn't at all certain what the people back in Britain thought of the war with the Zulus. Little did he know that no one, not even the Queen, had any idea that Sir Henry Bartle-Frere had started a war on his own; and thousands of British soldiers were now invading the kingdom of a former trading partner and ally. Indeed, both the High Commissioner and Lord Chelmsford hoped to have the matter decided before anyone in London could protest.

As Warren blew out the oil lamp, his tent lit up with several flashes of lightning. The crash of thunder portended the return of the summer deluges. He pulled his blanket over himself, worried that the pounding of rain and crash of thunder would deprive him of sleep. Yet within moments of closing his eyes, exhaustion took hold and his world faded to black.

Members of the Naval Brigade, HMS Active, at Fort Tenedos

Chapter V: A Forgotten People

Nthuli Territory, northeast of Lower Drift
18 January 1879

Zulu Inkosi

Like most rumours distorted through the fog of war, what Captain
Wynne had heard about a Zulu 'peace party' was grossly
exaggerated. King Cetshwayo had, indeed, hoped for a peaceful
resolution to the crisis, but the British rebuffed his overtures for
negotiation, demanding total surrender and compliance with the
ultimatum's impossible terms. The attack on the kraal of his close
friend and confidant, Sihayo, along with the slaughter of three-score
of his people meant the only resolution to the crisis would be
through violent expulsion of the British from Zulu lands.

The idea of going to war against those he'd long considered
friends was very distressing for the king. His uncle, the divine
Shaka, had once called King George IV his 'brother Georgie'. So,
too, did Cetshwayo view Queen Victoria as his 'white sister'. What
pained him most was *why* his regal sister would so grievously betray
him. What reason could the Queen have for wishing to bring
destruction upon the Zulus? In the end, it mattered not. War had
come, regardless of whether or not the king understood why.

The Zulu Kingdom was vast, expanding across the south-eastern regions of Southern Africa, uniting numerous tribes and clans under one ruler. In a way, this was not so very different from the British Empire. Within days, messengers reached the far corners of the realm, ordering every regiment of the *amabutho* to muster at the Royal Kraal of Ulundi. Every warrior, even those from the older married regiments that were only called up during the direst of circumstances, was ordered to the royal muster.

Among those heeding the king's call was the *inkosi* of the Nthuli clan named Godide kaNdlela. At seventy years of age, he was a peer of the king's senior generals, Ntshingwayo and Mnyamana, and had served in the same *ibutho* during their youth. The Nthuli were assimilated into the growing Zulu Empire during the reign of King Shaka, settling in the Thukela region not far from the Indian Ocean. Godide was named a member of the *izikhulu*—the royal barons— during the reign of Cetshwayo's father, King Mpande. He was held in high regard by the current king, who summoned him to his hut the night before the *impi* was to depart to face the invaders.

Godide entered the dimly-lit hut, keeping low with his hands held up by his face as he approached his sovereign. To gaze directly upon the king without his expressed permission was deeply offensive, as were any attempts to stand taller than the king. Cetshwayo was a colossal presence, both physically and psychologically. Standing over six-and-a-half feet tall and built like he could take down an elephant with his bare hands, he was an imposing sight, even when seated upon his throne. As the *inkosi* approached, Cetshwayo cradled a ceremonial axe in his lap; a symbol of his power. He also held a wide-bladed *iklwa* spear, said to have once belonged to the great Shaka himself.

"I have come as you commanded, *Ndabazitha*," Godide said, using the term of address similar to the British title, 'your majesty'.

"Please rise, my friend and noble teacher," the king said, slowly raising his hand.

Godide allowed himself to look upon his ruler, though he remained seated at the base of the amaZulu throne. He held his hands up by his face in a form of salute. "What would you command of Godide and the Nthuli?"

"A task no less perilous, yet devoid of the glory that awaits Ntshingwayo and the our great *impi*," Cetshwayo stated. "The 'eyes

83

of the king' have found another British force to the south, crossing the Thukela at *Mathambo*."

"A terrible sacrilege, that they would trample the very ground on which you won your birth right to the amaZulu throne, *Ndabazitha*."

The king nodded. "It is believed that the great *inkosi*, Chelmsford, accompanies their main army and has crossed the uMzinyathi at kwaJimu. There is another arm of their soldiers to the north not far from Chelmsford. It is likely the *impi* will have to face one or both. But, we cannot ignore the skulking band of red soldiers to the south and allow them to pillage our lands and threaten the Royal Kraal."

Cetshwayo paused for a moment and locked gazes with the old *izikhulu*.

The king then continued, "Regretfully, I do not have enough warriors to send with you to defeat this army. I have exempted warriors in the north, as well as the Thukela region in the south, from attending the royal muster, that they might defend their homes and delay these forces. This is what I need from you. You will take the uMxhapho Regiment and head for Mathambo with all haste. The *amakhosi* from two regiments in the region will fall under your command. I need you to delay and, if possible, defeat this unexpected threat. Once Ntshingwayo has dealt with Chelmsford, we will see if my white sister, Victoria, will come to terms."

"It will be done, *Ndabazitha*."

The king gave a slow and confident nod. "There are some abandoned structures near Eshowe that until recently belonged to those who sought to spiritually corrupt our people. To the south near the Inyezane River, the hills are beautiful and full of majesty. No doubt they are blessed by the spirits of the ancestors. I remember it well during the war against my traitorous brother, the pretender, twenty-three harvests ago. You will know the ground when you see it. Hold onto the heights, draw the white soldiers into attacking you, and the sons of Zulu will reap many tears from the enemy's widows."

"As you command, *Ndabazitha*."

Bowing low and averting his eyes once more, Godide left the royal hut.

Despite his advanced age, Godide was still a fit and able warrior much like his peers, Ntshingwayo and Mnyamana. The warriors of the uMxhapho *ibutho* were disappointed to not be joining the main impi in the fight against Chelmsford. Yet, they were also experienced warriors in their early thirties and at the peak of their physical prowess. The *izinduna* who led them understood the gravity of their task, and the importance of preventing the southern enemy column from threatening Ulundi. While their warriors chastised and goaded each other, each force proclaiming loudly which would first spill blood in honour of their sovereign and defence of the kingdom, Godide and Ntshingwayo quietly wished each other well.

"I fear you may confront an even greater challenge than I," Ntshingwayo said candidly. "I may be facing the *inkosi*, Chelmsford, but I bring 25,000 warriors against him. You have but a single regiment of 2,600 fighting men, plus whatever local forces you can muster, against an unknown enemy force."

"The Great Elephant said my task is not necessarily to defeat the British but to delay them," Godide added.

"A thankless, but necessary task. Whatever victories my regiments win, and no matter the honours our king bestows upon them, do not let that diminish the importance of your mission, my friend. The people in the Thukela region are still children of amaZulu. You go not only to protect the Royal Kraal but also the king's subjects. Do not let them become a forgotten people, at the mercy of the white soldiers in red jackets."

The old general's words brought both comfort and consternation to Godide. Fit as they may be, they were still both very old men, devoid of any grandiose ideas about an easy and glorious victory. They knew it would take a combination of superior strategy and overwhelming numbers to defeat the far better armed and equipped British redcoats. And numerical superiority was something Godide simply did not have. The local warriors of the Thukela region were mostly old men, whose regiments were depleted by long-forgotten conflicts and the natural attrition brought on by age.

On the morning of 18 January, the much smaller *impi* under Godide kaNdlela departed from the mustering fields near Ulundi. The warriors were accompanied by several hundred teenage boys, mostly their sons or younger brothers, who acted as mat carriers and drivers of the cattle that would serve as food for the regiment.

Four warriors of great renown accompanied his army, acting as his senior *izinduna*. The youngest of these was a royal *induna* named Phalane kaMdinwa. Godide was unfamiliar with the coastal region, but Phalane knew it well. He'd even met and traded with the now-traitorous John Dunn on several occasions. Just prior to the previous harvest, Phalane purchased a Tower percussion musket for three head of cattle from the 'white Zulu'.

Phalane was one of the most respected *izinduna* within the uMxhapho Regiment. Standing taller than most of his companions, with a lean, muscular frame that looked carved from onyx, his abilities as a leader of warriors was only matched by his natural charisma. He was also a very humble man, cognisant of his place within the *amabutho* hierarchy.

"We can reach the drift at Mathambo within four days," he explained to the *inkosi* and fellow *izinduna*. "Five if we run at a more measured pace."

"We need to save our strength for battle," Godide asserted. "But do not worry; I may be an old man, but I can still run with the best of our warriors."

"Of course. Once we rally our reinforcements, I recommend we make for the kraal at Gingindlovu. From there we can send out our scouts until we find the enemy."

It was a simple yet sound strategy. Though he'd never been that far south, Godide was aware of the old mission station at Eshowe. While it seemed logical that the British would head for and attempt to occupy it on their way to Ulundi, it was still purely a guess. The coastal regions varied considerably from the open grasslands that surrounded the Royal Kraal. The land near the mouth of the Thukela was extremely hilly with many dense forests throughout. It would be entirely possible, not to mention disastrous, for them to simply miss the British altogether.

Scouts had last seen the enemy column attempting to cross the Thukela River on their strange looking boat, suspended from a long rope. Their total strength was unknown, as so many of their troops were still on the Natal side of the river, partially hidden by the

86

expanses of trees along the bank. The scouts surmised there to be at least a thousand redcoats, with twice as many treacherous Natal warriors accompanying them. Godide cautioned his *izinduna* to be prepared for twice as many enemy combatants, and to be ready to face their hated cannon.

The problem with the information they'd received was not only were the scouts unable to see how large the British force was, but all the intelligence was now four days old. Who knew if the enemy had left Mathambo? And if so, how far they had advanced into Zululand?

"Our adversaries bring an absurd amount of equipment with them," Phalane stated, as he jogged next to his *inkosi*. "Great carts requiring many oxen to pull them. There are many rivers they must cross, and the weather will hinder them far greater than us. They are lucky to travel at even half the distance our warriors are capable of each day."

While the *induna's* reassurances were comforting, Godide loathed not knowing his enemy's fighting strength or where they were. He decided after the second day of their journey, he would send his fastest runners on ahead to scour the areas they would pass through each day. The last thing he needed was for his *impi* to stroll blindly into a British ambush!

During the first day of their trek, the *impi* reached a place called kwaMagwaza, approximately thirty-five miles south of Ulundi. It was still another forty-eight to the old mustering barracks at Gingindlovu. KwaMagwaza was a viable strongpoint from where they could rally every warrior in the region and send scouts out to find the British. Calamity struck, however, on the 19th when nearly a third of Godide's warriors were struck by a terrible stomach illness. Many lost control of their bowels, leaving an unholy stench around their campsites that night.

"It's all the damned meat we consumed at the king's feast," Phalane lamented. He clutched his stomach as he returned from his

87

latest bout of painful diarrhoea. "Our warriors have eaten so little over the past few months, and yet we gorged ourselves the night before we left Ulundi."

"We'll rest here for a day; two if necessary," Godide said. With a blanket wrapped around his shoulders, he sat next to his evening campfire.

The other three senior *izinduna* were gathered with him. The men huddled close to the fire, discussing the state of each company within the uMxhapho Regiment. Being in their early thirties, these were warriors in the prime of health. Godide was confident that within a day they would be ready to continue the trek. As they discussed the need to send runners to every homestead within twenty miles of their path to Gingindlovu, a stiff breeze blew in from the east. The old *inkosi* glanced over his shoulder. Storm clouds approached along the horizon.

Incessant rains would pummel them, just as it did their British adversaries. While the white soldiers donned their greatcoats during the day and had tents to protect them at night, the Zulus had neither of these. At night, they struggled to sleep with often only their shields to protect them from the torrential downpour.

"The weather spirits smile on us," Godide asserted. The first drops of the evening shower splashed upon his shoulders and caused his humble fire to hiss in protest.

"How is it a blessing?" one *induna* asked.

"The heavens have come forth to aid us in stopping those who would take the lands of the divine's chosen people. Our very name means 'people of the heavens'! The rivers will swell, and the ground will turn into an impassable quagmire. The misery we suffer under the rains is but temporary; a means of further forging our spirits for the coming battle."

"Our enemy's advance will be slow and exhausting," Phalane added. "They have to dig their ridiculously heavy wagons out of the mud every few paces. They have little choice but to follow the old roads established by that vile betrayer, John Dunn."

The *inkosi* continued, "Once we reach Gingindlovu, we will send our scouts out to find the British. We may lack the numbers of the great *impi*, even with the reinforcements who join us along the way; but we will be able to fight at a time and on ground of our choosing."

The rain was starting to fall heavier. Godide gave up on his campfire which now put out thick clouds of black smoke. He'd made a crude lean-to out of his shield and some brush stands. It gave him some protection from the punishing downpour. He'd established his sleeping space on a small mound, so the water might drain away from him.

The old warrior sighed as he laid on his sleeping mat which squished in the mud. His twelve-year-old grandson, who acted as his mat carrier, sat dutifully nearby. His head was bowed, sleep overtaking him. Godide smiled at the lad, recalling when he served as mat carrier. This had been during the reign of Cetshwayo's grandfather, King Senzangakhona. The idea of war was very different then. Indeed, their entire world had changed. And now, during the twilight years of his long life, would Godide kaNdlela see that world and the great empire raised by Senzangakhona's son, Shaka, destroyed by men who'd once called Zulus 'friends'?

Chapter VI: The Invasion Commences

Lower Thukela
17 January 1879

Stores and equipment waiting to cross Lower Drift

The unenviable task of getting all wagons and baggage across the river fell to the transportation officers. They should have been either quartermasters or commissariat officers who specialised in such matters. However, the army's commissariat was severely lacking in both manpower and resources. The responsibility fell mostly to young lieutenants from regiments on Home Service, who volunteered simply for the chance of adventure on active service. The learning curve was steep, the responsibilities vast, and the chance for recognition practically non-existent.

While on campaign, the army typically used mule wagons to transport its stores of food, ammunition, tents, and other equipment. With resources scattered throughout the British Empire, an ongoing conflict in Afghanistan, and with Her Majesty's government not anticipating a war against the Zulus, there had been little priority to furnish the Natal regiments with the necessary wagons and draught animals. Lord Chelmsford was compelled to either purchase or hire local ox wagons, often at extremely inflated rates, from local settlers. These were huge monstrosities, 18 feet in length, and nearly 6 in width with an empty weight of 3,000 pounds. Each required sixteen oxen, spanned in eight pairs, to haul them. Local Africans served as wagon drivers. Young *voorloopers*—often the sons of the drivers—walked beside the teams of oxen with long whips, keeping the jittery animals in line. The trouble with oxen was they were ponderously slow, requiring several hours of grazing per day with even more for rest to allow their stomachs to digest properly. While the mules the army did have were hardier animals who could haul the smaller wagons much longer and further in a day, the finicky beasts refused to graze and required vast amounts of fodder.

Under ideal road conditions, the ox wagons were rated to haul nearly 8,000 pounds of goods and supplies. However, roads inside the Zulu Kingdom were practically non-existent. Conditions for the No. 1 Column were most certainly better than their comrades to the north, as John Dunn had established a viable wagon trail for trade within the coastal territory. And yet, even this was a far cry from what one would consider a 'road'. The torrential return of the summer rains had also rendered what track there was into a near-impassable mire.

Despite all these difficulties, to say nothing of the pending threat offered by the Zulus, by the 17th of January, Colonel Pearson's No. 1 Column was ready to commence the invasion in earnest. Reveille sounded at 3.30. Under the soft glow of the pre-dawn, soldiers tore down their tents and rolled up their blankets and bed rolls. NCOs conducted final inspections of weapons and kit. Conductors and frantic transportation officers sorted out where each company's wagons were supposed to be.

It all seemed very chaotic; resembling a swarm of fire ants from a distance. Knowing they would be departing this morning, Sergeant David Fredericks had conducted a thorough inspection of his section the night before, ensuring none of his men had broken or missing pieces of kit. As he and his fellow section leaders made their way over to Colour Sergeant Bennet for their morning briefing and coffee, they were mildly surprised to see their officer commanding, Lieutenant Robert Martin, waiting for them. He personally took the time to fill his sergeants' cups with piping hot coffee of far better quality than the bitter sludge they'd been quaffing over the past few weeks.

"Special occasion, sir?" Sergeant Stirling asked.

"Of course," the lieutenant replied. He raised his cup. "Gentlemen, today, the war commences for us. Our objective is to reach old missionary outpost of Eshowe about thirty-five miles from here. I expect the Zulus will give us a rather warm welcome long before we arrive."

"Thirty-five miles might be a short jaunt back home in Blighty," Colour Sergeant Bennet added. "But you are all well-acquainted with the lovely state of the roads, plus the many hills between here and Eshowe; it could take us the better part of a week to reach the mission station."

"We'll be marching by fours on the right side of the column," the officer commanding continued. "Sharp-shooters and skirmishers will push out 200 yards on the flanks, terrain dependant of course. Expect a muddy slog. I anticipate we'll be fighting the weather as much as the Zulus." He then turned to Bennet. "Colour Sergeant, I'll leave morning parade to you. I'm to meet with Colonel Parnell and find out where our place is among the throng. Keep me informed. Once our wagons are loaded, we'll take up our position and be ready to march."

"Very good, sir."

The NCOs came to attention and exchanged salutes with their officer commanding.

David returned to his section to find Corporal Anderson had conducted a quick check of the men, while Monroe supervised the tearing down of their tent.

"Monroe!" Sergeant Fredericks called out.

The lance corporal stepped gingerly through the sucking muck, as he made his way over to his section leader. "Yes, sergeant?"

"You'll be on the flank with the other company skirmishers. Grab your kit and report to Corporal Knight."

"Understood," James replied. As he hoisted his pack onto his shoulders, donned his helmet, and picked up his rifle, he said to his mates, "Don't worry, lads, I'll give you ample warning before any Zulus come to stab you in the bollocks." He gave a tight-faced grin and nod to his sergeant.

There still lingered much of the boyish exuberance at the chance of action that one would expect from a nineteen-year-old soldier. But David saw the unmistakable darkness in Lance Corporal James Monroe's eyes. This paradox existed in many young soldiers who

92

cherished the playful innocence of their age, yet whose very souls became like old men the first time they killed for Queen and Country. The sergeant never said anything to his lance corporal but was well aware of the nightmares that plagued him every night. He knew because he, too, was sometimes visited by horrors from their violent past. *How much worse will they become after this is all over?* he thought. He shook his head, forcing such ideas from his mind.

"Get yourself and the boys through this alive, then worry about the nightmares," he said under his breath.

"Have I done everything to protect our lines of communication and stores?" Colonel Pearson asked his second-in-command.

He and Colonel Walker sat astride their mounts, surveying the assembly of men and wagons of the column's first division.

"The forts are sufficiently garrisoned," Walker said reassuringly. "And all stores are across. Colonel, I think we can say the column is ready to begin the advance on Eshowe."

They were soon joined by Lieutenant Colonel Parnell and Captain Wynne. His sappers would be right behind the advance guard and Native Pioneers.

"The Buffs are ready to march, sir." Parnell gave a sharp salute.

"Thank you, Henry," Pearson replied. "Captain Wynne, I expect a lot will be demanded from your sappers this day."

"That's why we're here, sir. Unless the Almighty deems to stop us, we'll make certain the road to Eshowe is clear."

Pearson nodded and checked his pocket watch. It was five minutes to 5.00. The sun was up with only a few clouds in the sky. He could only hope the fine weather lasted.

"Gentlemen, return to your units."

The men exchanged salutes. Colonel Charles Pearson and his staff officers rode off to take their place in the column.

The lead division was the stronger of the two, consisting of all eight companies from The Buffs, two 7-pounder cannon, the rocket tubes and Gatling guns from the naval detachment, the 2nd Imperial Mounted Infantry, No. 2 Field Company, Royal Engineers, the Stanger and Victoria Mounted Rifles, plus the Natal Hussars and 1st

Battalion of the 2nd Natal Native Contingent. Pearson intended to gain speed in the lead element's advance by leaving most of their baggage behind with the second division. Only fifty of No. 1 Column's near four hundred wagons would accompany the first division. The rest would be escorted by Lieutenant Colonel Welman's division consisting of two companies from the 99th and ten companies from the NNC. Much to his chagrin, the rest of his regiment had been broken apart, left on garrison duty at various locations. Two remained in Natal, with four guarding the two forts along the Thukela for the time being. Colonel Pearson's reasoned that somebody had to protect their supply and communication lines; he felt more comfortable having his veterans from The Buffs with him once the actual fighting commenced.

Nearly two hundred yards off the right flank of the column, Lance Corporal James Monroe and the sharp-shooters from A and H Companies walked through the tall grass, keeping their eyes open for any sign of the enemy. They were led by a corporal named James Knight. In addition to being Sergeant Stirling's assistant section leader, he was also in charge of the company's skirmishers and designated marksmen. Monroe spent nearly as much time with him and the other sharp-shooters as he did with his own section. They forced their way through the five-foot grass, still wet from the night rains and morning dew.

"Just walking through this shit is leaving me soaked," one soldier complained.

"You could always go dig wagons out of mud and shit," Corporal Knight countered.

"And hope we don't let the Zulus sneak up and put a spear through your neck," James added with a malicious grin.

Off to their left, they saw a team of sappers and Natal Pioneers hastily digging drainage ditches off a swampy section of road. Infantrymen heaved their wagons through the sludge. This occurred once more a bit further on. The column progressed less than two miles before having to stop for repairs to the rain-saturated road.

"I hear the centre column has no roads at all," a trooper from the Stanger Mounted Rifles said, as he rode next to Monroe.

"That will give them a spot of bother," the lance corporal chuckled. He noted the squishing of his shoes in the muddy earth.

The carbineer's section leader shouted down from atop a low ridge to 'quit arsing around' and take up his post on the far flank. The trooper kicked his horse into a gallop; hooves sending clods of mud and trampled grass into the young redcoat's face.

"Bloody twat," he grumbled. He wiped his face and checked his rifle. Since the first day of march towards the staging camp at Lower Drift, his normally black footwear remained completely filthy. The bottom few inches of his trousers were splattered with mud. Like the rest of the imperial redcoats, who'd all been in the same uniforms since their last resupply the previous April, his tunic and trousers were in a terrible state. He could feel drops of dew coming in past a patch on the right knee of his trousers where some stitching had come loose.

Corporal Knight was walking up and down the length of skirmishers. They were in loose order, with ten to twenty yards between each man. The column had been marching for just under an hour when a halt was called.

"We're stopping for twenty minutes," Knight called out. "Take a short rest and a smoke, if you wish, but keep your eyes open. We still have no idea where in the bleeding fuck the Zulus are."

"Saw a few this morning," James noted. "A pity they buggered off before we could properly say 'hello' to each other."

"I'm sure we'll get our chance sooner-rather-than-later."

Monroe took a deep breath in through his nose and let out a sigh. Lately, he found himself embroiled in internal conflict. He was both excited and filled with dread at the prospect of battle. His gut told him that before this matter with the Zulus was decided, he would have to kill again. Did all who had taken a life feel as wretched as he did? He never dared to ask. Instead, he tried to simply dismiss the matter, telling himself repeatedly, *'No one forced me to take the Queen's Shilling.'*

Towards the head of the column, Captain Warren Wynne led his No. 2 Field Company behind the Natal Native Pioneers. Leading the vanguard of mounted troops was Captain Percy Barrow, a regular Army officer from the 19th Royal Hussars.

"Splendid morning, Captain Wynne," the cavalry officer said, as he rode over to Warren and pointed to an open meadow near another abandoned mission called St Andrew's. "I'll recommend to Colonel Pearson that we halt there for breakfast. Lord knows, there will be heavy work once we reach the Nyoni River."

"A splendid notion," Wynne agreed.

Barrow continued up the column to where Pearson and the staff rode.

Warren turned to his senior subaltern. "Mister Courtney, pass word to the men. We'll be halting at the mission station for a spot of breakfast."

"If the Nyoni is anywhere near as flooded as the Thukela, the lads will need all their strength this afternoon," the lieutenant noted.

It was nearly 8.00 when the first division halted at the old mission. Like all the others within the Zulu Kingdom, it was abandoned soon after Cetshwayo's ban on foreign missionaries. The column had been on the march for nearly two-and-a-half hours yet travelled just three miles from Lower Drift.

Sergeant David Fredericks wiped his forearm along his sweaty brow and gazed back up the road, shaking his head in frustration. He could just barely see the site of their previous camp from that very morning.

"Could have crawled here faster than this," a private named Corble grumbled.

"Just you watch, we're likely to get pissed on before the day is done," another moaned.

This brought rebuking slaps across the helmet from one of his mates, Private William Dunne. "Would you shut your fucking arsehole! Don't be tempting fate like that."

Another man spoke up. "If we get soaked this afternoon, I'm blaming you!"

"Don't you sodding monkeys ever pay attention?" Corble snapped, removing his helmet and throwing it at Dunne. "We have a bloody river to cross, so we're going to get all soggy, regardless of what the weather does!"

The bickering continued as the soldiers established a large perimeter around the convoy, digging their breakfast of tinned beef and hard biscuit from their packs. David glanced over to Rob Anderson, who simply rolled his eyes and shook his head. The truth was, soldiers always found a reason to complain. If the weather was idyllic, they would gripe about the food; and if the food was palatable, they would whine about the roads; if the roads were smooth, they would complain about their shoes or how hot their uniforms were; though few would argue with the last point. Regardless, not a day passed without a litany of complaints that have been common since the dawn of professional armies.

"If they're not complaining, they're not happy," Rob said, with a chuckle to his section leader.

"In that case, we have some of the most content soldiers in all Her Majesty's armed forces," David added with a grin of his own.

He really could not blame his men for their bitterness regarding the weather and soggy living conditions. His own greatest fear was losing half his section to typhoid or dysentery or falling victim to fever himself. However, he also knew to keep his own complaints to himself. There was nothing he could say to the other section leaders or to Colour Sergeant Bennet that they were not already aware of.

An hour past noon, Captain Barrow's riders reached the Nyoni River. While the rains had mercifully not swollen the normally idyllic stream beyond its banks, they were extremely steep.

Barrow was no stranger to the difficulties involved in transporting so many men and materials across such rough terrain, offered his assessment to Colonel Pearson. "We'll have to double-span the wagons, sir," he asserted.

The column commander and staff surveyed the river from a low rise. The mounted vanguard and the two lead companies from The Buffs were wading across and establishing picquets from which to protect the rest of the division.

Double-spanning the wagons was an arduous process. An entire ox team had to be unhitched and then connected to the wagon that was crossing. Controlling sixteen pairs of the unruly beasts proved especially difficult for the wagon drivers and voorloopers. As wagons crossed over, scores of draught animals would have to be led back across the river and hitched up again. The already muddy riverbanks were churned up as the first wagon slogged through the waist-deep current. Teams of sappers and Natal Pioneers were established on both sides of the river. After every two or three wagons crossed, they would rush forward with their shovels and other tools to repair the damage. Knowing that crossing the river would take most of the afternoon, Pearson ordered the column to establish camp about 200 yards from the crossing point.

Captain Percy Barrow
19th Royal Hussars

At around 3.00 that afternoon, the winds picked up, blowing in dark storm clouds. Less than half of the wagons had made the crossing when the heavens opened, unleashing a punishing downpour upon the column.

"God…damn it, Corble!" Private Dunne shouted over the deafening roar of the pouring rain. "This is all your fault, you know!"

"Oh, piss off, or I'll command the rain gods to strike you with lightning," his fellow soldiered called back.

"Oy, watch the blasphemy!" another man bellowed.

The storm came upon them so quickly they were completely drenched before any could pull their greatcoats from their packs.

"Or what?" Corble countered. "The Almighty has already given us shitty weather, shitty roads…not to mention half of us have the shits!"

"Point your rifle barrels down." Sergeant Fredericks checked his men.

His soldiers complied, streams of water pouring out as they did so.

"Nothing bothers you, does it, sergeant?" Private Dunne asked. "I mean, I've never heard you complain."

"Nor will you," David stressed. "Any complaints I have are not your concern." He nodded towards the west where a thick mist engulfed the nearby hills. "Keep your eyes open, lads. I doubt the Zulus enjoy this weather any more than we do. But if they're out there, don't think they won't use it to mask their approach."

While most of the soldiers in H Company were veterans of the previous year's war against the Xhosa, there were a few new recruits who joined the Regiment just prior to the invasion. The sergeant found one of these men, Private John Harris, kneeling behind a short brush stand. The lad was huddled beneath his greatcoat, his Martini-Henry clutched close to his chest. He struggled to see more than a few feet in front of his face.

"Everything alright, Harris?" David asked, causing the soldier to jolt.

"Yes, sergeant," the private replied, quickly nodding his head. "Just can't see a damned thing is all."

Even through the pouring rain, it was clear something was troubling the young man. David waited for a moment while the private gathered his thoughts.

"Sergeant, I can't help but wonder, is this what war is really like? I mean, I joined the Regiment to fight for Queen and Country, for the glory of the Empire! When Mister Martin said the war began for us this day, I half expected to find thousands of Zulus waiting for us. I've not seen a single one since I've been in Africa, just rumours and hearsay from those who say they've spotted a few of their scouts watching us. Where are they, sergeant?"

"Bugger if I know," David replied candidly. "Something to remember; war is near endless tedium, with that rare moment of sheer terror. And regardless of our intentions or how meticulous the officers are in their planning; the enemy always has a say in the outcome."

The soldier nodded and fidgeted. He tried to find a way to be comfortable, kneeling behind a bush in the middle of a South African downpour. For his part, Sergeant David Fredericks recognised the young soldier's naivety. He had been the same not so long ago.

The rains continued unabated. Scores of soldiers sought out their company wagons and began unloading tents. The punishing storm made it difficult to see. Men tripped over tent poles, ropes, and other equipment that was hastily pulled from the wagons. While some fought to erect their tents, others took spades and dug drainage trenches, using their tools to scoop away the pooling water from where they hoped to sleep that night.

The officers shared in most of the same hardships as their men. They had camp beds and far more personal space, yet as Captain Warren Wynne was all-too-aware, even those holding the Queen's Commission could scarcely keep dry during the rain-soaked summer of Southern Africa. As officer commanding of No. 2 Field Company, he was fortunate enough to have a camp bed and was not required to sleep on the ground. However, this was a small comfort, as the cot was completely drenched when his batman drug it into the leaky tent. The canvas on his tent was torn in several places, the stitching coming apart near the centre pole. Without complaint, the engineer officer hung his greatcoat and tunic, taking a few moments to scrawl some notes in his journal before 'lights out'.

Mercifully, the bouts of illness which wreaked havoc on Godide's warriors subsided within a day. Fortunately, most of the older warriors, those exempt from the king's order to assemble that they might defend their homes, had not taken part in the great feasts at Ulundi. Their concern was because they'd missed the royal muster, they had not taken part in the days of purification ceremonies that would ready their bodies and spirits for battle. With no diviners, known as the *izinyanga*, available to conduct the necessary rituals and charms, Godide could only chastise the men, reminding them that their duty to king and nation would carry them through the coming trials.

By the evening of the 20th of January, the *impi* reached the old oNdini Royal Kraal, which was the former homestead of Cetshwayo before his rise to become king. Located between the Mlalazi River and Ngoye Mountain, it was seventeen miles from Gingindlovu. Like most of the homesteads in the coastal regions it was deserted. The Zulu wives had taken their children and the elderly, along with all their cattle and belongings, deeper into the mainland. Only a handful of warriors remained, that they might reinforce Godide's *impi* while keeping an eye on the advancing British forces. Unfortunately, none of the fighting men who joined them so far had seen the enemy, as they had all come from homesteads north of Gingindlovu.

"There is an abandoned Christian mission at Eshowe, about a day's hard journey from here," Phalane told the *inkosi* and fellow *izinduna* that evening, as their army established its camp along the mountain.

He then pointed with his spear towards the west. A few miles south of Ngoye, the ground opened into gently rolling hills and great expanses of farmland extending all the way to the ocean. To the west, however, the terrain was extremely mountainous and rough.

"And you suspect that is where the enemy is headed?" an *induna* conjectured.

"It's an ideal place for them to establish a stronghold," Phalane remarked. "It also puts them about halfway between were they crossed the Thukela River and Ulundi."

"Then it is good that we shall reach Gingindlovu by morning," Godide asserted.

Fortunately for Godide and his senior leaders, there were still plenty of old huts for them to sleep in, saving them from the nightly rains. Gingindlovu was a massive *ikhanda*, or barracks, which could house thousands of warriors. He hoped to give his men a couple of nights of rest without being tormented by the relentless rain before they faced the British in battle.

Chapter VII: The Grandmother of Gingindlovu

West of the Amatikulu River, twenty miles south of Eshowe
21 January 1879

Zulu *izinyanga* diviners

Bleary-eyed, tired, and irritable after all the scares and false alarms from the previous night, the men of No. 1 Column rose at around 3.30 on the morning of the 21st. Though just twenty miles or so from their objective at Eshowe, once they turned north the terrain became very mountainous. Distance had become relative. They had travelled only seventeen miles over the past four days. Their immediate obstacle was the Amatikulu River, which swelled from the recent rains to such an extent that the fording point was no longer passable.

Captain Wynne's engineers and the Natal Pioneers spent the previous day finding another viable crossing, which they cut a path to while digging out the steep riverbanks and building earthen ramps to allow the wagons into the river without tipping over. There were also numerous large boulders to remove on the far bank. Through their extensive efforts, the sappers of No. 2 Field Company made the Amatikulu fordable once more. One could still expect the heavy wagons to sink in the mud and water, making for a labour-intensive day once the first division of the column arrived later in the morning. Oxen and mules would be extra skittish, being yoked to the monstrosities while sinking up to their stomachs in the river.

As elements from the first division made ready for departure, and with no one else to provide security for a time, Warren Wynne's sappers found themselves wielding their rifles nearly as much as their tools. Due to the arduous obstacle provided by the Amatikulu River and the poor state of the roads, Colonel Pearson decided it made the most sense that day to have Wynne's company travel immediately behind the vanguard of mounted troops. Two companies from The Buffs immediately followed, ready to provide infantry support in the event of a crisis. It also meant the sappers would be at the heart of any pending action.

At around 6.45, the lead elements of the column reached the Amatikulu. Inexplicably, the water level had dropped considerably overnight, making the original ford now passable.

"Still, it was nice of Captain's Wynne's lads to give us another crossing point," a mounted trooper said with a grin.

Even with the lowered water levels, it would take most of the day for their baggage to cross over. Colonel Pearson and the column staff arrived soon after and surveyed the crossing points.

"Another day of march, another river to cross," a staff officer noted, stretching his arms behind his neck.

The column commander simply gave a nod of acknowledgement. They would continue the advance in two divisions with the intent of establishing their next camp just beyond the Amatikulu. Anticipating possible contact with the Zulus, Colonel Pearson ordered the artillery, rockets, and Gatling guns to cross immediately following the sappers and two companies from The Buffs. While the first companies of redcoats forded the crossing, their rifles and packs held high out of the water, the column staff was joined by an officer from the NNC named Lieutenant Robarts.

"Your pardon, colonel," he said, with a salute. "Some of my warriors have informed me of a Zulu *ikhanda* just a few miles to the east."

"*Ikhanda?*" the colonel asked.

"Think of it like a barracks or mustering field, sir," Lieutenant Robarts explained. "The locals call it Gingindlovu."

"No simplicity with their damned names, is there?" Lieutenant Colonel Parnell remarked with agitation.

"It literally means, 'swallower of the elephant'," the NNC officer observed. "Cetshwayo had it built to commemorate his bloody victory of his brother, Mbuyazi, twenty-two years ago. It's no longer used by the king, but it is still very much intact. At least, it was when we came through here six years ago."

"When you came through here?" a staff officer asked.

Robarts nodded. "I was an escort with Sir Theophilus Shepstone's deputation for King Cetshwayo's coronation."

Henry Parnell shook his head. It seemed strange that two nations, which had just recently been staunch trading partners and friends, were now at war. That a British colonial official had even crowned the Zulu King felt even more absurd.

"An ideal place to stage their regiments," Colonel Pearson remarked, his focus on the nearby Zulu stronghold. He then ordered the two companies from The Buffs to cross the river and secure the far bank.

With infantry no protecting the crossing, Captain Wynne divided his sappers into two elements, leaving half on each side to conduct repairs to the fording points as needed. As he was overseeing the passage of some of his equipment carts, a staff officer rode over to him.

"Your pardon, captain. We just received word from Surgeon Norbury. Seems a pole on the hospital wagon has broken."

"How far back are they?"

"About two miles."

Warren nodded and said it would be taken care of. He found one of his NCOs who was overseeing the nearside fording point. "Corporal Smith!"

"Sir?" the man replied, coming quickly to attention.

"Take one of the men and head back up the road. See what you can do about a broken pole on the hospital wagon."

"Right away." The corporal then called out to one of his sappers, an Irishman named O'Leary. The two took a donkey cart full of carpentry tools and started back up the road.

"To be honest, I'm surprised we got this far without any number of the wagons breaking," Lieutenant David Courtney said, joining his officer commanding.

104

Warren concurred. "The rivers are a great unknown. At least on the roads we can see what's coming. The rivers are a real gamble. We don't know if the greater risk is our wagons sinking in mud or if there are great boulders just beneath the surface, waiting to break an axle."

Despite the hours in blistering sun—that is, when the column wasn't being tortured by endless rains—Lieutenant Courtney could not help but notice his officer commanding was looking rather pale. "Are you alright, sir?" he asked rather candidly. "You seem to have lost colour in your face. When was the last time you slept?"

"I managed a couple hours last night," Warren replied.

Courtney shook his head. "You know, sir, if you collapse from exhaustion, they'll leave me in charge of the company."

The men shared a short laugh at this, though the lieutenant's expression quickly became serious. Warren sought to reassure his senior subaltern.

"I appreciate your concern, Mister Courtney, but I am fine. Thankfully, my entire family is known for their robust health. My father turns eighty in a couple months, and he still manages well enough." Noting Lieutenant Courtney's lingering apprehension, he added, "I promise I'll allow myself a few more hours each night, once we're established at Eshowe."

"Just do us a favour, sir, and remember to delegate. You've got me, Willock, and Main, not to mention Colour Sergeant Smith and all of our non-comms." Though not entirely convinced by his officer commanding's reassurances, David Courtney decided to let the issue lie for the time being. In truth, sleep was a commodity that no one seemed to get enough of in the field.

This was why coffee and tea were the life's blood for the army!

On the far side of the river, NNC warriors, along with a score of Captain Barrow's mounted volunteers rode in the direction of the Zulu stronghold to ascertain the rumours about an enemy force converging in the area. Colonel Pearson, meanwhile, had dismounted his horse and was talking a short walk to stretch his legs. It was a maddeningly slow process getting the wagons across the river, even though the water level had dropped substantially. Still, as slow as their progress was, the column was continuing to move forward towards their objective.

He was soon joined by Lieutenant Colonel Parnell, who was returning from checking his two companies that were providing over-watch for the crossing.

"No sign of the enemy, sir," Henry said. "It feels as if the entire country is just deserted."

"The Zulus know we're here," Pearson replied. "I suspect they've taken their wives and children and driven their cattle herds further inland." Just then he saw a rider approaching from the east. Recognising him as Lieutenant Robarts, he added, "It looks like we'll soon have an answer regarding the enemy barracks."

"Colonel, sir," the lieutenant said, as he reined in his horse and saluted.

"What news?" Pearson asked.

"We could only get to within about half a mile of the kraal, sir," the officer explained. "It is still very much intact with eight-foot palisades surrounding the compound. It's very large, sir. I daresay it could easily house 5,000 men. We spotted the smoke from many campfires, both in and around the kraal. Even if the main *impi* is determined to engage Colonel Glyn's centre column, I daresay they've still got plenty of friends for us to deal with."

This report, vague as it was, filled Pearson with both irritation and excitement. He was naturally anxious to engage the Zulus in a decisive battle; however, he was greatly disappointed by the lack of detail. Given the complete absence of professional cavalry in Natal, the invasion columns had to rely on locally-recruited volunteers, most of whom knew nothing about how to conduct a proper reconnaissance.

He decided a more robust and lethal form of investigation was needed. "Colonel Parnell, send two companies from The Buffs to assault the kraal. Both rocket tubes, the 7-pounders, half our Naval brigade, the Stanger and Victoria Mounted Rifles, and two companies of NNC will be in support."

"Very good, sir," Parnell said, acknowledging with a salute, despite his reservations about the plan. A quick calculation and he reckoned the detachment would have, at most, 600 men; of whom less than one third would be professional infantry. To send such a small force into the unknown with the real possibility of thousands of enemy warriors waiting for them was extremely dangerous. In his mind, it would be more prudent to wait until all The Buffs were over and then send the entire battalion. However, orders were orders, and he understood Colonel Pearson's desire for expediency. As it was, it would be close to dark by the time the taskforce returned, even if they did not run into a large force of Zulus.

"Captain Jackson!" he shouted, summoning over the commander of C Company. They and G Company were the only ones who had crossed thus far.

"Sir?" the captain asked, as he rode his horse over.

"C and G Companies are leading an expedition towards a Zulu kraal, five miles east. Mounted troops will screen your front with NNC on the flanks. The 7-pounders and naval rockets will be in support."

The captain nodded. "What do we know of enemy forces in the area?"

"Almost nothing," the colonel replied, shaking his head dejectedly. "Scouts have seen the smoke from numerous campfires but nothing substantial. Both companies will advance in skirmishing order. But be ready to form into squares on the guns at a moment's notice."

"We'll keep them close, sir," the captain reassured him.

It was nearly 1.00 by the time the taskforce was organised and ready to advance. Another company from The Buffs along with several of NNC warriors replaced C and G Companies on picquet duty. Even at a brisk walk, it would take the redcoats and artillery a couple of hours to traverse the heavily saturated five miles of ground between them and Gingindlovu. Meanwhile, the rest of No. 1 Column continued its laborious crossing over this latest river.

"I say, where are they off to?" a private asked, as the soldiers from H Company of 2/3rd Buffs heaved their tent and ammunition wagons through the sinking muck at the bottom of the Amatikulu.

In the distance, they could see the two companies of redcoats, hundreds of NNC warriors, a couple of rocket tubes, and two 7-pound cannon departing the camp and heading east.

"Off to have a little fun, from the looks of it," Private Corble observed.

"Lucky bastards," another man grumbled.

He and several mates were struggling to heave a wagon wheel over a large rock hidden beneath the surface of the water.

Corporal Robert Anderson had taken a thick plank and was using it for leverage to help the wheels over submerged obstacles and through the thick mud. He first removed his pack, jacket, and various kit, leaving them and his rifle in the back of the wagon. Any time they came upon another obstacle, the corporal would submerge himself up past his chest and wedge the brace under the wheel. It was awkward yet effective. H Company's wagons progressed across the river in minimal time.

"Might also save us a broken wheel or axel." He grinned at Sergeant Fredericks as their tent wagon reached the far bank.

One of the company subalterns, Lieutenant Willock, was waiting for them. "Keep following the track about 400 yards. Colour Sergeant Smith will show you where to stage the wagons."

"Yes, sir," David replied.

The sergeant then closed his eyes and turned his face up towards the sun for a moment. He removed his helmet and ran his fingers through his sweat-matted hair. As much as they struggled to keep their uniforms and equipment dry during the constant rains, it was on blistering hot days like this that David was grateful for the chance to cool off in the river.

Captain Jackson's detachment advanced towards Gingindlovu at a reasonably quick pace; the ground holding firm beneath their feet despite the recent rains. A few soldiers noted that the tall grasses they trampled through gave them far greater purchase than the calf-deep mud of the wagon track. The captain and his fellow officers remained mounted. Jackson constantly scanned with his field glasses for any signs of the enemy.

"Look lively, lads," a sergeant spoke up. "None of you want to get skewered in the bollocks by a kaffir lurking in the grass."

It was nearly 3.00 when the *ikhanda* came into view. The plumes of campfire smoke—if that's what it was—had mostly dissipated.

"Impressive," one soldier noted, gripping his rifle close.

The palisade stakes surrounding the large complex were tall logs, eight feet in height, and sharpened at the top. From a distance, they gave the appearance of a long row of teeth.

At a quarter mile, with no sign of the enemy, Captain Jackson ordered his men to load their weapons and make ready to advance on the compound.

"With your permission, sir," one of his subalterns spoke up. "I'll take a few mounted troops and see if we can draw the enemy out."

"Alright," the captain concurred. "Just be careful."

Jackson then ordered the cannon placed in the centre with the two rocket tubes on either flank. With the NNC and mounted volunteers deployed on the wings, the two infantry companies formed into a long skirmish line.

The captain nodded to his lieutenant, who along with two other subalterns from The Buffs and a few mounted rifles, spurred their horses into a gallop, riding straight for the large opening along the western rampart of the large kraal. Redcoats nervously scanned the palisade, not knowing if they were manned by enemy troops or simply for appearance and to keep in cattle.

After a few minutes, the officer rode out of the kraal, waving his helmet over his head. "This place appears to be deserted, sir!" he shouted to his captain.

Captain Jackson let out a sigh of relief, though he was somewhat disappointed the enemy had decided not to turn out this day. "Alright lads, stand easy." He then directed the section leaders of both companies to sweep the compound.

Mounted troops were then directed to ride beyond the kraal, searching the immediate vicinity for any sign of the enemy. NNC warriors clustered close together, kneeling with their shields and weapons ready.

"This place has been deserted for some time, sir," Jackson's colour sergeant reported about half an hour later. "Anything of value was pilfered long before we got here. Most of the huts are in disrepair and crawling with spiders. If any Zulus were here recently, they didn't stay for long."

"Here, look what we found!" The excited voice of his senior subaltern shouted. He and a pair of officers were riding over to them with a crawling mass hobbling beside them. It wasn't until they reached the captain that he realised it was, in fact, a very old woman stooped over and covered in a ratty shawl.

"Thought we spotted a large porcupine," the lieutenant said with a laugh, noting the woman's ratted hair. "What should we do with her? Think the chaplain will want to keep her as a pet?"

The lieutenant and a few others derided the woman with a slew of cruel terms. Captain Jackson took pity on her. This was no animal, like his subaltern suggested, but somebody's grandmother. Still, he agreed, somewhat, with what his officer suggested.

"Reverend Robertson knows these people, and he speaks their language. Perhaps he can get some information from her. If she is by herself, it's just as likely the local Zulus don't even know she's here." He then spoke gently to the old woman, trying to recall what few words of isiZulu that he knew. He hoped he was telling her she would not be mistreated. She nodded and spoke a few hoarse words he could not understand.

The captain then turned to the petty officer in charge of the naval rocket tubes. "Be a good man and send a pair of rockets into the compound," he ordered. "The huts are clustered together. A couple of incendiaries should sort it out."

"Sir!" the petty officer said, snapping off an excited salute. He called to his men, "Section…action front! Two rockets at 400 yards!"

Like most army officers, Captain Jackson had little regard for Hales rockets. Notoriously inaccurate and wildly unpredictable, they did little except make a lot of noise. But given the size of the compound, he reckoned even they would be hard-pressed to miss.

With impressive speed brought on by endless drills and rehearsals, the sailors loaded the 24-pound rockets into their tubes, set the fuses, and did a final elevation check. When two of the leading seamen acknowledged they were ready, the petty officer gave an excited shout of *'Fire!'*

With a loud 'whoosh' the rockets flew from their tubes, a burst of sparks and smoke in their wake. Both landed inside the kraal with a loud boom. Despite the recent rains, the thatch caught fire relatively quickly. Within minutes the entire compound was being devoured in a blazing inferno.

With a good-natured grin, C Company's senior subaltern nodded towards the burning compound. "Well, now that that's sorted out, we can return to camp just in time for supper."

Officers of the HMS Active
Commander Henry Campbell seated in the centre

The column of thick, black smoke was visible from the newly-established camp not far from the river. Colonel Pearson scanned the area with his field glasses but saw little more than the billowing smoke. It was enough, and he allowed himself a satisfied smile.

Two hours later, Captain Jackson's detachment returned. The soldiers and sailors had mixed feelings about the expedition. While it was certainly satisfying to have laid waste to one of the enemy's most important strongholds in the region, the Zulus were conspicuous by their absence. Because it was the naval rocket battery that set fire to Gingindlovu, most of the redcoats were disappointed they had done little except stand and watch the spectacle.

That evening, Reverend Robertson sat with the old Zulu woman whom he had taken into his care. She was emaciated, and she seemed very addled. She claimed to have no knowledge of the war between the Zulus and the British. When told of the invasion, she simply said, "A pity that we must fight the friends of the Great Elephant."

"You refer to Shaka?" Robertson asked, recalling that the *Great Elephant* was one of the names given to the legendary Zulu king.

He had no way of guessing the woman's age, and even she didn't seem to know for certain. Judging by the deep wrinkles in her face and the vast history that seemed to hide behind her eyes, it was conceivable that she lived through the reign of the Zulu Kingdom's most famous ruler, his father, Senzangakhona, and possibly even his grandfather, Jama.

"No other man, before or since, has been worthy of such a title," she explained. "Many called him 'tyrant', yet he loved my brother and avenged his murder."

"Who was your brother?"

"Dingiswayo of the Mthethwa."

This revelation drew an appreciative whistle from the reverend, though he doubted anyone else in the column would even know the name.

"The only man who Shaka ever acknowledged as his overlord and teacher," he noted.

The woman nodded and cracked a tired smile in appreciation that a white man would recall her revered brother, murdered more than sixty years before.

"Shaka served Dingiswayo as a loyal general, and the Zulus were loyal friends of the Mthethwa. My brother appreciated his genius and knew he was the rightful heir to the Zulu Kingdom. He aided Shaka in claiming what was rightfully his after the death of King Senzangakhona. In return, the Great Elephant avenged my brother when the dark monster, Zwide, murdered him. Soon after, the Mthethwa were united with the amaZulu under Shaka's divine rule."

Reverend Robertson was very familiar with the history of the Zulus and the neighbouring kingdoms. He had read several times the works of the adventurer, Henry Fynn. As a young man, he was among the first whites to make contact with Shaka. The leader of the expedition, a former Royal Navy lieutenant named Francis Farewell, had even secured the rights to what would become Port Natal from King Shaka. And decades later, Fynn's son, also named Henry, was now a magistrate along the Natal-Zulu border.

This woman, who evaded any questions about her own name, knew much about the history of the Zulu and Mthethwa. But, her answers became vague the closer Robertson's questions drew to the present. Any mention of King Cetshwayo was met evasively. The woman's only memory seemed to be of 'the dear little boy' who was Shaka's nephew and son of Mpande.

Colonel Pearson visited the reverend later that evening, while the old woman slept on a blanket near his wagon. The colonel was rather surprised by the level of detail which Robertson recalled of the woman's story.

"Do you believe all that?" he asked, uncertain what to think of it.

"She has no reason to lie to us," the reverend said with a shrug. "I mean, what does she have to gain? I think she was taken aback that I even knew who her brother was. Some of the tales she told me matched the descriptions in Fynn's book. And while she cannot even tell me her name much less her age, she is clearly very old."

"And you believe that she has no knowledge of the enemy's movements in the area?" Pearson asked.

"Judging from her withered state, I imagine her family is either long dead or has abandoned her. She made no mention of a husband or any children, so perhaps she never married."

"She could very well have wandered back here long after the kraal was abandoned and was simply presumed dead by her family," Pearson speculated.

"A shame, really," the reverend added. "Her mind is mostly gone, it seems, yet she clearly remembers the age of Dingiswayo and Shaka."

Chapter VIII: Where Are They?

West of Gingindlovu
21 January 1879

A Zulu *ikhanda*

It was nearly nightfall when Godide's army reached Gingindlovu. The column of smoke was visible for miles, and it filled the Zulus with dread to think the British had advanced this far into their country. Godide ordered some of his fastest runners ahead to assess the devastation and see if the British were still in the vicinity.

"The fires still burn fierce, *inkosi*," a runner reported when the *impi* was about four miles from Gingindlovu.

Companies of warriors from every *ibutho* formed into battle lines, anticipating finding the British at any moment. Warriors from the older regiments and local volunteers kept in the centre. The younger warriors from the uMxhapho formed the 'Horns' on the flanks.

"Then they were only recently lit," Phalane surmised.

Godide concurred. "Which means the enemy cannot be far." He then addressed his *izinduna*. "My friends, I am sorry I cannot offer our warriors shelter this night. Clearly, the red-jacketed soldiers are travelling quicker through our lands than we first expected. But they are close. And tonight, we shall hunt them."

At the camp, it was after dark when the wagons from their second division finally crossed the Amatikulu. The soldiers providing escorts were wet and exhausted by the time they unpacked their tents and sat down to their humble rations of hard biscuit and tinned beef for supper. The only mercy this night was the sky was clear and devoid of rain clouds.

Just outside the command tent for No. 2 Field Company, Captain Wynne was joined by his senior subaltern, Lieutenant Courtney. Warren was brewing tea over a small fire, and he offered Courtney a cup. The two had thus far forged a strong working rapport, aided in part because they were close in age and experience. In many ways, Warren viewed David Courtney as more of a peer than a subordinate.

"A fortunate turn of events for the detachment the colonel sent out," Courtney conjectured.

"What do you mean?" his captain asked.

The lieutenant paused for a moment, suddenly regretting his candour. He gave an imperceptible nod and explained. "No disrespect intended to Colonel Pearson. After all, I am no infantry officer. Yet I cannot help but think his dividing of our forces the way he did was a mistake, and a potentially lethal one at that." He waited for a moment, gauging his officer commanding's response.

Wynne remained silent.

"We were several hours from getting our wagons across, with over half the column on the other side of the river. Had the Zulus been at that stronghold, God only knows what sort of trouble the lads could have gotten into. And suppose they had attacked us here, instead? Again, I do not mean to question the colonel's judgement. Yet, I cannot help but think that dividing our forces, especially when we have no viable intelligence as to the enemy's strength or disposition, is inviting disaster." Courtney took a moment to take a drink from his mug of tea. At first, he thought perhaps he had gone too far in his criticism of their column commander.

"Like you, I am no infantry officer," Wynne replied after gathering his thoughts. He was having similar misgivings. "We both understand basic military strategy, as expected by all who hold the Queen's Commission. I confess that I also felt the decision to send such an understrength force towards Gingindlovu was ill-advised. We should have waited until the entire column, or at least the first division, was over. On the morrow we could detach a robust reconnaissance force to ascertain the enemy's whereabouts. I cannot foresee them simply letting us walk all the way to Eshowe without taking a moment to say 'hello'." He took a moment to refill his mug. "But, neither you nor I are in command of this column. We can only look after our own and give advice to the colonel that is within our expertise and experience."

In truth, the colonel's decision troubled Captain Wynne more than he let on. Charles Pearson was a highly-experienced officer, *mentioned in despatches* several times during the Crimean War. He had, thus far, shown great attention-to-detail regarding the logistics and transportation needs of the column, keeping his infantry and horsemen ready to face the enemy at any given time. Had he simply been careless this day? Was he underestimating the Zulu threat?

He decided to heed his subaltern's request and laid down that night earlier than usual, hoping to get a few hours of sleep devoid of interruption. Warren felt a touch of guilt. He had neglected to update his journal over the past couple days, as well as his next letter to Lucy. His diary, which he had written with meticulous detail since he was assigned to take command of No. 2 Field Company, was intended to serve as both a chronicle of the war and a possible training aid for future officers. Field manuals about warfare in Southern Africa were severely lacking in detail. Captain Wynne intended to chronicle whatever lessons he learned fighting against the Zulus.

"I'll make time for it tomorrow," he whispered. He shut his eyes and within moments was fast asleep.

It was nearly midnight, and a cacophony of voices called out in the all-consuming darkness from the picquets which encircled the camp from about 200 yards. Every two hours, the corporals-of-the-watch would take fresh troops to each post. Challenges and passwords were shouted back and forth between the sentries and their replacements, and the next shift would begin.

Sentry duty was an extremely tedious, yet necessary, detail a soldier could be assigned. Two hours could feel like twenty, especially for soldiers who'd been up all day, marching, digging wagons out of the muck, and fording endless rivers. No soldier was ever at a post by himself but, at minimum, in pairs or groups of four. It was not uncommon for men at the various posts to talk to each other, often-times calling out phrases like, *'It's 12.15 an all's well!'* These would be repeated back. Sometimes with a rather coarse or profane response attached. It was a matter of passing the time, as well as helping the weary soldiers stay awake. On this particular night, it served an even greater purpose than anyone in No. 1 Column would know.

The noise coming from the passwords being shouted by the midnight shift alerted Phalane and his band of warriors. The Zulu *impi* had easily found the tracks left by the British redcoats and their cannon, making it a simple task of following them back to their bivouac. Godide kept his army close until they found the enemy encampment. They were to utilise the cover of darkness to quietly deploy the 'Horns of the Beast' and completely encircle their quarry.

It was a sound stratagem, albeit one fraught with its own difficulties. Having not actually seen the British, and arriving at Gingindlovu just before dark, the Zulus had no way of knowing how far away their enemies were encamped. And they still had no idea just how large the British force was. It was the night before the New Moon, and the enclosing darkness worked against them as much as it did the redcoats.

With subsequent shouts echoing in the night, Phalane and his warriors dropped down to one knee and stared hard into the darkness. It was impossible to see more than a few feet. Voices carried far, making it difficult to judge how close the British were. The *induna* waved for his nearest warriors to follow him and continued to crawl forward, keeping low in the tall grasses. Though he could not see them, he was confident the rest of their warriors

117

were executing the *inkosi's* intent and slowly surrounding the enemy. It bothered Phalane to not know the size of the British army. Their own forces numbered around 6,000. For all they knew, the redcoats might actually outnumber them.

'*It matters not*,' the *induna* quietly reassured himself. '*Once we surround them, we'll gut every last one before they even know we've taken their camp!*'

Suddenly, there was a loud shout not twenty feet from where Phalane knelt. This was answered by another call about fifty feet to the left. None of the Zulus spoke English. They had no way of knowing these were simply '*all's well*' call-outs coupled with various bits of banter.

Signalling to his nearest warriors to halt and remain hidden, Phalane crept back between his companies, seeking out his commanding *inkosi*. There was to be a series of signals, such as bird whistles, to be passed up the lines and allow Godide to know once all regiments were in position. With the constant shouts coming from the imperial redcoats, Phalane was suddenly filled with doubt about their proposed attack.

He found Godide fifty yards behind the rear companies of the uMxhapho Regiment. Various *izinduna* from the other *amabutho* had gathered around the *inkosi*. Several were whispering the same concerns Phalane now had.

"The enemy knows we're here," one protested. "I don't know how, but they've seen us."

"Why do they not open fire?" another asked.

"They're luring us into a trap!" the first *induna* insisted.

Godide remained silent for the moment, looking to his most trusted advisor. "And what does Phalane kaMdinwa say?" he finally asked.

"I am not certain the British are luring us into a trap, *inkosi*," he stated. "Nor can I say why they have held their fire. I, myself, almost ran straight into their lines. It is uncertain if these are merely lookouts or if they've deployed all their soldiers, who are now waiting for us. I do believe they know we're here. Perhaps they are goading us into attacking."

It bothered Godide that the normally self-assured Phalane was filled with doubt. If they waited until morning to attack, when they could clearly see the British strength and disposition, so too could their enemy see them. The terrain was mostly flat, open grasslands, making it the perfect killing ground for the redcoats and their long-ranged rifles. Nor did he think it was wise to attack an unknown force who, most likely, knew they were there.

The old *inkosi* recalled what the king had told him. "The branch of leaves, which extinguished the fire," Godide began, referring to King Cetshwayo by one of his praise names, "spoke of a place not far from here; beautiful hills where we can attack the invaders from a place of strength."

"I know of where he speaks," Phalane said, finding his confidence once more. "One is called Wombane near where the old track crosses the Inyezane River. The British will have to cross there if they intend to reach Eshowe."

"But *inkosi*," one of the *izinduna* said. "Tomorrow is the night of the new moon, the blackness of *mnyama*, when disruptive spirits plague the land. We cannot give battle on the *mnyama*!"

"I understand the spiritual risks," Godide replied firmly. "But if we allow our enemies to simply walk past Wombane, then we will have disobeyed our king. He can quell the angry spirits on our behalf. The divine power of Cetshwayo, the king of amaZulu, is greater than that of the *mnyama*! If the British march on Wombane, the blackness will consume them, while the sun of amaZulu protects us."

Willing to take their chances against the disruptive spirits, the assembled *izinduna* quietly crept back to their respective regiments. Phalane knew the mountainous terrain near Wombane. It was the perfect place to launch an ambush against the invaders. Their 6,000 warriors holding the high ground, coupled with the spiritual powers of the king, would send the white betrayers to a bloody grave!

As he returned to his men, Phalane heard another call-out coming from the imperial forces. Unbeknownst to him, it was simply a password being shouted as the 2.00 relief took over the picquets.

119

Chapter IX: A Day of Battle

The Inyezane River, fifteen miles from Eshowe
22 January 1879

The hills near Inyezane

Reveille sounded at 4.00 for the soldiers of the Southern Column. Colonel Pearson knew they were within a day's march of Eshowe, maybe two. Despite the terrain becoming more mountainous, the roads were better. The weather was promising and he was anxious to reach the old mission before the rains returned. Unbeknownst to him, a hundred miles to the north, Lord Chelmsford was marching away from No. 3 Column's camp at Isandlwana with over half his force, intent on engaging what he thought was the main Zulu *impi* at a place called Mangeni Falls.

"A beautiful morning," a staff officer noted. He nodded towards the rising sun in the east.

The place where they camped, four miles from the Amatikulu crossing, was known to the Zulus as kwaSambabela. A natural rise which made for an ideal defensive position for the large camp, it overlooked a picturesque valley of rolling grass hills, dotted by brush stands and small groves of trees. Neither of the officers knew the entire camp had been surrounded by thousands of Zulu warriors just a few hours before.

Like the previous days, Pearson divided his column into two divisions. At Lieutenant Colonel Welman's urging, he detached three companies from The Buffs to the second division to provide extra security on the wagons. They had yet to find the Zulus, but the further they marched inland, the greater the chance of an encounter became. Colonel Pearson acknowledged that Welman's two companies from the 99th were not sufficient to protect the second division's long train of wagons. Over a short breakfast, the colonel briefed the staff and senior commanders on the order of march that day.

"NNC warriors will form the vanguard," he directed. "They will be supported by the Stanger and Victoria Mounted Rifles, as well as the Natal Hussars. Colonel Parnell, two of your companies from The Buffs will immediately follow."

"Yes, sir." Parnell checked his battalion rolls. "That will be Captain Jackson's C Company and Lieutenant Martin's H Company."

"The two 7-pounder cannons will follow next," Pearson continued, "supported by two companies of sailors from the HMS Active, as well as a half-company from the Natal Pioneers."

"Yes, sir," Commander Campbell of the naval detachment confirmed. "I'll accompany this element myself. What of Mister Coker's Gatling gun?"

"Place him at the head of the wagons behind Captain Wynne's sappers," the colonel answered, before addressing Wynne. "Captain, I've kept you in the vanguard for most the trek, but I think we need you more at the river crossing now that the roads have had a chance to dry over the past few days."

Warren nodded and made some remarks in his notebook. He'd seen Midshipman Lewis Coker a few times; the eighteen-year-old naval officer in command of the Gatling gun crew. This peculiar weapon was an American invention, first produced at the end of their civil war. Consisting of seven barrels which rotated around a central shaft, it was fired by a hand crank. Bullets were fed via a large cylindrical magazine seated on top. The Royal Navy purchased a number of the newest 1876 model, though they had yet to see actual service in combat. Midshipman Coker was anxious for his gun to be the first used against an enemy of the British Empire.

121

Colonel Pearson concluded his briefing by ordering a company of Royal Marines to support Coker's Gatling crew. Two more companies from The Buffs were to follow the first division's wagons with two companies of NNC providing the rear guard. Lieutenant Colonel Welman and the second division were to break camp two hours after the first departed.

Gatling gun crew from HMS Active

Like every other morning, soldiers roused themselves from their bedrolls as the buglers sounded reveille. And like every other morning, this was met with numerous complaints laced with all manner of creative profanity.

"Quit your bloody complaining," Corporal Anderson chastised, his own voice dripping with irritation. "It didn't rain last night, so none of you have to worry about soggy kit today."

Sergeant David Fredericks then added, "And thanks to the generosity of Her Majesty's government, you get another hearty breakfast of tinned beef and hard biscuits. I even have our section's allotment of lime juice and sugar, as an added treat."

That their NCOs could find humour in the squalid daily life in the field, all the while sharing in the same hardships as them, quelled the private soldiers' bickering for the time being. Like every morning, David grabbed his dirty tin mug and went to his meeting

122

with Colour Sergeant Bennet, while Corporal Anderson oversaw the striking of the tent and kit inspection.

The entire No. 1 Column knew they were getting close to their destination. Every soldier shared in Colonel Pearson's anxiousness to reach Eshowe. Sergeant David Fredericks was just thankful the rains had stopped for the time being.

The colour sergeant and section leaders were joined this morning by Lieutenant Martin. He informed them that C and H Companies were providing the bulwark of infantry for the lead elements of the column.

"If the vanguard finds the Zulus, we'll be the first to get stuck in with them," the officer commanding explained. "I've ordered Colour Sergeant Bennet to make certain two of our ammunition boxes have their screws loosened. Each section will designate a pair of riflemen to act as runners, in the event any of you require hasty resupply of cartridges."

Though no one in the company had seen any Zulus the previous night, rumours abounded of bands of warriors creeping up on their camp only to be scared away by the call-outs from the picquets. Who witnessed any of this was unknown, but Lieutenant Martin was not taking chances. Captain Jackson of C Company issued similar orders to his NCOs.

The striking of tents and positioning of wagons for the first division was done with surprising speed, and the mounted vanguard departed at 4.30. The two companies from The Buffs followed about twenty minutes later. Soldiers marched along the track of dried mud, their rifles at port arms, watching the nearby hills and glades for any sign of the enemy.

Like every morning for the past week, Lance Corporal Monroe was detached to the company sharp-shooters. They advanced along the ridge to their right, providing security for the vanguard's flank. In addition to scanning the horizons, David constantly walked up and down the column, keeping an eye on the soldiers in his section, making certain there were no stragglers. The other NCOs of the company did the same. The silence was periodically broken by berated shouts towards any who fell behind or were otherwise careless. Occasionally, he would have a quick word with either Corporal Anderson or one of his fellow sergeants. But for most of the morning, he quietly studied the hills, listening to the sounds of marching feet, braying oxen, the squeal of wagon wheels, and the muttered conversations between his soldiers. A strange silence had fallen over his section with little of the usual banter.

"The lads are awfully quiet." Anderson walked over to his section leader. "There's something in the air here. Can you feel it?"

"Hair on my sodding neck is standing up," David confessed. His gaze kept falling on the vedettes and sharp-shooters up the hill on his right flank. "How long will the Zulus allow us to trod all over their lands before they decide we are no longer welcome?"

The road, unfortunately, was not in as good of condition as Colonel Pearson hoped. Captain Wynne's sappers were called forward three times to conduct hasty repairs during the four-mile trek to the Inyezane River. Near the head of the column, the lead mounted troops crossed the river, noting the familiarity of the terrain.

"The same track we followed for the king's coronation," Lieutenant Robarts recalled to Captain Barrow. "There is a flat space of open grassland not far from here."

"Any chance it will be suitable to conduct a halt for breakfast?" the captain asked. Despite the relatively short distance travelled, he knew the column would be on the march for several hours by the time they crossed the river. And with an immediate departure following reveille, there had been no time for the men to eat. The oxen would also need to graze and take on water.

"Possibly," Robarts said, scrunching his brow. "Forgive me, sir, but it's been six years since I last passed through this way. I remember the flat plain. I cannot quite say if it is a suitable place to halt the column, as I do believe there is a lot of brush and surrounding hills."

"We'll just have to clear it first and make certain no Zulus are waiting for us," Barrow surmised.

As they rode through a section of brush that crawled right up to, and in some cases over, the wagon track, Captain Barrow ordered his troopers to spread out and scour the potential hiding places for any enemy warriors. There appeared to be no sign of the Zulus. At length they reached the grassy plain surrounded by straggling brush with a long rise further north. There was also a hill a few hundred yards from the brush-covered ridges.

"Wombane," Robarts recalled. "At least, I think that's what the Zulus called that little hill."

Captain Barrow took a few moments to assess the layout of the land before giving his nod of approval. "It's not ideal, but it will have to do. Disperse the vedettes and make ready to receive the rest of the column." He scribbled a brief note to Colonel Pearson which he gave to an aid.

It was half an hour before the column commander made his way up to the plain. While he harboured many doubts as to its viability, especially with high ground covered in trees and brush to the front and right, Captain Barrow sought to reassure him.

"Sir, we still have a long trek if we intend to reach Eshowe this day," he explained. "And according to Lieutenant Robarts and the others who came this way with Cetshwayo, the track becomes very steep beyond here. It will be a hard slog, mostly uphill, before we reach the plain that leads to Eshowe."

Knowing he could not always choose the most ideal place to rest his troops, Colonel Pearson gave a reluctant nod. "Very well," he said. "Disperse your picquets and then give the men time to rest themselves and their horses."

"Your pardon, sir," an officer from the Victoria Mounted Rifles spoke up. "With your permission, I'd like to give any of my men who are not on vedette duty a chance to take their breakfast."

"Just make certain we keep enough of a presence along any approaches that the Zulus don't surprise us," the colonel stressed. He turned his horse about and rode back towards the main column.

Soon the first of the wagons arrived at the designated halting point. Oxen were un-spanned and led by voorloopers to graze. Vedettes were rotated so troopers had time to have their breakfast and feed and water their horses. Some even took the chance to bathe in one of the numerous small streams flowing down from the heights. Men laughed and splashed about as they washed their filthy bodies and clothes.

Godide's spies, hidden within the stands of trees and thickets, spotted the first wave of mounted troops crossing the Inyezane. Any misgivings the *inkosi* and his warriors had about fighting on the day of the new moon quickly vanished. The restless spirits they offended would have to be dealt with later. Once the British were defeated, the *inkosi* would send word for diviners to come and purify their warriors and quell any angry spirits. But for now, the redcoats were coming.

Though Godide intended to use the standard 'Horns of the Beast' tactic, he needed to make concessions for the terrain. The 'Chest' would attack the British column head-on, supported by the 'Right Horn' which would move to hit the enemy's left flank. The most crucial element, however, was the 'Left Horn'. The terrain his other two forces would need to cross was extremely rough. The left could simply follow the long ridgeline which extended south past Wombane Hill. A rapid pivot and sprint down the steep slopes, and they would quickly smash the enemy both on the right and from behind.

"Everything depends on the 'Left Horn'," Godide stressed to his assembled *izinduna*. "Drive the redcoats into the river, and we will have ample plunder to take with us back to Ulundi!"

The Zulu leaders quickly dispersed to lead their respective companies into position. As the youngest and largest element, the uMxhapho Regiment detached six of its one hundred warrior companies to spear-head the 'Chest'. The remaining 2,000 warriors would make up the 'Left Horn'. As one of the fittest men within the *ibutho* plus the vital importance placed on his role, Phalane elected to accompany the flanking force. Three additional companies of local volunteers led by another of Godide's senior *izinduna* would occupy Wombane Hill. They would act as a mobile force, ready to support either the 'Chest' or 'Left Horn' as needed. Phalane was deeply concerned about the 'Right Horn', as it was mostly old men who had not attended a royal muster in many years. The ground they would need to traverse was steep, rocky, and covered in thick brush. The royal *induna* reckoned there was little that could be done. So long as the 'Left Horn' succeeded in flanking the redcoats and driving them into the river, then it mattered little if the old regiments took part in the battle at all.

The sun crested the ridgeline behind Wombane. Twenty or so mounted soldiers appeared riding up the trail. These were the first imperial soldiers that most of the warriors had seen. Many of the younger fighters sneered in contempt, anxious to spill the invaders' blood. Much to their surprise, the enemy horsemen halted at a large clearing. While a few rode off in each direction to survey the brush and groves of trees, most of the rest dismounted. After a brief discussion between the mounted men's leaders, some of them decided to sit down for breakfast. Perhaps most absurd of all, several even made their way down to a small tributary, stripped out of their clothes, and started to wash themselves.

"It is good they cleanse themselves before we send them to the afterlife," one warrior mused.

At around 8.00, a corporal from the vedettes rode quickly down from the northern picquet. Captain Barrow was in discussion with Lieutenant Robarts and another volunteer officer regarding the terrain to the north.

The NCO rode up to them and saluted. "Zulus spotted to the north, sir."

"How many?" the captain asked, curtailing his excitement at finally having contact with the enemy.

"No more than a dozen. They were spread out and keeping low in the brush."

"Probably scouts," Robarts conjectured. "They likely have friends nearby if they're wandering anywhere near our vedettes."

Captain Barrow nodded. "Tell your men to look alive, corporal." He then sent a rider back to Colonel Pearson, who was arriving with the 1/2nd NNC.

Leading the Natal warriors was a regular army officer named Shapland Graves; a battalion major from The Buffs, attached to the NNC. Acting as his second was the column staff officer, Captain Fitzroy Hart; another regular army officer from the 31st Regiment who, unfortunately, only spoke a few words of Zulu. This was more than could be said for his NCOs, who were all white settler volunteers. Many of these men were Dutch or German. Their grasp of English was scarcely any better than their knowledge of the local languages.

The three officers were quickly alerted to Barrow's messenger, who sprinted his horse towards them.

"Colonel!" he said excitedly. "Captain Barrow's compliments, sir. Zulus have been spotted near Wombane Hill."

"Looks like we may have, at last, found the enemy," the colonel replied. A pleased grin crossed his face. "Major Graves, send your men forward and see if they can shake these 'grouse' out of the brush."

"Yes, sir," the major replied. He ordered Captain Hart to take a company forward in a reconnaissance towards Wombane.

This order was met with much enthusiasm by their assembled warriors, for the 2nd NNC Regiment consisted of many warriors from iziGqoza; the cousins of the Zulus who had been crushed by Cetshwayo during the war between him and Mbuyazi. Most of these men had been children then, having escaped from the slaughter at Mathambo near Lower Drift. They were anxious to avenge their fathers, mothers, and other kinsmen slain by 'the butcher', Cetshwayo. Far more courageous than many of the Natal locals, the regiment was still handicapped by the insistence of Lord Chelmsford that only white officers and NCOs would lead them. Because so few within the European settler community had bothered to learn any of the local languages, communication proved to be extremely difficult.

Finally, Captain Hart shouted, *'Zulus!'* and pointed his sword towards Wombane. This was met with a loud war cry from the iziGqoza. They raised their spears high before starting their advance on the hill.

Riding behind the lead rank of warriors, Captain Hart pointed them in the direction of Wombane, using what few words of their language he could remember. Near the saddle between the hill and the high ridge behind, six Zulus emerged. Several of the NNC warriors shouted excitedly, pointing with their spears and knobkerrie clubs. The Zulus waited a few moments, no doubt trying to gather whatever intelligence they could about the slowly arriving British column. After about a minute, they disappeared into the brush.

"At the quick step!" Captain Hart shouted, waving quickly with his drawn pistol.

None of the warriors spoke English, nor did many of his European NCOs, but the message was clear. The company advanced at a jog towards the heights.

The iziGqoza were alert and suddenly aware of what sounded, to the whites, like a buzzing of bees in the brush ahead. Knowing that this was not the noise of insects, but the murmur of warriors hiding in the brush, several warriors desperately tried to convey this to their officers. Unable to understand what was being said, the Europeans berated them and waved for their men to continue onward.

The NNC warriors' suspicions about a pending trap were soon confirmed when a Zulu *induna*, in all his regalia, stood and shouted, *"Usuthu!"*

Hundreds of warriors rose from the brush, echoing the loud war cry. The NNC froze, as did their officers. Zulu marksmen unleashed a volley from their muskets before throwing them down and brandishing their spears. Perhaps the only saving grace for Captain Hart and his men was that the enemy was overanxious and attacked while the NNC company was still a couple hundred yards away. As such, their musket volley was largely ineffective. Even more terrifying for the allied warriors was the sight of so many Zulus rising up to meet them.

Hart drew his sword and shouted, *"Baleka!"* He thought it was the isiZulu word for 'charge!' Unfortunately, the word literally meant 'run'. Horribly outnumbered by this emerging threat and thinking their officer had ordered them to retreat, the entire company turned about and fled down the hill. It was doubly unfortunate that Lieutenant Raines, one of the few officers who could have understood his captain's mistake, was among those killed in the initial volley of musketry. A shot smashed into his forehead, killing him instantly. His body lay twitching in the grass, blood and brain matter oozing from his smashed skull. Several of the European NCOs were also struck down. Captain Hart, realising the calamity he was in, rode down the slope, attempting to rally his troops into reforming their battle lines. As the charging Zulus swarmed over the bodies of the fallen, they stabbed each corpse repeatedly, reminiscent of a hunting ritual known as *hlomula*.

What was intended as a short rest for the No. 1 Column was now evolving into the savage fight they'd been waiting for. The Battle of Inyezane had commenced.

The echoing of Zulu musketry alerted the Stanger and Victoria Mounted Rifles, many of whom were still enjoying their bath in the stream. Troopers splashed out of the stream, hurriedly throwing on their boots, trousers, and tunics, as they sprinted to their horses. Forming into skirmish lines, they drew their carbines from their scabbards.

"Hostiles front!" an officer shouted.

Numerous black warriors in a disorganised mob were rushing up a nearby ravine. A sporadic volley erupted from the mounted troops, startling their horses as well as the approaching Africans. It was only by a stroke of fortune that none of the rattled carbineers had adjusted the sights on their weapons. Their shots mostly sailed well over the heads of their intended targets.

"Cease fire, damn you!" a voice to their front shouted.

To their collective horror, the troopers realised it was not the Zulus to their front but the remnants of Captain Hart's detachment.

"Oh, bugger me," a carbineer said with much regret.

There was no time for remorse or speculation as to whether they had shot any of their own men. Large bands of Zulus were now appearing. The distressed Captain Hart managed to keep his wits about him as he pointed his sword in the direction of this emerging threat.

Over by the wagons, Surgeon Norbury had the perfect vantage point to ascertain the scope of the enemy attack. Zulus were bounding down from the various heights in a wide semicircle. The doctor was familiar with the 'Horns of the Beast' method of battle and was filled with both awe and terror to see it demonstrated first-hand. He assumed one element was the 'Chest' and the other the 'Right Horn'. What he could not see yet was the 'Left Horn'.

"Colonel!" the doctor shouted, as he saw Pearson riding towards him. "Zulus to our immediate front with more on the left."

Colonel Pearson was now fully aware of the threat to his column. Nearly half of his first division and all of the second were spread out along the march. He was facing what every officer in charge of a column dreaded most. It was impossible to tell how many Zulus he was up against. He rightly assumed there were many he could not even see yet.

"Captain Jackson, Lieutenant Martin!" he shouted, to the officers commanding the two lead companies from The Buffs. "Secure the knoll on the right, and do not let them flank us!"

"Sir!" Captain Jackson acknowledged. Though they could not yet see any Zulus on their right, the infantry officer was also familiar with the 'horns' tactic and knew the slope on their right would soon be teeming with enemy warriors.

Meanwhile, the Mounted Rifles and other cavalry were dismounting on the knoll itself, while Lieutenant Lloyd's two 7-pounder guns were unlimbered.

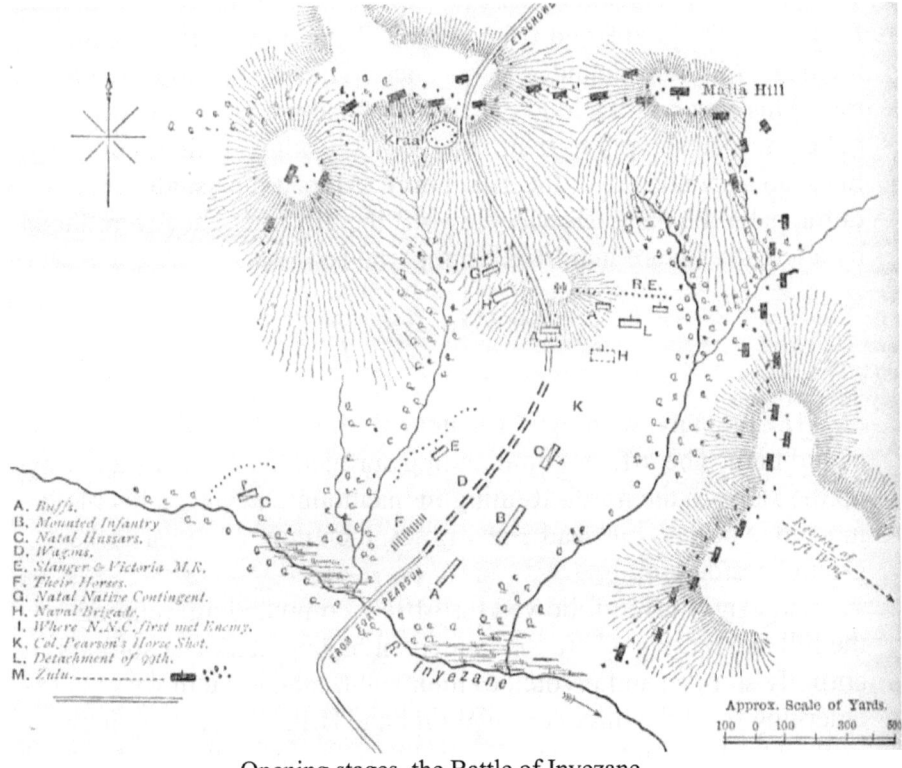

Opening stages, the Battle of Inyezane

131

Phalane cursed under his breath when he heard the initial salvo of shots ringing out from skirmishers in the 'Chest'. The uMxhapho companies forging the 'Left Horn' were not in position. He knew the overly excited warriors in the centre must have executed their attack too soon. His own men followed behind him in several long files; 2,000 warriors altogether. They kept behind the reverse slope of the long ridge extending south past Wombane, lest they expose themselves and their intentions prematurely to the enemy. However, this also meant, for the moment, they could not see the British either.

Phalane had intended to lead his warriors to where the ridge ended, at a low saddle near a stream leading away from the river. This would have ensured that the 'Left Horn' was able to strike their foes both in the flank and from behind. Time now worked against them and his heart pounded in his chest. The *induna* stopped and raised his spear with a loud cry. With drilled precision, his warriors halted, turned sharply to their right, quickly adjusted their company lines, and bounded over the hill. Terror gripped the usually unflappable Phalane. Down below off the dirt road, they were faced by a lengthy line of hundreds of imperial redcoats.

"H Company, with me!" Lieutenant Martin shouted, raising his sword high. The officer commanding sprinted his horse a short way up the slope to the north. Reining in his mount, he waved his blade in a circle around his head a few times, then pointed towards the ground beside him.

Sergeant Stirling followed his officer commanding, running up the hill and halting where the lieutenant had pointed. His soldiers abruptly stopped and pivoted to their right, facing the threat emerging from the direction of Wombane Hill. The NCO quickly walked back down the line of his soldiers, ensuring they had adequate spacing and ordering them to either kneel or find cover. David Fredericks' section was behind Stirling's with the remainder of H Company behind him. They hunkered low in the tall grass, as they advanced up the hill. Every few paces, soldiers would halt and scan the horizon for enemy warriors.

Lieutenant Martin was now riding back down the line, directing his remaining sections into position. Meanwhile, Colour Sergeant Bennet ordered the company's ammunition wagon to position itself just off the main road behind a short rise. The company's senior NCO pulled a pair of heavy boxes to the tailgate of the wagon, making certain the screws were loosened. He calmly, yet purposefully, made his way to each section, informing his sergeants where their ammunition wagon was.

It was then that a black wave of Zulu warriors crested the high ridge to the east. *"Skirmishing order!"* Lieutenant Martin shouted. *"At 400 yards, fire and adjust!"*

Rather than unleashing his soldiers to 'fire at will', the officer commanding was ceding control of his men to the section leaders. With his men spread out in skirmishing formation in a frontage extending nearly 200 yards, he had little choice but to direct his sergeants and corporals to control their soldiers' fire. Despite still languishing as a lieutenant, Robert Martin was an experienced officer who explicitly trusted his NCOs. He rode down to the ammunition wagon where he dismounted and tethered his horse before returning to the line. Shots were ringing out from his soldiers, as well as from Captain Jackson's C Company.

"Bastards are impossible to spot," Private Dunne muttered. He tried to set his sights on any of the numerous Zulus who appeared briefly before disappearing into the bush.

"Steady lads!" David called out. "Controlled shots…remember your drills!"

"Mark your targets before you fire," Corporal Anderson added. "Only engage what you can hit."

In the terror and excitement of battle, even the most experienced veterans needed a steady hand to keep them focused and disciplined. Of all his duties as a non-commissioned officer in Her Majesty's Armed Forces, Sergeant David Fredericks understood this to be the most important of all. And above all, he himself needed to keep a level head, even when the abject fear of death nearly caused him to soil his trousers.

133

His soldiers found cover behind boulders, patches of scrub brush, or low rises in the earth. All the while, the two NCOs of the section constantly bounded from position to position to check on their men. David also kept a close eye on Sergeant Stirling's section on his left.

"A spot of fun, this!" Stirling shouted with a whoop as the two sergeants hunkered behind a thick stand of brush. His face was flushed, an inane grin creasing his face. He jerked open the chamber of his rifle, ejecting a smoking spent cartridge. "Trying to find me a Zulu dancing partner, but they keep dropping out of view. Bashful bastards!"

"Yes, rather unsporting of them," David muttered.

A thick branch snapped as it was struck by a Zulu musket ball. Hundreds of enemy warriors now lined the slope, with thick clouds of wafting smoke obscuring them. David raised his rifle and fired in the direction of where he thought he saw a muzzle flash. At such a range with smoke, tall grass, and brush stands obscuring much of the hillside, it was impossible to tell if he'd hit anything.

"Oi, looks like Captain Wynne's engineers are moving up to anchor our extreme right," Stirling then noted. "How goes it with your lads?"

"Same as you. Just a 'hard pounding' at the moment. We need to keep engaging at maximum range and not let them get close enough for their muskets to be effective. And above all, they cannot be allowed to mass for an assault!"

"Agreed," Stirling concurred. "Spread thin as we are, if they can charge us in massed formation, we're fucked. Then again, if they do manage to launch a concerted attack, that defilade to our front ought to slow them a bit. Who's on your right?"

"Corporal Roberts. Sergeant Davies is on our extreme right."

"Bugger me," Stirling replied with a derisive laugh. "Would hate to see him get killed when he's this close to retirement!"

David snorted. Satisfied that his left was secured for the moment, he took a deep breath and sprinted a short way over to a small mound of earth, diving behind it as musket balls slapped into the ground and whistled overhead. At such an extreme range, the Zulus were compelled to simply lob their shots rather than trying to aim. Still, if they could bring enough muskets to bear, the sheer volume of fire would be extremely hazardous for the redcoats down the slope. This was emphasised as David heard a loud cry from off to his right.

"Corble's hit!" a voice shouted. *"Fuck, I think he's dead!"* The distressed private first thought to check on his friend, who lay on his back, blood streaming from his forehead.

"Keep your goddamn head down!" Corporal Anderson shouted. "There's nothing you can do for him!"

Fredericks let out a relieved sigh that it was not one of his men. This sense of relief was tempered with a trace of shame. Private Corble was still a fellow soldier of The Buffs, not to mention from the section of his friend and mentor, Sergeant Milne. Since being detached to Rorke's Drift, Milne's section was being ran by his assistant, Corporal Jonathan Roberts, whose face was ashen as he fought to control the emotions of his soldiers.

Rifle shots continued to echo all around him, and David took a moment to assess the Zulus up on the hill. Thus far, they had made no attempt to mass their numbers to charge, having been driven to ground by the barrage of musketry from The Buffs. His ears ringing with the reports of rifle and musket fire echoing off the hills, it was impossible to orient on any one sound. Instead, he relied on his vision. He thought he saw a waft of smoke come from behind a bush about 300 yards up the hill. Checking his sights, he chambered a round and aimed for the centre of the bush. He took a deep breath to calm his nerves as the front sight of his weapon danced about. After a moment or two, the movement subsided and he squeezed the trigger. His rifle erupted with a loud crack, the heavy recoil slamming the buttstock against his shoulder. It was impossible to tell if he'd struck his target or simply driven the enemy warrior to ground. Satisfied that particular threat was sorted for the moment, he chambered another round and continued searching for Zulus. There was, perhaps, a score of warriors visible to his front. All were lying sprawled in the grass like contorted shadows. He could only assume they were dead.

"Not so anxious to attack now," he noted. He then fired once more at a puff of smoke in the distance.

Chapter X: Fighting Sappers

The ridge south of Wombane
8.30 a.m.

Zulus advancing in skirmishing order

Towards the crest of the hill, Phalane lay on his stomach, surveying the battle. With the ongoing chaos and clouds of acrid smoke, it was impossible for him to know how the battle went for the 'Chest' and 'Right Horn' of the *amabutho*. What he did know was that the 'Left Horn' had executed its attack way too soon. Scouts had told them the British force was divided. It had been Godide's intent to have the 'Left Horn' attack the rear of the lead division, enveloping these companies and driving a wedge between the two forces. Instead, the regiments caught sight of redcoats down below and, in their excitement, pivoted towards them and readied to attack. From his current position, it was clear they should have advanced at least another half mile south before turning to attack the column.

In the ensuing chaos, Phalane lost much control over his men. Warriors were now reluctant to press the attack head-on with so many red-jacketed soldiers facing them. Skirmishers wielding old muskets had contented themselves to hide in bushes or behind small knolls and lob their shots towards the enemy.

"We do not win a battle by hiding from the enemy!" the *induna* roared, standing tall and defiant. British bullets kicked up clods of dirt around him. "With me, lest you dishonour your king and ancestors!"

Whether goaded on by his words of shame or inspired by his unfaltering bravery, the warriors of the uMxhapho rose up as one. With battle cries of *'Usutu!'*, they followed the royal *induna* down the slope. They maintained their discipline, not allowing themselves to cluster and keeping their company lines intact. They were far from reckless, bounding from one piece of cover to the next. In the event neither brush nor earthen mounds were available, they slinked low, using the tall grass for concealment.

The slope was exceptionally steep. The further they bounded, the more unstoppable their momentum became. This added a greater ghastly effect whenever a warrior was struck down by the heavy bullets loosed from British rifles. Those struck in the legs or stomachs would often summersault down the hill, until their shattered bodies crashed into a mound or thicket. Any who were hit in the chest or shoulders spun about, unable to stop themselves as they continued to fall down the hill. And given the size and smashing power of the Martini-Henry bullet, Phalane witnessed one poor fellow have his arm torn clean off, just above the elbow. The man screamed as the severed limb was ripped away in a spray of blood; the fingers still clutching his assegai.

What was especially unnerving was the accuracy of the enemy's rifles. Still roughly 400 paces away, the English soldiers were at least four times beyond the effective reach of the Zulu muskets, yet their own shots were felling warriors with startling frequency. And while the uMxhapho had the redcoats drastically outnumbered, the brutal killing and maiming of their friends made them hesitant.

Upon reaching the ravine, skirmishers immediately found what cover they could and commenced firing at the redcoats once more. While they were now much closer, it was the British who were afforded the decisive advantage of holding the high ground. Boulders and thickets impeded the Zulu warriors' ability to mass their numbers for a charge. Even when they were able to do so, they were met by concentrated volleys from the redcoats who were now within a hundred paces.

To their extreme right, beyond the line of imperial soldiers, Phalane heard the thundering boom of British cannon. He squinted

137

his eyes and saw a cluster of men around these monstrosities. They were not dressed in red jackets, but in blue and white uniforms with peculiar white hats adorning their heads. Their cannon were firing at the right flank of the Zulu 'Left Horn' anchored off of Wombane.

Keeping low, the *induna* rushed along the extended lines of his *ibutho*, seeking to find a weak point in the enemy position that he might exploit. Despite the punishment his warriors were taking from the redcoats to their immediate front, it appeared the fighting was fiercest near Wombane Hill and the British cannon.

While sailors from the Royal Navy brought their 7-pounder cannon into action, Captain Wynne ran at the head of his men, noting a danger to the exposed redcoats on the right flank. Soldiers from the Imperial Mounted Infantry were hurriedly leaping, and in some cases falling, from their horses while rushing for cover. Warren ordered his men to halt. All dropped down to one knee while he sought out the IMI's officer commanding, Captain Barrow. It was not difficult to find him. He was the only one who remained mounted, near-constant clips of musket balls catching on the trees and brush all around him. Despite the fraying of his nerves, he outwardly remained calm. He ordered his troopers to anchor off the right of Lieutenant Martin's H Company of The Buffs.

"Captain Wynne," the officer acknowledged when he spotted Warren. "By God, it is good to see you, sir."

"And you, sir," Warren replied. "We'll dress off your right, using those fallen logs and patches of rocky ground for cover."

Barrow concurred. "Splendid! Good to know your sappers can fight, as well as build bridges and dig us out of the muck. I just hope the Zulus don't have friends behind that hill, ready to flank us."

"If there are, we have at least two more companies from The Buffs behind my lads. They should be on the field within the next ten to twenty minutes."

"It'll have to do." Barrow allowed himself a slight wince, as a musket shot smacked into the tree ten feet from where he sat. He then shouted to some of his nearest soldiers, "Would somebody pot that fellow already? He's making my horse nervous!"

Soldiers of the Imperial Mounted Infantry
Battle of Inyezane

Several IMI soldiers began firing in the direction of the Zulu attempting to unseat their officer. Wynne allowed himself a nervous grin as he ran back to his company. They had taken cover in a short defilade parallel to the far ridge.

"Mister Courtney! Take the left, dressing off the IMI."

The senior subaltern nodded and shouted for half the sections to follow him.

"Mister Willock," Captain Wynne continued, "you will be on the right. Keep an eye out for our friends from The Buffs. And Mister Main, you will take the centre."

"Sir!" the subalterns acknowledged, before rushing to their positions on the line.

Both the captain and Colour Sergeant Smith paced along a patch of low ground lined with several fallen trees. Smith was exceptionally tall, and it was no small wonder many of the enemy's shots were directed at him. He remained calm, almost genial, with his booming voice reassuring his sappers.

"Look to your front; check your sights; mark your targets and control your fire."

Most of their men took up positions behind whatever cover they could find. Sergeant Small seized the initiative to have his men drag whatever logs, branches, and other forms of cover could be utilised to improve their positions. He directed each sapper's sector of fire, ensuring they overlapped with the men on their left and right. Perhaps most surprising was that for one with a reputation for being excitable and overly-anxious at times, Sergeant Small was surprisingly tranquil, the tone in his voice unflinching.

"Seems the good sergeant is most relaxed when someone is trying to kill him," Colour Sergeant Smith chuckled.

Captain Wynne was pleased with the discipline of his young sappers, none of whom had served on Foreign Service, let alone a battle. The relatively poor marksmanship of the Zulus likely aided in calming their nerves. It seemed their enemies were making a lot of noise with little effect. Despite the hundreds of warriors now occupying the ravine directly to their front, most of the Zulu shots sailed high, well over even Colour Sergeant Smith's head.

"Here come Captain Harrison's boys," the colour sergeant noted. The officer commanding from D Company of The Buffs was conversing briefly with Lieutenant Willock before ordering his men to find cover and engage the enemy skirmishers still on the heights.

A mass of Zulus along the ridge appeared to be forming into company lines to attack. Several concentrated volleys from Harrison's men tore into them, driving the survivors to seek cover. A second company of imperial infantrymen were spotted about a quarter mile further on, racing towards the ongoing fray.

"Bugger...shit!" one sapper shouted, lurching back from his position, his rifle clattering on the rocks. His right cheek was cut and bleeding, though he seemed to not notice.

"Dawkins, you hit?" Sergeant Small asked, chancing a glance his way.

"I don't think so," the sapper said, his nerves clearly rattled. He grabbed his rifle and sprawled behind a rotten log. He made ready to aim his weapon when it dawned on him what had just happened. "Well, I'll be damned. Bastards shot the sight off me sodding rifle!" He reached up and felt the dampness of the blood on his cheek; the result of either a shard of musket ball or shattered chunk from his broken sight. Shaking it off, he chambered a round and continued to engage as best as he was able.

Though trained predominantly to build bridges, roads, and forts, Wynne's sappers were required to possess the same basic skills in drill and musketry as the rest of Her Majesty's soldiers. He walked the line, shouting words of encouragement; occasionally pointing out the positions of various Zulus on the hillside and in the ravine. Warren was impressed by the cool discipline his soldiers exuded. They took their time, aiming carefully before firing, making a point to not simply sling bullets at the hillside as fast as they could reload. When he reached the far right of his position, he found Lieutenant Willock directing the fire of several sappers towards a cluster of warriors about 200 yards away, behind a short knoll.

"Captain Wynne!" A voice shouted off to his right.

Warren turned to see Captain Harrison of The Buffs.

The red-jacketed officer sprinted over to him, his pistol drawn. "We think we've found their flank. Colonel Parnell wants mine and Wyld's companies to exploit it."

"Understood," Wynne replied. "My lads will lay suppressive fire and cover you as best we can."

"Just make certain you cease fire we reach the ridgeline," Harrison stressed. "I didn't come all this way to get shot by a bullet from Birmingham."

Chapter XI: Charge of the Jack Tars

The knoll, west of Wombane Hill
8.30 a.m.

Midshipman Lewis Coker
HMS Active

"Right, lads, with me!" The words came from the very young naval officer, Midshipman Lewis Coker, as he urged his Gatling crew on. One sailor carried a pair of large cylindrical magazines. Five more helped the midshipman wheel the multi-barrelled gun to the top the knoll. The two 7-pounders were already in action. Accented by a pair of loud booms, they fired in quick succession, their explosive shots flying in a high arc towards where the Zulu 'Chest' had first engaged the NNC. Captain Jackson's company from The Buffs was to their left with Lieutenant Martin's redcoats on the right.

Behind the cannon was Colonel Pearson and several staff officers. The commanding officer of No. 1 Column remained astride his horse, constantly scanning the battlefield with his field glasses, sending messages to the various company commanders as needed. "Mister Coker," he acknowledged, lowering his glasses and nodding to the midshipman. "Good to have you with us."

"Aye, sir!" the excited young officer said, taking a moment to catch his breath.

Pearson pointed his field glasses in the direction of Wombane. "Those fellows on that hill are causing us a bit of distress. Even our cannon cannot seem to dislodge them. See if you can sort them out."

"Yes, sir!" Coker said, standing tall and snapping off an enthusiastic salute.

Pearson almost dismissively returned the courtesy, though he did allow himself the briefest of smiles. He reckoned he wasn't much older than the midshipman when he fought his first action at the Siege of Sevastopol. He, too, had been filled with zeal and excitement. Now he would see if the young officer's professionalism matched his fervour.

As his men wheeled the gun into position and performed some quick function checks, Coker surveyed the situation. The Zulu 'Left Horn' appeared to be sufficiently checked for the moment. To the immediate right of Martin's company was another from The Buffs, along with the dismounted IMI, Natal Hussars, and No. 2 Field Company. Adding to the Zulu woes, two more companies from The Buffs were rushing into position to Captain Wynne's right flank, pouring greater volumes of musketry into the beleaguered enemy attackers.

To Coker's left, just past Captain Jackson's company, his fellow sailors from the HMS Active were performing splendidly. The controlled volleys under Commander Campbell stopped the advance of the Zulu 'Chest', while the 'Right Horn' seemingly disappeared.

"We're in position, sir," one of the sailors reported. "Function checks complete. Ready to engage, at your command."

The midshipman nodded. "Focus on the slopes of Wombane. The saddles on either side will be your left and right limits."

"Understood," the gunner replied.

Another crewman mounted the large magazine.

Coker was now grinning absurdly, filled with excitement at fighting his first action, and as commander of a gun crew, no less!

"At 300 yards!" he shouted, his voice cracking slightly. He drew his sword. "Action front…fire and adjust!"

143

The Battle of Inyezane, from *The London Gazette*

With a turn of the crank, the Gatling erupted into a relentless salvo of rapid fire shots; 300 rounds per minute. As a cloud of smoke enveloped their front, the young midshipman watched the rounds impact through his field glasses, giving minor corrections as needed. All the while he held his breath, praying for no breakdowns or misfires. While its effects were devastating and morale-shattering, the Gatling was by no means a flawless weapon. Prone to malfunctions, especially when overheated, the extractor arm was known for ripping the ends off brass cartridges swollen from the heat, causing a stoppage. However, Coker was obsessive about his gun. He personally conducted the most minute of inspections and maintenance daily. His attention-to-detail was now paying dividends. The relentless barrage of rounds tore into the bodies of enemy skirmishers on the far hill.

After a full minute of firing, with the first drum magazine expended, Coker gave the order to cease fire.

"That broke 'em, the filthy bastards!" one of his crewmen shouted excitedly.

"Take up your rifles and pick off any survivors," Coker directed. His ammunition stores were limited, and with no knowledge as to the enemy's total strength and disposition, he did not wish to expend another magazine on a few stragglers.

Satisfied with how his crew and their gun performed, the midshipman glanced over his shoulder towards Colonel Pearson who simply nodded. It was all the reassurance Lewis Coker needed.

At the same time as Midshipman Coker's gunners were picking up their rifles to drive off what remained of the Zulus along Wombane, his commanding officer, Commander Henry Campbell, sought out Colonel Pearson. He was observing the battle from astride his horse, not far from where the Natal Pioneers and the artillery were posted. Every minute or so, one of the guns would emit a loud boom, leaving the crew engulfed in a cloud of smoke as an explosive shot sailed towards the suspected Zulu positions to the east.

"Colonel, sir." The naval officer saluted.

"Commander," Pearson acknowledged, lowering his field glasses. "I see Mister Coker's Gatling has driven most of the Zulus off Wombane. Splendid bit of shooting there."

"Yes, sir. And now, with your permission, I'd like to finish this fight. Infantry companies are driving in the enemy flank off to our extreme right, yet I believe the Zulus are clustered on the far side of Wombane where those huts now burn."

"Yes, I've ordered up Captain Forester's company from The Buffs. They should be here any minute. They will support your advance, along with Captain Hart's NNC. Drive the enemy from Wombane, and we'll put an end to this little game."

The commander saluted once more and rode back to his men.

The colonel turned to one of his ADCs. "Order a general advance on the right. Captain Harrison has already turned the flank; the rest of the lads will now move up to support."

Commander Campbell's blood was boiling, as he returned to the naval brigade. He assembled his company commanders and quickly briefed them. "Half of B Company will remain to protect the guns. Marines will stay with the Gatling. The rest of the brigade will rally on me." Giving his officers a few moments to sort their men, he then drew his sword and bellowed loudly, "Alright, Jack Tars, time to put an end to this! We'll advance in skirmish order. *Fix bayonets!*"

With a series of echoed orders from the officers and petty officers, nearly 200 sailors from the HMS Active drew their long blades and fixed them to the ends of their rifles. Captain Forester's company of redcoats had just arrived, having practically sprinted more than a mile to reach them. There would be no reprieve, however. They were ordered to support Campbell's advance.

And despite their harrowing encounter at the start of the battle, coupled with nearly being shot by their own troops, Captain Hart's NNC company made ready to storm the ridge. Once all company commanders reported they were ready, Campbell raised his sword, and without another word stepped off.

The 'Jack Tars' gave a loud battle cry as they followed the commander up the slope. They ran at a very quick step and soon found themselves outpacing both The Buffs and NNC warriors. Salvoes of musket fire rained down from the heights, as well as from their left-front. The Zulu skirmishers frantically tried to drive the assailants away. The attack stalled for a moment when several men were hit. Two of these were black sailors from West Africa, known as *Kroomen*, who were recruited into the Royal Navy. A white sailor cried out as a bullet struck him in the thigh. He fell to the ground, dropping his rifle, and clutched at the terrible wound already bleeding profusely.

"Right boys, down!" the commander shouted. "Reform the lines and fire by volley!"

"Stand firm, The Buffs!" The voice of Lieutenant Colonel Parnell alerted the officers commanding of both H and C Companies.

The soldiers continued to fire relentless volleys against the Zulus on their right. The report of a cannon shook the ground.

The battalion commander for 2/3rd Buffs called over his subordinate officers. "Captain Jackson! Lieutenant Martin! C and H Companies will support the advance on the right. I will lead Captain Forester's company in support of the attack on Wombane."

"Very good, sir," Jackson replied, snapping off a sharp salute.

Lieutenant Martin was dismounted and rushed back to his company, brandishing his pistol. "H Company, on your feet! Are we going to let Captain Jackson's lads beat us to the top?"

"No, sir!" the entire company shouted in unison.

"Fix bayonets!" Colour Sergeant Bennet shouted.

This was echoed in turn by his sergeants and corporals.

David Fredericks drew his long blade from its scabbard and attached it to his weapon with a loud click. Unlike the triangular spikes used by enlisted soldiers, NCO bayonets were shaped like a short sword. Though ostensibly a measure of their status, so they might be more easily spotted on the firing line, David hated the sword bayonet. It was not nearly as sturdy as the spike and more prone to breaking. About the only advantage it offered was one could slash with it, which was usually impractical when it came to bayonet fighting.

"With me!" the officer commanding shouted, waving the men forward with his pistol.

Unlike the eager men from the naval brigade, they moved at a quick but measured walk, constantly searching for any signs of the enemy, often pausing to fire a shot before continuing. Though the Zulus had been mostly driven from the ravine, the redcoats hunkered low. The subsequent storm of musketry from the ridge told them the Zulus were not yet out of the fight. What puzzled Sergeant Fredericks was that the enemy had not massed for a counterattack. Advancing uphill, over mostly open ground and only able to fire the occasional shot, the imperial infantrymen were left vulnerable. And yet, no massed ranks of warriors appeared on the horizon. Having never actually faced the Zulu *amabutho* before, David could only reckon the barrages of Martini-Henry fire had broken them.

"Adjust your sights!" he shouted to his section. "Set for 200 yards!" Following a quick slide of the bar on his rear sight, the sergeant reloaded and raised his weapon again.

Many of the Zulus were now turning to run, some pausing to fire parting shots. David's rifle gave him a brutal kick as it fired with a loud bang. He continued up the hill, chancing a quick glance at his section, making certain none were extending too far ahead of the company. It was then he saw Private Dunne double over. The soldier cried out as he fell to his side, clutching at his stomach.

"Bill!" one of the man's friends cried out, falling to his knees beside him.

David rushed over and grabbed the man by the shoulder. "Keep up the advance! We do *not* stop for anyone!"

The soldier gritted his teeth. With a quick shove from his section leader, he grabbed his rifle and ran to catch up with the rest of his mates. David took a moment to assess Private Dunne.

Blood was oozing between his fingers where he clutched his stomach, his face contorted in agony. "Bastards fucking got me, sergeant."

"Take it easy, son, just breathe. Stretcher bearers will be here to fetch you shortly." He then waved to Colour Sergeant Bennet, who nodded in acknowledgment and called back for the bandsmen carrying the stretchers. It was their job to ferry the wounded from the battlefield.

David pitied the young man. Gut shots were horrifically painful and nearly always fatal. There was nothing else he could do. He patted the soldier reassuringly on the shoulder before re-joining his section.

Lieutenant Colonel Parnell rode ahead of Captain Forester's company. He spotted a lone naval officer bounding down the hill towards him. He recognised the man as Campbell's adjutant, Lieutenant Craigie. "Damn it, man, where do you think you're headed?" he asked incredulously. "The battle is that way!"

"Your pardon, sir. The attack has stalled, and Commander Campbell ordered me to bring up the rest of our companies plus the marines."

"Off with you, then. And don't worry, my lads from The Buffs will get your lot unstuck." Shots rang out behind him. Several soldiers from Forester's company were firing at suspected Zulu positions in the distance. "Captain Forester, make certain your lads mark their targets before they fire! Remember, there are friendlies to our front!"

These redcoats were soaked in sweat, their faces crimson as they tried to catch their breath.

"Just how in the bloody hell do the damned Zulus run so far and then fight a battle?" one soldier grumbled through gasping breaths.

"For starters, they're not wearing these fucking wool sweat-suits," one of his mates reasoned, grabbing at the front of his jacket.

As the battalion commander caught sight of Campbell's detachment, he turned to order Captain Forester to wheel his company to the left. Before he could say a word, his horse bucked violently, shrieking as it was struck by a rifle shot. Parnell was thrown from his mount, the wind knocked from him. He landed hard on his back, his head smacking a large rock. His vision blurred for a few moments, and he was suddenly grateful he'd worn his helmet rather than his patrol cap that day. Rolling onto his stomach and letting loose a violent cough, he was aware of Captain Forester who rushed to his aid.

"Are you hit, colonel?"

"I'm fine, dash it all! Just get your company to the top and help Campbell break those black devils!"

As the captain waved his company forward, he spotted a pair of bodies in the grass; two of the unfortunate sailors who'd fallen from Zulu musketry. He then heard a scream to his left and turned to see one of his soldiers falling to his knees. Blood streaming through his fingers, he clutched at his shattered face. Sergeants were exhorting their men onward. His colour sergeant sprinted ahead to find the left flank of Campbell's detachment. No sooner had Captain Forester and his men halted than the naval commander—heartened by the sudden arrival of reinforcements—ordered the assault to continue. A pair of volleys in rapid succession socked them in with smoke.

All the while, Campbell stood tall, brandishing his sword as he gave the next order. *"Charge!"*

The 'Jack Tars' gave a loud cry, which echoed across the hills. Their bayonets levelled, they swarmed the last hundred or so yards to where the Zulus made their final stand.

Captain Forester paused. He was filled with both surprise and admiration at their discipline and courage. "Such a splendid display," he said, as he was joined by one of his subalterns.

"Those lads joined the wrong branch of the forces, sir," the young lieutenant added in appreciation. He then informed his officer commanding, "The NNC have rolled up the left flank. The Zulus are retiring everywhere."

"Very good. We'll advance in good order and sort out any stragglers that get past Campbell's boys."

For H Company of The Buffs, the battle was also sputtering to an end. The slope they'd climbed was extremely steep. Many struggled to maintain their footing. They spotted soldiers from Captain Harrison's company walking along the ridgeline. They had attacked the Zulu flank long before H Company's advance.

"They've all hoofed it, sir!" a sergeant shouted down to Lieutenant Martin.

"Cease fire!" H Company's officer commanding shouted.

The last smattering of parting shots echoed off the hills.

He nodded to Colour Sergeant Bennet who ordered the section leaders to get a count on how many cartridges each of their soldiers had remaining. David's men had shown excellent fire discipline, and most had between forty-five and fifty cartridges in their pouches. Checking his own pouches, David counted four ten-round packets remaining in his reserve pouch with fifteen loose cartridges in his ready pouch.

Rob Anderson was checking each man, not just for ammunition expenditure but to see if any were injured. A few were bleeding from various cuts and scrapes though nothing serious. One had been grazed in the forearm by a stray musket ball. In his excitement, the private was not even aware of his torn sleeve or that he was bleeding.

Three soldiers in David's section had only recently arrived in Southern Africa and, therefore, just fought their first action. It was these three that the sergeant sought out as the company reorganised itself and prepared to continue the march to Eshowe. Eighteen-year-old Private John Harris was red-faced, sweaty, and trembling slightly while he checked his ammunition pouches. His mouth was parched, and he kept licking his lips.

"Take it easy, man," David said.

The soldier fumbled with his ready pouch and dropped a couple of rounds into the dirt.

"Drink some water and take a few breaths. I hope you weren't shaking like that during the battle."

"N...no, sergeant," Harris stammered. "Kept me nerve right up until the lieutenant ordered us to cease fire." He paused for moment. "I think I got one, sergeant. Did as I was taught; indexed the range, took a breath, let it half out, and slowly squeezed the trigger. Saw what looked like a puff of mist come off one of those bastards, before he tumbled down the hill. It was the damndest thing I've ever seen; not at all like how I envisioned it."

"Trousers got a little wet, I see," the sergeant added with a disarming grin.

Harris glanced down in embarrassment. The front of his trousers was soaked and covered in mud. "Fell into a puddle right when the shooting started. Of course, I may have pissed myself, too. Honestly, I can't say for certain." He gave a short laugh and grinned. David patted him on the shoulder, reiterated for him to drink some water and check his weapon, before moving on to the next man. It was the same for his other new soldiers; both were shaking with nervous excitement but otherwise unharmed.

He made his way back down the slope that was now littered with the bodies of fallen Zulus. Many lay behind stands of brush and thick shrubs, their heads burst open, limbs shattered, and guts ripped asunder. Such was the destructive power of the Martini-Henry rifle. Those poor souls struck by explosive shot from the cannon were in an even worse state, many with bodies ripped to pieces. David saw one corpse that was perfectly intact, except the head was missing. The body lay sprawled backwards down the hill, a steady stream of blood and bodily fluids still streaming from the stump that had once been his neck.

The stench from the shattered bodies was terrible, and David had to supress the urge to vomit. More than a few soldiers found the pungent smell unbearable and spewed up the remains of their previous night's supper.

"Well, I don't know about them, but I'm hungry now," Sergeant John Stirling stated loudly, a mischievous grin on his face.

About 200 yards further down the hill, David's own smile of relief quickly faded. Colour Sergeant Bennet was standing over poor Private Dunne. The terribly wounded soldier was being gently lifted onto a stretcher by a pair of bandsmen. David jogged his way down the grassy slope over to them. Bennet held his helmet under his arm and was wiping his forearm across his brow.

"Anyone else in your section hit?" the colour sergeant asked.

David shook his head. "No. Just a few cuts and bruises."

He then nodded towards the stretcher bearers who were trying to make their way down the broken terrain without dropping their charge. "How is he?"

"I'm afraid he's not long for this world," Bennet replied candidly. "Surgeon Norbury is one of the best, but even he cannot perform miracles."

In truth, H Company had been extremely fortunate given the ferocity of musketry from the Zulus. Besides Dunne, Private Corble, who'd been shot in the head, was their only other serious casualty. Much to the surprise of everyone, he was still alive, though he'd yet to regain consciousness. Conversely, the redcoats from H Company left scores of enemy warriors either dead or dying from their terrifyingly accurate rifle fire. The blinding clouds of smoke, tall grasses, and brush stands had done much to conceal their foes. They were therefore surprised to see just how many Zulus had fallen to their musketry.

David was astonished at the level of compassion shown by the soldiers checking the enemy wounded. A private from Sergeant Stirling's section knelt next to a Zulu who'd been shot through the bowels. The exit wound where the bullet burst through his side had left a hideous gaping maw of shredded guts, bone splinters, and flesh. The man's face was sweaty. He trembled violently, as the soldier placed a hand on his shoulder.

"Rest easy, *abanesibindi abaqawe*," the private said, referring to the warrior with the Zulu term best described as 'brave hero'.

"A far cry from those who refer to the enemy as 'apes' or 'niggers'," Colour Sergeant Bennet said, nodding towards the soldier.

"When one makes the enemy less-than-human, it can ease their conscience," David observed. "Personally, I am glad to see that not all of our men have lost their humanity."

Much like his sharp-shooter, Lance Corporal Monroe, after every battle he'd ever fought, the sergeant's thoughts returned to the first time he killed. It was towards the end of the Ninth Cape Frontier War when H Company was skirmishing in the thick brush, attempting to flank a Xhosa ambush. Unable to see more than a few feet in front of him, David and an enemy warrior were equally surprised to nearly crash into each other. He had no recollection of any conscious thoughts going through his mind, only of instinctively shouldering his rifle and firing. The heavy calibre bullet had

152

smashed into the base of the warrior's throat, spraying his killer with blood and gore. He was thrown into a tree behind him, where he collapsed in a heap, his body convulsing violently, eyes wide open as death took hold. Though he'd had just a moment to gaze upon the man's face, it was burned forever into David Frederick's memory. Should he live to be a senile old man, the image of the first man he killed would never leave him. He often wondered about the warrior. The black head ring he wore denoted that he was married. Did he have children? Did his friends ever find him? Or was his body left to rot with his loved ones never knowing his fate?

That he had feelings of remorse seemed illogical. After all, had he not fired, the Xhosa would undoubtedly have disembowelled the sergeant with his assegai! And yet, the one thing David wished for more than anything after that day was forgiveness. Whether it was forgiveness from God for committing murder or from the warrior himself, he could not say.

He had thought it would become easier. Yet he knew that each time he fired a fatal shot, it would bring back memories of the face of the first man whose life he so abruptly ended. Every soldier or warrior killed was a human being with his own loves, beliefs, and dreams.

On the hill, he saw one of his soldiers remaining. Unsurprisingly, it was James Monroe. He stood with his rifle cradled in his arms, gazing at the body of a dead Zulu. The side of the enemy warrior's head was missing, sheared away by a shot from the lance corporal from far below.

"Thought I'd missed this bastard completely," Monroe said quietly. "Instead, I took half his head off from 400 yards." He shook his head. "I'm too fucking good at this, sergeant. It's not natural."

"No, but it is effective," David countered. He placed a hand on his shoulder. "Come on, James, we're leaving. I need an ammunition count from you, and then you can report back to Corporal Knight and the sharp-shooters."

Monroe nodded and quickly turned away from the man he'd slain. He knew his sergeant was deliberately taking him away from that scene of death, and in his battered heart he was grateful. Barely nineteen years old, after every battle, Lance Corporal James Monroe felt more and more like an old man. Each time he wondered if he would ever feel young again.

153

As he returned to his section, Sergeant Fredericks' addled mind started to piece together all the actions of the last couple hours. He reckoned he might have shot a Zulu this day, maybe two; yet the smoke had been thick. With so many rifles firing in the same direction, it was impossible to say for certain. Privately, David was glad he did not know whether he had killed again.

Sketching of the Battle of Inyezane by Lieutenant Charles Knight, 2/3ʳᵈ Buffs

Chapter XII: A Bloody Morning

Near Inyezane
9.45 a.m.

The Gatling Gun and crew from the Battle of Inyezane

The column's volunteer chaplain, Reverend Robertson, sat on the bench seat of his wagon, his rifle across his knees, head resting in one hand, and a Bible clutched in the other. His nerves were frayed, and he was shaking badly. This was noticed by Lieutenant Main from No. 2 Field Company. His face etched in concern, Main walked over to the wagon and placed a hand on the bench.

"Everything alright, reverend?" the officer asked.

"If only it were," Robertson answered. His face was red, eyes wet with tears. "Twenty years I've spent in the Cape, and I can now say I have never made a single genuine convert to Christianity."

Main said nothing but gave the pastor a puzzled look.

Robertson was quick to explain, "My driver has been with me for years and is easily my most zealous convert. Yet when he came to my wagon, covered in blood, eyes filled with rage, and a grin that only the devil could love…" He shuddered. "Do you know what he told me? He said that he had found his own brother amongst the Zulu wounded, and that he killed him without pause or remorse. It

155

was with graphic detail and malicious glee that he described disembowelling the very man who came from the same womb as he. Tell me, Mister Main, what kind of Christian would commit such an act of barbarism with unbridled joy?"

Though he knew of countless times when white Christians had committed similarly heinous acts of murder, the lieutenant diplomatically remained silent. Surely the reverend had to understand that savage murder in battle was no less barbarous when it was committed by white Christians. Granted, the deranged man had been one of the reverend's own converts. And he had killed not just a badly wounded enemy warrior, but his own brother.

"I'll tell you this, lieutenant, I no longer know what my purpose is in this accursed land."

At the knoll where the artillery and Gatling gun were being limbered up, Colonel Pearson saw Midshipman Coker and his crewmen conducting a few function checks on their weapon. Rather than simply supervising, the young officer's hands were covered in black powder residue and oil as he personally removed and checked the gun's bolt.

"An impressive display, Mister Coker," Pearson said, leaning over the saddle of his horse.

The startled midshipman quickly came to attention and rendered a sharp salute. "Colonel, sir. Just conducting a bit of maintenance before we continue to march. Don't want to risk a malfunction should the Zulus return. We'll have the gun properly cleaned once we reach camp."

"Very good, do carry on." Pearson started to turn his horse away when he stopped and looked back to the officer and his sailors. "Oh, and I'll need a full report from you; sent up through Commander Campbell, of course. I do believe this is the first time a Gatling gun has been used in actual combat by Her Majesty's forces. Both the Admiralty and Horse Guards need to know about its effectiveness. Be both thorough and candid, Mister Coker."

"Of course, sir."

The midshipman's face turned a touch red in disbelief. To his best recollection, at no time in the history of the Royal Navy had a midshipman been tasked with writing an official despatch from a command capacity. As soon as he helped replace the bolt and conduct a final function check, he dug into his pockets and pulled

156

out his tattered notebook. He quickly scribbled a few notes, his greasy fingers leaving streaks on the pages. He sought to recall every detail regarding the gun's performance. While the Gatling had proven to be a fearsome weapon both physically and psychologically, he knew better than most about its many mechanical issues. His report could very well be the first that would lead to improvements being made, both to the gun and the ammunition it fired.

The only prisoners taken had come from the naval brigade, when their unexpected charge overran the Zulu positions. Those from the 'Left Horn' who could escape had done so long before the hodgepodge of companies stormed the ridge to the east. Numerous trails of flattened grass, often streaked with drying blood, told of the Zulu wounded who'd been dragged or carried away by their mates. Those left behind were either already dead or had injuries that would soon send them to their ancestors. As Lieutenant Lloyd of the naval brigade interrogated one of the men, the vastly differing perspectives between combatants became clear.

"We thought we were winning this battle," the warrior said through an NNC interpreter, "until those awful men in the white trousers showered lead upon us. The diviners had blessed our weapons with charms and spells. We could not see through the smoke, but we knew we had to be raining death upon you."

Fortunately for the British, the Zulu muskets were old and in terrible disrepair. Most had only been given rudimentary instruction in musketry, and this was confined to reloading and basic firing. It was assumed that if the *izinyanga*, who the British referred to disdainfully as 'witchdoctors', had properly blessed their firearms, their bullets would fly true. Despite the warriors from the 'Left Horn' having closed to within a hundred yards of the British right, most skirmishers knew nothing about proper aiming. Hence, their bullets mostly flew high over the redcoats' heads.

Further interrogations would reveal that the entire Zulu force had numbered about 6,000 fighting men. The captured warrior explained that their *inkosi*, Godide, understood that he could not stand toe-to-toe against an evenly matched force of redcoats.

"Everything depended on the 'Left Horn'," the warrior explained with surprising honesty. "Godide ordered them to get between your two columns, divide your forces, and allow the 'Chest' and 'Right Horn' to destroy the lead elements. After they split from the main *impi*, we never saw them again. It would seem they failed in their mission."

"You could say that," Lieutenant Lloyd replied.

Though he made no mention of it, as the officer played out the actions of the battle in his mind, he surmised that their victory had been as much due to a tactical error on the part of the 'Left Horn', as it was a triumph of British firepower. Had they executed their phase of the attack as planned, it was very possible the Zulu left would have, at minimum, overwhelmed Captain Wynne's sappers, while destroying much of their wagons and stores. Though he hated to diminish the scope of their victory, the naval officer could not help but feel that No. 1 Column had simply been lucky.

"But then, fortune favours the bold," he said quietly to himself.

From his position atop the knoll, Colonel Pearson could not be any more pleased with the performance of his column. He had smashed a sizeable Zulu army with only half his forces. The discipline and valour displayed by Commander Campbell's naval brigade was especially noteworthy, as was the havoc inflicted by Midshipman Coker's Gatling gun. The only men who left disappointed by the day's action were those of the 99th Regiment. They were confined to guarding the wagons and had missed most of the fighting. Only a handful had been sent into the fray. And their only role was to help Harrison and Wyld's companies turn the Zulu left flank.

As he assessed the reports his ADCs were bringing to him from the various regiments, Colonel Pearson's gaze fell upon Lieutenant Colonel Parnell of The Buffs. His horse was nowhere to be seen, and he was walking with a limp.

"By God, colonel, are you alright?"

"I'm fine, sir, though sadly I cannot say the same for my horse." Parnell held up a lead slug that had mushroomed from impact and was covered in flecks of dried blood. "I extracted this from my poor mount."

"This is no musket ball," Pearson noted, as he took the slug and turned it over in his hand.

"No, sir, it's a Martini-Henry round." Parnell shook his head in bemusement. "I thought the Zulus didn't have any of our weapons!"

The thought of Cetshwayo acquiring modern breach-loading rifles, whose effective range was roughly eight times that of archaic muskets, was terrifying to ponder.

"We'll sweep the field for any enemy firearms," Pearson directed. "If they've somehow managed to acquire modern rifles, we need to inform his lordship at once."

"Your pardon, sir," the sergeant major from The Buffs said. "I recommend we take the time to conduct ammunition resupply. The lads were in the thick of it for well over an hour-and-a-half, and their cartridge pouches are severely depleted."

"Agreed," Pearson said. "Once we've swept the field and sorted out any enemy firearms, we'll rest for two hours. To be honest, I had hoped to have us at Eshowe by nightfall. However, the enemy seems to have had something to say about the matter." He chuckled softly before giving similar orders to the IMI and other mounted troops.

Captain Hart's NNC were ordered to dig a single grave for the British dead. There were twelve altogether, though it was suspected that the gravely injured Sergeant Oscar Hydenburg of the NNC and Private William Dunne of The Buffs were not long for this world. Imperial redcoat, European volunteer, and African ally alike were buried together. The spot chosen was in the shadow of a large shade tree to the left of the wagon track. Two of Captain Wynne's sappers cut a makeshift wooden cross, inscribed with the names of the fallen. Most were from Captain Hart's NNC detachment who were overwhelmed early in the fight.

"I hope we can eventually return to give them a more charitable memorial," Warren remarked.

Lieutenant Courtney nodded. "Provided the Zulus do not desecrate the marker or their grave."

Colour Sergeant Smith joined the two officers. "Such is not their way. The Zulus have great reverence for the dead, even their enemies."

"One would not know it, given the state of those poor souls from the NNC," Courtney remarked. "I saw what they did to them. Their bodies were stabbed and bludgeoned dozens of times long after they were dead. I don't think there was an inch upon them not desecrated with a spear thrust."

"It's called *hlomula*," Smith explained. "As barbaric as it may be to us, to the Zulus it is how they honour a worthy foe or beast during the hunt."

Courtney looked at him with an expression of horror.

Smith shrugged. "I didn't say I understood or condoned it, sir."

Having lost his horse to a Martini-Henry bullet, Lieutenant Colonel Parnell was anxious to see if any such weapons were found among the Zulu dead. His entire battalion formed a line from the base of the road to the ridgeline. Scores of muskets were visible lying in the brush and near the bodies of many of the slain.

In a surprising act of charity, numerous soldiers filled their helmets with water from the nearby Inyezane River to give to the Zulu wounded.

"What have we found so far?" Colour Sergeant Bennet asked his section leaders after half-an-hour of searching the field.

Dozens of battered and rusted firearms were laid into a large pile near one of the wagons.

"Mostly Tower muskets," Sergeant Davies remarked. He fumbled through some of the various weapons. "From the few you can still read the manufacture markings on, many are continental European. Danzig, Mutzig, Tulle." He then paused as he hefted one that caught his attention. "This says 'Manchester', though I'm not sure what the 'NH' after it means."

"Manchester, New Hampshire," Sergeant Stirling spoke up. "A bloody American weapon, that."

"And at least forty years old," the colour sergeant noted.

David Fredericks spoke up as he joined the men, a trio of flintlocks cradled in his arms, "What's a bitter pill, is that most of what we've found are Tower muskets."

"Meaning we've been getting shot at by our own damned weapons," Stirling grumbled.

"But at least no Martini-Henrys," the colour sergeant observed. Bennet then nodded towards a mounted officer riding over to them.

"Lieutenant," he said with a quick salute, as he recognised William Robarts of the Victoria Mounted Rifles.

"Colour Sergeant," the volunteer officer replied. "Any weapons of value in this lot?"

Bennet shook his head. "They're mostly old bits of junk. You looking for a souvenir, sir?"

"Actually, I'm trying to find a suitable rifle for my servant, Gingwayo. He's a capital fellow, very loyal, and I thought to show him my appreciation."

"Here's an Enfield, sir," Sergeant Fredericks remarked, hefting a percussion cap rifle that was in a far better state than most of the other muskets. "It's got some mild rust-pitting, but it looks sturdy enough. At least the stock has not succumbed to termites yet."

"Splendid!" Robarts said excitedly, as David handed him the rifle. "I see it requires percussion caps."

"There's some bags and pouches piled over there." Colour Sergeant Bennet pointed over by another wagon. "Perhaps you'll find some there."

"Yes, much obliged." The lieutenant quickly saluted the men and walked his horse over to the other piles of loot.

In the end, he managed to find a powder horn, a pouch with percussion caps, and six bullets. He'd hoped to find more shots for the rifle. But when he presented it to Gingwayo later that morning, the young man's face lit up, and Robarts swore he never saw him quit smiling afterwards.

Nearly 200 firearms were recovered from the ridge and Wombane Hill. All were aged muskets in terrible states of disrepair.

As they looked at the large pile of firearms, shields, and assegais, the battalion's senior NCO, Sergeant Major Green, bluntly stated what had now crossed his commanding officer's mind. "It would seem your poor horse was not shot by a Zulu after all."

The loss of the beloved mount he'd had for over ten years distressed Parnell greatly. Losing her to a careless shot from one of his own soldiers upset him further. "It seems I need to have a word with Captain Forester," he said coldly. He shook his head in frustration. "It's as much my fault as theirs. Riding between my own troops and the enemy, obscured by clouds of smoke, what did I think was going to happen?"

Green said nothing. Privately, he was still angered by what had transpired. He recalled the story he'd heard the previous year during the Xhosa War, when a captain from the 24th Regiment was accidentally shot in the back by one of soldiers.

The colonel continued, folding his arms across his chest, "At least now we can assume the Zulus are not in possession of modern firearms."

"Surgeon Norbury also informed me that every shot he extracted from our wounded came from muskets. If the Zulus were in possession of Martini-Henrys, sir, we would have taken it far worse than we did today. And speaking of the surgeon, I recommend you go see him about that nasty crack to the head."

"I'll be fine, sergeant major," Parnell asserted. "Might have a beastly headache for the next couple days, but nothing like poor Private Dunne, who's been shot through the guts."

With a nod of understanding, Sergeant Major Green then handed his commanding officer a sheet of parchment. "The tally of our losses, sir."

Two privates from Captain Forester's company of The Buffs were slain. Two more were severely injured. Lieutenant Martin's company suffered three critically wounded, the worst being Private William Dunne. Friends of Private John Corble were surprised to find that, despite being shot in the head, he was still alive. The musket ball had punched clean through his helmet; however, it smashed into his skull at an angle instead of straight on.

Over by the hospital wagon, Lieutenant Martin met with Surgeon Norbury regarding the badly injured Corble.

"Provided he doesn't suffer from brain swelling, he should eventually recover," the doctor explained. "He'll need to be on bedrest for at least the next two weeks, then light duty for another month. I'll have to check his wound every couple days to see how the skull is knitting back together."

"Thank you, doctor," Martin said appreciatively. He asked sombrely, "What of Private Dunne?"

"I've made him as comfortable as I can," Norbury replied. "Even if I could extract the bullet, which is lodged deep in his guts, there's been too much tearing. I'm afraid he'll die of septic shock within the next day or so."

It was no small relief for Colonel Pearson to learn that rumours about the enemy possessing modern rifles appeared to be completely unfounded. The column was given two hours to rest, take on water, and replenish ammunition, while his staff sorted through the hastily-scrawled reports from each commanding officer.

"It's turning into a beastly day," Colonel Walker said, removing his helmet and wiping a handkerchief across his sweaty brow.

"Still, better than another day of downpour," Pearson reasoned. He then acknowledged Major Graves of the 2nd NNC Regiment.

"We've finished interrogating the prisoners, sir," the officer said.

"Any intelligence?"

"One man claimed to be from Cetshwayo's personal regiment, the uThulwana. Yet he said the main *impi*, including most of his regimental mates, were all headed for a place called kwaJimu. I've never heard of it."

"It's their name for Rorke's Drift," Colonel Pearson explained.

"Ah, well, that makes sense now. I was amazed at this old warrior's candour. From what we could gather, the entire enemy force sent against us amounted to no more than 6,000 men."

"They're fighting a delaying action," Colonel Walker conjectured.

Pearson nodded. "Well, I don't want them to think they've delayed us at all. The column will have until noon to rest and refresh. After which, I want us on the march again. If the enemy still has some fight left in them, then this is the worst possible ground for us to occupy."

"And, of course, it won't take long for the flies to gather and those bodies to start to stink," Walker added.

"Was there anything else?" the column commander asked Graves.

The major shook his head and started to walk away once Pearson dismissed him. He paused and turned back to his commanding officer.

"Actually, there was one thing, sir. The old boy seemed to know they were beaten before the battle even started. When asked why they fight at all, his response was, *'And what would you think of a people who would desert their king?'* To be honest, colonel, I have to admire them for that."

"As do I, major. As do I."

For Godide and the southern *impi*, the Battle of Inyezane had begun with great promise, only to end in disaster. Phalane was proud of his warriors for maintaining their discipline and resolve. Once it became apparent they could not break through the British lines, and with enemy reinforcements threatening their left flank, the uMxhapho Regiment withdrew from the field quickly and orderly. Those badly wounded during the retreat were carried away by their mates. Sadly, the dead were left where they fell.

All the while, Phalane led the survivors up a narrow and exceptionally steep saddle towards the sounds of chanting and war dances in the distance. He knew of a hilltop that was relatively flat about four miles away. From there, one could just barely see the site of the battle.

"Those old women chant and dance about like they've won a great victory," a warrior growled, as he helped his badly-injured friend up a particularly slippery piece of ground. "Instead, they left us to die!"

The wounded warrior had been struck in both the outer thigh and the side by enemy bullets. Though glancing shots, they'd torn away ghastly chunks of flesh and cracked the man's ribs, making it extremely painful to breathe let alone walk. Phalane stepped onto a rock outcropping, reached down, and helped the warrior heave his injured friend upwards. The wounded man's face was etched in agony, sweat beading off his forehead. Yet he made not a sound.

While his warriors doggedly trudged on, the *induna* kept glancing back to make certain the British were not pursuing them. That they seemed content to defend their wagons and drive the Zulus off perplexed him, at first. But in their position, he likely would not have gone chasing after the enemy through steep and unknown terrain, lest they walk straight into an ambush.

As he continued to help his men in aiding their stricken comrades, Phalane listened. He heard more and more curses towards the old warriors who were supposed to reinforce the 'Chest' and 'Right Horn' of the attack. Though they could not see what had transpired, the only assumption any of them could reach was that Godide and his centre regiments had faltered, thereby abandoning the uMxhapho Regiment to destruction.

The battle had ended around 9.30 a.m., and by noon No. 1 Column was once again on the march. The frayed nerves of those who'd taken part in the fighting began to calm. There was the added air of sadness from those who'd lost friends that day. The decisiveness of their victory could not fully assuage the numbing sorrows of the friends of Privates John Bough and James Kelleher, nor those from the NNC's fallen. All knew it could have been much worse. The survivors quietly gave prayers of thanks it was not their time that had come this day.

"Imagine how it must be for the Zulus," Rob Anderson said to David Fredericks. They continued to march, all the while searching for any more signs of the enemy.

"Many tears will be shed for their dead this day," the sergeant concurred.

The NCOs and their soldiers kept glancing skyward as the column lumbered its way up the steep track. Colour Sergeant Bennet had mentioned reading about a solar eclipse for that day.

"I recall the Xhosa felt that fortune was portended by the phases of the moon," Rob recalled. "I wonder if the Zulus have the same superstitions."

"I would argue that superstitions are not limited to the natives," David remarked. "Some say that an eclipse of the sun during battle is a terrible omen, though I'm not certain for whom."

"As if the eyes of God were being closed in sorrow," the corporal stated. He then looked up at the heavens once more.

"Well, a good thing we concluded our little scrap before we could offend the Almighty," the sergeant added.

Though it was a cloudless day, since around midday the sky had been gradually darkening. What surprised David the most was that the temperature dropped significantly. This came as a bit of reprieve to the sweat-soaked soldiers in their stifling wool tunics. It was now nearly 4.00 and just a small crescent sliver of the sun remained.

"Perhaps some greater calamity in this land is causing God to look away in mourning," David said with a nervous laugh.

"Yes, well, Sergeant Milne will be filled with jealousy when he hears about our exploits this day," Corporal Anderson said after an awkward silence.

David laughed as he thought about his old friend and former mentor haplessly detached to working the ponts at Rorke's Drift. As a breeze blew over the men, their grins faded. Neither the sergeant nor his corporal could explain why they were suddenly on edge. They each tried to dismiss the feeling as nerves following a battle, yet this was different. Fear gripped the heart of Sergeant David Fredericks. He clutched his rifle close. He kept silent lest he embarrass himself by voicing his absurd feelings. He shook his head in frustration, unable to explain his premonition of dread.

It was not only Sergeant David Fredericks who struggled with feelings of anxiety. Despite his elation at their significant victory, Colonel Charles Pearson was similarly bothered as the eclipse of the sun reached its apex around 4.00 that afternoon.

"Everything alright, colonel?" The voice of his ADC, Major Porter, startled him.

"Yes, yes," he said quickly. He glanced skyward. This would not be a total eclipse, and a defiant sliver of sunlight shone behind the black splotch of the moon. Though not a superstitious man, he could not shake the sense of foreboding.

He quickly focused his attention on sorting out their camp for the night. He decided upon a stretch of ground atop a high ridge. Though it offered superior views and was a naturally defensible plateau, it simply did not have sufficient room for the column's massive wagon train and their tents.

"Looks like we'll be sleeping under the stars tonight," the colonel said to his staff officers. "Let us hope the rains spare us for one more night."

That evening, Colonel Pearson sat on a camp stool behind his battered old field desk. An oil lamp lit the pages of despatches, as well as a faded and scribbled on map he'd acquired from a local trader prior to the invasion.

"The last of the rear guard have reached the camp," Forestier Walker said. He pulled up a stool next to his fellow colonel.

Pearson checked his watch. "Nine o'clock. It's been a long day for them."

"That it has. They were the advance guard this morning and are only now able to have supper. I suppose they'll sleep well tonight, provided the Zulus don't come crawling back for another scrap."

"They're likely having second thoughts after this morning," Pearson speculated. "I've finished my despatch to Lord Chelmsford, though looking at this map, I cannot help but think he'll have the entire war decided before it reaches him."

"That old boy we captured even said it; the Zulus want what we do, a decisive battle."

"They're not equipped to fight a protracted campaign," Charles remarked. "Even less so with their harvest imminent."

Their thoughts were interrupted by Major Porter. He came to attention before his commanding officer. "Beg your pardon, sir. This may seem like a trifle, but there's been a lot of speculation among the camp as to what we should call the battle we fought today. Surely, it has to have a name."

"I say we call it Victory Hill," Walker suggested. "In reference to the hill where Mister Coker's Gatling drove the enemy off."

"That was one of the suggestions, sir," Porter said.

Pearson nodded thoughtfully. With only half his column, he turned what could have been a disastrous ambush into a decisive victory. No. 1 Column had suffered fifteen dead and roughly thirty wounded, mostly NNC warriors and European carbineers.

Seven of Commander Campbell's sailors were among the wounded, though none fatally. Surgeon Norbury performed brilliantly in saving the life of Ordinary Seaman George Doran. He'd been shot in the left thigh and nearly bled to death before he could be carried to the hospital wagon. The most critically wounded were Privates Dunne and Corble from The Buffs and a sergeant from the NNC named Oscar Hydenburg.

By comparison, estimates from the sweep of the field concluded that at least 400 Zulus were killed, with two to three times as many wounded. The battle had been decisive. It baffled the British to learn that prior to the charge of the Jack Tars, the Zulus were convinced they were winning the exchange. Still, Colonel Pearson had doubts as to what to call their battle.

"*Victory* is such an over-used word," he finally said. "While I commend our soldiers and sailors for their efforts today and feel it was, indeed, a great victory, I find it improper that we should attempt to give our battle this day the same name as Lord Nelson's flagship." He squinted his eyes and pointed to his map. "Now then, the name of the river we crossed this morning prior to the attack…"

"Inyezane, sir," Major Porter informed him.

"Then let the papers and history books record that on the 22nd of January 1879, Her Majesty's Forces did defeat those of Zulu King Cetshwayo at the Battle of Inyezane."

"Long may it be remembered, sir."

The initial grave marker for the British dead, Battle of Inyezane

Chapter XIII: On to Eshowe

Five Miles from Eshowe
23 January 1879

The March to Eshowe, from *The Illustrated London News*
Mounted officer in foreground presumed to be Colonel Pearson

The day began at 3.00 a.m. for Colonel Charles Pearson and the No. 1 Column with an immediate order for 'stand to'. Soldiers quickly donned their red tunics and tea-stained helmets before hefting their rifles and sprinting towards their respective sections' positions along the defensive laager. The hour just before dawn, the rising to blind those looking east, was a dangerous time for any army and the likeliest when an enemy would attack. Indeed, the Zulus called it *'The Horns of the Morning'*. All remained still. Only the occasional boar or giraffe crossed into the soldiers' view. At 3.45, a bugler sounded reveille. With the column ordered to start its final push to Eshowe at 5.00, the men had just enough time to choke down some cold coffee and hard biscuits before striking their tents and making ready to march.

Colonel Pearson was joined this morning by his column staff, the battalion commanders of his regular infantry, as well as Captain Wynne of the engineers over a hasty breakfast which consisted mostly of lukewarm coffee. He had also summed Captain Shepstone

169

of the Durban Mounted Rifles, who would act as the advance guard for the column.

"Gentlemen," the colonel said. "We are five miles from our destination at Eshowe. I had hoped to arrive there yesterday until our friends, the Zulus, so rudely interrupted us."

This was met with a few forced chuckles from the assembled officers. Warren Wynne wondered if Pearson knew how close they had come to disaster. His company of sappers had been completely exposed. Had the Zulus advanced just another half mile behind the ridge before pivoting to attack, the captain reckoned he would not be standing here. His company would likely have been butchered and the divided column in a fearful state from which to extract itself from.

"I want the column ready to march by 5.00," the colonel continued. "Captain Shepstone, have our vedettes found any signs of the enemy?"

"No sir. It would seem *Inkosi* Godide has had his fill of the Martini-Henry for one day."

Though it was only five miles to Eshowe, the going was painfully slow. Captain Wynne's sappers were kept busy, having been called forward four times to repair the sodden and broken track. While soldiers and horses could readily navigate through the churned up boggy mess, the same could not be said for their ox-drawn wagons and artillery. At one point, engineers and Natal pioneers with spades spent over an hour shovelling dirt and gravel to make a crossing fordable, only to have the entire patch crumble under the sinking weight of the first wagon.

The advance guard, consisting of Captain William Shepstone's Durban Mounted Rifles, reached Eshowe around 9.00. Warren Wynne, who'd accompanied the lead element to within a mile of the old mission site, was surprised to see how idyllic the scene was. Even from this distance, one could clearly see the steeple of the small church, several houses, and a slew of gardens full of various fruit trees.

"Would you look at that?" a trooper said. "Who'd have thought the trappings of civilisation could be found in such a barbaric wilderness as this?"

Captain Shepstone ordered two of his sections to advance in a screen line through the settlement, while the rest of his troopers fanned out to cover the flanks. The mounted soldiers rode quickly yet cautiously, lest the Zulus be waiting to surprise them. All was quiet. The only sounds came from their horses and a score of shrieks and calls from various birds.

The grounds of the Eshowe mission were 120 yards long and about 80 wide, sloping down from west to east. The small church, built of sun-dried bricks with a corrugated iron roof occupied the highest ground, overlooking the rest of the mission. A school and workshop were nearest the church. These were also built of bricks, covered in plaster, with thatch instead of iron roofs. A large house with a veranda sat at the bottom of the gentle slope, surrounded by an orchard of lush orange trees.

"This place has been deserted for months," a trooper noted. "I'm amazed it's still here."

"The Zulus neither occupied nor destroyed it," one of his mates added. "It's as if God himself were preserving it for us."

After sending a rider back to inform Colonel Pearson that the mission was intact and free of Zulus, the column commander, staff officers, Lieutenant Colonel Parnell, and Captain Wynne rode into the depot, joining Captain Shepstone on the high ground nearest the church. A south-easterly running stream ran behind the orange grove. Some of the troopers dismounted to water their horses. An additional two houses were seen just beyond the junction, with a third to the southwest.

"Your thoughts, Captain Wynne?" Pearson asked.

His engineer officer stood with his arms folded across his chest, his calculating eyes taking in the layout of the mission station and the terrain. "Your pardon, sir, but the ground here is terrible," he replied candidly.

"How so? The mission occupies a fine piece of high ground."

"That may be, sir, but there are thirty-foot rises all around. And that steep drop-off to the west is a terrible blind spot, chock-full of brush. The enemy could get within seventy yards of this place before we knew they were there."

This assessment annoyed Pearson. He viewed Eshowe as a strong defensive position. "Duly noted, captain. However, here we have ample buildings to house our stores. And aside from the blind spot to the west—where we can place sentries to over watch—the Zulus cannot get closer than four hundred yards along any of those high points before we spot them."

"Understood, sir," Wynne said. "The trouble we now face is that we have no building materials. There aren't enough trees to build palisades, and I can't very well use the wagons since they're needed for bringing up more supplies."

"You're an engineer; make do."

Wynne nodded, saluted the colonel, and took his leave. He'd made his concerns known. It was all he could do. Fortifying Eshowe would be a much larger undertaking than Fort Tenedos.

Captain Wynne paced the perimeter, deep in thought as he conceived how to build up his defence works. Colonel Pearson decided to erect his headquarters near the orange grove. Wynne's No. 2 Field Company would encamp on the mission station itself. Most of the column would have to position itself in defensive positions overlooking any potential blind spots or suspected avenues-of-approach.

Around 10.00 the first elements of the column arrived. Like the troopers from the Durban Mounted Rifles, the soldiers were in awe of the tranquil setting in the midst of the harsh Zulu wilderness. There was little time for them to take in the view, however, as staff officers and engineers quickly directed them to their places within the camp's proposed defences.

While the column's lengthy convoy of wagons and men slowly made their way into the mission site, Charles Pearson decided to take a look inside the church. It was plain and unadorned, with only some old pews covered in dust and a couple of tables. Spider webs clung to the ceiling rafters.

"Nothing a short sweep won't sort out," Major Porter said, as he joined his commander.

Pearson allowed himself a grin and stepped back out into the sun, thankful the rains had spared them the previous night. He then heard, *'Rider approaching!'*, shouted from near the southern approach. The messenger was a young subaltern from the 99th Regiment. His gleaming helmet plate was visible from a mile away.

"Colonel, sir!" the young officer said. Quickly dismounting, he handed his horse to one of Pearson's orderlies and came to attention. "Compliments of Colonel Ely. He wishes to inform you that his convoy of sixty wagons, bearing rations and other resupplies, crossed the Thukela River yesterday morning."

While this news normally would have been welcome to Pearson, it filled him with concern. Though No. 1 Column had at last reached Eshowe, with a decisive victory against the Zulus, the very presence of such a large enemy force made him question the security of Ely's convoy. He ordered an aid to find Lieutenant Colonel Parnell.

Parnell appeared a few minutes later. "You sent for me, sir?" The commanding officer of 2/3rd Buffs had spent much of the morning overseeing his companies and the chaos that ensued from having so many wagons and draught animals to contend with. He'd just met with his quartermaster to determine where the battalion's ammunition stores would be centrally located, when the column commander summoned him.

"As you know, Colonel Ely is bringing up the first of our resupply convoys," Pearson explained. "He has only three companies from the 99th and a handful of troopers from the Alexandria Mounted Rifles to act as his escorts. Given what we faced yesterday, I fear he is too exposed. We gave the Zulus a damn good thrashing, but I'm certain they will be back once they've finished licking their wounds."

Henry Ely was a battalion major with the 99th Regiment. With his recent brevet to lieutenant colonel, plus Henry Welman's seniority on the Army List for promotion to full colonel, it was anticipated he would be Welman's eventual successor. He was tasked with overseeing resupply and keeping lines of communication open between Eshowe and Lower Drift.

"A lightly-defended convoy would make the perfect target for retribution," Parnell concurred. "I suspect the Zulus have learned a thing or two about how we fight. I doubt they will make the same mistakes twice."

Pearson nodded. "Order two of your companies ready to depart in the morning. I'll task two companies of NNC and some mounted rifles to act as vanguard and flank security." He then addressed the subaltern from the 99th. "Inform Colonel Ely he is to advance no further than the Msunduzi River until he's sufficiently reinforced."

"Very good, sir." The young officer saluted and remounted his horse. It took him several minutes to negotiate his way past the scores of wagons, hundreds of protesting draught animals, and numerous soldiers who inadvertently blocked his way.

After receiving a few additional instructions, Henry Parnell returned to his battalion headquarters tent. He tasked Captains

Jackson and Forester with executing the column commander's intent. Though there would be numerous grumblings from the ranks over having to march all the way back towards the Thukela, the two officers understood the necessity. Captain Forester, still reeling from embarrassment regarding his commanding officer nearly being killed by his soldiers, was glad for the distraction.

At the naval brigade's camp, Midshipman Lewis Coker finished writing his report for Colonel Pearson. His hand was shaking as he handed it to Commander Campbell, who took his time reading it over.

Sir,

I have the honour to report I was placed in rear of the leading column with the Gatling gun. About two hours and a half after leaving the camping grounds, the head of the column was engaged. A report having come in that the natives were threatening the rear of the column, I placed my gun on a hill, in a good position for firing if necessary. I brought my gun into action...no natives appearing, I moved on with the wagons...on arriving at the foot of the hill, where the headquarters were, I was ordered by Colonel Pearson to bring the gun up and place it opposite a hill where some natives had taken up position. I immediately opened fire on them; they were retiring in the bush. I ceased firing, having expended about 300 rounds.

Lewis Coker, Midshipman

"I have penned a separate report regarding the specifics of the gun's functioning and a few recommendations," Coker remarked.

"Very good, Mister Coker," Campbell said approvingly. "You did well yesterday, son."

"Th...thank you, sir!" Lewis replied, letting loose the last shreds of nervous tension, he allowed himself a sigh of relief. "With your permission, I'll return to my crew."

The commander nodded, the two exchanged salutes, and Coker hurried back to where his Gatling gun sat along the perimeter. Campbell smiled in admiration at the young man. Of all the officers and men under his charge, Lewis Coker exuded more energy and determination than any. His relentlessness was equalled only by his sense of duty. Though only eighteen years of age, his six years spent as a midshipman aboard training vessels had educated and experienced him beyond his years. Once the fighting with the Zulus was over and they returned to duty aboard the HMS Active, Commander Campbell was determined to help Coker prepare for his lieutenant's exam.

A View Inside the Fort, by Lieutenant Charles Knight, 2/3rd 'Buffs' Regiment

That evening, as he stood outside his tent, watching his camp slowly come together, Colonel Pearson was alerted to a runner approaching from the northwest. The man was a black African who wore a red scarf around his head, denoting him as a member of the Natal Native Contingent.

"Message for Colonel Pearson," the man said. His English was surprisingly good with only a hint of an accent.

"What news?" Pearson asked, hands on his hips.

"From Captain Cherry," the messenger said, handing a note to the colonel.

Captain Charles Cherry was a regular army officer from the 32nd Light Infantry who assumed command of the 3rd Battalion, 1st NNC Regiment at the start of the war. Part of Lieutenant Colonel Anthony Durnford's No. 2 Column, they had been left at Kranzkop between Lower Drift and Rorke's Drift to protect against a possible Zulu counter-invasion.

Pearson chuckled softly as he read the message:

Colonel,

Large force of Zulus, numbering possibly 6,000 warriors, sighted moving towards Lower Drift. Suspect they intend to oppose your advance.

C. Cherry, Capt.

"You can thank Captain Cherry and let him know I've already taken care of this force of Zulus," the colonel said. His voice brimmed with smug confidence.

He dismissed the man, informing him that he could camp with the mounted volunteers. Pearson told the man to make his way back to Middle Drift in the morning, once the colonel penned his reply.

Charles was glad for this bit of news, even if it was redundant. Being a hundred miles to the south of the centre column, he was essentially blind to all that was transpiring with Lord Chelmsford. But since Captain Cherry had sent no news regarding the centre column, Pearson could only speculate that the invasion was proceeding according to his lordship's plan.

Pearson then went over his map, trying to speculate just where the other columns were. Colonel Wood's northern No. 4 Column had crossed near the town of Utrecht and would likely be somewhere in the vicinity of the large mountain called Hlobane; the stronghold of the abaQulusi. Last he'd heard, Colonel Glyn's centre No. 3 Column was heading due east, and had likely made it at least as far as the mountain of Isandlwana, perhaps even as far as Mangeni Falls.

Given what Pearson learned the previous day from the old Zulu warrior, that King Cetshwayo's intentions were the same as the British. Pearson could therefore not help but wonder if the decisive engagement desired by both sides had already occurred. In the absence of information, all he could do was carry on with his own mission.

Pearson's own No. 1 Column had to be strong enough to face a large enemy force on its own, though their primary purpose was logistical. Lord Chelmsford intended for Pearson to establish several supply depots along his axis of advance, with the ability to provide support to Glyn as necessary. Eshowe was to be but one of these; the next possibly at another old mission called St. Paul's, another twenty-five miles on.

Lieutenant Colonel Durnford's highly mobile No. 2 Column would essentially be the eyes of the invasion force, preventing the Zulus from serving up any nasty surprises to supply convoys dispatched from Pearson's column.

"Strange that Captain Cherry sent the message from Middle Drift and not Durnford," Colonel Walker noted.

"Given his need for mobility, perhaps he was not at the drift at the time Cherry received his intelligence. Regardless, tomorrow I will send Durnford a message. In the absence of countermanding orders from the GOC, he needs to be ready to support us, as we are furthest away from friendly forces."

"Agreed."

Lord Chelmsford's original invasion plan

No. 1 Column (Pearson) to advance on Eshowe and establish supply depot before advancing on Ulundi

No. 2 Column (Durnford) to act as mobile reserve force, ready to assist either Glyn or Pearson

No. 3 Column (Glyn) to head straight for Ulundi, with the intent of meeting the main Zulu *impi* in a decisive engagement

No. 4 Column (Wood) to harass the Zulus in the north, while acting in concert with Glyn

No. 5 Column (Rowlands) to garrison Natal, while providing any necessary reinforcements to Wood

Just after evening parade, the men of H Company, 2/3rd Buffs learned that Private William Dunne had passed away. That night, instead of the usual banter over card games and cigar smoke, a sombre pall hung over the section. The following morning, as Sergeant David Fredericks walked along the line conducting a quick inspection of his soldiers' kit, he could feel just how hard Dunne's death had struck his soldiers. The private's closest friends kept a stoic demeanour during the day, only at night allowing their tears to fall. A likeable fellow who many within H Company viewed as a friend, William Dunne was six months from the end of his enlistment when a Zulu musket ball ended his life. That he had lingered for so long in extreme pain before death came for him only added to the bitter feelings of his mates.

"All he wanted was to see the white cliffs of Dover once more," Private Howard Walters said glumly after morning parade. He leaned against the company's ammunition wagon; his rifle resting on the bench seat.

"You know he told me recently that he intended to become a fisherman, once he was back in Blighty," another soldier remarked. "Silly bugger couldn't even swim, yet he was determined to make a living on the seas."

"Walters, you're on first sentry watch," Sergeant Fredericks said, as he walked over to the men. "You'll be replacing Corble. He's in pretty rough shape."

"Rough shape?" Private Peters asked. "I thought he was dead."

David shook his head. "He's alive but not looking well. Surgeon was able to remove the musket shot and patch him up, but it did a number on his skull."

"He should be glad the Zulus don't have Martini-Henrys," another private reasoned. "Would have blown out the back of his head."

Walters said nothing. He continued to lean against the butt stock of his rifle, staring with bloodshot eyes into the morning gloom.

Sergeant Fredericks would usually severely chastise a man for failing to respond to his directives immediately. This time, he felt a slightly gentler approach was needed. "Walters!" He tapped the man on the shoulder with his notebook.

179

The startled private immediately came to attention. "Sorry, sergeant." He fumbled with his weapon. "Sentry duty, you said?"

"Yes, you're replacing Private Corble. Report to Lance Corporal Monroe and he'll get you sorted."

Walters gave a short nod and turned his gaze outward.

David grabbed him by the tunic sleeve. "Keep your head about you," he said sternly. "You cannot honour Dunne's memory if you get yourself, or any of your mates, killed needlessly."

With no defence works in place yet, additional designated sentries remained on watch, while the rest of the company stood down and started to see about their coffee and breakfast. Walters wordlessly grabbed his Martini-Henry and made his way through the camp to find Monroe. David was about to speak to the rest of the section, when one of the officer commanding's aides walked briskly over to him.

"Your pardon, sergeant," the private said. "But Mister Martin has called for you and Corporal Anderson to come at once."

Fredericks gave a curt nod and called over his shoulder, "Rob!"

"I heard him," the corporal replied. He was seated against the side of the ammunition wagon, running a bore brush down the barrel of his rifle and checking for any signs of rust pitting. He quickly stood and accompanied his sergeant as they sought out their officer commanding.

Lieutenant Martin had established the company's headquarters, which consisted of little more than a few camp stools and a hastily dug fire pit, approximately ten yards behind the centre of their section of the perimeter. His batman was feverishly trying to light the damp wood in order to make his master's coffee. The officer commanding was standing off to the side, having a private discussion with Colour Sergeant Bennet.

David was surprised to see Sergeant Stirling also waiting to see the lieutenant. "John, what brings you here?"

"No idea," his fellow sergeant said with a shrug.

David suspected his commander wanted to talk to him about Private Dunne's death. However, if he also wanted to see Stirling that made him doubt this theory. As far as he could recall, none of Stirling's soldiers had fallen during the battle. Besides Dunne and Corble, the only other casualty from H Company that he could recall was Private Henry Walker from Sergeant Davies' section, who'd been shot in the leg by an enemy marksman.

"Gentlemen." The lieutenant waved the NCOs over.

All three quickly walked up to the officer and came to attention.

"At ease. You're no doubt wondering why I needed to see you."

"To be honest, sir, I thought you wished to discuss Private Dunne's death," David said hesitantly.

The officer gave him a perplexed look. "What? No, that's not it...though I am sorry. He was a good man."

His placid expression made the sergeant doubt these last words. He wondered if his officer commanding even knew who William Dunne was. He then shook off such thoughts as unfair. After all, though the company was well understrength, Lieutenant Robert Martin had over seventy soldiers under his command. And given the deliberate distance which lower enlisted were kept from the officers, one could not expect him to know every man by name. Indeed, the few times when he did have to deal directly with private soldiers was mostly when doling out punishments or commendations.

"As you are aware, we've been a bit short-handed on NCOs since Sergeant Milne was detached to Rorke's Drift," the commander explained. "Corporal Roberts assumed charge of his section; however, he has fallen ill with a terrible fever and is no longer capable of leading the section." He nodded to Rob. "Corporal Anderson, you will replace him as section leader until Sergeant Milne returns to us. It could be quite a few months; possibly through the duration of the war. I'm therefore appointing you to lance sergeant. I know you are ready for promotion to full sergeant; however, the battalion does not have any vacancies at the moment. But do well, and I'll see to it you are elevated into the first permanent section leader billet that comes available."

"Thank you, sir," Anderson replied. "It is an honour."

"Sergeant Stirling," the lieutenant continued. "I'm taking Private Norton from your section and promoting him to lance corporal with an appointment as Lance Sergeant Anderson's assistant."

"Very good, sir."

"And Sergeant Fredericks."

"Sir?" David asked.

"I'm relieving Lance Corporal Monroe of his duties as sharp-shooter and reassigning him as your assistant section leader. If he

181

wants to earn that second chevron, he needs to learn how to be more than just a solid shot."

"Understood."

Colour Sergeant Bennet tossed a single white cloth chevron to Anderson. "We don't have any lance sergeant stripes. Stitch that above your corporal chevrons and make it look as proper as you can."

"Yes, colour sergeant."

Bennet nodded for Rob to follow him. "Come with me. We'll let the lads know you're their new section leader."

Lieutenant Martin dismissed the two sergeants who came to attention before departing.

"Well, how about that," John said with a bemused chuckle. "All this time you've been saying Rob Anderson was ready for promotion. Yet it only came when one sergeant got tasked to be a 'water taxi' at the sodding ponts, and his corporal came down a severe case of the shits."

"Your man, Norton, will be thrilled," David noted.

Private Terrance Norton had completed his six-year enlistment two months prior. He had elected to remain with the Colours, not wishing to miss out on the promise of battle against the Zulus.

"He'll probably run around naked, whooping and hollering after I tell him." Stirling paused for a moment before turning a slight shade of red. "Oh wait, that's how *I* celebrated my first promotion."

"I remember that," David laughed. "Colonel Parnell damn near had you brought up on charges of drunk and disorderly conduct."

"Well, once I was able to convince him that I was completely sober, he told me to put my trousers on and quit embarrassing him. Colour Sergeant Bennet saw to it I was tasked with corporal-of-the-guard for a week straight."

The amusing memory brought a much-needed laugh from both men. Dark clouds, with their promise of another downpour, had blackened the collective mood of No. 1 Column. Something neither mentioned, but both were keenly aware of, was how lucky they had been two days earlier. Every man in the Regiment understood the basics of Zulu warfare. Given where the enemy engaged them, David reckoned the element the Buffs had faced was the 'Left Horn'. The lead division's firepower had been concentrated at the head of the march with their two companies, Lieutenant Lloyd's 7-pounders, and Midshipman Coker's Gatling gun. Had the Zulu 'Left

Horn' continued a few hundred yards further south, they could have hit the division from behind, chopping up the Natal Pioneers with the very distinct possibility of surrounding an annihilating Captain Wynne's engineer company. The simple fact was, the Zulu 'Left Horn' had executed the brunt of their attack far too soon after the 'Chest' drove in the NNC and mounted vedettes. Instead of flanking the British column and driving a wedge between the two divisions, they ran straight into a merciless wall of Martini-Henry firepower. As for the Zulu 'Right Horn', they never seemed to materialise during the battle.

The sun was now just over the distant mountains and the two sergeants gazed over the defences towards the road to the south. Just a few miles away, hundreds of enemy warriors lay dead or slowly dying in the tall grass and stands of trees near the Inyezane River.

"I wonder how many of them are mourning the loss of their mates," David thought aloud.

Chapter XIV: From Beauty to Desolation

Eshowe
24 January 1879

The Fort at Eshowe

For the second night in a row, the garrison at Eshowe suffered a terribly rainy night. Many grumbled that the two days of reprieve before and on the day of the Battle of Inyezane had seemed too good to last. It was on the soggy morning of the 24th that Colonel Pearson penned a pair of messages. The first was a despatch to Lord Chelmsford, informing him of the column's decisive victory at Inyezane and subsequent arrival at Eshowe. He further implored his lordship to adjust the No. 3 Column's avenue of advance further south to support his own advance through the Mhlatuze Valley. *'A hundred miles separating our columns gives the enemy ample room to manoeuvre between us,'* he wrote.

Normally, this message would have gone to his fellow column commander, Richard Glyn. However, Pearson was very much aware that the notoriously micromanaging Chelmsford had usurped all control of the column from Colonel Glyn. So, Pearson chose to write to the GOC directly.

The second message was addressed to Lieutenant Colonel Durnford, who he assumed was still near Middle Drift. While a highly mobile force of both indigenous African and white European horsemen, it was understood that Durnford's primary mission was to provide support to both columns and assist in keeping lines of communication open. No. 2 Column did not report directly to Colonel Pearson, but it was still within his prerogative to direct where Durnford was needed unless countermanded by the GOC.

Lt Col Durnford,

I know your original plan was to cross at Middle Drift and occupy the eNtumeni mission station west of Eshowe. In light of recent developments, including a decisive battle fought by my column at Inyezane, I recommend you instead cross at Lower Drift. The route is longer, but safer from ambush.

Please advise once you've established at eNtumeni.

C. Pearson, Col

Pearson did not know Durnford was ordered up to Rorke's Drift by Lord Chelmsford a few days earlier; leaving behind Captain Cherry's battalion to secure Middle Drift and thereby depriving No. 1 Column of his support. Captain Cherry had no knowledge that his commanding officer was dead and most of No. 2 Column annihilated. It would come as bitter irony over the coming weeks that Charles Pearson knew nothing of the recent string of catastrophic and tragic events that had recently transpired. On the same day as his decisive victory at Inyezane, disaster struck both Richard Glyn's and Anthony Durnford's forces at Isandlwana. Yet on the evening of the 24th, the mountain under whose bloody slopes the accomplishments of No. 1 Column would be forever consigned to the shadows was little more than a scribbled point on Pearson's map; most likely misspelled.

Unbeknownst to any man at Eshowe, the strategic situation in Zululand had disastrously changed.

While Colonel Charles Pearson and the No. 1 Column were oblivious to the tragic disaster that occurred at Isandlwana, recriminations simmered amongst Godide and the *izinduna* following their defeat at Inyezane.

"We knew the English soldiers evenly matched us in numbers," Godide said coldly. "And yet we fought them on ground of our choosing. They were divided and scattered; ripe for the harvest of slaughter." He glared at Phalane. "The uMxhapho attacked too soon. Instead of driving a blade between their two forces, you led your men straight into a wall of enemy rifles!"

Enraged by this accusation, the *induna* leapt to his feet. Nearby warriors were alarmed by this and rushed to Godide's side.

Phalane ignored them. His gaze bore into the old *inkosi*. "Do *not* try to place the blame on my men! I will accept responsibility for the uMxhapho's premature attack. But where were the rest of the *amabutho*? And where were you, *inkosi*?"

"You forget yourself," one of the older *izinduna* snapped. "This great warrior is our *inkosi*; appointed by the king as our commanding general!"

"And I am a royal *induna*," Phalane retorted, his anger deepening. "The great Cetshwayo has placed special trust in me because of my abilities, not because of who my father was." He opened his arms and addressed the entire assembly. "What then will the *little branch of leaves* say when he learns the uMxhapho fought the English alone on the slopes of Wombane?"

"You did not fight the white soldiers alone!" the older *induna* shouted back.

"But you ran," Phalane snarled. His voice was calm, yet his gaze filled with fury. "Oh, I have spoken with many of your warriors. You left them leaderless, with no hope of support once the enemy's blue-jacketed fighters attacked." He shook his head and spat on the ground. "I am done with this. Let the king send an *inkosi* who is not afraid to fight, and I will follow him. I leave it to you to explain our defeat to Cetshwayo."

The following morning, Phalane and the uMxhapho *ibutho* marched away from Godide's camp. Knowing the British were now occupying the abandoned settlement at Eshowe, the royal *induna* and the survivors of his regiment headed north. They encamped near a lake fed by the Mhlatuze River, about twelve miles from the old mission. Their journey was slowed by scores of wounded who served as a reminder of the terrible price paid. Phalane place the blamed on Godide's hesitation and the cowardice of the old warriors.

186

One of the senior *izinduna* to accompany Phalane was the Nzuzu chief, Matshiya kaMshandu. His people's lands were nearest to Eshowe, and he knew the region well. It was his warriors who were driven from Wombane Hill by the repeating gun, the likes of which the Zulus had never seen before. Matshiya suspected Godide was likely finished as their commanding *inkosi*, and so he and some followers joined Phalane and the uMxhapho. For his part, the royal *induna* was glad to have a guide who was familiar with the territory. He was determined to keep a watchful eye on the English while harrying their column as much as possible, until the king was able to send sufficient reinforcements.

Two days had now passed since the disastrous engagement against the white soldiers. Just before dawn, Phalane decided to bathe in the river. The water was cool, and he found it invigorating as he washed away the grime from the last few days. He was joined by Matshiya and a few other warriors who'd risen early.

"I've sent twenty of my best scouts to keep watch on the English," Matshiya explained. "Once we learn their intentions, we can decide how to best deal with them."

"The orders from our king remain unchanged," Phalane remarked. "Godide may have failed, but we are still sons of Zulu. Our mission is to delay this enemy force until the main *impi* has dealt with those treacherous invaders near kwaJimu."

Matshiya paused and took a moment to wash his face, contemplating his next words. He and Phalane were essentially peers, each with their own independent command. They needed to cooperate with each other, especially in light of abandoning their *inkosi*, Godide.

"The old warriors may have been hesitant, but we still share in the blame," he finally said. "I am as guilty as you, my friend, for allowing my warriors to engage in nothing more than an exchange of gunfire with the English. The smoke was thick, and we thought we were getting the best of them. We did not understand that their weapons have a far greater reach than ours, and their accuracy is terrifying. How many of our friends did we leave dead on the slopes of Wombane? Three hundred? Perhaps as many as four? And how many of them did we fell with our muskets?"

Phalane averted his gaze downward. "It is true. I failed, perhaps even more so than the *inkosi*. And I have let my pride fill me with resentment and hate. Even if we did attack too soon, I should have planned for that and ordered my skirmishers to suppress the English, while I led a concentrated attack between their two columns of wagons."

His friend walked over to him, the cool water splashing around his ankles, and placed a reassuring hand on his shoulder. "We suffered a terrible defeat, but the war is far from over, my friend. Let us be mindful of the painful lessons learned and wait for word from the *impi* and our king."

They would not have long to wait. Despite being nearly a hundred miles from Isandlwana, news travelled fast within the Zulu Kingdom. Messengers called out in loud voices from mountaintops, passing the word to every corner of Cetshwayo's realm.

'The swallows lie butchered on the slopes of Isandlwana!' was one such cry; the term 'swallows' being first coined by the divine Shaka as a term for the whites. Details were sparse. Much of the message gave praises to both King Cetshwayo and the great *inkosi*, Ntshingwayo, who led the *impi* to great victory. As he and his *izinduna* sat around a large campfire that night, Phalane let out a sigh of relief.

"The swallows have had their wings plucked," he said, with perhaps his first smile since the war began.

Work would soon begin on the entrenchments at Eshowe, under the watchful eye of Captain Warren Wynne and his sappers. Colonel Pearson only intended to remain at Eshowe until Lord Chelmsford updated him on the centre column's status and directed him to advance to his next proposed supply depot at St. Paul's. The actual fort at Eshowe was intended to be similar to what Captain Wynne constructed at Fort Tenedos, with a permanent garrison of about 400 soldiers.

The trouble Wynne found was the entire perimeter, if it were to encompass all the buildings at the old mission, was 450 yards; far too large to be effectively manned by 400 soldiers and a pair of cannon. He expressed his further misgivings to Colonel Pearson. "We simply cannot provide any fields of fire into the ravine to the west. And the stream to the north runs through a valley that is one massive blind spot. While I know we can over-watch these with picquets, there is one place where we cannot."

Pearson stared hard at the grove of trees, remembering well the promise he made to the Norwegian missionary, Ommund Oftebro. "I told the reverend we would be good stewards to his mission," he said, a trace of regret in his voice. "He especially loves his fruit trees, and I can see why."

"They do add much beauty to this place, sir," Wynne concurred. "Believe me, I do not make this recommendation lightly. But given the high ground surrounding this place and the dead ground to the north and west, I feel we have little choice. An entire Zulu regiment could march through that grove in the middle of the day undetected, let alone at night."

The colonel gave a sad nod of resignation. "If possible, save what trees you can that are closest to the buildings. But do what you think is necessary, Captain Wynne. You have my full support."

"Yes, sir. A pity this war compels us to turn a place of such beauty into desolation."

Without sufficient trees or stones to construct walls and palisades, the column's only option was to dig into the earth. Like the Roman legions of antiquity, they dug great trenches around the camp, using the earth to build up the ramparts. Engineers then used their tools to sculpt the piles of dirt into viable firing platforms for both infantry and artillery. While work began in earnest on the southern rampart, large details were dispatched to cut down trees and clear away the thick stands of brush and undergrowth along the western ravine.

It was the destruction of the fruit grove that saddened the soldiers of No. 1 Column the most. Not only did it provide an idyllic setting, but the idea of adding fresh fruit to their otherwise bland diet had been a substantial morale boost for the men in the ranks.

"Enjoy it while we can," Lance Sergeant Robert Anderson said, as he and his section went through the grove, plucking as many bananas, apples, and oranges as they could stuff into their packs. He then picked up and peeled a fresh orange, taking a deep bite as the juice sprayed out the corners of his mouth. "At least I know I won't catch scurvy for at least another week or so!"

On the evening of the 24th, with felling axes still echoing, Lieutenant Martin summoned his section leaders to his command tent. In addition to Colour Sergeant Bennet, they were joined by one of the battalion staff officers, Lieutenant Julius Backhouse. Backhouse was twenty-four years old, having served four years as a subaltern with A Company before being reassigned as one of Lieutenant Colonel Parnell's aides just prior to the Xhosa War.

"Gentlemen," Lieutenant Martin began. "I know we've had a long journey to reach Eshowe, coupled with a battle, no less. But now that the Zulus have made their presence felt, Colonel Pearson feels our resupply convoys require stronger escorts."

"And we drew the lucky lot," Colour Sergeant Bennet finished.

The officer commanding gave an affirmative nod. "It will be us and B Company, along with two companies from the 99th, two from the NNC, and ten mounted infantry soldiers to act as vedettes."

"Who's leading the convoy, sir?" Sergeant Stirling asked.

"Lieutenant Colonel Coates of the 99th."

At their commander's answer, the sergeants of H Company thought they saw Lieutenant Backhouse's face twitch.

"Most of you know Mister Backhouse," Lieutenant Martin continued. "He has been reassigned to us. Mister Backhouse, welcome to H Company."

"Thank you, sir, it is good to be with you," the younger officer replied.

"We have forty-eight empty wagons to take back to Lower Drift," Martin continued. "Speed is key to this phase of our mission, and so we will be leaving our tents and ammunition wagons here. We'll bring an emergency stock of eight boxes of cartridges, should we run into a spot of trouble. As our column's primary purpose is establishing supply depots for the rest of the invasion force, we can count on a lot of these types of missions. And as we saw two days ago, the Zulus are more than keen to put up a fight. Have your men rest up tonight and be ready for an early start tomorrow."

"Sir," all the NCOs said, as they collectively came to attention.

When he returned to brief his section, Sergeant David Fredericks was greeted with some of the expected groans from a couple of soldiers. Threats of additional guard duty quickly quelled any further grumblings.

"What of Corble?" Private Peters asked. "Is he coming with us?"

David shook his head. "Private Corble has yet to fully regain consciousness. Colonel Parnell offered to take him on as an orderly, once he sufficiently recovers."

Between William Dunne's death, Corble's terrible wounding, and Rob Anderson's reassignment, Sergeant David Fredericks' already understrength section was down to fourteen soldiers, including him and Lance Corporal Monroe. H Company's total strength at the moment was sixty-two men, to include both officers and other ranks, against an authorised strength of a hundred.

"Well, at least we have more room to stretch out at night," James Monroe said, with his perpetual good-natured grin.

A section of the entrenchments around Eshowe

Hopes of a sound night's sleep were quickly dashed. Around 8.30, a picquet from the 99th sounded the alarm as a pair of shots were fired into the darkness. Soldiers spilled forth from their tents in various stages of undress. The sun had set an hour-and-a-half earlier. With only a sliver of moon in the cloudy sky, men tripped over tent ropes and bumped into each other. Curses and profane insults added to the confusion.

David Fredericks found his section's place on the line behind one of the empty wagons. He then grabbed Private Walters by the shoulder, and shoved him towards his position, while similarly guiding the rest of his section to their places.

The last to come out of their tent was James Monroe, who was making certain no one lingered. "All accounted for," the lance corporal said, his eyes tired, struggling to remain alert. He was nearly naked, except for his underpants, ammunition pouch, and boots, which he'd thrown haphazardly onto his feet without bothering to lace up.

David gave an affirmative nod before telling his second to take his place on the line. He quickly found Colour Sergeant Bennet and informed him his section was set before returning to his position. In the encompassing darkness, it was difficult to determine which section of soldiers was his. At one point he nearly ran into John Stirling, who was pacing the line behind his men.

"Dash it all, old boy," Stirling said, once over his surprise. "If you want to get that close to me again, you'll have to buy me supper first!"

"With the way you smell, you're not even worth a stale biscuit and tin of rancid beef." David laughed nervously.

"And I'm sure you smell like a fucking lavender bush!" his friend retorted.

Such crude banter was commonplace amongst soldiers in the ranks, particularly during moments of great strain. Every man knew a substantial number of Zulus had fallen during their last battle, but the majority had escaped to fight another day. With so many blind spots surrounding Eshowe and their defences yet to be completed, it came as no surprise to anyone that the enemy would attempt to exploit their weaknesses.

David slowly walked the line behind his men, keeping a watchful eye on them, as well as what might be approaching the camp. As H Company occupied part of the western ramparts, the hateful ravine was just a few dozen yards from their position. The sergeant felt the same frustration as his soldiers. He squinted his eyes and tried to see something, anything at all, in the suffocating darkness.

"Bastards could walk up and stick me right in the neck, and I'd never know it," Private John Harris muttered under his breath.

"Let your ears tell you what your eyes cannot," David whispered. He strained to listen for any sounds of Zulus crashing through the thickets that still covered the ravine, the pounding of his heart seemed to echo in his ears. After about twenty minutes, the feelings of nervous anxiety turned to boredom.

192

"Don't tell me those jittery twats were firing away at shadows again," a private bickered. The man's assumptions would eventually prove correct, and word soon passed that it was yet another false alarm.

"Clear your weapons, lads," Sergeant Fredericks ordered.

He and Monroe personally checked the chamber on each soldier's rifle before sending them back to their beds.

"So much for the Zulus wanting to dance with us again," James remarked with a loud yawn.

"We may deal with a thousand false alarms during this campaign," David speculated. "But God help us if we become complacent on the night the Zulus decide to attack."

Chapter XV: Return to Lower Drift

Eshowe
25 January 1879

A Wet Night at Lower Drift, from *The London Gazette*

Perhaps the only good news from the previous night was they were spared from another night of soaking rain. Just after reveille, most of the camp made ready to begin another day of backbreaking labour building up the Eshowe fort. Meanwhile, the first convoy of forty-eight empty wagons was readied for the return to Lower Drift to bring more supplies. Officers commanding from The Buffs, 99th, and NNC companies met with Lieutenant Colonel Coates. He directed them to their places.

Though the convoy was substantially shorter than the gargantuan divisions Colonel Pearson had been obliged to divide his column into during the initial march, the entire train stretched for well over half-a-mile. B and H Companies from The Buffs led the convoy, marching in columns of four on either side of the road with skirmishers thrown out on the wings. The NNC companies took the centre. The 99th provided the rear guard. The section of mounted infantry vedettes were ordered to keep close to the wagons, riding ahead as needed to scout terrain where a Zulu ambush could be waiting.

Twenty minutes before their scheduled departure, Private Peter Davies sought out his section leader. "Beg your pardon, sergeant, but if it's alright with you, I'd like to go say goodbye to Bill."

David smiled sadly. "See if any of the others wish to join you. Just be back here in five minutes."

"Yes, sergeant...and thank you."

Private William Dunne was buried inside the fort's perimeter. He was not alone. He shared his eternal resting place with Sergeant Oscar Hydenburg of the NNC who also died of wounds suffered at Inyezane. David watched as Davies and several of his mates walked over to where the makeshift wooden cross jutted out of the ground. David had spoken the previous day with Colour Sergeant Smith of the engineers. He promised to have a proper headstone erected for their fallen soldiers.

"So long, Eshowe," James Monroe said, glancing over his shoulder. The company formed into their column of march. "Can't say I'll miss the place."

"With all the walking we've done, I just hope my boots last until April," Private Walters said, lifting the heavily scuffed and well-worn sole on his right foot.

At the shouted command of the conductors, the first of the wagons lurched forward. The draught oxen brayed and snorted. The young African lads acting as voorloopers controlled the temperamental beasts with their long whips. The morning passed uneventfully. The sky was grey, and though they'd so far been spared from the rains this day, the air felt hot, heavy, and extremely humid. By the first half-mile, every redcoat in Coates' convoy was soaked in sweat. Even the officers sitting astride their horses were feeling the effects of the stifling heat and humidity.

"At least we're mostly travelling downhill," Lieutenant Backhouse mused. He and Robert Martin rode at the head of their company. Approximately fifty yards to their front were the ten mounted infantrymen.

In addition to the armed escorts, the convoy was accompanied by the column's senior medical officer, Surgeon-Major Thomas Tarrant. The forty-eight-year-old doctor had been practicing medicine for twenty-four years and served in Malta, the Crimea, Turkey, and India, in addition to numerous years on Home Service. Tasked with establishing medical aid stations along the route from Lower Drift to Ulundi, he was returning to retrieve more supplies for the next phase of the column's advance and to provide medical support should the convoy come under attack.

Three hours into their trek, at around 8.30, Lieutenant Colonel Coates ordered the convoy to halt for breakfast. They had travelled roughly seven miles; more than they accomplished most days. Picquets were sent out two hundred yards to protect the flanks, while everyone else sat down to a hasty breakfast of cold coffee and tinned beef. Lance Sergeant Rob Anderson still had several oranges from the fallen fruit trees in his pack. He shared these amongst his section before taking the last one over to his former section leader, David Fredericks.

"Thought you could use something a bit less bland with your breakfast." The lance sergeant smiled.

"Thank you," David said appreciatively. He sat with his back against a wagon wheel and removed his helmet.

Rob knelt next to him and rested his rifle against the wagon.

The sergeant ripped away the orange peel and pulled off a wedge. He closed his eyes for a moment, as he took a bite. After weeks on campaign, with little but hard biscuits and tinned beef, something as simple as an orange was like a taste of heaven.

Every man in the convoy was soon glad they had their breakfast when they did. At 9.15 the bugle calls ordered the collective soldiers to make ready to march once more. Picquets were recalled, and as soon as every section leader had accountability of his soldiers, the order to continue the trek was given. A mile further on, a stiff breeze blew up from the south, carrying with it an unholy stench that nearly caused many of the men to vomit.

"Oh, bugger me with a sodding fish fork!" one private blurted out. "What in the bleeding fuck is that smell?"

"Have you forgotten what we went through three days ago?" Sergeant Fredericks asked. The wafting aroma of rotting death assailed his nostrils, and he struggled to maintain his stoic demeanour in front of his soldiers.

About the only man in all of H Company that appeared unfazed was Lance Corporal James Monroe. "A dead enemy always smells sweet." His face broke into a mischievous grin.

"I think this stench is rotting your brain, lance corporal," Private Peters said through the handkerchief he held up to his face.

"It's just something I read once," James explained. "My father loved reading to me about the Romans. I recall during one of their civil wars a general, or maybe even the emperor, made a similar remark. Apparently, he was the only member of his entourage not to become ill when they came upon the bodies of their slaughtered enemies."

"In that case, we should call you 'Emperor' Monroe!" Private Harris called out. He then doubled over in a coughing fit, as he fought to keep his breakfast down.

They rounded a bend, and the scarred battlefield came into view. Corpses littered the slopes of the long ridge, many already bloated and starting to rot. Carrion birds circled the hills. Numerous bodies were partially devoured by wild beasts. It puzzled the redcoats that the Zulu dead remained unburied after three days.

"Why would they abandon their mates this way?" Private Harris asked, his face ashen and countenance aghast.

Sergeant Fredericks could only shake his head, his feelings both of revulsion and pity.

"Sir, it looks like we've got a live one here!" a mounted trooper called back to Lieutenant Martin.

"Go and see about it, Mister Backhouse, if you would be so kind," the officer commanding directed.

Julius nodded and galloped his horse over to the brush stand about ten yards off the road. It overlooked the ravine where they'd pummelled so many enemy warriors with enfilade fire. Two troopers had dismounted and were kneeling next to the badly stricken man. His right arm and right leg were broken and peppered with numerous gashes.

"Poor bastard got hit by cannister shot from the looks of it," one soldier observed.

"He's lucky he wasn't cut in half," his mate replied.

"Lucky?" the first man mused. "I'd say, given he's been left out here these past three days without food or water, he probably wishes he'd been disembowelled by our cannon."

"*Ngicela...amanzi*," the man said, pleading through parched lips.

"What's he saying?" the second trooper asked.

"He's asking for water," Lieutenant Backhouse spoke up. He climbed out of the saddle and knelt next to the warrior. He nodded to one of the troopers. "Give him some from your water bottle."

197

As the Zulu thirstily drank, the soldier asked, "What should we do with him, sir?"

"We'll splint his arm and leg and place him in one of the wagons."

It was with mild surprise that Lieutenant Martin acknowledged the return of his subaltern. He was walking his horse while four troopers carried the badly injured warrior. The man's face was pale. He was in obvious agony, yet he made not a sound.

"High threshold for pain, this lot," one of the soldiers sadly admired.

They lifted the warrior into the back of the nearest wagon.

Lieutenant Backhouse reached into his saddlebags and pulled out some hard biscuits and gave them to the Zulu. As he re-mounted his horse, he saw his officer commander looking at him, his head cocked slightly to one side. "Couldn't just leave him there," Julius asserted with a shrug. "Wouldn't be right."

Martin nodded and both officers continued to ride at a slow trot. They were alerted by a couple of piteous cries from somewhere off to their left, down in the ravine.

"Nothing more we can do here," the officer commanding said.

Backhouse shot him a quizzical look.

"It's not our fault their friends deserted them."

The Inyezane River had fallen substantially over the past three days, making crossing with empty wagons substantially easier for the convoy. What had taken an entire day before was accomplished in just over two hours. The mounted vedettes continued to ride ahead. As the last of the wagons splashed its way through the Inyezane, shouts of *'Hostiles front!'*, followed by a spattering of carbine fire, alerted the column.

"Spread out!" Colour Sergeant Bennet shouted.

Soldiers scattered.

"Sergeant Stirling!" Lieutenant Martin called out. "Cover our front. The rest of the company will protect the flank."

"Sir!" John waved his arm forward, ordering his section to follow him.

A section from the 99th company on their left was following their lead, deploying one section forward, the rest covering the flank.

No sooner had all soldiers in the convoy spread out and dropped to one knee, they heard a voice bellowing, "Cease fire, goddamn it! Those are friendly kaffirs!"

Soldiers groaned.

David Fredericks shook his head. "That's the second time we've nearly shot our own bloody natives."

"Won't be many wishing to die for Queen and Country if they get shot by our own damned bullets," Rob Anderson added. The lance sergeant, who was perhaps the strictest enforcer of fire discipline and attention-to-detail David had ever met, was absolutely furious.

"It's only filthy niggers," a private scoffed.

This brought a sharp backhand slap across the face from the lance sergeant.

"Those 'filthy niggers' are our allies," he snapped. "Forget that again and I'll have you shovelling shit for the remainder of the war."

Rob Anderson was one who rarely raised his voice or used profanity, and his furious retort caught the soldier completely off-guard. The private turned red in embarrassment, quietly stammering, 'Sorry, sergeant' and wishing he could find a hole to crawl into. It wasn't that he regretted his words, exactly. However, firing on allied troops was as unforgiveable as it was reckless, especially to an NCO like Lance Sergeant Robert Anderson.

Remarkably, the small group of African men, numbering four total, seemed none too concerned about what could have been a catastrophic mishap. One was a messenger from Lower Drift, carrying a despatch for Colonel Pearson.

The message was from Royal Navy Senior Lieutenant Anthony Kingscote of HMS Tenedos. As the senior officer remaining at Lower Drift, he was left in command of the crossing and its pair of forts.

Fort Tenedos came under attack on evening of 23 January. Zulus were quickly driven off by a pair of cannon shot and salvo of musketry. No bodies were found the next morning, though there were a few drag marks in the grass. Will increase our patrols and maintain a robust sentry watch.

A. Kingscote, Lt, RN
HMS Tenedos.

199

Lieutenant Colonel Coates quickly read the despatch before sending the men on their way. It was 5.00 in the evening when the convoy halted for the night. Because their wagons were empty and less prone to getting stuck in the mud, they had managed seventeen miles; nearly twice what they achieved on their best days during the initial trek to Eshowe. They now encamped on the same patch of ground the entire column had occupied on the evening prior to the Battle of Inyezane.

"If all goes well, and provided the weather cooperates, we might very well reach Fort Tenedos by tomorrow evening," Coates informed the convoy officers that night.

"What of the attack on the fort?" a captain from the 99th asked.

"Probably just some locals causing mischief," the colonel said dismissively. "I doubt it's the same army that attacked us, unless the Zulus decided to run thirty miles south after the thrashing we gave them."

"Could have also been jittery sentries popping off at nothing," Lieutenant Backhouse muttered.

Though he did not reply out loud, Robert Martin gave a nearly imperceptible nod of concurrence. Anxiety and nerves could get the best of sentries even under ideal conditions. Very little was known about the Zulus, and what intelligence there was to be had was critically lacking in detail. As far as any of the officers could recall, the only piece of valuable information regarding the enemy *impi* in the region reached them after the column had already defeated them in battle.

The camp was less than a quarter of the size of what last occupied the flat plateau on the 21st. This made laagering the wagons much easier, albeit still a confused and labour-intensive process. Hasty earthworks were dug around the camp with the draught animals corralled in the centre of the laager. Sentry shifts were established. Sergeant David Fredericks was assigned as sergeant-of-the-guard for the first two-hours after sunset. He established himself in the back of an empty wagon, lighting a small oil lamp so he could be readily found.

He placed the lamp on the driver's bench and decided to take a few minutes to write a letter to his wife; the first since they had crossed the Thukela River. Though he expected H Company to remain at Lower Drift for only a couple of days, he could leave his letter with one of the orderlies at the forts.

Lillian Fredericks and the other families from 2/3rd Buffs resided in the port city of East London, nearly 500 miles from the Thukela crossing. Being so far removed from the war, especially when compared to the families of the 24th Regiment in and around Fort Napier and Pietermaritzburg, David wondered what sort of news had reached his beloved. Did Lillian even know that her husband's regiment had fought a battle recently? No doubt she was concerned for his safety, just like every other wife, child, or parent whose loved ones were part of Lord Chelmsford's invasion force. And what of the families back home in England? David had not spoken to his brother or sister since he joined the Army. He now regretted not taking the time to reconnect with them prior to his departure for Southern Africa more than two years prior. Though he swore he would never return to Whitstable, David decided whenever the battalion returned to Home Service in Britain, he would take some leave and seek out his brother and sister, as well as his father, provided any of them were still alive.

The chaotic plethora of thoughts filled his mind. He squinted in the pale lamplight, writing everything he could think to tell Lillian about his latest 'adventure' with The Buffs. He then checked his watch. It was five minutes to 8.00. He set down his quill and parchment and rubbed his eyes. It was nearly time to make his rounds and check all the guard posts. The sergeant donned his helmet and picked up his rifle. As he climbed out of the back of the covered wagon, there was a bright flash of lightning followed two seconds later by a crash of thunder. David let out a sigh of resignation, even before the first drops of rain splashed off his helmet.

"I knew our reprieve was too good to last," he said under his breath, as he pulled his greatcoat from his pack. He had barely enough time to run his arms through the sleeves before the heavens opened with a punishing deluge.

The rains fell upon British and Zulu alike with the same punishing force. At his camp along the river north of Eshowe, Phalane sat by his small campfire, partially protected by a high brush lean-to. A messenger arrived that evening, bearing more detailed accounts of the terrible slaughter that took place at Isandlwana. It was the great victory the king had hoped for; over a thousand red-jacketed white soldiers and their Natal allies were slain. But, it had come at a terrible price. Given the destructive power of the British rifles, the royal *induna* could only guess just how many from the main *impi* had departed this life and joined their ancestors.

It was with little surprise when Phalane learned that Godide had been stripped of his command by King Cetshwayo and sent home in disgrace. The king had concurred with the *izinduna* within the uMxhapho Regiment. The older warriors had held back and acted shamefully, abandoning the 'Left Horn' to its ignominious fate. The *induna* felt no satisfaction in this knowledge, only shame and sorrow. His conscience was deeply troubled by his own failures during the battle and the subsequent disgraceful public berating of his *inkosi*. He would soon learn he was not the only senior leader within the *amabutho* needing to seek redemption.

The following morning, with a thick mist clinging in the air, Phalane emerged from his makeshift hut and stretched his arms overhead. Thus far, the only elements of the British army to leave Eshowe was a large convoy of empty wagons heading south. He rightly assumed they were returning for more supplies. This reinforced the great weakness that plagued the invaders; their total reliance on ponderous ox-wagons. While he certainly longed for the chance to catch the redcoats out in the open and launch a proper ambush against them, Phalane also saw opportunity, so long as the British remained at Eshowe.

He and his warriors began to prepare their breakfast, when a lookout shouted that a rider and small band of warriors was approaching from the north.

Though he expected this to be another message from the king, possibly some reinforcements to help him deal with the redcoats slinking about Eshowe, he was taken aback when he saw the rider. "Prince Dabulamanzi." He bowed.

The king's brother nodded. He sat astride his horse, his percussion musket draped across his lap. "The English have been whipped and driven back across the uMzinyathi, yet they continue to desecrate our coastal lands." He then stressed, "*My* lands."

"They are currently contained in the abandoned mission at Eshowe," Phalane explained. "Will you and your warriors join me for breakfast?"

The prince dismounted his horse. "Yes, thank you."

Dabulamanzi's countenance was grim and not what the *induna* expected from one who'd fought with the *impi* that destroyed Lord Chelmsford's forces at Isandlwana.

Dabulamanzi was a few years older than Phalane, and the two were only moderately acquainted. Still, the prince knew of Phalane's reputation as an *induna*. Given all that transpired over the past few days, he knew this man was his best chance at gaining a friend and ally. "You may have heard there were two battles fought against the treacherous *inkosi*, Chelmsford."

Phalane's mat carrier stoked their camp fire, while finishing cooking his master's breakfast.

"Only rumours," the *induna* stated. He offered a gourd of beer to the prince.

Dabulamanzi took a long drink before continuing. "Let us just say, you are not the only one who was betrayed by the old warriors. I know Godide and the cowardly women abandoned you and the uMxhapho at Wombane. He has rightly been punished by my brother, our divine king. And while the *amabutho* won a great victory at Isandlwana, Ntshingwayo and the *amakhosi* abandoned me and the Undi Corps, leaving us to attack the enemy stronghold at kwaJimu alone."

Dabulamanzi failed to mention that, by attacking kwaJimu—known to the British as Rorke's Drift—he had disobeyed his brother's expressed orders about crossing into Natal. If Phalane knew about King Cetshwayo's directive, that their forces were to remain on the Zulu side of the uMzinyathi, he made no mention of it. KwaJimu was anything but a stronghold. Consisting of little more than a pair of buildings 500 yards from the river crossing, it had been converted into a makeshift fortress by the small garrison of resourceful redcoats, utilising mealie sacks and biscuit boxes.

Dabulamanzi's mentions of 'betrayal' confirmed what Phalane suspected. The attack on kwaJimu had failed. This, coupled with the

203

southern *impi's* defeat at Inyezane, had most certainly dampened King Cetshwayo's elation regarding their victory at Isandlwana.

Phalane decided to remain silent, taking a more diplomatic approach to his dealings with the prince. The two men needed each other as the war against the British entered its next phase.

Prince Dabulamanzi kaMpande with a pair of attendants

The night out in the rain was utterly miserable for Lieutenant Colonel Coates' convoy. Soldiers spent the night huddled beneath the wagons. A fortunate few were able to climb in the backs, where the battered canvas tarps offered at least some protection from the elements.

A thoroughly soaked four companies of redcoats and two companies of NNC warriors paraded before their officers the following morning. The choking pre-dawn mist threatened to smother them.

Prior to inspecting his section, Sergeant David Fredericks pulled James Monroe off to one side, that they might check each other's kit for any deficiencies.

"Can't very well discipline one of our men for a shoddy weapon if my own is pitted with rust or other defects," David said. He

204

opened the breach of his Martini-Henry and handed it to the lance corporal.

Monroe, who understood firearms better than any man in H Company, quickly but meticulously ran his fingers over the rifle, checking the breach, cocking lever, front and rear sights, as well as making certain the barrel was secured in place.

"No signs of rust or black powder residue," he said. He then pointed to the left side of the rifle near the breach. "You've got a loose rivet here. Shouldn't cause you any grief unless another one gives way. We can fix it easily enough once we reach camp."

David nodded and thanked his second-in-command. The rivet James mentioned was only barely loose, to the point that most would fail to even notice. This made the sergeant even more glad to have the knowledgeable lance corporal as his assistant.

"You're looking surprisingly refreshed," David observed. "I take it you've been sleeping better?"

James shrugged. "It's the damnedest thing, really. The nightmares ceased right after Inyezane. I've slept like the dead the last few nights. I doubt the dark spirits have left me, just gone dormant is all. So long as there is a war going on, my mind seems to know that it needs sleep if I'm to remain among the living."

"You went into the wrong profession," David remarked. "You should have gone to university to become a doctor specialising in the human mind."

"Sadly, lads like me who grew up in the gutter don't get to go to university," the lance corporal observed. "I was much like you, sergeant. I marked an 'x' on my enlistment papers and only learned how to read after I joined the ranks."

The clinging fog delayed their departure, with the convoy only able to continue its journey around 9.00. This allowed the men time to make themselves a proper breakfast, though the previous night's rains soaked any available timber, meaning they had to take their coffee cold. With the mist finally beginning to dissipate and the promise of a scorching day, the convoy continued its trek. They had only proceeded about a mile when the vedettes called back that there was another column of wagons approaching.

"Ah, that will be Colonel Ely," Coates surmised. He rode forward to meet with his fellow officer from the 99th. After about ten minutes, he rode back to inform his company commanders that the stream had swelled during the night and there was only one viable fording point.

"As they are bringing supplies back to Eshowe, Colonel Ely will have priority," he explained.

The fully loaded wagon's coming up from Lower Drift would require a substantial portion of the day to cross. The officers then understood they would not be reaching Fort Tenedos that evening.

While the convoy waited on the north side of the river, Surgeon-Major Tarrant sought out the commanding officer. "It's our Zulu friend," he explained. "The arm and leg have become infected."

"I understand," Coates replied. He then checked his watch. "I estimate it will be at least another four hours before the last of Colonel Ely's wagons are across the river. Do what you need to, doctor."

None of Tarrant's orderlies had accompanied him. It therefore fell to volunteers from the convoy to assist the surgeon. An English-speaking warrior from the NNC was brought to the wagon to interpret for the doctor. Tarrant explained slowly that the arm and leg had become badly infected, and the only way to save the warrior's life was to amputate both limbs. The Natal African slowly translated, gesturing with his hands what the doctor meant to do.

"Let him know that this will render him unconscious, that he might be spared the pain," Tarrant said, holding up a small vile of chloroform and a rag.

The Zulu warrior shook his head and spoke a few words in his native tongue. "He says, he wishes to keep his wits about him," the translator said.

"Suit yourself," the doctor said. He directed the four soldiers to hold the man down; two on his arms, and two more on his legs.

As he retrieved his scalpel and bone saw from his bag, the Zulu spoke to him again. "What's he saying?"

"He says, 'may his ancestors guide your hands'," the Natal man translated.

Outside the wagon, a soldier was stoking a fire to heat an iron bar used to cauterise amputated limbs once the surgeon finished. Nearby soldiers expected to hear shrieks of pain coming from within the wagon. Without so much as a sniff of chloroform, the Zulu made not a sound.

Company commanders were gathered nearby with Lieutenant Colonel Coates, as they sat down for lunch. Lieutenant Martin grimaced as he watched the soldier at the fire retrieve the red-hot iron bar, his hands wrapped in thick rags. The sound of searing flesh coupled with the nauseating stench wafted forth from beneath the wagon cover. It was only then that they heard cries of pain coming from the Zulu warrior. Surgeon-Major Tarrant soon emerged, wiping a rag across his brow. A private took the amputated limbs downstream and threw them into the river.

"How is he, doctor?" Coates asked.

"Finally succumbed to the pain and fainted," the Surgeon-Major replied. "I reckon he has as much of a chance as any man who's lost an arm and a leg. Though the infection was terrible, it had yet to become fully gangrene. Provided it didn't spread into his bloodstream, he may live."

"What's to become of him?" a captain from the 99th asked.

"Provided he doesn't die on us before we reach the Thukela, we'll hand him over to the Natal authorities," Coates answered. "Though not a threat to anyone, I suspect they'll keep him as a prisoner-of-war until this little dispute is settled."

An hour later, with the sun breaking through the lingering clouds from the previous night, another NNC warrior was spotted running up the road from Lower Drift. The man carried a small leather pouch, which he held over his head as he forded the river. Upon reaching the far side, he was taken over to the convoy commander.

"Message for Colonel Pearson," the warrior said in heavily accented English.

"Let me see it first," Coates demanded. The messenger produced a single folded parchment from his pouch. The colonel's countenance fell as he read the short missive. He then returned the message and ordered the man to make for Eshowe with all haste.

"What did the despatch say, sir?" Lieutenant Martin asked.

"There's been a terrible disaster," Coates replied. "Colonel Durnford is dead."

Chapter XVI: To Fight or Run

Eshowe
26 January 1879

Lieutenant Colonel Anthony Durnford

Work on the fort at Eshowe was scheduled to continue later that morning. As it was Sunday, a full parade of the column was ordered, and Reverend Robertson read a short service. While the pastor led the men in a final prayer, the messenger reached the fort. Pearson's staff officer, Major Porter rushed over and whispered in his ear that there was an urgent despatch waiting for him. The colonel, along with Parnell and Welman, quietly took their leave of the service.

The messenger had run through the night and was covered in sweat, exhausted, and very hungry. He did his best to come to attention as he pulled the single page from his pouch, handing it to Pearson. This was the first despatch Charles had seen giving him some sense of the calamity that struck their brethren in the north. Like Lieutenant Colonel Coates, he was baffled that it came from the High Commissioner, Sir Henry Bartle-Frere. It was dated the 24th of January; its vagueness and brevity causing more confusion and questions than it answered.

Lt Col Durnford killed, his black troops defeated and scattered. Lord Chelmsford has won a victory against the Zulus. Both actions took place on 22 January.

H.B. Frere
High Commissioner, Natal

"The same day as our action at Inyezane," Lieutenant Colonel Parnell noted, after Pearson handed him the despatch.

"Yes, but it does not say where either action took place," the column commander noted. "The last I knew, Durnford was at Middle Drift. If his forces were defeated there, it places the Zulu *impi* between us and No. 3 Column."

"Perhaps, though we both know these damned natives are notoriously unreliable," Parnell reasoned. "They could have simply run off, leaving poor Durnford at the mercy of the Zulus. It could be that his lordship has beaten the main Zulu army."

Charles gave a nod, though he was far from convinced. If Chelmsford had bested the main *impi*, then why such a short and cryptic message from the High Commissioner? Why not a despatch from the GOC himself?

"Your pardon, colonel," Welman spoke up. "But could the damned High Commissioner have been any more ambiguous? He's told us nothing except Colonel Durnford is dead and his column, I assume, destroyed. We don't know where it happened, or for that matter where his lordship, Colonel Glyn, and No. 3 Column are. Or what this 'victory' was and against who." The commanding officer of the 99th Regiment then shook his head in frustration.

There was hope these questions would be answered when another messenger arrived later that afternoon. However, this was quickly dashed. Though the despatch was from Lord Chelmsford, it was dated the 21st, before any of the fighting took place.

Colonel,

I've ordered Durnford's column to Rorke's Drift. No. 3 Column has set up temporary camp at Isandlwana. Will continue towards Ulundi as soon as supplies reach the camp. Continue to keep me informed as to your progress.

Chelmsford

"At least now we know Colonel Durnford was not at Middle Drift," Colonel Walker remarked.

Pearson unfolded his battered map and looked over the scribblings denoting Rorke's Drift and Isandlwana, which was ten miles east of where No. 3 Column had crossed the uMzinyathi.

Charles furrowed his brow in contemplation. "If Durnford was ordered to Rorke's Drift, then it is likely he met his defeat somewhere between there and Isandlwana. But where was No. 3 Column? Were they at Isandlwana, or had they already moved on?"

Ironically, Pearson was technically correct on both counts. Lord Chelmsford had taken half of the column in pursuit of what he thought was the main *impi* on the morning of the 22nd. The remainder were left to guard the camp at Isandlwana. What neither he nor Walker knew was how serious the defeat of Durnford was.

Frere's message was meant to imply Isandlwana, calling it a defeat of Durnford, as he was the senior officer present. Yet none of this was made clear in the message. The victory eluded to was the Battle of Rorke's Drift, but no mention of location was given, nor that Chelmsford was not even present during this action, but twenty-five miles to the east. The battle had in fact been won by a single company of redcoats from 2/24th Regiment, led by Lieutenant John Chard of the Royal Engineers.

Furthermore, no one understood that the very purpose of Frere's message was political rather than strategic. It amounted to little more than a subtle ploy by Frere to protect Chelmsford from recriminations while casting blame for the disaster upon Durnford. For all Colonel Charles Pearson knew, Richard Glyn's No. 3 Column was still completely intact and executing its mission to attack the Zulu Royal Kraal at Ulundi.

A third despatch reached Eshowe that evening, this one from Senior Lieutenant Kingscote, detailing the Zulu 'attack' on Fort Tenedos. There were no casualties to report nor were any dead Zulus found the next day. This report irritated the colonel. It seemed plain to him that the gun crews at Fort Tenedos had gotten jittery during the night and opened fire on nothing more than shadows.

"A waste of good powder and shot," he grumbled, as he tossed the message aside.

He then ordered his secretary to pen a message for the column, informing them of what transpired to the north, as best as he could disseminate. On the morning of the 27th, when all companies formed up for their morning parade, their officers commanding read it to them.

Colonel Glyn's column, accompanied by the General, have had an encounter with a large force of Zulus on the same day as ours victory, and routed them. There is no doubt that two such reverses as the Zulus suffered with this column will tend to discourage the enemy. The news of Colonel Durnford's death is very sad.

Though he detested being vague or misleading, the column commander had nothing else to tell his men. He could only hope their victory at Inyezane and whatever defeat the GOC had inflicted on the Zulus would be enough to drive the enemy into disarray. He hoped his lordship had a more detailed account for him soon, along with whatever orders were needed to conduct the next stage of the invasion.

On the morning of the 27th, the forty-eight-wagon convoy reached Lower Drift. The two companies from The Buffs were ordered across with the wagons and told to remain at Fort Pearson until it was time to return to Eshowe. The NNC and redcoats from the 99th would camp outside of Fort Tenedos on the Zulu side of the river, using the empty wagons as a laager. As soon as H Company reached the Natal side of the river, Lieutenants Martin and Backhouse sought out the garrison commanding officer, while the company lounged in the shade of a tree grove near the pont. Colour Sergeant Bennet, meanwhile, pulled aside his section leaders, wishing to speak with them in private. The company's senior NCO removed his helmet and scratched his fingers through his thick, sweat-soaked hair.

"I don't need to tell you that the course of this war has changed drastically. That much is obvious. We don't know is exactly what has transpired or how it will affect us. The lads will doubtless be consumed with rumours and hearsay. That's unavoidable. But I need each of you to stress what exactly we know, and that is all. We don't fight a war based on rumour. Quash any outlandish stories that may pervade the ranks until we receive more thorough official despatches. I will, however, make one prediction that I want kept just between us; I don't think we'll be returning to Eshowe anytime soon."

With their tents left at Eshowe, the men of H Company were compelled to improvise some form of shelter. Sergeant Stirling recommended taking a detail back across the Thukela to acquire tarps from empty wagons to make lean-tos. Six men could sleep under each of these and it would offer some protection from all except the most torrential of downpours. They were in the middle of the South African rainy season; every soldier resigned himself to having to sleep in his greatcoat each night.

"A pity about Colonel Durnford," Private Peter Davies said, after Colour Sergeant Bennet dismissed H Company to their breakfast.

"What the bleeding fuck do you care if some officer snuffs it?" one of his mates chastised.

"I met Durnford once," Davies explained. "Wasn't intentional, of course. He came upon me when I was on sentry duty, and we actually spoke for a few minutes. He was very kind; not the sort of officer who looked down on us poor rankers as being beneath him."

The other private snorted as they ate a hasty breakfast of tinned beef and biscuits.

Meanwhile, nearly half the company accompanied Sergeant Stirling back across the river. It was only when they returned with a dozen tarps that he mentioned anything to Lieutenant Martin and Colour Sergeant Bennet.

"Best we took these before anyone noticed," the sergeant explained. "Or worse, before those twats from the 99th came up with the same idea."

At Eshowe, a sense of urgency gripped the remaining garrison. They increased their labours to make the fort impenetrable. The remaining six companies from The Buffs were tasked with taking what lumber was available and building a stockade along the southeast corner of the camp, between two large gum trees. At 17 feet high, this would allow two tiers of riflemen who could pour an enfilade of savage musketry into any enemy forces coming from the southeast. This also made it the most defensible position at Eshowe.

Sometime around midmorning, a loud explosion shook the compound. Though they had been briefed at parade that the engineers would be conducting demolitions, it still rattled the column. Many soldiers ran for their weapons.

"Damn it all, it's just Captain Wynne's lads having a bit of fun!" a corporal chastised his men. Several of them had fallen from the stockade onto their stomachs and were now feeling a bit foolish.

The source of the explosion came from Colonel Pearson's order that the two furthest outlying houses destroyed, lest the Zulus use them to establish positions for their marksmen. Knowing it would be a long and tedious ordeal to level the structures with pickaxes, Captain Wynne received permission to allow his sappers a bit of practice with explosives.

As the garrison settled in for the possibility of a siege, rumours of the disaster reached the Southern Column. Though the Zulus had thus far kept their distance from the stronghold, the shouts and ovations of their runners echoed from the surrounding hilltops. None of the white soldiers understood their meaning. The NNC warriors, on the other hand, were much troubled by what they heard.

"What the devil is the matter with them?" Captain Wynne asked in exasperation, as he oversaw a labour detail to fortify the defences.

"It bodes ill, whatever it is," Colour Sergeant Smith replied, his face as impassive as ever.

Another despatch from the GOC arrived that evening. Though he had intended to clarify the situation, his message was once again vague and cryptic. Likely he did not know about the despatch from Bartle-Frere, and he had furthermore assumed that Colonel Pearson already knew about the horrific defeat at Isandlwana. In reality, Pearson was not aware of this, nor that Richard Glyn's column was completely shattered.

Colonel,

Consider all my instructions as cancelled and act in whatever manner you think most desirable in the interests of the column under your command. Should you consider the garrison of Eshowe too far advanced to be fed with safety, you can withdraw it.

Hold however, if possible, the post on the Zulu side of the Lower Thukela. You must be prepared to have the whole Zulu force down upon you. Do away with tents, and let the men take shelter under the wagons, which will then be in position of defence, and hold so many more supplies.

Chelmsford

The message was somewhat alarming, and Pearson could detect a sense of panic in the GOC's words. His grand scheme of invasion, which had taken months of meticulous planning to put together, was now being abandoned. And while he and Colonel Wood had been spared from being micromanaged like Richard Glyn, Chelmsford had dictated every major course of action they were to take during the initial phases of the invasion. Now, his lordship seemed at a complete loss and was leaving it to his column commanders to determine how to proceed.

The commanding officer of No. 1 Column was left with feelings of indecisiveness. Though he would not publicly admit it, he did not know what he should do. He decided to hold a council of war. While not unheard of, this was extremely rare. However, as feelings of foreboding overcame Charles Pearson, he needed the experience and candour of his senior officers, lest his column fall victim to whatever disaster had befallen poor Anthony Durnford.

All staff officers and battalion commanders met at the column commander's tent that night. The message from Chelmsford was passed around with a few moments given for the assembled leaders to digest the contents.

"I thought Durnford had moved up to Rorke's Drift?" Colonel Walker asked.

"Apparently not," another staff officer remarked. "Can we assume that Durnford was defeated at Middle Drift, and that the Zulus have invaded Natal?"

"If that's the case, then Colonel Glyn's column has likely been withdrawn to check them," Pearson concurred. "The question now is, what do we do? Our northern flank is exposed, and we cannot count on support from either the No. 2 or No. 3 Columns."

"We should dig in here and draw the Zulus into a fight," Lieutenant Colonel Wellman of the 99th said with enthusiasm. "My lads are eager for a brawl, and if the Zulus want to attack our stronghold, I say let them."

Lieutenant Colonel Parnell of The Buffs, who was a far more experienced veteran, expressed his doubts. "The Zulus don't have to attack us here. We know Cetshwayo has nearly 40,000 warriors. If even half of those are sent this way, they can simply invest the mission station and wait for us to starve." He then spoke directly to Pearson, "Colonel, I recommend we withdraw to Lower Drift. Fort Tenedos is a much stronger position, plus we can get resupplies via the ponts. If we stay here, we accept far too great a risk with little to gain strategically."

"I cannot believe you are suggesting we abandon all we've strived for without so much as a fight," Wellman countered indignantly. He then addressed a concern that even Parnell had to concede. "His lordship's message states the battles happened on the 22nd. It is now the 29th. If indeed Cetshwayo can launch his entire army against us, they could be here, well…now. And even if all the road repairs are still holding—which we know there is no guarantee of that—it will take several days for us to reach the Thukela. That's several days strung out in a long column of march, just begging the Zulus to ambush us."

Parnell then countered, "With respect, Colonel Welman, we saw what my lads from The Buffs were able to do in the face of a Zulu ambush."

"While there is no doubt your men performed admirably at Inyezane," Colonel Walker quickly said, before Welman could offer a retort, "we were facing a force that was evenly matched with ours. I doubt we would handle them so soundly should their numbers be magnified tenfold."

"All the same, Lower Drift would be a much stronger point of defence," Colonel Pearson finally said. "If we remain here, there is no guarantee of any resupplies reaching us."

Just as he was about to order the column to pack it in and make ready to retreat, Captain Warren Wynne joined the meeting.

"Your pardon, sir," he said, removing his patrol cap. "I was inspecting the southern ramparts when I received your summons."

"Before you make your decision, colonel," Walker spoke up. "I think we should hear what our engineer officer thinks of Eshowe's defences."

Pearson gave a nod of consent. The captain then read over Lord Chelmsford's despatch.

"You were previously of the estimation that this station was in a poor state should the Zulus attack," Pearson stated. "Opinion is divided as to whether we should retreat to Lower Drift or make our stand here. As our chief engineer, I think you are in a unique position to give us a viable perspective, captain."

Warren paused for a few moments, reading over the message. However, he made no hesitation in giving his recommendation. "We risk being caught out in the open and chopped to pieces if we try to retreat, sir." His words brought a grin from Lieutenant Colonel Welman and a scowl from Parnell. He took it a step further by stating what had been on his mind ever since Inyezane. "And if I may add, colonel, while we routed the Zulus during our last encounter, we were lucky. From where I stood, it was plain that the enemy commanders made a grave tactical error, running right into Colonel Parnell's riflemen. Had they not done so, they could have easily gotten behind the lead division and…well, I would not be here to discuss this matter with you. My instincts tell me that they will not make the same mistake twice."

216

"Luck is simply a matter of preparation meeting opportunity, captain," Parnell rebuked. "You are an engineer officer not an infantryman. I trust you will remember your place."

"Your pardon, sir," Warren replied. "I was merely making observations from my position during the battle."

"Enough," Colonel Pearson interrupted. "What of the defences here, captain?"

"I confess, I found the location less than ideal," Wynne said bluntly. "However, we've made great strides in improving the ramparts, as well as observation posts. The fort is not ideal, sir, but it is tolerable. I also fear what will happen to the morale of our men, should we abandon this position and hand it over to the Zulus. Of course, if we stay, there will be the issue of rations and ammunition resupplies."

Pearson looked to the column's assistant quartermaster general, Captain MacGregor, who had thus far remained silent.

"I agree with Captain Wynne," the logistics officer stated, in answer to the unasked question. "For the foreseeable future, it would be safest if we remain here and strengthen our defences. I think that the issue of rations will be answered once Colonel Ely's convoy arrives."

"Thank you, gentlemen, that will be all for now," Colonel Pearson said. The men all stood and came to attention as they were dismissed. Pearson, who initially considered retreating to the Thukela, was now having second thoughts.

The following morning, a message reached Eshowe from Ely's column informing Pearson they were about half-a-day's journey away. Bearing food, medicine, and other much-needed supplies, their arrival gave Charles Pearson the confidence he needed to dig in and prepare to defend against the coming Zulu onslaught. However, even these added stores would not be sufficient for a drawn-out siege, nor was there room for all troops and animals within the confines of the stronghold, originally only intended to hold 400 troops. He ordered Percy Barrow, who led the column's mounted troops, sent to him.

"Colonel, sir," the cavalry officer said, coming to attention, his helmet tucked under his left arm. "We've just returned from patrolling a stream about six miles to the north of here. We spotted a band of about forty Zulus, though they seemed content to simply skulk about the woods on the far side."

Pearson seemed to not hear him, instead handing him the despatch from Lord Chelmsford.

"Damn it all," Barrow said, his face turning pale. He then added reassuringly, "If the Zulus do intend to attack, they are not here yet. We saw only the occasional roving band, usually no more than a couple dozen. I think they are waiting to see what we do next."

"As I understand, it is the time of their harvest," Pearson noted. "However, with Colonel Durnford's command wiped out and no word regarding Colonel Glyn and No. 3 Column, we must prepare ourselves for the worst. If we withdraw the camp to behind the redoubts, then we will need to downsize the garrison. Therefore, I need you to take your mounted troops and make ready to ride for Lower Drift. The NNC will act as your escorts."

The captain nodded in understanding. It was now mid-afternoon, and his staff officers passed the word down for all troopers to make ready to ride at once. So great was their desire for haste that they left most of their personal belongings in their tents. The NNC, who were oblivious to what was transpiring, yet had heard the shouts of triumph from Zulu messengers calling from the hilltops, were too glad to be leaving Eshowe.

Colonel Pearson gave Barrow a short message to be sent directly to the GOC. In it he stated why he decided to hold at Eshowe, and that he hoped he was making the right decision. He also stressed, *'We are still in the dark as to what happened.'*

The colonel hoped by spelling it out so bluntly, Chelmsford would give him a more detailed account of what had transpired with Anthony Durnford and Richard Glyn's columns.

Though there was little time to prepare for departure, Barrow's staff officer, a lieutenant from the 20th Hussars, offered to take any letters from the garrison to be sent home. There were a few hastily scribbled notes to loved ones, namely stating that they had fought a battle against the Zulus but were alive and in good spirits. Captain Warren Wynne, who'd been writing a string of letters to his beloved Lucy, was especially grateful to have these taken by the young officer.

It was 2.15 p.m. when the mounted troops rode away from the stronghold, and Captain Barrow was determined to reach the Thukela by nightfall. He ordered his troopers to deploy a screen line to their front. The NNC would form vedettes on the flanks, while others would drive the hundred head of draught oxen that Pearson had sent to assist Ely's convoy. It had not been an easy decision for Colonel Pearson to make. He would now have only a handful of mounted troops at Eshowe.

About six miles from the mission station, Barrow's vanguard came upon Lieutenant Colonel Ely's convoy.

The captain quickly rode over and saluted. "Sir, it is good to see you've made it this far unmolested by the enemy." His voice was etched with a touch of nerves.

"Thank you, captain," Ely replied, returning the salute. "The only Zulus we've seen are those dead fellows near the Inyezane crossing. You can smell them from miles away."

"I'm afraid there are a lot more heading this way," Barrow explained. He briefed Ely on the despatch from Lord Chelmsford, and said he needed to make his way to Eshowe with all possible speed. "I've brought fifty pairs of oxen to assist you, sir."

"Much obliged," Ely replied. If he was shaken at all by the distressing reports from the GOC, he was doing his best not to show it.

Wagon drivers shouted to their voorloopers, who quickly took the pairs of oxen and yoked them to the already lengthy spans hauling each wagon. The two officers then wished each other all speed, and Barrow's troopers continued to ride away at a modest canter. Though many wished to sprint their horses all the way to the Thukela, they had roughly thirty miles to trek. "We need our horses fresh, should we run into the Zulus," the captain explained.

With the departure of the escorts for Lieutenant Colonel Coates' convoy, plus that of Captain Barrow's mounted contingent, the garrison remaining at Eshowe shrank from over 4,700 troops to roughly 1,500. While the departure of so many would lessen the strain on their supplies, the fort at Eshowe would still be extremely cramped, as the remaining garrison was nearly four times what was intended.

Throughout the camp there was much chaos. Orders and reports became exaggerated with soldiers adding their own thoughts to the disseminated despatches. Many were of the mind that the Zulu *impi* was headed straight for them and would arrive at any minute. And so, haste was made to strike the tents, shove all personal belongings into their packs, and hurriedly take up positions behind the defences. As the ramparts were not complete, bands of infantrymen and sappers picked up the shovel and pickaxe, intent on at least completing the outer trench before nightfall.

Colonel Pearson ordered all wagons brought within the compound and placed in a line, ten yards behind each of the earthen ramparts. In the event of the entire fort being surrounded, this would offer some protection to the defenders against being shot from behind. So great was the urgency and desire for self-preservation, even the officers took up shovels and toiled beside the enlisted ranks.

By nightfall, with Lieutenant Colonel Ely's much welcomed resupply convoy being guided into the fort, the men of No. 1 Column settled in for a long night. With unseen hosts of Zulus now lurking in the dark, the Siege of Eshowe had begun.

Chapter XVII: Stronghold under Siege

Fort Tenedos, Lower Drift
27 January 1879

Officers from 3rd Regiment of Foot (The Buffs), circa 1870
Seated (L to R): Lieutenant Upton, Colonel Pearson, Captain Jackson, Surgeon
Walker, Captain Alexander, Captain Hamilton, Major Parnell
Standing (L to R): Lieutenant Addison, Captain Lefroy, Lieutenant Backhouse,
Quartermaster Cleary, Lieutenant Newham-Davis, Lieutenant Gordon, Lieutenant
Martin, Captain Gelston

As night fell and the Thukela River drew ever closer, the men of 2nd
Squadron, Imperial Mounted Infantry, along with the volunteer
horsemen, increased the gallop of their horses. The numerous river
crossings were particularly nerve-wracking, especially after the sun
had set. With very little star or moonlight, the lead riders of the
vanguard nearly fell straight into the water before they could even
see it. There was also the incessant fear of Zulus hiding in the brush,
waiting to spring an ambush. Even Captain Percy Barrow, a usually
calm and level-headed officer, struggled against feelings of
skittishness each time they crossed a body of water or came upon
large brush stands or groves of trees. He quietly reminded himself
that the only Zulus they had seen were those near the Inyezane; the
putrid stench of death even more vile than he could have anticipated.

221

So anxious were the mounted troops to reach Lower Drift that they soon began to outdistance their escorts from the Natal Native Contingent. The NNC warriors took great umbrage at this, losing their bearing and clustering into small bands. While Barrow was concerned that some of the warriors may choose to desert, he knew they first had to reach the Thukela River. A Natal African was no safer in Zululand than the white British soldiers they fought beside.

For the men of H Company, 2/3rd Buffs, there were conflicted feelings of relief at not being among those now trapped at Eshowe, countered by frustration and guilt at being powerless to do anything to help their mates who remained behind. Lieutenant Martin had ordered picquets posted near the pont, ready to assist the garrison across the river at Fort Tenedos, if need be.

"There's no way the Zulus are crossing this," Private Harris muttered. He sat against a tree, his rifle cradled in his lap. "Bastards across the river will get to have all the fun should the Zulus turn up."

"Anxious to sate your bloodlust again?" James Monroe asked. The lance corporal had been placed in charge of an eight-man picquet consisting of soldiers from their section and Lance Sergeant Anderson's.

While Harris had been certain he'd brought down a Zulu at Inyezane, the fact that so many rifles were fired at the enemy skirmishers had subsequently given him doubts. "I just want to take one of their fucking heads off and not have someone else able to claim the kill."

The lance corporal snorted and shook his head. He then took a few minutes to check each one of their soldiers, making certain they had their allotment of ammunition, as well as full bottles of water. With their tents left at Eshowe, their greatcoats would be all that protected them from the elements.

A rustling in the brush behind them alerted Monroe. He quickly turned to see it was Rob Anderson carrying a small oil lamp.

"How are your men managing?" the lance sergeant asked.

"We're fine," James replied, stretching his arms overhead. "I have them in two-hour shifts; two awake, six asleep." He then

222

cocked a grin. "A pity we don't see much of you since you took over your own section."

"Technically, I'm only acting section leader until Sergeant Milne returns to the Regiment," Rob corrected.

"He's a hundred miles away at Rorke's Drift," Monroe recalled. "I doubt we'll be seeing him until the war is over. Still, I cannot help but wonder if he's all caught up in that spot of bother with the Zulu *impi*."

"Unfortunately, we know very little about what's happened, only that No. 2 Column was routed."

"I would think that Rorke's Drift would be as secure as our position here," James conjectured.

"There's no fort there," Rob reminded him. "And the uMzinyathi is not nearly as wide as the Thukela."

"Well, a lot can happen between now and whenever this little brawl is decided," the lance corporal persisted. "Not that I bear any ill intentions towards Sergeant Milne. It's just that I am very close to earning my second stripe and that can't happen if you return to the section."

"If it makes you feel any better, should I return to your section I'll not be keeping my lance sergeant stripe either."

Anderson was chuckling quietly at this. In truth, he cared very little about what insignia he wore on his right shoulder. His concern was performing his duties to the best of his ability while keeping his soldiers alive and in as sound of health as could be expected under the austere conditions. Promotions, medals, and recognition could sort itself out once the fighting was over. "Alright, I need to check Corporal Knight's post." He then pulled out his battered pocket watch; a gift from his wife just prior to their departure from East London. It was now 11.00.

As he picked up his rifle and lamp, a series of alarms were shouted from across the river. "Damn it all," Anderson whispered, hastening to the next guard post. He quickly called over his shoulder, "Look alive, Monroe!"

The lance corporal did not need reminding. He shook each of his sleeping soldiers by the shoulder and told them to 'look alive'. Having checked to make certain that Corporal Knight's sentries were awake and alert, Lance Sergeant Robert Anderson hastened to his officer commanding's tent to wake up Lieutenant Martin.

Given the numerous false alarms that had plagued No. 1 Column since the war began, the commander of H Company ordered his night picquets to only wake him when the alarm was sounded across the river. Only after it was ascertained that there was a viable threat to Fort Tenedos would he order 'stand-to' for the rest of the company.

Rubbing his tired eyes throwing on his boots, the lieutenant followed Anderson down to the pont. They were soon joined by Corporal Knight and Lance Corporal Monroe.

"Do we know what's happening?" Martin asked.

"Just some shouting is all, sir," Monroe answered. "Can't understand a damned word of it."

The officer strained his ear and then heard someone on the far side barking, "It's Captain Barrow of the IMI; hold your fire, damn it all!"

Letting out a sigh of relief, Lieutenant Martin nodded to Anderson. "Looks like Colonel Pearson has sent the Imperial Mounted Infantry back to the drift. Stand your men down, lance sergeant."

Though just a young subaltern during the Siege of Sevastopol during the Crimean War, Charles Pearson could still recall in graphic detail the horrifying effects of a lengthy siege. There were two issues that were of equal or, perhaps, greater significance than their physical defences. The first was logistics. Despite their vast convoys of stores, supplies of rations, ammunition, and other amenities were not unlimited. On the morning of the 29th, two days after dispatching Barrow back to Lower Drift, he met with his second-in-command and the column's senior commissariat officer.

"Colonel Walker," Pearson said. "We need a thorough inventory of all stores. Direct all battalion commanders to inventory their ammunition and ration. Commissary Heygat, I need you to do the same with all recently-arrived supplies from Ely's convoy."

"Very good, sir."

With 1,500 men now occupying the cramped defences at Eshowe, the brunt of his fighting strength were the 600 soldiers from 2nd Battalion of The Buffs and 380 from the 99th Regiment.

Having sent two companies from The Buffs and two more from the 99th to act as escorts for returning supply wagons to Thukela, Pearson was now missing their added firepower.

Though his soldiers demonstrated splendid fire discipline, they had expended large quantities of cannon shot and Martini-Henry cartridges. A sizable portion of the day was spent with company subalterns and colour sergeants overseeing the inventory of ammunition boxes. Since the four companies from Coates' convoy were compelled to leave their wagons behind, this gave the garrison an added supply of approximately 80,000 additional cartridges. Having sorted through all the various reports, Commissary Heygat estimated that each rifle had 340 rounds available to include what each soldier carried on their person. There were thirty-seven 24-pounder rockets and forty-six 9-pounder rockets. The four 7-pounder rifled muzzle-loader (RML) cannon had a combined 200 rounds of shrapnel, 254 common shot, 20 double shell, and 33 case shots. The column's chief artillery officer, Lieutenant Lloyd, mentioned that the NNC left copious quantities of black powder for their personal muskets behind, which he intended to put to good use. Additionally, Midshipman Coker still had 127,000 rounds for his Gatling gun.

Colonel Pearson took solace in knowing that, for the moment at least, he had ample quantities of ammunition. As a precautionary measure, he ordered all commanders to strictly oversee their soldiers' food rations. Confident that he had sufficient firepower to thwart any attack from the Zulus, Pearson knew his greatest potential nemeses would be disease and hunger.

Around noon, as his sections were taking turns at their midday meal, Captain Wynne heard sentries shouting, *'Zulus!'* Soldiers from all over the compound rushed to the ramparts, badly disrupting the earthworks which were still very loose.

The engineer officer snatched his field glasses from his saddlebags and rushed to the north wall where Lieutenant Courtney and several of his NCOs hunkered behind the defences next to a company from the 99th.

"Over there, sir," the subaltern said. Though he did not have his own glasses, his vision was very acute. He could see the large mass of black figures about four miles distant.

Wynne brought up his glasses and tried to get a count of the enemy force. They were moving laterally at a rather leisurely pace. "It's as if they're out for a Sunday stroll," he muttered.

Colonel Pearson rushed to see for himself the perceived threat. Warren just happened to be the first officer he spotted. "Captain Wynne! What do you see?"

"Zulus, sir. A few hundred, perhaps. It's difficult to say for certain."

"Are they moving to attack?" the colonel asked anxiously.

The captain took a moment to scan the enemy formations before answering. "No, sir. It's as if they are oblivious to our presence."

"What the devil are they playing at?" Pearson asked in frustration. He joined the men on the ramparts and searched the horizon with his own field glasses.

"To be honest, sir, I don't think they're playing at anything," Wynne conjectured. "If they were planning to attack, they would not allow themselves to be so casually spotted. It is also doubtful they would launch an assault in the middle of the day."

Pearson gave a short nod of reluctant acceptance and returned to his headquarters. In addition to now being cut off and possibly surrounded by a large force of unseen Zulus, he was doubly frustrated that Chelmsford left him essentially blind to what transpired in the north. He tried to play out every possible scenario that could have occurred, yet his instincts told him the reality was far worse than what his decades of military logic dictated.

No sooner had Warren returned to his camp stool to finish his lunch, he heard someone shouting, *'Fire!'*, by the church. The captain had to stifle a groan, as he saw flames coming from the thatched roof.

"What's happened, sir?" an anxious subaltern from the 99th asked, rushing over to Warren. "Are the Zulus inside the camp?"

Captain Wynne sighed with a touch of embarrassment. "It's just one of my lads, gotten a little too keen while trying to smoke out a bees' nest." He ordered Sergeant Small to form a firefighting detail, hauling buckets of water up onto the roof. The only reason the entire structure was not ablaze was the constant rains left the thatch completely soaked. Only the outer layer was able to fully dry during the hot, sunny days. What could have ended in disaster became little more than a case of embarrassment, not to mention a severe berating, for the careless sapper.

The rest of the day's labours continued without further incident. The Zulus spotted by the sentries disappeared by mid-afternoon, and the fire on the church roof was extinguished later that night. Warren sat behind his small camp table, finishing the letter he'd begun at breakfast to Lucy.

28 January 1879

My own darling wife,

Perhaps at the same time as you receive this you will read in the newspapers some bad news of the expedition into Zululand; at least Colonel Pearson has today received a telegram from the General commanding, which was not explicit, but full of ill forebodings, leaving Colonel Pearson free to retreat at once to the frontier.
It was expected that the whole Zulu force would be down upon our column, and that the other columns (so we must gather) had gone back. At any rate, we must look for no help.

It was at first decided to retreat at once. I was one of the minority to insist on remaining, as I looked upon a retreat of 37 miles as likely to be most disastrous. It has been decided to remain and fight to the last. Our provisions will suffice for some time with care. And though ammunition is rather scarce, I hope it will last, if they only send some force to our relief. My fort is more than half finished, and we are straining every energy to complete it, at any rate roughly, by tonight.

Do not trouble your heart, my darling. Hope the best; and if I am taken, it will be, through God's mercy, into His Paradise of Love. To Him I commend you, my sweet precious wife, and my darling children. Love to all dear ones.

Your fond husband, Warren Wynne

There was a sense of openness in the words to his beloved that Captain Warren Wynne never expressed to anyone else. As far as every man at Eshowe was concerned, the column's chief engineer was calm and placid, regardless of the threat or emerging crisis. Penning a few candid words to his wife, not knowing when or if he could get them to her, was cathartic.

While Captain Wynne penned his letter to Lucy at the column's headquarters located in the storehouse, Colonel Pearson met with Colonel Walker, Commissary Heygat, and the column's transportation officer, Captain Clarke.

"It does not look like we will be leaving Eshowe for some time," the colonel remarked. "Until Lord Chelmsford can inform us as to the greater strategic situation within Zululand, it is prudent that we continue to reinforce our stronghold here." He then looked to his commissariat and transportation officers. "Which brings me to the issue of all the excess beasts of burden we have living within the compound."

"Yes, sir," Captain Clarke acknowledged. "Draught animals require an extreme amount of forage each day, and there simply is not enough within a mile's span of Eshowe to feed 1,200 oxen."

"What's more, we cannot leave them outside the defences each night lest the Zulus wander off with them," Colonel Walker added. "And leaving so many within the fort is already becoming unsanitary. One can scarcely walk a few yards without coming across piles of dung, and it's already starting to attract flies. Disposing of human waste from our own men is difficult enough."

"These damned beasts have been more trouble than they are worth," the colonel muttered. "At first light, we'll send a thousand of them and most of the mules back to Lower Drift."

"Sir, if the Zulus are out there our animals will likely be captured," Captain Clarke noted.

"A risk we will have to accept. We lack the means to graze them properly. And if we slaughter them all, we'll have to bury most of the carcasses or the meat will rot long before it can be consumed. And if the Zulus do capture them...well, we'll just have to take them back once his lordship reinforces us."

The ADC simply nodded, though the colonel thought he heard the man mumble, '*If* he reinforces us.'

It was around midnight when Pearson dismissed the last of his staff officers and sought to get a few hours of sleep. No sooner had he dozed off when there was another great disturbance, though this time not from another false alarm regarding a Zulu attack. Loud animal groans and shouted curses from soldiers on guard duty echoed throughout the camp. Ironically, it was a horde of about ninety draught oxen, kept as emergency slaughter, that had gotten loose and were now trampling over the earthworks.

The colonel emerged bleary-eyed and in his shirtsleeves. He let out a tired sigh when he saw what was transpiring. He turned to one of his ADCs who stumbled out into the blackness in a frenzy. In the darkness well beyond the ramparts, they heard the excited shouts of Zulu scouts.

"Well, sir, that answers whether the Zulus are out there," the ADC observed.

As the morning dawned on the 30th of January, soldiers within the garrison watched with bemusement as African wagon drivers and voorloopers led hundreds of draught oxen and mules out of the fort.

"Well, there goes our chance at fresh meat for supper," Sergeant Small of No. 2 Field Company said, with a mirthless chuckle. He walked over to one of his mates who stood with his arms folded, watching the chaotic scene. The last few days had been mercifully devoid of rain, and the ground had dried considerably. Clouds of dust kicked up as the protesting beasts were driven out of the camp, while Natal Africans shouted at them and drove them on with their long whips.

"Of course, had they stayed, the entire camp would be filled with shit within a week," another sergeant remarked. "Besides, have you ever tried eating ox meat? Bastards are stringy and tough. It's enough to rip one's teeth out."

The two NCOs saw Captain Wynne rushing about, addressing several of the sappers as he pointed to various points along the ramparts that had crumbled during the last couple days. The destruction caused by the rampaging oxen the night before left a sizeable breach in one of the walls.

"That man seems to be everywhere at once," Small observed. "I wonder if he ever sleeps."

"Ah, Sergeant Small, good," the captain said. He hurried over to them. "I've spoken with Colonel Parnell. He's tasked C Company of The Buffs with providing a labour force to repair the breach. I'll help re-stake everything but will need your sappers to oversee the detail."

"Of course, sir," the NCO replied. "You know, captain, I can re-stake the markers. I have all the measurements in my notebook. You know you don't have to be everywhere at once." The engineer sergeant could not help but notice the haggard countenance of their officer commanding.

Warren's eyes were bloodshot, his face pale and clammy. "Thank you, sergeant, but these defences are my responsibility not yours. Get your men ready and go find Captain Jackson from The Buffs. He's already expecting you."

"Yes, sir."

A man who was proud of his robust health and physical constitution, Warren was not about to let a few sleepless nights prevent him from performing his duties. The disruption of the earthworks during the last couple days emphasised their inherent weaknesses. He knew they needed to be improved, lest they fail to protect the column during an actual Zulu attack.

There was also the matter of a kraal for the column's remaining cattle. Though the draught oxen and mules had been released, Colonel Pearson ordered the cattle remain as a source of food. Having sent Sergeant Small on his way, Captain Wynne found two more of his sergeants whom he directed to supervise the improvement of the nearest defence works. Satisfied that his company was gainfully employed at making the necessary improvements to the stronghold, he briskly made his way over to a small ravine.

"Ah, Mister Courtney, I believe this will be the ideal place for the cattle kraal. Do you concur?" he called out.

His leading subaltern was waiting for him. "I do, sir. The low-lying ground will be simple enough to laager our beasts in. There is ample grazing for them. It's also within full view of our sentries. Should the Zulus attempt to rustle any of them away, they'll get a bullet in the face." He then paused for a moment, noting his officer

230

commanding's exhausted expression and bloodshot eyes. "Are you…are you alright, sir?"

"Fine, fine, never better. I swear, between you and Sergeant Small…" Wynne took a deep breath. As he let it out, sweat formed on his brow. "Actually, I could do with a sit-down for a few moments." Without warning, he doubled over and began to vomit uncontrollably.

A corporal standing behind grabbed the captain by the shoulders, preventing him from falling onto his face. Courtney and the NCO helped sit the captain down. Wynne's eyes were glazed over, his mouth agape.

"Easy there, sir," the subaltern said, keeping his voice calm. As the corporal held their commander upright, Courtney removed Warren's helmet and undid the top three buttons of his patrol jacket. He took the captain's water bottle from his belt and helped him take a few sips.

Warren sputtered and coughed, his eyes blinking quickly as his vision returned to him. "Damn it all, that was embarrassing." He looked up into the faces of nearly a dozen of his men, who'd rushed to his aid.

"It's alright, lads," Courtney said to the startled band of sappers. He pointed to two of them. "You men help get the captain to his bed. The rest of you back to work."

"Yes, yes," Wynne concurred with much reluctance. "I suppose it wouldn't hurt if I lie down for an hour or so…"

Henry Parnell witnessed the incident. As Warren was led away by a pair of his sappers, the colonel walked over to Courtney. "Everything alright, lieutenant?"

"The captain's just a bit worn, sir," Courtney replied reassuringly. He then glanced down for a moment under Parnell's hard gaze. "Actually, sir, I don't think he's slept a wink since Inyezane. He's a meticulous perfectionist, and I don't think he'll allow himself a proper rest until the defences can hold off the hordes of Genghis Khan."

"I'll never fault a man for his determined sense of duty," Parnell said slowly. "But, Captain Wynne needs to realise that he is no good to us if he works himself to death. As an engineer officer, he should understand better than any the risks we're already taking with illness and disease in these confined conditions."

There was an unmistakable trace of irritation in his voice. The commanding officer of 2/3rd Buffs was still angry that the engineer officer had overridden what, in his mind, was Colonel Pearson's good sense. If Parnell had had his way, the entire No. 1 Column would already be well on its way back to Lower Drift. From there, they could make a stronger defence devoid of worry about rations and ammunition stores. Lieutenant Courtney knew none of this and assumed the colonel was simply concerned over a fellow officer. This was, in part, true. Henry liked Wynne and respected his skills as an engineer. That said, he also felt that Warren's current state of ill health was his own doing.

"Zulus!"

The cry of a sentry snapped the two officers out of their reverie.

"I wish these bastards would just attack and be done with it," Parnell moaned. He sought out his nearest company commanders.

Lieutenant Courtney made his way out of the ravine and scrambled up the nearest earthworks. This time he brought his field glasses. The enemy force in the distance was much larger, possibly a thousand warriors. Shouted alarms from other places around the large fort told him there were similar bands along the perimeter.

"They're toying with us," the lieutenant surmised.

The Zulus were clearly checking out their defences while maintaining a safe distance. Inyezane had taught them the destructive power of the Martini-Henry Rifle.

Courtney knew the enemy could conduct a throughout reconnaissance of their positions with only a few warriors, who could get within a few hundred yards of the fort without being spotted. That the Zulus were probing them with such large numbers told him they were playing mind games with their foes.

A few designated marksmen were given permission to loose a few rounds at the enemy. The loud crack of sporadic rifle shots echoed to the engineer officer's left. The Zulus were roughly a thousand yards from the fort. It was doubtful any of the shots hit, and if any enemy warriors did fall, Courtney did not see them.

"Save your bullets, lads," the lieutenant said under his breath. "All you're doing is letting them know their provocations are working."

His thoughts were echoed by the berating shouts from Lieutenant Colonel Welman, whose overly-eager soldiers from the 99th had fired the shots.

"The maximum authorised range for our sharp-shooters is 800 yards," he sternly reminded his company commanders who'd allowed the men to engage. "Those bloody kaffirs are well beyond that."

Courtney chuckled under his breath, climbed down from the ramparts, and made his way back to No. 2 Field Company's place on the line. The afternoon would be filled with numerous such alarms, as large bands of enemy warriors made appearances, thereby disrupting the work on the fort's defences and improvements. The Zulus were playing a mental game with their British foes, and they were winning.

Alarms at Eshowe, from *The Penny Illustrated Paper*

Morale in the garrison took another blow later that afternoon when a band of about thirty NNC warriors came running back up the southern road towards the fort. They were talking excitedly, and the soldiers guarding the entrance heard them say *'Zulus'* repeatedly. One of the men who spoke a little English told the guards, "Zulus have taken cattle. Many hundreds were waiting for us."

Though another setback for No. 1 Column, it was hardly surprising. Colonel Pearson speculated that these particular enemy warriors may have been headed for the Inyezane to bury their dead comrades. Pearson met with the senior officers over lunch to discuss this latest setback.

"There can be little doubt that the enemy has us completely invested," Lieutenant Colonel Parnell said disdainfully.

"The question now is how many are there?" Colonel Walker asked.

"We know this is their harvest season," Pearson observed. "With our advance halted, I suspect most of Cetshwayo's warriors have returned home to see about their crops."

"They don't need a large army to keep us penned up while harrying our lines of communication," Walker noted. "I suspect that once their harvest is taken in, probably within the next month, they will reform their armies and come at us in force. We can only hope his lordship is able to reinforce us before then."

Charles Pearson's thoughts turned to his friend, Colonel Richard Glyn, and No. 3 Column. With nothing but vague reports from Lord Chelmsford and Sir Henry Bartle-Frere, he knew nothing about the status of the centre column. Lieutenant Colonel Durnford was dead and his mounted column destroyed, so there would be no reinforcements coming from them. Surely if his lordship knew No. 1 Column was now besieged at Eshowe, he would send Henry Pulleine or Henry Degacher's battalions of redcoats from the 24th Regiment to support them. The concept of being left blind all this time, both to the enemy's disposition and that of their own army, was maddening for Colonel Charles Pearson.

Chapter XVIII: Return to Rorke's Drift

Rorke's Drift
30 January 1879

Lieutenant General Sir Frederick Augustus Thesiger, Lord Chelmsford
General Officer Commanding (GOC), British Forces in South Africa

While Captain Warren Wynne and his engineers fortified the stronghold at Eshowe, his friend, Captain Walter Jones, and No. 5 Field Company continued their arduous trek towards Rorke's Drift. Much like the southern column, they had been left unaware of all that had transpired within the Zulu Kingdom over the past few weeks. Since the two engineer officers had departed company, there was little to occupy Jones' mind except the daily slog through the quagmire that was the sodden and churned up road. The first leg was a gruelling hundred miles from Port Durban to Greytown. From there, it was another seventy to Rorke's Drift. But unlike his friend, Warren Wynne, Walter Jones would learn of the disaster that had befallen the centre column almost as soon as it happened.

It was on the evening of the 22nd when they heard the first news from the war. The company was readying to make camp for the night, when picquets alerted Captain Jones to the arrival of a frantic rider wearing the cord breaches and riding jacket of one of the volunteer mounted units.

The man halted his exhausted and near-dead mount just short of Captain Jones and saluted. "Captain, sir," he said breathlessly; his voice shaking and complexion pale. "Lieutenant Harry Davies, Natal Carbineers."

"You're a bit lost," Walter replied, returning the salute. The look of strain upon the rider's face unnerved him. "You do know you're riding away from the war."

Davies did not reply at first but dismounted and removed his hat. "Your pardon, sir, but there has been a terrible disaster. I'm not sure where to start…"

"At the beginning would be nice," Jones replied, folding his arms across his chest.

"Yes, sir."

The lieutenant quickly told Jones and his assembled officers as much as he could recall. As part of Durnford's No. 2 Column, the Natal Carbineers had ridden from Rorke's Drift to Isandlwana that very morning. He further detailed the disastrous battle that followed, his own return to the camp to find ammunition, and subsequent escape from the slaughter. As the officer spoke, a few enlisted sappers ceased in their labours of setting up camp to listen to his frantic words. Their corporal sought to berate them, only to stop short at Davies last statement.

"The camp's been overrun and Colonel Durnford killed."

This caused Walter Jones' facial expression to fall. He closed his eyes for a moment, fighting to remain stoic. He felt as if he'd been kicked in the guts by a mule. He had fond memories of his time serving under then-Major Durnford and was particularly looking forward to a reunion with his old commanding officer. "What of the rest of the column at Isandlwana, or the camp at Rorke's Drift?" he asked, regaining his composure.

"I have no idea," Davies confessed, shaking his head. "Most of us who survived crossed at a drift about ten miles south. We could still hear the volleys of musketry coming from the infantry. I doubt they could have held for long. While Lord Chelmsford was off chasing shadows, the entire Zulu army swarmed the camp. When our mounted troops ran out of bullets and fell back towards the camp, the entire right flank collapsed." The volunteer officer was clearly shaken. He removed his hat, wiping a rag over his face and forehead. His lips parched, he went to take a drink from his water bottle to find just a few drops remaining.

Walter took his from his hip belt and handed it to the lieutenant, who drank thirstily.

"Much obliged, sir," he said, handing the drained bottle back to the captain. He continued, "I saw one poor company of redcoats who'd come up to support us, being swarmed in the flank and from behind. No thousand men, regardless of how well trained and armed, could last for long against 25,000 Zulus, especially as spread out as they were and with their right flank gone." He then detailed their harrowing escape towards the lower drift. Many of the riders and NNC warriors were overwhelmed by the pursuing mass of Zulus and cut to shreds. "After we crossed—those fortunate among us not to be run down and gutted—our transportation officer, Lieutenant Cochrane, said he was going to head for Helpmekaar where we expected to find two companies from 1/24th still en route. I volunteered to ride for Pietermaritzburg to warn the high commissioner. But as you can see, captain, my horse is damned near shot. If you could oblige me with a fresh mount, I would be in your debt."

"Of course," Jones said, quickly nodding while trying to digest all that he'd been told. There was another rider with Lieutenant Davies, and he ordered his farrier sergeant to exchange horses for both men. Trying to not create too much of a stir, he summoned his senior subaltern, Lieutenant Richard Porter, along with the company's acting-colour sergeant, James Ellis.

"We heard," Porter said, saving his captain from having to explain the situation again.

"As did half the lads," Ellis added. He glanced over his shoulder to see a handful of sappers talking hurriedly amongst themselves.

"Which is why we need to address the facts as we know them," Walter asserted. He then shook his head. "There's nothing for it. Colour Sergeant, parade the men."

In addition to the tragic news, of which they had few coherent details, Captain Jones was further concerned about Lieutenant Chard and his detachment. He'd sent them on ahead with a light equipment wagon more than a week prior. Friends of the sappers who accompanied Chard were especially worried about their mates.

"Unless we receive countermanding orders," the captain explained to his assembled company, "we still have our mission to perform. And right now, that mission is to make our way to Rorke's Drift."

He half-expected hesitation from his sappers. Instead, there was a renewed sense of enthusiasm and purpose. The men of No. 5 Field Company were determined to reach the drift; and if something happened to Lieutenant Chard and his sapper team, they would avenge them.

A day-and-a-half later, No. 5 Field Company was making headway between Greytown and Rorke's Drift when a mounted entourage was seen approaching from the north.

Lieutenant Porter pulled out his field glasses and scanned the mass of men. "By God, sir, it's his lordship!"

Lord Chelmsford and his entourage were headed for Pietermaritzburg when they came across Captain Jones and his sappers. They were still about a day's march from Helpmekaar. Despite the rains, the roads along this stretch were more manageable than the quagmire they'd slogged through since leaving Greytown.

"My lord!" Walter said as he rode up to Chelmsford and saluted sharply. "By God, sir, it is good to see you still among the living."

"Indeed," the GOC replied. His eyes were bloodshot, and the captain surmised he hadn't slept in days. "And I will feel much relief once you are encamped at Rorke's Drift and begin work on the fortifications."

"So, the depot was not overrun by the Zulus?"

Chelmsford shook his head. "No. In fact, it was your man, Mister Chard, who led the defence. Not the most interesting character, but he proved to be the right man for the job. He and the men of B Company, 2/24th barricaded the mission station with mealie bags and biscuit boxes, withstanding the onslaught from an entire Zulu corps of about 4,000 warriors. You'll be pleased to know that I am personally recommending him to Her Majesty that he be awarded the Victoria Cross."

"That is splendid news, sir," Walter replied with a nod, albeit the confusion on his face was evident. Lieutenant John Chard was quite possibly the laziest and most boring officer he'd ever known. He was tempted to ask Lord Chelmsford if he was certain he had the right man. He quickly thought better of it and decided to use what little time he had with the GOC to ask something far more pertinent. "Is it true, my lord? Was the centre column destroyed, and is Colonel Durnford dead?"

Chelmsford abstained from stating his innermost thoughts; he held Anthony Durnford personally responsible for the disaster at Isandlwana. He knew it would be a poor showing to decry the slain colonel in front of a subordinate officer; not to mention Walter Jones was a fellow engineer and former protégé of Durnford's.

"Regrettably, yes," he replied slowly, choosing his words carefully. "Thankfully, only one company from 2/24th was at Isandlwana, so Colonel Degacher's battalion is mostly intact. Sadly, Colonel Pulleine and most of 1st Battalion were wiped out along with hundreds of our volunteers and native warriors. The two remaining companies are now under command of Major Russell Upcher. You'll find them at Helpmekaar. The remaining infantry companies and mounted troops are at Rorke's Drift. They'll be glad to have proper fortifications instead of rotting mealie sacks. Now if you'll excuse me, captain…"

The sappers marching on the road parted, eliciting loud cheers as their commanding general rode past. Chelmsford appeared to not even notice them. Captain Jones let out a deep sigh of relief, as his baffled subaltern walked his horse over to him.

"Did I hear that right, sir?" he asked.

Walter nodded.

Porter let loose a laugh and shook his head. "So, it seems our Mister Chard has written his way into the history books."

Shiyane Mountain, overlooking the depot and river crossing at Rorke's Drift

It was not until the 30th of January, a full week after the battle, that Captain Jones and No. 5 Field Company finally reached the mission station. Rorke's Drift was in a terrible state. A large mass grave to bury the Zulu dead was dug not far from the charred ruins of the hospital; yet patrols were constantly finding bodies of slain warriors further afield. The British dead were buried behind the depot near the base of Shiyane Mountain. Much of the surrounding grassy fields were flattened and streaked black with dried blood. And after the first few days, one needed to only follow the swarms of flies and the stench of rotting flesh to find more slaughtered enemy warriors. While there was a macabre sense of satisfaction at finding more of their dead adversaries, it also served as a stark reminder of the 1,300 British and allied Africans whose bodies still lay exposed on the slopes of Isandlwana.

As Captain Walter Jones and No. 5 Field Company lumbered their way into the depot, he found the entire mission station to be downright depressing. No one had any tents. Even those belonging to the garrison company had been destroyed. For the rest of 2nd Battalion of the 24th, most of their personal belongings and kit were lost when the Zulus sacked the main camp at Isandlwana, leaving them utterly exposed to the hostile elements. One of the buildings, which Walter later learned had acted as the depot's hospital, lay in charred ruins. The storehouse remained, but its thatched roof had been taken down. Only a large tarp over the small attic provided cover against the rain.

As he dismounted near the crude stone fortifications that now butted up against the storehouse, he sought out his wayward subaltern. Instead, the first man he found was the officer commanding of B Company, 2/24th, Lieutenant Gonville Bromhead.

"Captain, sir," he said with a salute.

Jones returned the courtesy. "I hear you were in a bit of a scrap about a week ago."

"That we were, sir, but we got the Zulus sorted." The infantry lieutenant then dropped his gaze for a moment, seemingly uncertain of himself. "You'll want to see Colonel Degacher. He's in the old storehouse."

Walter nodded and made his way through the small, squalid camp. Though Colonel Richard Glyn had resumed his duties as commanding officer of No. 3 Column following Lord Chelmsford's departure, it was apparent Lieutenant Colonel Henry Degacher of 2/24th was the one overseeing the day-to-day running of the garrison.

"Ah, Captain Jones," Degacher said, rising from his camp stool and extending his hand. "Glad to have you with us."

"It's good to finally be here, sir," the engineer officer replied diplomatically. "Might I ask where Lieutenant Chard may be found?"

"Regrettably, he's no longer here," the colonel responded. "I'm afraid fever and dysentery have taken a toll on what remains of the column. With the hospital burned to the ground and no tents available, we had to send the wounded and sick to Ladysmith. His lordship feels that after all Mister Chard did to save the depot, he deserves a bit of a rest."

Ladysmith was west of Rorke's Drift and Helpmekaar. Walter surmised that he'd missed the hospital convoy, including his subaltern, by just a couple days. "What of my sappers who came here with him?"

"Regrettably, only Driver Robson survived. The rest were ordered up to Isandlwana on the morning before the battle. Colonel Pulleine intended to use them to repair the roads leading from the camp to Mangeni Falls."

"Beastly bad luck for Corporal Gamble and the lads," Walter said sombrely.

"Indeed. Come, I'll take you to Colonel Glyn."

It was now nearly noon. They found Colonel Richard Glyn and the senior surviving officers of No. 3 Column seated on biscuit boxes having their lunch.

Major Dunbar, now acting as quartermaster for the column, was briefing the colonel on the state of their rations and the procurement of ammunition to replenish their exhausted stores. "We sent wagons back to Greytown. Hopefully they've arrived by now."

"They most likely have," Walter spoke up. He then came to attention and addressed Colonel Glyn. "Your pardon, sir. Captain Walter Jones, No. 5 Field Company, Royal Engineers."

"You are a welcome sight, captain," Glyn said. He pulled himself tiredly to his feet and clasped Walter's hand.

"Ah, so you've come from Greytown," Major Dunbar remarked.

"Yes, sir," Jones replied. "Your wagons passed us when we were about two days shy of Helpmekaar. Being empty, they managed well enough. However, even if the rains cease, they'll sink into the mud once they're fully loaded. Given how long it took us to arrive here, I suspect it will be at least a week to ten days before they return."

Glyn nodded and waved for Jones to take a seat, while he and his staff continued their meeting. For a regimental meeting, it was sparse on participants. From what Walter garnered, none of the officers from 1/24th survived the battle. Along with Lieutenant Colonel Pulleine, every staff officer, company commander, and subaltern were killed. Among these was Henry Degacher's brother, William, who had been acting as battalion major.

As the meeting broke up, Degacher pulled Jones off to the side. "I take it no one has briefed you on the larger strategic situation."

"They have not, sir. We met with Lord Chelmsford on his way to Pietermaritzburg. All he said was there was a disaster at Isandlwana, but the lads here made quite the stalwart stand."

"Yes, and proud of them we are." Degacher sighed, his words unintentionally sounding dismissive. No doubt the Battle of Rorke's Drift would inspire the public and, perhaps, ease the horrific shock of the tragedy at Isandlwana. With numerous Victoria Crosses and Distinguished Conduct Medals being recommended for the defenders, he had little doubt that the battle would become a thing of legend in the history books.

However, he understood that in the overall scheme of the war, the defence accounted for very little. "To put it bluntly, captain—and please pardon my language—the situation we found ourselves in is utter shit. At the start of the invasion, between our No. 3 Column and Colonel Durnford's mounted troops, we had over 5,000 fighting men and six cannon. Thirteen-hundred are now dead; their bodies tragically left to rot where they fell. The Zulus captured two of the cannon. We subsequently suffered mass desertions from our natives, and Commandant Lonsdale was compelled to disband the entire 3rd NNC Regiment. Which means we now have scarcely a thousand troops garrisoned between here and Helpmekaar and almost no ammunition to speak of."

"Understood," Walter acknowledged. "Then I'd best get to work on fortifying the drift. And if I may ask, sir, what of the northern and southern columns? I arrived in Durban with Captain Wynne's No. 2 Field Company. Last I knew, they were headed towards Lower Drift to join up with Colonel Pearson's column."

"We've heard nothing from Colonel Pearson. As he's more than a hundred miles to the south, this is hardly surprising. I believe Lord Chelmsford intends for him to withdraw to Lower Drift. Colonel Wood's No. 4 Column is about the only effective fighting force we have left. But his numbers are too few to continue prosecuting the war on his own. Fortunately, he's managed to withdraw his column back to Utrecht sixty miles north of here."

Walter shook his head glumly. "And to think, my greatest fear was that the war would be over before I even reached Rorke's Drift."

"We all thought it would be over quickly," Degacher stated. "But now it seems the Zulu War has only just begun."

With the arrival of No. 5 Field Company, proper work on the two forts at Rorke's Drift began in earnest over the following week. The stronghold at the supply depot was named Fort Bromhead by the men of B Company, 2/24th, after their officer commanding. The other, which overlooked the ponts, was named Fort Melvill after the brave adjutant from 1/24th who died while trying to save the Queen's Colour. There was a brief reprieve in their sombre deportment when a patrol recovered the Queen's Colour from its watery grave, not far from where Melvill and Lieutenant Neville Coghill were killed.

For the men of No. 5 Field Company, there was the added sadness of their own losses. Corporal William Gamble, along with Sappers Harry Cuthbert, James Maclaren, and Michael Wheatley had eagerly volunteered for the mission to Rorke's Drift. Echoing Captain Jones' words, all the men could say was that it was *'beastly bad luck'* that the four had been ordered up to Isandlwana on the very morning of the battle. Driver Charles Robson was especially distraught. The only reason he was still alive was because, as Lieutenant Chard's batman, he was ordered to return with him to Rorke's Drift about an hour before the Zulus were first spotted by the unfortunate garrison left at Isandlwana.

"We need to do something for them," Colour Sergeant Ellis said to Captain Jones on the evening of 5 February. It was yet another rainy night. He found his officer commanding sitting on his camp bed, pouring over sketches he'd made of the forts. "I know we have no bodies to bury. And I suspect we'll never find and identify any. But we should give the lads a chance to pay their respects and say goodbye."

Walter concurred. "There's a civilian chaplain here, Smith I believe is his name. I'll speak with him and with Colonel Glyn."

After dismissing his colour sergeant, he lifted the flap of his tent and looked towards the fort, where several hundred soldiers from 2/24th huddled beneath their greatcoats and whatever else they could find to protect them from the hateful downpour. Having only just arrived, No. 5 Field Company were among the few to even have tents. Walter sighed and shook his head. Though he pitied the men, there was little he could do for them.

The following morning, Captain Jones ordered his men to cease in their labours for an hour while they gathered down at the drift. The remainder of the garrison dutifully kept their distance, and the men of No. 5 Field Company paid their last respects to their fallen friends. From the ponts, one could clearly see the peak of Isandlwana on the skyline about ten miles away. It was painful to see the mountain, knowing that their friends' bodies lay unburied on its slopes. Yet there was nothing they could do about it, so long as the Zulus controlled the lands east of the uMzinyathi.

The sky was grey with thick clouds promising even more rain that afternoon. For the moment, it had ceased long enough to allow the sappers of No. 5 Field Company a few moments to remember the fallen. The grasses around the ponts had long since been trampled into the earth by thousands of soldier's boots and animal's hooves over the past six weeks. With the constant rainfall, the ground was slick with mud, every divot and gouge forming numerous puddles.

The company stood in parade formation and removed their helmets. They were joined by a civilian volunteer chaplain named George Smith. A burly man with a long, thick beard, the defenders of Rorke's Drift had taken to calling him *'Ammunition Smith'* due to his tireless ferrying of cartridge packets to the firing line over the course of twelve hours of battle. The reverend stood next to Captain Jones, who took it upon himself to lead the first part of the short memorial service.

"Corporal William Gamble, Sapper Harry Cuthbert, Sapper James Maclaren, Sapper Michael Wheatley…more than just names, and more than soldiers of the Queen, they were our friends. They were our brothers. They volunteered selflessly to come to this far-flung corner of the world to face their country's foes with steadfastness and valour. And in this forgotten land, where their mortal bodies lie, so too does the spirit of Britannia. Their duty to the Crown and the Empire done, may their souls find rest."

Jones then nodded to Reverend Smith, who proceeded to read from the Psalms like he had during numerous memorials for fallen British troops over the past weeks. As the reverend spoke, Walter's thoughts turned to his old friend, Warren Wynne. He could only hope Lord Chelmsford had gotten word to them by now! He'd spent much of the previous night pouring over a map of the region, hoping his friend and the rest of No. 1 Column were not wandering about blind to the calamity that had changed the very course of the war. Had they made it to Eshowe? And if ordered to withdraw, could the column extract itself back to Lower Drift?

A chill ran up Walter's spine. If the southern column reached their intended destination of Eshowe, that meant they were thirty-five miles inside enemy-held territory. He hoped they had had time to reinforce their position, lest they leave another thousand British corpses inside the Zulu Kingdom.

"...and so, we commit the souls of William Gamble, Harry Cuthbert, James Maclaren, and Michael Wheatley to you, oh Lord. Their duty done, may they rest in peace. Amen."

Chapter XIX: The Punishment Due

Lower Drift
31 January 1879

An officer from the Natal Native Contingent, along with a sergeant major from the
Natal Carbineers and various African volunteers

Captain Percy Barrow's mounted troops had reached the Thukela in
a single day. The men were ever anxious about a possible ambush
by the Zulus. Within a day they had outpaced the NNC, whose
warriors were indignant with a sense of abandonment. Though they
soon scattered into small bands, it was a testament to their loyalty
and discipline that they returned to Lower Drift rather than
abandoning the British altogether.

Unfortunately for Barrow and his men, conditions at Fort
Tenedos were scarcely better than those at Eshowe or Rorke's Drift.
While there had been a few days of reprieve from the rains, they
were replaced by the ceaseless heat from the scorching sun. This,
coupled with being so close to the slow-moving Thukela River, had
led to swarms of mosquitos and flies tormenting the garrison.

The fort on the Zulu side of the river was meant to be a supply
depot with a small garrison, and the mounted troops found
themselves to be little more than a nuisance to those stationed at the
fort. Captain Barrow, therefore, gave his troopers permission to
camp on the far side of the river. He also sent a rider with Colonel

Pearson's message for Lord Chelmsford in the direction of Rorke's Drift. More rumours awaited them regarding the defeat of Lieutenant Colonel Durnford. Yet even a week after the battles of Isandlwana and Rorke's Drift, substantive details were still lacking. Many continued to believe that the British defeat had happened at Middle Drift.

"A victory and a defeat with Colonel Durnford dead; that's all we know," Senior Lieutenant Kingscote, the Royal Navy officer commanding Fort Tenedos, remarked when pressed about any news from the other columns.

As a naval senior lieutenant and an Army captain were essentially the same rank, Percy Barrow was content to leave Kingscote in command of Fort Tenedos. He maintained responsibility of his own Imperial Mounted Infantry and the mounted volunteers. Lieutenant Colonel Coates assumed command of both sides of Lower Drift, though he remained detached, allowing the two forts to go about their daily routine without interference.

With no definitive tasks for his troopers, Captain Barrow ordered them to remain ready but gave the troop commanders free reign to dispatch riders to the various towns and homesteads of his men. Only the Imperial Mounted Infantry were regular Army redcoats. Most of the rest were volunteers from local militias and settler communities. Many of these men were married and wrote letters to their families, letting them know where they were and asking if they could send a few sundry items to replace what they had been forced to abandon at Eshowe. One such letter, written by Lieutenant Robarts to his wife, spoke candidly and harshly about the justification behind the war itself.

> *A retribution must overtake the Zulus which will destroy them as a nation. However, we must not forget that they are fighting fair and in a just cause, though they are opposed to us. They are fighting for their own country, as we are fighting for ours.*

"A terrible injustice," he said quietly, as he finished penning the letter.

Many of the colonial volunteers had only a passing affiliation with their native Britain. Men like Sir Henry Bartle-Frere, Lord Chelmsford, and the imperial redcoats under their command would eventually return home to England. Though battalions would often spend years assigned to the various colonies throughout the Empire, it was not their home. And once they departed South Africa, none would have to live with the consequences of the war. Yet for men like William Robarts, Natal *was* home. How the conflict with the Zulus ended would greatly affect his livelihood and that of his family and friends. He was, therefore, more likely to ask questions regarding the purpose of the war.

William was also quite active within Pietermaritzburg society and had eyes and ears in the Natal government. As best as he could tell, Sir Henry Bartle-Frere was pursuing his own agenda of confederating Southern Africa under direct British rule and using Lord Chelmsford's soldiers to bring about said confederacy by force. The young officer surmised that his lordship had to be privy to the High Commissioner's intentions. After all, Sir Henry could not order the GOC to invade Zululand. Most of the soldiers who found themselves in the middle of this war between the Crown and their former allies simply assumed that Lord Chelmsford's directives came from Horse Guards and Her Majesty's government. Lieutenant Robarts had his doubts.

"By God, have we all been dragged into their private little war against King Cetshwayo?" he quietly asked himself. He leaned against his saddle which he often used as a pillow when camping under the stars.

A small oil lamp gave him just enough light to write by. In addition to his feelings about the war itself, he further expressed his concerns to his wife regarding the imperial soldiers who stayed at Eshowe. He reckoned they had enough rations and supplies to last three months maybe four. This meant Colonel Pearson was taking a huge risk, should Lord Chelmsford be compelled to wait for reinforcements from Britain before launching an expedition to reinforce him. And like Pearson, Robarts was extremely frustrated by the lack of information to come from the centre column, as well as the GOC. Yes, they were a hundred miles away; however, given that Chelmsford had already sent a message to Pearson, vague as it was, surely the men at Fort Tenedos should have been made abreast of the situation! Sadly, the naval lieutenant in charge of the depot knew no more than he did. Even in the age of telegraph and semaphore, a profound lack of viable information led to the spread of wild rumours; a nemesis when fighting colonial wars on the furthest-flung corners of the Empire.

The following morning, the summer rains returned with renewed vengeance. Doubling the misery of the newly-arrived forces at Fort Tenedos and those remaining at Eshowe was the lack of tents or other shelter. At Eshowe, there simply was not room within the compound for tents to house 1,500 men. As for those who'd hurriedly made their way back to the Thukela, their tents had been left at Eshowe. A fortunate few would find some shelter under the wagons each night, while Sergeant Stirling had procured a few wagon tarps to serve as lean-tos. For most, there was little except their greatcoats to protect them from the elements each night.

That evening, three men from David Fredericks' section were tasked with sentry duty. The rain was particularly hellish, coming down in sheets and threatening to wash away the entire camp. John Stirling was sergeant-of-the-guard, so David tried to get a few hours of sleep. This proved futile. Though he was able to find shelter beneath an ammunition wagon belonging to the 99th's garrison at Fort Pearson, resting his head against one of the spoked wheels, a steady stream of water was pooling beneath him. By midnight it was three inches deep. His bottom and legs were completely soaked and numb. By this time his senses had finally succumbed to fatigue, and he dozed off. Less than an hour later, he was shaken awake.

"Oh, bugger all," he grumbled. He wiped his eyes and turned to see who'd so rudely interrupted his sleep. It was so dark he could not even see the outline of the man who knelt next to the wagon.

"Beg your pardon, sergeant." It was Private Peters. "You need to come at once. It's about Private Walters."

"What about him?" David asked with annoyance. "He's on sentry duty, is he not?"

"That's just it, sergeant. He was supposed to be."

The sergeant muttered a few profane curses, slapped his soaked helmet on his head, and followed the soldier through the blackness of the camp. In the torrential downpour, torches were useless and oil lamps nearly impossible to keep lit. Near the company headquarters, David was able to see a lone soldier standing at attention being dressed down by Colour Sergeant Bennet. Lieutenant Martin stood by observing, his arms folded across his chest. As David hastened to them, a hand was placed on his shoulder, stopping him abruptly. He turned and was just able to make out the distressed face of Sergeant Stirling.

He was carrying the errant soldier's rifle, in addition to his own. "I'm sorry, David," he said. "I had no choice. You would do the same in my position."

Sergeant Fredericks said nothing but turned his attention to the unfortunate Private Walters.

The colour sergeant was now standing right next to him, shouting into the soldier's ear. *"You abandoned your post, private! Do you know what danger you put the lives of your fellow soldiers in? Shut up! You don't get to fucking speak!"*

Lieutenant Martin then noted Sergeant Fredericks, and he waved him over before addressing Walters. David rightly surmised that the private had been unable to handle the constant deluge anymore and had sought shelter. While he could not exactly fault the man for seeking relief from his extreme distress, every man at Lower Drift and Eshowe was subjected to the same torments from the weather. Even the officers were not protected from the elements. Abandoning one's post was among the worst crimes a soldier could commit short of cowardice, theft, or murder.

"This is a serious offence, Private Walters," the officer commanding said, his voice straining to be heard over the downpour. "According to Queen's Regulations you could be shot for this. Not only do I have to report this disgrace by despatch to Colonel Parnell and Colonel Pearson, I have to waste another man guarding you. You are hereby under arrest until such time as Colonel Pearson decides your fate."

As another soldier led Walters away, David walked over to the lieutenant and came to attention.

"Sergeant Fredericks, it pains me to see such a breach in discipline coming from your section," Martin said reprovingly.

"Yes, sir. I accept full responsibility for Private Walters' actions. He has not been the same since Private Dunne's death."

"Men die during war, sergeant," the lieutenant said coldly. "You know this as well as any."

"Yes, sir. His actions were inexcusable, but so too were mine. I should have been firmer with him and, if needed, had him replaced

251

on sentry duty until we got him sorted. He's never been a problem for me, never late to formation, follows orders without question…"

"Except when ordered to maintain his post," the officer commanding countered.

"Yes, sir." David swallowed hard. There was little he could say in his soldier's defence.

"Breaches of discipline are inevitable even among the best soldiers," Colour Sergeant Bennet spoke up. He had to practically shout to be heard over the torrential rainfall, yet his tone had changed considerably. "And a siege only exacerbates matters. That is why we must meet any lapses immediately and firmly."

"That means Walters will die," David observed, struggling to hide the distress in his voice.

"That's for Colonel Pearson to decide," Lieutenant Martin replied. "And if we are unable to get a despatch to the column, then as the senior officer at Lower Drift, Lieutenant Colonel Coates will decide Private Walters' fate."

David took a moment to compose his thoughts. Before his officer commanding could dismiss him, he quickly said, "Sir, I request permission to speak with Colonel Coates."

"Denied," the lieutenant said without hesitation. "If you wish to make a case for Private Walters, come find me in the morning. I will decide whether to bring it to Colonel Coates, who will then determine if it warrants presenting to the column commander."

"Yes, sir."

Any hopes David Fredericks had for sleeping that night were dashed by the unfortunate incident involving Private Walters. "Of all the lads for this to happen to," he muttered. He huddled beneath his greatcoat and slumped into the growing puddle. All the while, the rains continued to beat their vicious cadence on the bed of the wagon.

About an hour before dawn, the deluge finally ceased, and the sergeant both longed for and dreaded the bugle call that would announce reveille.

He found Lieutenant Martin drinking a tin cup of cold coffee, for there was no possibility of getting fires lit within the swamp that had become Lower Drift. The Thukela River swelled considerably during the night, rising past its natural flood plain and soaking the camp. The officer commanding of H Company was alone, having sent Lieutenant Backhouse and Colour Sergeant Bennet away. Like David Fredericks, he looked as if he had not slept at all.

"Lieutenant, sir," David said, coming to attention.

"Stand at ease, sergeant. Now, tell me exactly why I should make a case to save Private Walters from the hangman's noose."

Sergeant Fredericks thought to implore Lieutenant Martin to intercede. Walters had previously been an exemplary soldier with no disciplinary problems during his time with the regiment. He had just received his good conduct pay and was contemplating remaining with the Colours, when his enlistment expired in another year. However, his previous service only made his offence even more unscrupulous in the eyes of his officer commanding. Instead, he gave the only argument he could find even remotely compelling.

"Because we need every rifleman we can muster," he said bluntly. "We're already understrength, sir, and the men's health is far from ideal. Seven of our soldiers are down with fever. And while I may not be privy to the strategic situation, my instincts tell me every last one of us will be needed to break the siege of our friends at Eshowe."

"And that is the same argument I used with Colonel Coates," Martin replied.

"You've already spoken with him?"

"Of course, I have!" the lieutenant asserted. "Make no mistake, Private Walters' punishment will fit his crime, but his life will be spared."

It was a sombre day for the soldiers of H Company. All shared in the shame of their mate's misconduct. The company stood in parade formation in a large square facing a weather-beaten tree about a hundred yards from the pont. Walters was led by a pair of soldiers over to the tree. He was bare-chested, his expression passive. David had been allowed to come see him the night before and told him of his sentence. Walters knew he was fortunate to still be alive, and he accepted his fate stoically. Lieutenant Colonel Coates was tasked with overseeing the punishment.

Colour Sergeant Bennet read the sentence. His booming voice echoed loud enough for all within a mile to hear.

"Private Thomas Walters; you have been found guilty of abandoning your post, thereby placing the lives of your fellow soldiers in grave danger. By order of Lieutenant Colonel Coates, on the authority of Colonel Pearson, commanding officer of No. 1

Column, you are sentenced to fifty lashes and ordered to forfeit three months of good conduct pay."

The colour sergeant then turned to Lieutenant Colonel Coates who nodded. Walters' arms were placed around the trunk, and his hands bound.

Flogging, long considered barbaric in most civilised armies, had been abolished on Home Service by the British Armed Forces years before. However, given the often-severe nature of campaigns on the frontiers of the Empire, the practice was still allowed on Foreign Service. A whip consisting of numerous cords was most often used. The wounds cut deep and could lead to severe blood loss or infection. The shock alone of being subjected to fifty lashes in one session could prove fatal. For this reason, Private Walters would be given fifteen lashes this day with the remainder doled out over the coming weeks, after his back had sufficient time to heal. There was also the chance that the commanding officer would consider remitting the remaining lashes.

David had only witnessed one flogging during his years with the Colours. The suppressed memories made his stomach turn as he watched a corporal from B Company make ready to commence the punishment. With a signal from Lieutenant Colonel Coates, the NCO swung the whip in a hard slap across the condemned soldier's back. David winced. He could see a series of cuts and deep welts already forming. Walters remained stoic, stifling the urge to cry out. By the eighth blow, his back now streaked in blood, he let out a sob of agony. He beat his head against the tree, burying his face to hide his shame as the lashes continued. And despite the disdain he felt, even the corporal carrying out the sentence felt a trace of pity. He pulled his last three blows slightly, abruptly stepping away when finished. The soldiers who had escorted Walters immediately rushed to either side of him, untying his bindings and helping him away. Surgeon-Major Tarrant would stitch up and bandage the wounds. That at least two more such sessions awaited Private Walters nearly made his mates wretch. The chilling torments of endless night-time rains were a trifle by comparison. As distasteful as the affair was, all were fairly certain no one at Lower Drift would abandon his post again.

It was not just the garrisons at Fort Pearson and Fort Tenedos who were dealing with lapses in discipline. A similar, almost identical, incident had occurred on the same night as Private Walters' transgression. The entire garrison was turned out to witness the punishment, yet the actual flogging of the delinquent soldier was far different. A pair of bandsmen were tasked with carrying out the sentence. Their whips barely even struck the exposed flesh of the man's back, leaving only a few red marks and not a single cut. Still, Colonel Pearson hoped it made its point. He knew the longer the siege continued, the more difficult discipline would be to enforce.

Chapter XX: Death and Disbandment

Eshowe
1 February 1879

Colonel Charles Pearson, taken during the Zulu War

One man not on-hand to witness the previous day's flogging was Captain Warren Wynne. His boundless energy and tireless worth ethics had finally succumbed to the endless weeks of work with little to no sleep. Lieutenant Courtney took charge of the company, following his commander's detailed notes and instructions, while Warren slept all through the afternoon and into the following morning.

Not only was Warren oblivious to the punishment of a delinquent soldier, he was completely unaware of the Zulu incursions which compelled Colonel Pearson to post the entire column at 'stand-to' throughout much of the night. Under such circumstances, with the entire garrison huddled beneath the wagons in full kit, scarcely a man got any sleep. It was, therefore, a complete reversal of roles when Warren returned to his duties, eyes clear and his senses restored. He was still feeling a little weak from his dreadful experiences of the previous days, but at least his vomiting and diarrhoea had stopped for the time being.

The return of his strength and vigour was especially welcome, as every day more soldiers were placed on the sick list. The column also suffered its first fatality since arriving at Eshowe. Private Arthur Kingston from C Company of The Buffs had taken ill with fever just prior to the Battle of Inyezane. His condition worsened, and on the evening of 1 February he breathed his last.

With the death of the young soldier, Captain Wynne was suddenly more acutely aware of his own health issues. He took his time, walking more slowly as he accompanied Colonel Pearson and his staff officers on a tour of the fort. The entire ground was like a giant puddle; the mud churned up from the endless footfalls from over a thousand imperial soldiers. The smell was awful, though few noticed anymore.

"As you can see, sir, we've cleared this ravine for the cattle," Warren said, pointing with his riding crop. "I've also ordered a gateway constructed along the western ramparts with a drainage running down the eastern slope."

"Drainage is something we desperately need," Colonel Walker said, looking down at the two inches of water in which he stood.

Pearson said nothing but nodded his approval. All along the perimeter, soldiers laboured with pickaxes and shovels to widen and deepen the surrounding trench.

As they reached the northwest corner of the fort, Warren pointed towards this section of the trench. "As a matter of hygiene, we must address the stabling of the officers' horses. The cattle are properly contained, and we've done away with the unnecessary beasts of burden. However, given the confined space of our new home, our mounts will foul up the fort within days, bringing flies and disease."

"What are you suggesting, captain?" Colonel Walker asked.

Warren nodded towards a widened section of the trench which had been flattened at the bottom. "We 'stable' our horses here at night," he explained. "Extra sentries can be posted to prevent their being stolen or running off. We'll make the bottom of the trench wide enough to give them some measure of comfort and emplace posts for them to be tethered."

"It's less than ideal," Pearson stated. "However, it will have to do. We have enough issue dealing with human waste from over fifteen-hundred men, many of whom are down with dysentery, let alone our horses."

Sixty-four horses belonging to the officers and what few mounted troops remained were at Eshowe. The only one devoid of a mount was Lieutenant Colonel Parnell, whose poor beast had been killed by a stray bullet from one of his own men at Inyezane. Despite the measures taken to care for their animals, the officers knew it was inevitable that the occasional horse or cow would break loose and escape. Curses and shouts would often precede a soldier having to scramble over the ramparts in pursuit of a wayward beast. And though the initiative was appreciated, orders were given for soldiers not to venture more than four hundred yards beyond the camp to fetch a horse. This number was shortened to one hundred yards at night.

As they continued to inspect the defences, they came upon the old storehouse. Though there were several large buildings at Eshowe, these were not for the comfort of the soldiers or their officers. Instead, they were piled from floor to ceiling with grain sacks, boxes of biscuits, and tinned beef, as well as the stores of rifle cartridges and artillery rounds. Because the cannon were older muzzle-loaders, it was even more crucial to keep their sacks of powder out of the elements. Many of the wooden boxes used to carry the tinned beef and biscuits were emptied, filled with earth, and used to build more stable defence works.

As he surveyed the ramparts and parapets constructed under the watchful eye of Captain Wynne and his sappers, Colonel Pearson felt confident that Eshowe could withstand an assault by the entire Zulu *amabutho*. "Now if only they would attack," he said to Colonel Walker, as they stood atop the wooden stockade along the eastern defences.

"They've toyed with us a few times," his fellow colonel remarked. "And no doubt a few have paid the price for their brazenness."

"What troubles me is that we are completely blind here," Pearson stated. "We know nothing about the enemy's strength or disposition. And we still have no answers regarding the nature of their victory over Colonel Durnford or their subsequent defeat."

The Fort at Eshowe with the western ravine in the foreground

Though he had initially feared that having a brevet colonel as his second would lead to potential conflicts, Pearson was glad for Walker's company. The higher one rose within the military's hierarchy, the lonelier it became. For Evelyn Wood and Richard Glyn, who had no peers of equal rank with their columns, there was no one for them to vent their concerns or frustrations. To do so in front of subordinates was a gross breach of Queen's Regulations, not to mention completely unbecoming. Even a lance corporal knew to never complain in front of a private! And though Walker's colonelcy was a brevet rather than substantive, it still placed him in a position as a peer, allowing Charles Pearson to confide in him freely.

"Communication has never been his lordship's strong suit," Walker replied with surprising honesty. "However, I cannot help but think that any intelligence from the centre column would be irrelevant to us. The Zulus can cover great distances in a short time, yet they cannot be everywhere at once. And we know they are not stupid. I doubt that Cetshwayo has the numbers to fully engage us and is likely committing all his available assets to strike at Glyn and the centre column. From what we saw at Inyezane, I think the Zulus in this region intend to delay, rather than defeat us."

"An astute point," Pearson conceded. "However, it is all speculation. We must assume that No. 2 Column is no longer an operational asset, and we know nothing about the status of Colonel Glyn's No. 3 Column. If they've also been badly bloodied, and Cetshwayo no longer views them as a threat, he may very well turn his attention towards us."

"Like you said, we are completely blind," Walker emphasised. "Until such time as his lordship sends a runner to us, I think it's safe to say we cannot rely on any actionable intelligence to come from the north. We'll have to find a way to gather our own."

While Pearson contemplated how to make the best use of what few mounted troops remained at the station, they were joined by the column's doctor.

"Surgeon Norbury," Pearson said with a nod.

"Colonel, sir," the doctor replied.

"Something vexes you?" Charles asked, noting the worried expression on the surgeon's face.

"It's my medical stores. While I have ample instruments and bandages for the time being, I fear my supply of medicines will be quickly depleted. Dysentery and typhoid are a much greater threat to us than the Zulus, and they've already begun to take their toll."

"Yes, poor Private Kingston," Colonel Walker recalled. "Lad spent most of the journey from the Inyezane in the back of your ambulance wagon."

Two men who died of their wounds received during the battle, Sergeant Oscar Hydenburg and Private William Dunne, were buried near the old church. At the surgeon's recommendation, Pearson ordered a plot of land outside the stronghold designated as a cemetery. Arthur Kingston may have been the first British soldier to succumb at Eshowe, yet the colonel knew he certainly would not be the last.

"The Volunteers left all of their personal belongings here," Pearson said, after a few moments' contemplation. "While I will not suffer thieves, we do need medicines. I will authorise Colonels Parnell and Welman to personally oversee an inspection of their bags for any remedies they may have."

After dismissing the doctor and Colonel Walker, the commanding officer of No. 1 Column returned to the old church. He had portioned off a section to act as his headquarters. He sat behind his small camp desk and began to pen another message to Lord

Chelmsford. Though some of his entreaties seemed redundant, there was no guarantee that any of his despatches had even made it to the GOC, especially with large bands of Zulus spotted in the vicinity. After the incident with the cattle they'd tried to send back to Lower Drift, there could be little doubt they had roving bands of warriors watching the southern road.

In his latest note to Chelmsford, Pearson again made plain his distress at not knowing the full strategic situation. As one of the three column commanders, it was imperative that he be kept abreast of any significant developments surrounding Colonel Glyn or Colonel Wood's forces.

My Lord,

We continue to establish our fortifications at Eshowe. Unfortunately, our attempt to drive cattle back to Thukela failed, when they were intercepted by Zulus. We can get no word of you whatsoever. Our messengers keep returning, saying they cannot get through the Zulus, who are now all around us. Large bodies are often seen coming in different directions, mostly towards Natal. I hope this reaches you, that you can make us aware of what has happened with the other, and how we can best exercise your intent.

C.K. Pearson, Col

He let out a tired sigh, as he finished his latest letter to the commanding general. Normally, he would dictate such messages to one of his ADCs; however, he wished to keep the strain he felt at the column's predicament between himself and the GOC. He then summoned an orderly, Lieutenant Knight, and told him to find the fastest runner they had. The few black Africans who remained with the column were now Colonel Pearson's messengers. They were less conspicuous and had a better chance of outrunning the Zulus. A young man, probably in his early twenties, was brought before the colonel. He was tall and lanky and said to be of the iziGqoza. They were not only fierce fighters, but among the most reliable warriors within the NNC. Pearson gave the man the despatch with explicit instructions to first head to Lower Drift, and from there make his way to Rorke's Drift, as he assumed that Lord Chelmsford was still in the area.

It was a grey and drizzly morning when Private Arthur Kingston was laid to rest. There was no wood for a coffin, so his mates wrapped his body in a large flannel blanket. Adding to their sorrows was the way their friend had perished; not in a hail of bullets or Zulu spears, but from an unseen menace he could do little to battle against.

"It's not right to go out this way," one soldier muttered.

The battalion stood to attention as a party of six soldiers carried the fallen soldier's body to the freshly-dug grave just outside the fort.

"Far manlier to die at the hands of one's enemies," another private concurred.

Their words were etched with a trace of fear, that they too might fall victim to any number of diseases festering within the squalid fort. Like their column commander, every man within the 2/3rd Buffs knew that poor Private Kingston would not be the last of them to find his final resting place at Eshowe.

Seven riflemen formed a guard of honour on the far side of the grave. These men stood to attention, a lone sergeant standing behind them. Lieutenant Colonel Parnell authorised the men to fire a single volley in a final salute to their brother-in-arms. And while he did not wish to speculate on which of his soldiers would not survive the ongoing siege, he briefed his company commanders that this would be the last time he would allow soldiers to fire a salute over the graves of the fallen.

"After today, the living will need the ammunition more than the dead."

Chapter XXI: Disastrous Despatches

Eshowe
2 February 1879

Soldiers of the 88th Connaught Rangers, serving in the Imperial Mounted Infantry,
by Charles Fripp

Following the short funeral for Private Arthur Kingston, the garrison at Eshowe continued about their daily duties. The rain was now predictably coming at night and into the early morning, with the sun beating down on them through the afternoon. With no room for tents, and the constant alarms that further deprived the men of sleep each night, they were compelled to sleep near their posts, underneath the wagons, or wherever else they could find cover. There was almost none to be had, and whenever a soldier rose up from his fitful slumber, he was usually covered in sticky mud.

A point of pride for Colonel Charles Pearson was the extreme resilience displayed by his men. Soldiers are highly adaptable and able to improvise. Despite the terribly uncomfortable, not to mention unsanitary living conditions, they made the most of an all-around dreadful situation. Canvas tarps and other materials were stretched off the sides of the wagons to form large lean-tos which gave the redcoats more room for sleeping than their tents. Drainage cuts were dug with pickaxes around each section, with officers and NCOs enforcing that their men could only urinate in designated areas outside the ramparts. And while it was impossible to keep completely dry, such improvements helped give them some small measure of comfort.

It was now the morning of 2 February. Companies were finishing morning parade and inspections when a pair of runners were spotted coming up the southern road. These men were iziGqoza warriors from the centre column. They were among the few that remained after the 3rd NNC was disbanded. They were completely soaked, having run all night through a torrential downpour, which gave them the best chance of slipping past the Zulus. Their eyes were bloodshot, and their breathing came in deep gasps.

"Urgent message for Colonel Pearson," one of them said in heavily accented English.

The corporal-of-the-guard escorted the two warriors to the column headquarters. Pearson breathed an audible sigh of relief at finally having news from the rest of the army. The pained expression on the runners' faces alarmed him, and he dismissed the corporal as he took the soggy despatch from the lead man.

"Terrible disaster," the warrior said, his gaze falling.

What the colonel did not know was these men had been with Lord Chelmsford at Mangeni, while many of their tribesmen had remained at Isandlwana. Unlike many of the Natal Africans who'd fled during the Zulu onslaught, most of the iziGqoza remained stalwartly at their posts, fighting with extreme courage, and dying next to their white brothers in red jackets. These two survivors were filled with anguish and shame at not having been able to stand with their kinsmen.

As Pearson read the note, his face turned pale. He suspected something terrible had happened, what with Lieutenant Colonel Durnford being killed. He never could have imagined the calamity that had befallen their brethren from the 24th Regiment.

264

Colonel,

It is with much regret that I must tell you of the disastrous engagement that took place at the mountain of Isandlwana, ten miles east of Rorke's Drift, on the same day as your victory at Inyezane. Lt Col Durnford's column was brought up to Rorke's Drift on the 21st, then the following day to Isandlwana. One battalion of NNC remained at Middle Drift.

Over half of the column, acting on viable intelligence, sought out the Zulu impi on the morning of the 22nd, while 1/24th under Lt Col Pulleine, along with other attached troops, as well as Col Durnford's mounted forces remained to guard the camp. The Zulus swarmed down from the hills, surrounding the camp. Durnford over-extended his forces and was overrun. Despite the gallantry displayed by our soldiers, five companies from 1/24th, and one company from 2/24th, along with Cols Durnford and Pulleine, all battalion staff officers, and several hundred attached troops were completely annihilated.

I anticipate our losses at 1,300 dead, No. 2 Column effectively destroyed, and No. 3 Column no longer effective. Surviving forces have fortified Rorke's Drift against an enemy counterthrust. B Company, 2/24th has already repelled one such incursion by over 4,000 Zulu warriors, slaughtering several hundred during an attack on the mission station. I must insist that you withdraw to Lower Drift, as the enemy now controls all territory on the Zulu side of the rivers. In short, if you become endangered, I am not in a position to support you and won't be for at least six weeks.

Chelmsford

It was by far the longest despatch Pearson had ever received from his lordship, and far more detailed than the message the GOC had sent to London. But, Chelmsford understood that his column commanders needed to know the unvarnished truth, no matter how unpleasant. Colonel Wood was made aware of the disaster's extent even before Chelmsford fully grasped the situation. Captain Alan Gardner, a survivor of the battle, had ridden from Helpmekaar through the night to find No. 4 Column, which had elements conducting missions just twenty-five miles north of Isandlwana.

His hands trembling, Charles Pearson was clearly shaken by the catastrophic news, and he quickly dismissed the messengers. He slumped onto the rickety stool behind his camp desk, his left hand crumpling the despatch. His own regiment of the 3rd Buffs had fought beside the 24th during Xhosa War, and they had been garrisoned together at Cape Town for a time. He considered Richard Glyn a personal friend and took some solace in not seeing his name listed as killed. There was no comprehensive list, however. Pearson reckoned that at the time he sent this, Lord Chelmsford may not have known who among his officers was living or dead. Sadly, for the men in the ranks, the brave souls who stood shoulder-to-shoulder with their bloody bayonets towards the enemy were lost to posterity, consigned to anonymity and oblivion.

The colonel summoned his battalion commanders and senior staff officers to a private meeting. He shared Lord Chelmsford's alarming despatch and gave them a few minutes to fully come to grips with the distressing contents.

"So, Colonel Durnford was not at Middle Drift after all," Henry Parnell said, with a mirthless chuckle and a shake of his head.

"How could this have happened?" Welman asked in exasperation. "No force of Zulus should have been able to get even close to a concentrated force of Martini-Henrys!"

"I'm certain his lordship is asking the same question," Colonel Walker conjectured. "Unfortunately, we may never know what happened."

"The GOC seems to be casting responsibility onto Durnford," Captain Wynne remarked. The only officer below the rank of lieutenant colonel at the meeting, his position as chief engineer gave him greater responsibility and made his input invaluable to the column commander.

"Well, he was the senior officer present," Parnell observed. "I guess now we know what Sir Henry Bartle-Frere meant when he mentioned 'Durnford's defeat'. Still, he could have taken a moment to specify that it was not at Middle Drift but with the No. 3 Column! It's been eleven days since our battle at Inyezane. If this all occurred the same day, who knows what's happened between then and now?"

Henry Welman then added, "And eleven days is plenty of time for the Zulu *impi* to make its way here. After all, they are not hampered by wagon convoys and can run thirty or so miles a day."

"At least we now know what happened to our friends with the centre column," Henry Parnell said. He suddenly choked up and roughly pulled a handkerchief from his pocket, which he vigorously wiped over his eyes and coughed into. During the Xhosa War and their later shared time in Cape Town, he and his wife had developed a close friendship with Major William and Julia Degacher. William had served as acting commanding officer of 1/24th during the Xhosa War and was only superseded by Pulleine, another close friend of Parnell's, five days prior to the Battle of Isandlwana. If Pulleine was dead, he could only assume William Degacher was, too.

"Poor little Henrietta," he whispered, suddenly recalling William and Julia's new-born daughter.

There were a few moments of silence as the officers struggled to come to terms with the calamity. Adding to the sorrow and horror over such a tragic loss of life was the dilemma it now placed them in.

"I owe you an apology, colonel," Warren Wynne said at last. "It would seem my recommendation to remain here and fortify the mission station was ill-advised."

"The decision was still mine to make, captain," Pearson reassured him. "One can only give advice based on what they know at a given moment."

"I don't see how we can withdraw to the Thukela," Henry Parnell stated. "If the risks were substantial before, they are infinitely more so now. We still know nothing about the state of the Zulu *impi*, their remaining strength, how many casualties they've suffered, or even where they are."

Pearson then noted, "As much as we would like to think that our friends in the 24th made a stalwart stand with the Zulus paying a fearful price in blood, it would be prudent to assume they are still at full strength. Even if they did lose several thousand warriors, it is reasonable to expect they could field a force that outnumbers ours at least ten-to-one. Such odds can be readily faced behind fortifications, but not spread out on a column of march."

"And if we assume that Colonel Wood has withdrawn his forces safely to Utrecht," Henry Welman said, "with Colonel Glyn now holding Rorke's Drift, that leaves us as the only remaining British forces in Zululand. Which means we can expect their main *impi* to come for us."

"At minimum, we would have to shoot our way through the Zulus already massing to the south of us," Colonel Walker added. "And as fast as these devils can run, their friends can be on us as soon as they hear the sound of our guns. Our wagons and stores would have to be abandoned, meaning making a mad dash of over thirty miles with no more than what the lads can stuff into their packs."

"The Army has already lost a thousand soldiers," Pearson replied. "I'll not have us lose a thousand more, nor will I allow *'Eshowe'* to bear the same ignominy that will surely be placed upon the name *'Isandlwana'*."

One reason the column commander only wanted his most senior officers present was due to the delicate position he was now in. If he blindly followed Chelmsford's directive of withdrawing back to Lower Drift, in all probability his column would meet the same fate as poor Durnford and Pulleine, with another 1,500 redcoats added to the war's cost. However, he needed to exercise diplomacy and tact if he were to defy the GOC without being brought up on charges of insubordination. Moreover, none of this could be made known to the column at large. As far as the company-grade officers and other ranks knew, they were still executing the commanding general's intent by remaining at Eshowe.

The other reason behind his meeting was deciding how they would let their men know what had happened to their brothers in No. 2 and No. 3 Columns. Like their officers, the men in the ranks had formed close friendships with many of their fellows in the 24th Regiment during their time in Cape Town. That so many of their mates were most likely dead was something they could not keep secret.

"How should we tell the men what's happened?" Henry Parnell asked.

"Tomorrow is Sunday," Pearson replied. "The day that the entire column parades together so the chaplain can address them and see to their spiritual needs. That is when we will let them know about the poor lads from the 24th."

At Lower Drift, news of the disaster was met with the expected shock and disbelief; that an army of 'savages' armed with spears and shields could annihilate a thousand of the best professional soldiers in the world, equipped with modern rifles. In light of this, it was equally baffling that on the same day, a garrison of only a hundred men somehow withstood the onslaught of several thousand Zulu warriors.

"It baffles me," Lance Sergeant Rob Anderson said, as he and David Fredericks sat on the grassy slope leading down to the pont late that afternoon. "We routed the Zulus at Inyezane. A single company does the same at Rorke's Drift. And yet over half of No. 3 Column gets fucking slaughtered at Isandlwana." He shook his head, unable to come to terms with the news.

"Had the message not come directly from Chelmsford, I would not have believed it either," David remarked. He sat with his hands folded in his lap, his gaze fixed upon the slow-moving current of the river.

"You're worried about Sergeant Milne, aren't you?" Rob deduced.

David could only nod in agreement. Frederick Milne, his old friend and former section leader, who taught him how to read and later mentored him as an NCO, was tasked to supervise the ponts at Rorke's Drift. David could only hope that no one in No. 3 Column had decided to send him up to the camp at Isandlwana! And while the garrison at Rorke's Drift had withstood the subsequent Zulu onslaught, there had been no word on casualties.

"Well, I suppose we should look on the bright side. If Milne has copped it, at least you know your promotion is assured." David gave an awkward grin, deciding that a touch of morbid humour was appropriate given the dreadful circumstances.

Rob snorted and grinned. "Well, if we wait too long to extricate our friends at Eshowe, you'll be up for sergeant major!"

"Only if Colour Sergeant Bennet meets with an 'accident'," David remarked, supressing a laugh brought on by his battered nerves.

"Don't forget, I still have seniority, you twat!" the voice of Sergeant John Stirling called from behind them. They turned to see their friend standing with his hands on his hips, trying to look stern, though his face was twisted in a bemused smirk. "Now if you two are through planning the demise of everyone in the sodding battalion who outranks you, Lieutenant Martin needs to see us."

David hoped their officer commanding would have more news for them, but instead he only wished to review the guard and work details for the next few days. While the sergeant loathed the idea of 'busy work', he knew they needed to keep their soldiers occupied until they were called upon to re-join the fight. In addition to sentry duty and whatever work details were needed to maintain their humble camp each day, Lieutenant Martin ordered them to conduct refresher training on musketry and bayonet drills.

"Additionally, Mister Backhouse has offered to lead patrols along the riverbank," the officer commanding continued. "Given the swollen width of the Thukela, and the understanding that Zulus can't swim, the area is reasonably secure. However, we don't want to take any chances with raiders harrying the local settlements."

"Tell your lads they should be grateful for the chance to stretch their legs a bit," Colour Sergeant Bennet added. "We may not have our tents to sleep under, but we've got it far better than those poor sods remaining at Eshowe."

In addition to keeping the redcoats' time occupied, the question now became what to do with the various companies from the 2nd Regiment of the Natal Native Contingent. There had been much confusion since their departure from Eshowe. Many warriors simply assumed their duty was finished and headed home. There were still others, especially among the iziGqoza, who longed for another chance to bloody their spears in the guts of their hated Zulu cousins. These warriors remained encamped on the Zulu side of the river, setting up their makeshift brush shelters near the plain where their people had been slaughtered by Cetshwayo's warriors during the Zulu civil war.

Their commanding officer, Major Shapland Graves from The Buffs, had received a telegram from the commissariat officer on Chelmsford's staff, ordering him to give the NNC warriors one month's pay, allow them to keep their blankets, and return home. However, they were expressly ordered to be ready to return at a moment's notice.

"You are still warriors in the service of the Great White Queen," the major said, through an interpreter. "Those among your brethren who have already returned home are under the same orders.

However, as you have proven your loyalty by remaining at your posts, you will receive a month's pay in advance, with Her Majesty's thanks."

The translator had a touch of difficulty with some of the phrasing, which had no direct equivalent in isiZulu. Instead, he simply told the assembled warriors that they had the gratitude of the White Queen and they needed to be ready to fight again soon. The warriors all raised their spears in salute, shouting praises to both Queen Victoria and Lord Chelmsford.

Lance Corporal James Monroe watched the spectacle from a distance with mild amusement. With him was Private Thomas Walters, who was in his shirtsleeves, having been placed on light duty for a week by the camp doctor following his flogging. Though the scabs over the various cuts itched terribly, with a constant ache that required him to sleep on his stomach, the soldier's pride was far more wounded than his back. Sergeant Fredericks ordered Walters to assist Monroe with whatever he needed during his week of light duty. This was also because he wanted the lance corporal to keep a watchful eye on him. Walters' mourning for his friend, William Dunne, was compounded by his shame at failing in his duty to his mates.

"I've been in South Africa for just over a year," James recalled. "There are those back home, and here too, I suppose, who think one black-skinned kaffir is the same as the next. But those fellows are different."

"They've got guts," Walters concurred. "And they're certainly not afraid of the Zulus."

"After what the Zulus did to their families not half a mile from where we now stand, it's no wonder their hatred of their kinsmen outweighs any sense of fear."

The private simply nodded. Though four years older than the lance corporal and having been in Natal since the battalion's arrival in 1876, he was rather embarrassed to see that Monroe appeared to know far more about the indigenous peoples of the region than he did.

"How's the back?" James asked, changing the subject.

"It hurts, though not as much as my pride." The soldier lowered his head and stared at the ground.

Feeling a touch of impatience, the lance corporal grabbed him beneath the chin and forced him to look up. "Enough of that shit,"

271

he said. "Alright, so you fucked up. You paid the price, and it's done. You're not doing us any good, nor are you honouring Bill Dunne's memory by sulking around feeling sorry for yourself. Get your head sorted out. We're not done with these damned kaffirs, especially after what we learned about our mates from the 24th."

Walters bit the inside of his cheek, took a deep breath and nodded. "Thank you, lance corporal. I think I needed that."

"Sorting you lads out is what Her Majesty pays me for," James replied with a grin. He then remarked, "I'm sure Sergeant Fredericks will be briefing us after supper, but I understand we're leading a patrol along the Thukela tomorrow."

The weather played havoc on Colonel Pearson's plan to inform the column about Isandlwana, as the morning of Sunday, the 3rd of February, was met with yet another deluge of rain. The column-wide parade was cancelled, and it would be another day before Pearson could address his men. In the meantime, he penned a despatch to Chelmsford stating that if they left Eshowe now they would, *'Likely have the entire Zulu army on our backs and be compelled to either destroy our ammunition and stores at Eshowe or abandon them to the enemy during the march.'* He requested that the two companies from The Buffs, who had escorted the empty supply wagons back to Lower Drift, along with the five companies from the 99th still on the Natal side of the river, be sent at once to Eshowe. Pearson further recommended that twenty of the wagons he'd sent to Lower Drift be loaded with supplies and that the seven companies of infantry act as their escorts. He stressed that in order to maximise his combat power and lower his overall numbers, half the engineers, the Natal Pioneers, along with any wagon drivers and voorloopers not immediately needed would be sent back with the return convoy.

"Think this will earn his lordship's ire?" he asked, as he let Walker read the message.

"Does it matter?" his fellow colonel asked in turn. "Your responsibility is the safety of our men and the integrity of the column. Lord Chelmsford understands that the tactical situation drives our overall strategic objectives. You are doing right by making him fully aware of our situation and the practical dangers we face. I recommend you reiterate that we will follow his orders should he decide to overrule your council."

"Let us hope he sees reason. Otherwise, I might be up on charges of insubordination when all of this is over."

It was with remarkable speed that the iziGqoza warrior not only managed to sneak past the marauding bands of Zulu warriors between Eshowe and Lower Drift, but also make it to Rorke's Drift in three days. When informed that Lord Chelmsford was in Pietermaritzburg, he made the subsequent journey in just two more days. He arrived thoroughly exhausted, having deprived himself of sleep to reach his destination with all haste.

It turned out that Lord Chelmsford had sent a near-simultaneous despatch, reiterating his orders for Pearson to withdraw most of his column back to Lower Drift and leave a small garrison of about 600 soldiers at Eshowe. While he sympathised with Pearson's plight, the despatch from No. 1 Column changed nothing in Chelmsford's mind. He was further irritated when he received another message from Pearson stating the entire region was swarming with Zulus. He requested the GOC confirm his orders by the 16th so the column could begin its withdrawal. It was then that all communications ceased with the trapped garrison.

When an African runner returned to Pietermaritzburg empty-handed, having been chased by nearly a hundred Zulus five miles from Fort Tenedos, the GOC's irritation soon gave way to dread.

"By God, Crealock," Chelmsford said, to his ever-loyal chief staff officer. "It would seem we are facing an even greater potential disaster than Isandlwana."

"To be fair, my lord, I think Pearson may have been correct in his decision to remain and dig in," the colonel replied, though he too was filled with apprehension. "A hasty withdrawal would have required his leaving of provisions for the enemy, stretching our resources even further than they already are. And there is no guarantee that he would have made it to Lower Drift before being chased down by the entire Zulu *impi*. We have no idea where they've run off to since we last saw them."

The garrison at Eshowe was approximately the same size as that left at Isandlwana. The thought of adding 2nd Battalion of the 3rd Buffs, along with the companies from the 99th, Captain Wynne's sapper company, and the naval brigade to the already fearful death toll was unendurable. The only thing the two officers could take solace in was that Pearson's column was dug in behind strong earthworks, whereas Durnford and Pulleine had been caught out in the open.

Crealock made note of this. "Captain Wynne came to us highly recommended as an engineer officer," he remarked. "With the time he's had to build Eshowe into a stronghold, Cetshwayo would risk losing half his army, should he try to take it."

"But he doesn't need to take it," Chelmsford countered. "He only needs to invest it and prevent anything from entering or leaving. Which it seems he has now done. While I am put out that Colonel Pearson failed to withdraw his entire column to Lower Drift, at least he was prudent enough to send back all but essential combat troops to preserve their ration stores. We can only hope that they are able to hold long enough for us to form a relief column."

There were other British forces in Natal, and the colony was by no means helpless. However, there was still the very real issue of another potential uprising, especially considering the recent defeat at Isandlwana. The very reason for leaving Colonel Hugh Rowlands' No. 5 Column in Natal was to prevent another rebellion from the Xhosa, or other disgruntled provincials, while Chelmsford dealt with the Zulus. Now he would have to draw from these battalions in order to relieve the trapped No. 1 Column.

"At least we can assume Horse Guards will no longer deny us reinforcements," Crealock observed.

Chelmsford nodded. He'd sent his message to London on 27 January, yet he knew it could take up to two weeks for any despatch to reach the telegraph station on Madeira. The earliest he expected news of the disaster to reach Horse Guards was the 11th of February. Regardless of the umbrage he could expect to bear the brunt of, both from the General Staff as well as Her Majesty's government, he knew that, once at war, the British Empire was determined to see the matter through to whatever end. He'd specifically requested three entire regiments of infantry, two more of cavalry, and another field company of engineers. Given the time to hastily assemble sufficient troops and all their ammunition and stores, procure transport, and make the long journey to the Cape, he did not expect any waves of reinforcements to reach Natal until the first two weeks of March at the earliest.

Even after deciding which units already in Natal could be spared, the logistics involved had plagued the British Army since before the war began. Their greatest enemy now was time. Soldiers were garrisoned all over the Cape, some hundreds of miles away, and no rail system to speak of in Southern Africa. It would take weeks to assemble his forces at Lower Drift, possibly even longer than for fresh troops to arrive from Britain.

"We need Colonel Wood to take some of the pressure off both Glyn and Pearson," the GOC said, referring to the commanding officer of the northern No. 4 Column, who'd withdrawn his forces to Utrecht. He then dictated messages to both Wood and Colonel Rowlands ordering all troops near Utrecht be reassigned to No. 4 Column, who were to conduct raids and harassment operations, drawing the focus away from Rorke's Drift and Eshowe.

As he finished penning the despatches, which he gave to his lordship to sign, Lieutenant Colonel Crealock wondered if the general had gotten any sleep since the 22nd of January. Both men knew recriminations from London were forthcoming, quite possibly including the sacking of Lord Chelmsford and Sir Henry Bartle-Frere. To his credit, the GOC was less concerned about political reproaches and more with saving the lives of Colonel Pearson and No. 1 Column, who were now completely cut off and surrounded.

TRANSVAAL

SWAZI-
LAND

Rowlands

luneburg

Utrecht

Wood *Kambula*

Umkute

Bëmba's Kop

Buffalo *Blood* *Black*

White

Rorke's Drift *Isandlwana* *Ulundi*

Helpmekaar **Glyn**

Umfolozi

Klip

Z U L U L A N D

Tugela Ferry

Umhlatuzi

Pearson

Keate's Drift *Krantzkop* *Eshowe*

I N D I A N   O C E A N

Greytown *Tugela*

Mooi *Umvoti*

N A T A L

Chelmsford

Pietermaritzburg *Umgeni*

DURBAN

The distribution of British Forces following the Battle of Isandlwana

Political difficulties were not confined to the British. Within the
Zulu Kingdom the situation was extremely complicated. One of
King Cetshwayo's concerns was the Swazi Kingdom to the north.
Their young king, Mbandzeni, viewed British and Zulu alike as
potential rivals. Both had eyed his lands for annexation and he was

276

waiting to see who the eventual victor would be. Chelmsford was well-aware of the cool relations between the Swazi and Zulu; however, any hopes of the Swazi aiding him were dashed following Isandlwana. For the time being, Mbandzeni remained neutral, though he did pledge to allow King Cetshwayo to relocate over 5,000 head of cattle from the royal herds to his lands for protection.

The task of driving the remaining British forces from Zululand and destroying their garrison at Eshowe fell to Prince Dabulamanzi. The king's favoured brother was still reeling from the shock and disgrace following his utter failure to smash the garrison at kwaJimu. He was all-too-aware of how fortunate he was that this was not the age of their uncle, Shaka. Had one of the *great elephant's' amakhosi* so blatantly disobeyed his expressed orders, at the cost of hundreds of brave Zulu warriors, he would have been impaled in the royal kraal for all to see. That he not only lived but was allowed to lead the Zulu forces besieging the redcoats at Eshowe, angered and perplexed many within the Zulu nobility.

"Have Ntshingwayo or Mnyamana lead the *amabutho*! At least they know how to win a battle!" These derisive statements, among others, were muttered within the kraals of numerous *amakhosi*. Dabulamanzi was saved from even greater shame by having departed royal kraal at Ulundi so soon after informing his brother of the ill-fated attack on kwaJimu.

If the prince wished to storm the ramparts of Eshowe, he was prevented from doing so simply because he did not have the numbers necessary. The *impi* that attacked Isandlwana may have mustered 25,000 warriors; however, they were greatly diminished. The campaign against the British centre column had exhausted their strength. The Undi Corps, in particular, was completely shattered after its disastrous attack on Rorke's Drift. There was also the matter of the harvest, which most of the *amabutho* had returned home to attend to. When it came time to drive the remaining British forces from his lands, Dabulamanzi could only muster the 5,000 surviving warriors from Godide's *impi* plus an equal number from the Isandlwana regiments.

277

Chapter XXII: Shadows in the Night

Mounted Patrol, southeast of Eshowe
9 February 1879
***

Though he had felt it necessary to send the mounted troops back to Lower Drift along with the NNC, Colonel Pearson was now without any organised reconnaissance troops at Eshowe. Just prior to Captain Barrow's departure, Lieutenant Harry Rowden of the 99th Regiment volunteered to raise a section of mounted infantrymen. There had been no shortage of volunteers, particularly amongst the young soldiers of his regiment who were anxious for action, as well as the chance to escape the tedium of life in the fort.

In all, twenty men joined this detachment. Subalterns were directed to 'lend' their mounts, as sufficient horses were lacking. Some of the men had no riding experience at all, as was made evident the first time they tried pulling themselves into the saddle. Most fumbled with and dropped their weapons. A couple were nearly kicked by the fidgety horses.

"What the bleeding piss is this?" Sergeant Lewis, the section's loan NCO, said in disbelief to one soldier who had fallen out of the stirrups several times just trying to get mounted. "Haven't you ever ridden a horse before?"

"To be honest, sergeant, I'd never *seen* a horse until I joined the army," the private responded sheepishly.

Thankfully, not every member of the mounted Volunteers had departed Eshowe. A small detachment of eleven men under Captain Charles Shervinton of the NNC remained. An adventurer, explorer, and a self-proclaimed freelance mercenary, he and his brother, Tom, had come to South Africa several years earlier in search of fortune in the gold fields. Both men befriended George Shepstone, son of the colonial statesman, Sir Theophilus Shepstone, who most notably had successfully annexed the Transvaal for the British Empire two years before. George introduced the brothers to Anthony Durnford as well as Charles Pearson, who had taken a liking to both men. Because the brothers received a decent education in their youth and had a basic understanding of Queen's Regulations from prior service as volunteers in New Zealand, they were offered local commissions

278

during the raising of the auxiliary forces back in November. As Charles had served as an officer before, he was commissioned as a captain. His younger brother was made a lieutenant. Poor Tom had come down with typhoid fever prior to the column's crossing of the Thukela River and was languishing at the hospital at Fort Pearson.

Training for this new troop of mounted soldiers was haphazard even on the best of days. Captain Shervinton directed his more experienced Volunteers to pair up with the redcoats who had little to no riding experience. There were also insufficient bandoliers and carbines with scabbards available, so the regular army soldiers had to make do with their existing kit, while slinging their rifles across their backs.

The men of the 99th were so anxious to prove their mettle, they took the inevitable bruising falls with as much good humour as they could muster. What's more, Colonel Pearson ordered their formation to be permanent, at least until the end of the siege, therefore exempting the men from fatigue details and guard duty. Instead, they would mostly ride in groups of three or four, forming a screen of mounted picquets roughly 2,000 yards from the stronghold.

"They're not pretty, but they'll do the job," Lieutenant Colonel Welman said reassuringly, as he and Pearson watched the horsemen conduct mounted drill and manoeuvre.

"At least the column has eyes again," Charles acknowledged. He folded his arms across his chest and privately cursed his foolishness for sending away his best horsemen. He resisted the urge to chuckle as one hapless redcoat inexplicably fell sideways from his mount, landing in a puddle with a splash, much to the derision of his mates.

It was a warm yet overcast morning when Captain Shervinton led out a patrol of his mounted troops. They referred to themselves as 'Uhlans', after the German, Polish, and Russian lancer regiments. The title was a bold statement with just a touch of self-deprecating humour. Despite their rudimentary training and lack of numbers, they performed admirably during their early patrols, surprising the occasional band of Zulus who were quickly driven off each time, even when the patrols were but three or four men. Just having eyes well away from the stronghold was reassuring to those who lingered restlessly at Eshowe.

On this particular morning, the captain took six men to investigate suspected activity in the direction of a tall hill to the southeast. There were several stands of trees dotting its crest which

279

made the perfect place to post enemy scouts. The hill also served as a blind spot to the fort behind whose cover the Zulus could muster their forces for an attack.

"Spread out, lads," Shervinton ordered, as they approached the hill. He rode in the centre with Sergeant Lewis about twenty yards behind him.

The other four troopers rode in pairs on either side of them, keeping a distance of at least twenty to thirty yards from each other.

The hill appeared deserted, yet the hair on the back of the captain's neck stood up as his instincts told him otherwise. This was confirmed when a single shot rang out from near the crest. He and his men quickly fell from their mounts, finding cover behind rocks, fallen logs, or thick brush. One of the Volunteers cringed, realising they had not designated anyone as a horse-holder. They would be in serious trouble should their mounts bolt, leaving them alone to face an unknown number of enemy warriors.

The loud crack of musketry erupted from the heights, as about a dozen firearms opened fire on the tiny detachment. Though unable to see the Zulus, wisps of black powder smoke were clearly visible. The captain drew his pistol. The enemy marksmen were at least 200 yards up the hill, and he knew his weapon was practically useless. Sergeant Lewis and their soldiers were able to engage, however. As they returned fire, they intended to make good on the superior range and accuracy of their Martini-Henrys. Even the Swinburne-Henry carbines wielded by the Volunteers were infinitely superior to any firearms the Zulus possessed.

After a few exchanges of gunfire over the course of several tense minutes, a loud shout in Zulu echoed from a brush stand near the top of the hill.

"*Ayeke!*"

The enemy skirmishers, still unseen by their British foes, immediately ceased firing.

The same voice then called down in heavily accented English, "*Enemies of Zulu! We shall meet tomorrow!*"

All was then silent. Captain Shervinton and his men waited nervously. None wished to stand up in case it was simply a ruse to draw them out. At the same time, the officer knew they could not wait indefinitely. Taking a deep breath and composing himself, he stood boldly, gritting his teeth. He expected a salvo of Zulu bullets to rip his body to pieces. When all remained silent, he called for his men to retrieve their mounts and make ready to ride. Two of the horses, one which belonged to the 99th's adjutant, Lieutenant Davison, had sprinted away. Luckily, they were found together about half a mile back towards the fort. Shervinton quietly cursed and made a mental note to ensure that all future patrols had designated horse-holders, should they become compelled to fight on foot.

To the southwest of the fort, Lewis Coker and his Gatling crew had just finished washing some of their clothes which they hung from a tall brush stand. The sailors lit a small cooking fire to brew coffee and heat up their tinned beef.

The midshipman kept grabbing his field glasses and scanning in the direction of the rifle fire coming from the east. As it was several miles away, he could see nothing except the rolling grasslands and occasional stands of trees. "Dash it all," he muttered. "Who's out there having all the fun?"

"Patrol approaching, sir," a sailor said, drawing their attention to the west, where a Volunteer trooper and two mounted redcoats from another patrol were riding at a canter.

"Look alive, sir," the trooper said, as they rode up to the men. "I daresay the Zulus are becoming bold."

"You've seen them?" the young midshipman asked excitedly. "How many?"

"Several hundred, maybe a thousand," the horseman replied. "About two miles from here. And if those shots to the east are any inclination, you can bet they have friends lurking about."

"Splendid!" Coker said, rubbing his hands together. "That's enough to keep our Gatling busy for a few minutes, eh lads?"

The other sailors shouted their concurrence coupled with a few profane epithets towards the Zulus.

Boredom had become the greatest enemy of the naval brigade. Midshipman Coker drilled his crew daily, ordering their gun torn down and cleaned whether it needed it or not. So devoted was the midshipman to his sense of duty, that he almost never left the Gatling's position, even sleeping next to it. Commander Campbell was concerned for the eager lad's health. He had come down with a severe coughing fit that lasted several days. However, he soon recovered, no doubt in part due to the natural constitution of being eighteen years old. He took up his duties with renewed vigour.

"Well, come on, men!" he said excitedly. "Let's finish up here and make ready to send a few bullets their way, with Her Majesty's compliments!"

The sailors quickly finished their coffee and devoured their bland rations before dousing the cook fire. All but Coker grabbed their wet trousers and jackets from the bush and briskly made their way back into the fort. Much to the sailors' dismay, the Zulus spotted by the patrol never materialised, leading to another round of coarse profanity as the men expressed their disappointment.

Despite their enemy's reluctance to come within view of the defenders, the 'Uhlans' remained busy the rest of the day. Bands of warriors were spotted encroaching upon Eshowe from nearly every direction. It was impossible to get a definitive count on the enemy, yet their bold announcement to Captain Shervinton's small group of riders had put the garrison on high alert. There were several other engagements of mounted troops exchanging shots with Zulu skirmishers. The 'Uhlans' remained unscathed with a few claims of having seen enemy marksmen fall to their shots; though these were impossible to verify.

The day's skirmishes coupled with the bold threats from the Zulus that attacked Shervinton's patrol had raised the alarm at Eshowe. Picquets were withdrawn. Soldiers remained in their kit, taking their supper in the fort near their posts on the cramped ramparts. Nightfall came early, and it felt as if it were swallowing up the entire garrison.

Along the southwest corner near one of Lieutenant Lloyd's 7-pounder cannon, a faint glimmer was seen in the distance. The artillery officer checked his watch, seeing that it was about 9.00 p.m. Thankfully, the clouds were sporadic, allowing the moon and starlight to give the garrison some visual beyond the defence works and encircling trench.

"What do you make of it, sir?" the battery sergeant asked.

Lloyd raised his field glasses yet could not discern anything definitive. "Might be remnants of a campfire," he reasoned.

"Zulus!" a nearby sentry from G Company of The Buffs shouted.

Men on the ramparts loaded their weapons. As more alarms were sounded, the sleepless garrison scrambled to their positions. Soldiers were crammed nearly shoulder-to-shoulder, searching frantically in the darkness for any signs of the enemy.

"There they are!" another voice called, pointing in the direction of the faint glow. It was impossible to make out any definitive shapes; however, almost everyone agreed that they could see movement near a small fire.

The first loud bang from a Martini-Henry tore through the stillness of the night. Others soon followed. While soldiers all along the perimeter took the occasional shot at what they thought might be encroaching Zulus, most of the musketry was unleashed in the direction of the glowing embers where shapes could be seen dancing about. A stiff summer breeze blew the clouds of acrid smoke over the mission station. After a few minutes the firing ceased. Soldiers concentrated their gaze closer to the fort. They expected to see Zulus crawling up on their bellies at any moment.

"Sergeant, break out the case-shot," Lieutenant Lloyd directed.

"Sir."

The NCO saluted sharply and started to bark the orders that his gun crew had memorised since their earliest days in the Royal Artillery. Crewmen stood ready as the powder bag and 7-pound shot were brought to the gun. Before they could begin loading, however, a loud voice was heard bellowing, *"Cease fire! Cease fire!"*

It was Henry Parnell, who was relaying the order from the column commander. He and Welman were walking briskly along their respective battalions' sections of the line, while staff officers sought out the naval brigade and other troops.

Not surprisingly, Midshipman Coker was terribly disappointed at once again not being able to bring his Gatling into action. He ordered his crew to unload the weapon but be ready at a moment's notice.

"In the meantime, get some sleep," he said. The young officer turned and leaned against the gun, letting out a dissatisfied sigh as he stared into the empty darkness.

"What about you, sir?" his petty officer asked, walking up beside him.

Coker shook his head. "No, you and the lads go ahead. Doubt I'll be able to sleep tonight anyway. I might as well take first guard shift."

"But officers don't take sentry watch, sir…" The petty officer caught the annoyed glare from the midshipman before nodding in concurrence and finding his place beneath a tarp, where he hoped to catch a couple hours of sleep. Though ten years older than Coker, with much experience both at sea and during land expeditions, the midshipman was still his superior. The petty officer could advise, but he could not order Coker. Still, like Commander Campbell, he was concerned about the young man whose sense of duty was putting his health at risk.

As he adjusted himself onto his sleeping mat, he thought he heard Coker stifling a cough. The midshipman had just recently gotten over an illness. If he did not get some sleep, he would be unable to fight off a recurrence. And yet, the petty officer's mind was numb with fatigue. He reckoned he would speak to his officer in the morning. Thankfully, there were no more alarms, and he managed about three hours of sleep before reveille.

Dawn came, and a series of reinforced patrols were ordered to scout the area for any Zulu casualties. A and G Companies of The Buffs and fifty sailors from the naval brigade conducted a sweep from the southeast to the southwest. The redcoats and 'Jack Tars' formed a long skirmish line, maintaining ten to twelve feet between each soldier and sailor. All was desolate with no signs of the Zulus at all; no blood trails, drag marks, not even a discarded assegai or knobkerrie.

A group of soldiers from A Company soon approached the still smouldering remnants of Midshipman Coker's cook fire from the previous day. A few embers were still glowing. This was likely the source of the faint glow the previous night.

A sergeant broke into a fit of laughter. "There's your Zulus, lads!" He shouted towards the men from G Company, as he pointed towards the thicket where a sailor's jacket and trousers hung. They were riddled with bullet holes.

"Blast it all," Lewis Coker was heard saying from just behind the line. He stood with his sword drawn and resting over his shoulder. Letting out a sigh, he muttered, "So much for my spare jacket and trousers."

Despite the much-needed levity at the fate of poor Midshipman Coker's laundry, and with no further sign of the Zulus, the garrison remained at 'stand-to' for much of the day. By the following morning, tedium began to set in once more.

Chapter XXIII: An Unseen Enemy

Eshowe
11 February 1879

A Colour Sergeant from 2/3rd 'Buffs' Regiment

The cramped conditions and extreme variances in weather played havoc upon the health of the garrison at Eshowe. Thirty were laid up in the makeshift hospital; one of the only tents allowed to be erected within the claustrophobic fort. Most of these suffered from terrible diarrhoea which Colonel Pearson feared would soon lead to dysentery. At Surgeon Norbury's suggestion, on days when the weather was cooperative, the sick were carried to the ramparts, so that they might take in some fresh air. Unfortunately, cooperative weather proved difficult to come by.

The 11th of February marked a dark day for the British garrison. Three more soldiers had died from either fever or dysentery, despite the best efforts to keep conditions as sanitary as possible. Cess pits were dug along the outer entrenchments and filled in daily. Designated urine barrels were placed along the edge of the stronghold, which were also emptied each day. And yet, it simply was not enough. Being crammed together each night with little shelter, facing extreme changes in the weather, and the incessant plague of flies and ticks, it seemed every soldier and sailor in the garrison was suffering from one form of ailment or another.

The air was heavy, the sky thick with black clouds, as the three poor soldiers who'd succumbed were laid to rest. Again, there were no coffins, only a blanket to wrap their bodies in. The dead men's mates took it upon themselves to dig the graves, their pickaxes and shovels bringing up thick clumps of clay and mud. Colonel Pearson had expressly forbidden the firing of volleys over the graves. Not only was he concerned they might need every bullet before the siege was over, but if the Zulus were familiar with British burial practices, he did not wish to publicly announce that their siege was working, and imperial redcoats were dying.

"Of course, any of their spies within half a mile of here can see us digging graves," he said quietly to Colonel Walker, as they watched the small burial service.

Reverend Robertson led the mourners in prayer and read a few verses from the Psalms.

"Four men we've lost since coming here," Charles continued. "Not from Zulu spears or musketry but from damned disease."

"You were at Sevastopol, weren't you?" Walker asked.

Pearson nodded. "Yes, except then we were the besiegers. I was just a boy, not much older than Midshipman Coker. I often wondered how maddening it was for the Russian garrison once we finally invested the city. How helpless they must have felt, knowing all they could do was wait and hope we would break before them." As Reverend Robertson finished leading the mourning soldiers in prayer, Charles turned to his second. "We need to draw the Zulus into a fight. And if they won't attack, then we'll start laying waste to the country."

Conditions were only marginally better for those forces remaining at Lower Drift. While three of their fellow soldiers were being laid to rest at Eshowe, David Fredericks was acting as sergeant-of-the-guard for his company's section of the defences near the Lower Drift pont. Of the twenty men who should have been on sentry duty, nearly a third were absent at any time, having hurriedly made their way to relieve their tortured bowels.

It was around 11.00 in the morning, the thick clouds having mercifully blown away towards the northwest. David was checking the sentries when he saw one rather pale and befuddled soldier returning to his post. His face was white and sweat dripped down his cheeks, despite it being an overcast and surprisingly mild day. The private was using his rifle to help pull himself up the ramparts; every step seemed to exhaust him.

"Private Rutledge," David said, walking briskly over to the man.

"Sergeant," the soldier replied, standing erect and bringing his heels together. He swallowed hard as the NCO stood about two feet away, looking him over.

David lifted the man's jaw and looked into his bloodshot eyes. "How many trips to the latrine have you made today, private?"

"Four or five, sergeant. Can't remember for certain. Had the shits bad for a few days now."

The sergeant nodded and waved the man to take up his post. He then found his runner and ordered him to find Lance Sergeant Robert Anderson, who was Private Rutledge's section leader. It took about an hour for the soldier to find him returning from a patrol west of the drift. Despite the close proximity which the company found itself in each night, it had been at least a week since David had spoken to his former assistant section leader.

"Sergeant Fredericks," Robert said with a good-natured grin. He removed his helmet and wiped his forearm across his sweaty brow.

David was not smiling. "That man needs to be taken off guard duty and sent to Surgeon-Major Tarrant."

"What's wrong with him?" the lance sergeant asked, confused.

"Aside from being severely dehydrated, and spending more time shitting his guts out than on duty, you mean?"

Robert's expression turned serious. He shouldered his rifle and walked over to where Private Rutledge leaned against the ramparts. They spoke a few words quietly, and the lance sergeant placed a hand on the man's forehead. He then called down to one of his soldiers, *"Private Morris! Get up here and replace Rutledge, at the double!"*

The severity in his tone told Private Morris something was amiss. And though he quietly grumbled at having to go onto guard duty right after a patrol, the soldier slung his rifle and scaled the earthworks to replace his mate. Another private from Anderson's section was detailed to help the sick man make his way to the hospital tent. The lance sergeant gritted his teeth when David nodded for him to follow him away from the ramparts.

"Why would you put a man on the cusp of dysentery on sentry duty?" the sergeant asked, once they were out of earshot from the other soldiers.

"He assured me he was fine this morning," Robert replied, though his voice lacked conviction. "I even asked him if he needed to go to hospital. Damn it all, there is scarcely a man in my entire section that hasn't been shitting his guts out at one time or another these past two weeks, including me."

"Of course, a soldier is going to tell you he's fine, even when he's not," David countered. "Weakness is not tolerated in Her Majesty's forces, and neither is negligence. As non-commissioned officers it is our responsibility to determine when a tough countenance becomes foolhardy. Damn it, Rob, you know better! The lads do us no good if they wind up dead from dysentery or fever, and I suspect Private Rutledge may have both. Disease is already wreaking havoc upon the column. We cannot allow any of our men to fall victim because we failed to look after them."

Robert nodded, biting the inside of his cheek in frustration and shame. It was true that he had asked Private Rutledge every morning over the past three days if he was fit for duty, and the young man had assured him that he was. The lance sergeant had known better, particularly on this day. The right thing would have been to order the soldier to go see Surgeon-Major Tarrant and have him replaced on sentry duty. The sound of a rifle volley startled him; a sombre reminder of the funeral service for another soldier from the column. He was being laid to rest at the cemetery near Fort Pearson.

David motioned in the direction of the firing. "That sound is something I pray neither of us has to hear for one of our own soldiers."

The only soldiers within the entire column to engage in any meaningful action against the Zulus were Captain Shervinton's 'Uhlans'. The day after their encounter with the enemy, they approached the same hill to the southeast and again came under fire. Given its location and elevation, it was plain the Zulus were using it as one of their chief reconnaissance posts. The NNC officer appealed to Colonel Pearson for infantry support for his next patrol. However, due to its distance from the fort, the column commander was unwilling to risk his riflemen in an excursion.

"Their harassment of your patrols could be an attempt to lure our men into a trap," he explained to the distressed captain. "For all we know, there could be an entire regiment lurking just behind that hill. Before I can commit our infantry to any operations in the area, I need to know more about the enemy's strength and what they are doing. That is what you are here for, captain."

Shervinton came to attention, saluted, and took his leave. The adventurous officer returned to his men and asked for volunteers. A corporal from the NNC named Adams, four redcoats from the 99th, and a loan trooper originally from the Victoria Mounted Rifles stepped forward.

"We need to know what the Zulus are doing," Shervinton explained. "And I suspect they are conducting most of their manoeuvres at night. Rest up today, lads. We leave after dark."

Though he would not authorise the use of his regular infantry, Colonel Pearson allowed Captain Shervinton to take some of his own men in a night mission towards the troublesome hill. He reckoned that should they get into trouble, the 'Uhlans' at least had their mounts to make their getaway.

It had rained for part of the afternoon. As the small detachment rode into the clutching darkness, they silently prayed that they would remain dry. There were only moderate clouds, yet all knew the weather during the Southern African summer could turn foul very quickly. Of equal concern to the captain was the possibility that the Zulus had left warriors on the hill. He thought this unlikely, as their own camps were probably several miles from the fort. Before he could gather any meaningful intelligence about the enemy's movements, he needed to first deprive them of use of this position.

At the base of the hill, near the same spot where he and his men had first encountered enemy skirmishers a few days before, Shervinton ordered his men to dismount. There was a small stand of trees nearby which sufficed to tether their horses. He hoped that should they find a larger force of Zulus than they could handle, they could reach their mounts in time.

All was deathly silent as they began the climb; rifles and carbines held ready. Setting the example, the captain took the lead, walking about ten feet ahead of his small band of volunteers. Near the summit they found a series of large rocks, previously unseen from below. The smell of spent black powder still lingered in the air, telling them this was at least one of the positions from which the Zulus had engaged them.

"A perfect firing position," Corporal Adams whispered. "Can't even see it from below, yet they can see for miles from up here."

They continued to scour the hill, each man holding his weapon ready as they searched behind every tree, rock, and brush stand. There was nothing to be found. The smell of burnt powder was the only sign that the Zulus had been there. Forming a semicircle towards the southeast, the small band waited with bated breath for the coming of daylight.

It was just before dawn, the faint glow of the imminent sun illuminating the ground, when they spotted their quarry. A group of eight Zulus, all carrying muskets, were making their way up the slope. That they were so few confirmed Shervinton's suspicions. This was a harassing tactic by the Zulus rather than part of a larger plan to draw the British into an ambush.

As quietly as they were able, each man loaded and leaned into his weapon using the rocks for support. The false glow of the predawn made it difficult to gage their exact distance, and so they waited. The sound of a twig snap, most likely from a wild animal about twenty yards from the British position, alerted the Zulus. They quickly raised their muskets, searching for any signs of their foe.

Fearing they'd been compromised, Shervinton fired his weapon. The rest of his men immediately followed suit. They quickly reloaded, loosing several volleys in the direction of the small band of warriors. The captain had watched one man fall, struck in the shoulder during the first salvo. Another warrior cried out as a chunk of flesh was torn from his thigh. As the Zulus tried to drag their friends away, a third man was shot in the side. He dropped his musket, clutching at the painful wound, which fortunately for him was little more than a graze. Two of the Zulus returned fire in the direction of their assailants, while the remainder helped their wounded companions back down the hill.

The small British detachment waited for any of their foes to return, yet all was silent. By the time Shervinton and his men made their way down to where they had spotted the Zulus, they were long out of sight. The splattering of blood told of the effects of their shooting.

"A pity we didn't do more than simply clip them," Corporal Adams said with disappointment, as he kicked a chunk of torn flesh.

"I was hoping to take at least one of them alive," the captain said, with equal displeasure. Any intelligence gathered from enemy prisoners would prove invaluable, especially since the column had been blind to the Zulus' strength and disposition since first crossing the Thukela a month prior.

"I doubt they'll be coming up here again," Adams reasoned with a shrug.

Satisfied they'd successfully completed their mission, Charles Shervinton and his men rode back to Eshowe. Having heard the sounds of musketry, the garrison was turned out with soldiers manning the ramparts in force once more. The order was soon given to stand down. The captain made his way over to Colonel Pearson, who was waiting for him by the south entrance.

Shervinton explained all that had transpired throughout the night and their skirmish with the Zulus.

"A pity you were unable to capture any of them," Pearson remarked, echoing the captain's disappointment.

"Yes, sir. We may have confirmed what I've suspected for about a week now."

"And that is?" the colonel asked.

"The Zulus don't mean to attack us, sir," Shervinton surmised. "I don't think they have the numbers for it. Mind you, there are hundreds of them out there, maybe even a couple thousand. But it is the time of the harvest. I suspect Cetshwayo has disbanded his regiments, that they might return home to take in the mealie crop. And after what happened at Rorke's Drift, I doubt any of their *izinduna* are too keen on attacking a fortified position. They've left just enough warriors in the region to harass and prevent us from leaving."

"Let's keep this between us for now," the colonel directed. "I suspect you may be right. That would explain why the Zulus have not done more to attack your patrols. But we need more information. Widen the arc of your searches, captain. We know so little about this region. There may be Zulu kraals and homesteads as yet unknown to

292

us. The men need a real mission, a chance to take the fight to the enemy."

At Lower Drift there was much excitement as word reached the garrison that Lord Chelmsford himself was coming to inspect the troops and defences. Many of the younger enlisted soldiers took this to mean that an expedition to relieve their friends at Eshowe was imminent. In anticipation of this, Brevet Lieutenant Colonel Coates ordered the men of the 99th and The Buffs to parade the day before. This was redundant, as soldiers paraded and were inspected twice a day by their respective officers and NCOs. There was little to be done about the ragged state of their uniforms, particularly among The Buffs, though they were told to at least have them washed in the river. Even the bright crimson jackets of the 99th were starting to fade. Though they had stubbornly kept their Foreign Service helmets white, with their brass plates still affixed, these were mostly streaked with mud, grass, and other various stains. And yet, despite the slovenly appearance of the soldiers, their weapons and kit were nearly immaculate.

Colour Sergeant Bennet explained, "It matters little if our lads look like paupers, so long as their weapons function and their kit is in order."

On the morning of the 12th, his lordship and all his staff arrived at Lower Drift. They were met by Lieutenant Colonel Coates, who asked the GOC when he wished for the men to be ready for parade.

"That won't be necessary," Chelmsford replied. His eyes were red, his face pale from the weeks of stress and lack of sleep. Given the disaster that had befallen the No. 3 Column, not to mention his lordship's own brush with death, this was scarcely surprising.

The GOC then made a short inspection of the defences at Fort Pearson. As this was on the Natal side of the river, and with no Zulu incursions expected anywhere along the Thukela River, Chelmsford only gave a cursory inspection. He spoke briefly with the sergeant-of-the-guard and a few of the enlisted soldiers before leading his entourage down to the pont the naval detachment had ready for him.

"Fortunately, the Thukela provides us with a natural defensive barrier," Coates asserted, as the men stepped onto the pont. "We send patrols along the river every day; however, my lord, I can assure you there isn't a suitable crossing point anywhere between here and Middle Drift."

These words brought a small measure of comfort to the GOC, though he made no mention of it. With his invasion plans in tatters, one of Chelmsford's gravest concerns was the defence of Natal. Simply put, he did not have the numbers to man the entire stretch of the vast border between the British colony and the Zulu Kingdom. Enemy incursions had occurred along the uMzinyathi River in the vicinity of Rorke's Drift, yet the Thukela region appeared relatively secure.

His lordship's military secretary, Lieutenant Colonel John Crealock, had his sketch pad out and made a few quick scrawls of what he could see along the drift as the pont was pulled across by a score of men from the naval detachment.

Upon reaching the Zulu side, Crealock's face twitched, as he cast his gaze upon the entrenchments and earthworks that made up Fort Tenedos. "By God, sir, look at it," he said, not bothering to hide the disdain in his voice. "Could Pearson have chosen a worse piece of ground?"

"I beg your pardon," Lieutenant Colonel Coates spoke up.

Crealock sneered at him. "Come now, colonel. Don't tell me that you, as an infantry officer, cannot see why the position of this fort is terrible. It is completely exposed to enemy fire from that hill not 300 yards off!"

"Fortunately for us, Zulu muskets can't reach 300 yards," Coates countered.

"Fortunately for you, the Zulus have not invested this place," Crealock shot back. "Otherwise we'd have several hundred more dead imperial soldiers and sailors, not to mention losing the one foothold we have in Zululand."

Lord Chelmsford, who had remained silent up to this point, gently placed a hand on his secretary's shoulder, ending the argument. At first glance he concurred with Crealock's assessment, but there was little to be gained by having two of his officers publicly squabble in such an undignified manner. "Colonel Coates," he said. "You will place a reinforced picquet atop that hill."

"Yes, my lord," Coates replied, feeling defeated and embarrassed.

"Also, I will require a mounted escort to accompany me north. If we are to reinforce Colonel Pearson at Eshowe, then I need to have a look at the lay of the land."

"Very good, sir."

Chapter XXIV: You're All Highlanders!

Barracks of the 91ˢᵗ Highlanders, Aldershot, England
11 February 1879

The Wellington Statue at Aldershot

The 11ᵗʰ of February was not just a day of turmoil for Her Majesty's forces in Natal, but also for the Queen herself, her government, and the British public at large. There was no hiding it anymore. Lord Chelmsford's despatches regarding the invasion and disaster at Isandlwana had at last reached London. Cries of sorrow came from the families of the dead as papers reported the calamity. The Army staff at Horse Guards, along with the Prime Minster and members of Parliament, were filled with outrage. Over a thousand British soldiers were dead, in a war that the Crown had neither authorised nor was even made aware of until nearly three weeks after the last shots were fired at Isandlwana.

As a means of salving the emotional wounds brought on by the needless loss of life, much praise was given, both in the Houses of Parliament and in the press, regarding the heroic defence of Rorke's Drift. The names John Chard and Gonville Bromhead were echoed throughout the officers' mess of every regiment, as well as in Whitehall. Even the names of heroic private soldiers such as Henry

Hook, John Williams, and Frederick Hitch were becoming known to the British public. Little, if any, mention was given to No. 1 Column's victory at Inyezane.

A great cause for concern, which only helped motivate the urgent call for reinforcements, was the siege at Eshowe. If Colonel Pearson's garrison failed to hold off the Zulus long enough for a sufficient relief force to arrive, 2nd Battalion of The Buffs and most of the 99th Regiment would soon be added to the already unacceptable death toll.

There was also a rather delicate political situation. Prime Minister Disraeli and the entire cabinet were furious with Sir Henry Bartle-Frere and Lord Chelmsford, with many calls in Parliament for their immediate sacking. The entire situation was of great embarrassment to Her Majesty, for Queen Victoria was a close personal friend of Chelmsford's. Though she never made her feelings known publicly, there could be little doubt the Queen shared in her ministers' anger.

There was, however, a practical impediment to immediately replacing the General Officer Commanding in Natal. Simply put, there was no one to replace him. With the war in Afghanistan, every officer of sufficient rank was already deployed on active service. And if three more infantry regiments were to be sent to the Cape, with an undetermined number of cavalry and other assets, an officer holding at minimum the rank of lieutenant general was needed. The only possible candidate was General Sir Garnet Wolseley. However, he was currently High Commissioner of Cyprus, a territory whose annexation the British Empire had achieved just nine months earlier.

Despite the indignant rage felt by the prime minister and the senior generals at Horse Guards, an immediate decision was made to send three regiments of infantry to Southern Africa with all haste. Lord Chelmsford would have his reinforcements after all.

It was a brisk and drizzly evening when the despatch rider from Horse Guards arrived at Aldershot, forty miles southwest of London. Commonly known as *'The Home of the British Army'*, Aldershot Garrison became the first permanent training camp for Her

Majesty's Forces during the Crimean War. It had also recently become home to the venerable 91st Highlanders.

A single-battalion regiment, its full name since 1871 was the *91st (Princess Louise's Argyllshire Highlanders) Regiment of Foot*. A Scottish regiment, made famous for their distinctive kilts and tartan trousers, they fell under the command of Lieutenant Colonel James Buchanan Kirk. Having spent many years overseas, as well as on Home Service at various depots throughout Britain, they were finally given permanent billets at Aldershot on New Year's Day.

The relocation of an entire regiment was fraught with personnel and logistical issues. In addition to having only arrived six weeks before, with much equipment and stores to still be sorted, they were terribly understrength. Between its eight line companies and staff, a battalion of foot was authorised nearly a thousand soldiers. However, on the evening of 11 February 1879, the 91st Highlanders had just 562 total officers and other ranks.

The messenger—a captain from the Royal Dragoons—dismounted and tethered his horse outside the officers' mess. There were only about a dozen men seated around the long table. As approximately half of the regiment's officers were married, many chose to spend evenings with their families. Others had taken a period of leave while the regiment relocated itself.

One man who had joined his brother officers for supper was Captain Robert Lyttle, the officer commanding for A Company. Slightly shorter with an average build, he'd served with the Regiment for just over seventeen years. He also possessed a thick, bushy moustache that he was particularly proud of. His brother officers often complimented him on his martial and 'manly' appearance. Ironically, his wife, Jane, hated it, though they had long since reached a compromise. Robert would keep his thick moustache so long as he promised to never grow a beard, not even while on overseas service.

The dragoon captain strode into the dining hall just as the main course of roast duck was being served.

"Stranger in the mess!" one of the officers called out

"Announce yourself," Lieutenant Colonel Kirk demanded, from his place at the head of the table.

"Captain Sullivan, 1st Royal Dragoons," the man replied, coming to attention. "I bring an urgent message from Horse Guards for Colonel Kirk."

The battalion commander held out his hand, accepting the sealed envelope, which he almost casually tore open as the cavalry officer stood close by. The other officers continued in their dinner banter, though Captain Lyttle kept his gaze fixed upon his commanding officer, gauging his demeanour. His expression remained unchanged, yet Lyttle thought he could see Kirk's face turn ashen.

"When did Horse Guards receive Lord Chelmsford's telegram?" the colonel asked.

"Only this morning, sir," Sullivan replied.

Kirk stood and gently struck his table knife against his wine glass several times. His fellow officers were immediately silent, now finding their curiosity piqued at the despatch brought from Horse Guards.

"Gentlemen," the colonel began. "It is my duty to inform you, as of the 11th of January, the British Empire has been at war with the Kingdom of the Zulus. By order of Field Marshal, His Royal Highness, the Duke of Cambridge, the 91st Highlanders are to prepare for an immediate departure for South Africa. We will be joining the 57th Regiment and 60th Rifles in reinforcing those forces in Natal under the command of Lord Chelmsford. A call has been sent out for volunteers to fill our ranks. We have until the 19th of this month to be ready for war."

Captain Lyttle shot a glance across the table to the Regiment's senior logistics officer who was glumly staring at his plate. Quartermaster James Gillies was that most unusual species of officer who came up from the ranks. Having earned his commission while the Regiment was posted to Edinburgh a few years before, he understood all-too-well the needs of the men in the ranks. He also knew the often-times extreme difficulty in procuring sufficient kit, rations, weapons, ammunition, and stores even under the best of conditions. He met Lyttle's gaze, and the captain nodded reassuringly. Though logistics were ultimately the quartermaster's responsibility, Robert Lyttle knew that Gillies would need the help of every man in the 91st to sort and inventory each piece of equipment they would need for the upcoming expedition.

Immediately following supper, Lieutenant Colonel Kirk met with his two battalion majors. Their adjutant, Lieutenant James St

299

Clair, was on leave in Edinburgh and would have to be recalled with all haste.

"We have just one week to fill our ranks with replacements and be ready to sail," Kirk explained.

Kirk's senior battalion major was forty-five-year-old Alexander Cunningham Bruce, a highly experienced officer who'd served twenty-seven years with the Colours. The other, Major William Gurney, was two years Bruce's junior. Both men had seen their commanding officer walking with a slight limp as of late and had grown concerned over his health. They suspected James Kirk had something else he wished to discuss in private with them.

"Well, gentlemen," he said. "I confess I had wished to wait until a better time to inform you of this, but there is no sense in delaying any longer. I am afraid I will not be accompanying you to South Africa."

"Is it because of your foot, sir?" Gurney asked. "I thought perhaps you'd just taken a tumble from your horse."

"If only that were the case. It is with profound regret that I must tell you the doctors have found a cancerous growth in my foot. It has spread rapidly, and the surgeon believes amputation is the only recourse."

"When will you have this done, sir?" Major Bruce asked, their pending deployment to the Cape momentarily forgotten. He was genuinely concerned for his commanding officer, who'd also been a friend and mentor to him for the better part of his career.

"Soon," the colonel replied. "Though I will wait until after the Regiment departs. I'll not have the lads see me legless and crippled." Kirk's eyes were filled with sadness. The issues of his affliction were compounded by the knowledge that his Regiment was being called to war, while he was obliged to remain in England. He quickly regained his stoic demeanour and stood tall, addressing his senior battalion major, whose promotion to lieutenant colonel he knew to be imminent.

"Major Bruce, once you leave for South Africa, the Regiment will be yours."

Captain Lyttle slept little that night. He knew he had much to do in a very short time to get his affairs in order. The first thing he did was pen a message to his wife. She was still in Edinburgh and hadn't expected to join the Regiment in Aldershot for another month. They had two children, Carol and Anthony, who were nine and seven. Robert longed to see them before he left. There was no way of knowing how long the conflict with the Zulus would last. Plus, there was the very real possibility that the Regiment would be left in Southern Africa or dispatched to another corner of the Empire in the aftermath. It could be several months or several years before he saw his family again. That is, if he wasn't killed in battle or died of any number of diseases prevalent in Natal.

As he finished the letter to Jane, he took some solace from Lieutenant Colonel Kirk's reassurance that a rider would be sent to Edinburgh in the morning. Many of the families that had yet to relocate to Aldershot were still there; as was the battalion adjutant, who they needed to get a message to. God willing, he would have some time to spend with his wife and children before he left, even if it was just a couple hours.

This was most certainly not his first time on Foreign Service. Robert first joined the Regiment in 1861 as an eighteen-year-old ensign. He'd been dispatched with a draft of replacements to join the 91st in India. Though he missed taking part in suppressing the Indian Rebellion, he spent the next seven years in the subcontinent. It was here that he and Jane were married, and Carol was born. Of his seventeen years in the Regiment, Robert Lyttle had spent all but four with A Company. Those four years were on the regimental staff as battalion adjutant, after which he returned to A Company in the spring of 1873. The timing proved ideal, as its previous officer commanding, William Gurney, was appointed battalion major. Lyttle received his long-awaited captaincy soon after and took command of his old company with relish.

Due to the discharges of his time-expired soldiers, and the inability of recruiting officers and sergeants to keep up with demand, by February 1879 there were only sixty-two men in A Company. Twenty-five were new soldiers with less than a year with the Colours. Even his non-commissioned officers were fairly young. Only one of the sergeants, Douglas McIntyre, was over the age of

301

thirty. The youngest was just twenty-one. He was further hampered by his complete lack of subalterns.

Where A Company did have ample experience was in its colour sergeant, a hulking mass of humanity named Stanley Clinton. The sixth son of a clerk from Glasgow, he joined the Army as a 'Boy' at the age of fourteen during the immediate aftermath of the Indian Rebellion. Even then he required the largest uniform the quartermaster could find to fit over his mammoth frame. He was also quite fit, never seeming to tire on company marches or runs, while said to possess the strength of ten men. Some of the soldiers took to calling him, *Goliath's Big Brother*. Now into his twentieth year with the Regiment, he was a year younger, albeit nearly a foot taller, than his officer commanding. His very presence was enough to inspire, as well as terrify, his soldiers. As intelligent and well-educated as he was massive, Captain Lyttle often said it was a shame he would never be considered to become an officer. With the lack of subalterns in the company, many of their tasks were shared between the captain and colour sergeant, with Lyttle noting that Stanley Clinton was as capable as any one holding the Queen's Commission. On one occasion the officer commanding admitted with surprising candour, "It is a shame that who one's parents were is more important than intellect or talent when it comes to earning the Queen's Commission."

The morning of the 12th saw the military town at Aldershot become a chaotic mass of activity. In just a day, despatches had been sent to eleven different regiments on Home Service, directing each to send volunteers to fill the Highlander ranks. A telegram had reached the adjutant, Lieutenant St Clair, in Edinburgh. He was expected to return that evening by train. Captain Lyttle had little time to think about his family. He hoped they received his letter soon and could take a train down within the next few days. His entire focus now was on readying his company for war. Lieutenant Colonel Kirk ordered the entire battalion paraded on the morning of the 12th, where he read to them the orders from the Duke of Cambridge. This was met with much excitement by the younger soldiers in the Regiment, especially those who'd yet to see active service. They were especially eager for 'adventure' and the chance for glory.

Numerous messengers began arriving at Aldershot bearing the rolls from each regiment tasked with sending volunteers. The task then fell to the adjutant and his assistants to sort the names into each company. By the evening of the 13th, two days after receiving their initial orders, Robert Lyttle and Stanley Clinton met to review the list of replacements.

"Forty-five volunteers for A Company alone," Colour Sergeant Clinton noted. "That will put us at full strength; a first for this company, I think."

There was a touch of apprehension on his captain's face. "So many of our lads are new to the Army. I cannot help but wonder how many of these are babies straight out of recruit training."

"Impossible to say, sir. We only know their names, ranks, and current regiments. And it would seem they're all privates…oh, except this one at the top. Looks like we're finally getting a subaltern."

"Lieutenant William Craufurd," Lyttle read aloud.

"Unusual spelling of his surname," Clinton noted with a furrowed brow. "You don't suppose he's related to General Craufurd?"

The man he referred to was James Robertson Craufurd. A 75-year old retired general, he was named Colonel of the 91st Argyllshire Highlanders nine years earlier.

"Could be his grandson," the captain said. "Doesn't matter. We'll get plenty of work out of him, regardless."

The two spent the rest of the evening meeting with their sergeants and corporals, assigning the new volunteers to their respective sections.

The question regarding their new subaltern was answered early the next morning. It was just after 5.00; an hour before reveille. Captain Lyttle had just finished dressing and was inspecting his uniform in a full-length mirror when there was a sharp knock on his door.

"Enter," he said, adjusting his collar.

An officer wearing the uniform of the Grenadier Guards walked into the room, stopped a few feet from the captain, and came to attention. "Lieutenant Craufurd, reporting for duty, sir!"

Robert took a moment to make a final few adjustments to his tunic before turning to appraise the man. He was slightly taller than average and well-built. His hair was neatly combed, moustache trimmed, and uniform immaculate.

"Stand easy, Mister Craufurd." After a moment's pause he asked, "Are you by chance any relation to General Craufurd?"

The lieutenant gave an almost imperceptible nod. "My great-uncle, sir. I confess, it was he who secured my commission with the Grenadier Guards…"

"And your posting with the Highlanders," Lyttle finished for him.

The young officer appeared almost embarrassed by this. "Yes, sir."

"How old are you, Mister Craufurd?"

"Twenty-six, sir. I've held the Queen's Commission for seven years, though regrettably never on active service. I do, however, know my duties as subaltern quite well and view my possessing the name *Craufurd* as a great responsibility, as well as a privilege."

"Indeed." Robert extended his hand. "Glad to have you with us, Mister Craufurd."

Over the next few days, small groups of redcoats arrived at the garrison, first reporting to the regimental headquarters. Runners would then send for the designated representatives from each company tasked with fetching their new soldiers. When asked about new uniforms, not to mention the distinctive tartan trousers worn by the 91st Highlanders, they were told that until the annual uniform re-issue in April, they would continue to wear the uniforms and kit they'd already been issued. In all, 374 volunteers from eleven different regiments flocked to Aldershot to join the 91st. As expected, the vast majority were new recruits; many had not even finished their basic musketry drills.

As he held parade for his own A Company, Captain Lyttle's face twitched at the sight of so many different uniforms, not to mention boyish faces, within his formation. Of the 107 men who stood at attention before him, nearly half were brand new volunteers.

"I'll be damned if a single one of them is over nineteen," he muttered quietly, as Colour Sergeant Clinton and his section leaders conducted morning inspection.

"When a regiment is told to send volunteers, they are unlikely to send their best and most experienced," Lieutenant Craufurd whispered back.

"I hope that's not true of the Grenadier Guards," Lyttle added.

Both men stifled a chuckle.

Within the regiments posted throughout Britain, there was certainly no shortage of soldiers anxious for adventure overseas. However, any volunteers needed to first receive the recommendation of their company commanders, and then approval from their regimental colonel. As most regiments were understrength, the orders from each to send so many volunteers to those deploying to the Cape was likely met with protest. And as Lieutenant Craufurd astutely noted, no commanding officer was keen to give up his most experienced soldiers.

"Company, 'shun!" The booming voice of Colour Sergeant Clinton snapped the captain out of his reverie. Clinton then did a sharp about-turn and waited for his officer commanding

Captain Lyttle walked over, exchanged salutes with his senior non-commissioned officer, and took charge of the formation. "Stand at ease!" He paced back and forth, a few steps from the lead rank of the company. "When others look at you, they see young boys. They see many different uniforms worn by lads who've never laid eyes on the highlands of Scotland. When *I* look at you, I see soldiers of the Crown; men who will soon be risking their lives in a faraway land for Queen and Empire. Know that I don't give a damn about your age, what regiment you came from, or whether you're Scottish, English, Welsh, or Irish. From this day forth, you're all Highlanders!"

It was on the morning of the 18th of February, the air crisp and a thick frost on the ground, that the entire 91st Highlanders paraded before Field Marshal Prince George, the Duke of Cambridge. The Commander-in-Chief of the Forces was keen to inspect the various regiments before they departed for South Africa. He was joined by the 91st's Regimental Colonel, retired General James Craufurd.

Standing with the Duke and General Craufurd, while taking the salute of his battalion, was Lieutenant Colonel Kirk. Though his visage was one of unbreakable stoicism, deep inside he was utterly crushed. He was compelled to support himself with a cane. The pain in his cancerous foot was becoming intolerable.

"A fine body of men, colonel," Prince George said appreciatively, as the companies marched past the reviewing stand. "And quite the array of uniforms amongst them."

"Yes, your Royal Highness," Kirk replied. "Apologies, sir. We've had little time and simply do not have sufficient proper garb for all our new soldiers."

"The uniforms they have are serviceable enough," General Craufurd spoke up. "So long as, while serving under our Colours, they fight like Highlanders."

"I promise they will make you proud, sir," Kirk said reassuringly.

The entire parade took less than an hour. Afterword, the Duke invited General Craufurd and Lieutenant Colonel Kirk to supper at Horse Guards.

"I will be on the 3.00 train back to London," Prince George explained. "And you are both welcome to join me."

"It will be a privilege, your Royal Highness," Kirk said. He clasped the Duke's hand before coming to attention and saluting.

As soon as the Commander-in-Chief had taken his leave, James Kirk slowly made his way over to where Major Bruce had ordered the Regiment to reform. The 91st was scheduled to depart the following morning, and this was the last opportunity for Lieutenant Colonel Kirk to address them as their commanding officer. He leaned against his cane; the pain in his foot was only matched by that in his heart.

"91st Highlanders!" he began. "It has been my distinct honour to have served as your commanding officer these past three years. It is with an even greater sense of regret that I cannot accompany you to Southern Africa. But I have known Major Bruce for many years, and I know the Regiment is in capable hands. You are all Highlanders and with that comes lofty expectations. Her Majesty expects much from you. Fight well, protect each other, and bring further honour to your Regiment, the Crown, and the Empire!"

Officers of the 91st Highlanders
Major Alexander Bruce is sixth from the right, seated with his right leg atop his left

Word would not reach the Cape that reinforcements were en route until just a few days before their actual arrival. Therefore, all Lord Chelmsford and the British forces in South Africa could do was wait and speculate that Horse Guards was, in fact, sending additional troops to battle against the Zulus. In the meantime, he ordered Lieutenant Colonel Francis Law of the Royal Artillery to Lower Drift to assume overall command of the garrison. As a substantive lieutenant colonel, he held seniority over the brevetted Charles Coates. One of the most experienced officers in Southern Africa, he'd seen service during the Crimean War, Indian Mutiny, as well as the Chinese War. He was therefore among the few who Chelmsford explicitly trusted.

Additionally, the GOC ordered the companies from the 99th, previously tasked with guarding lines of communication between Lower Drift and Durban, brought up the drift to re-join their regiment. The addition of these troops, Colonel Law's arrival, plus his lordship's continued presence at Lower Drift only made the men of the 99th and The Buffs more convinced that an expedition to Eshowe was fast approaching.

It was late afternoon of the 17th of February. Sergeant David Fredericks' section was returning to Fort Pearson following another patrol along the Thukela. The only eventful moment of the day was when one of his soldiers nearly stepped on a crocodile that was lurking in the tall reeds near the riverbank. Lance Corporal Monroe had been compelled to shoot the beast before it ripped the leg off the unfortunate soldier. Monroe and another soldier carried the tail back, intending to cook it that evening as part of their supper.

"What in God's name is that?" Lieutenant Backhouse asked, having walked out to greet the returning patrol.

"Supper, sir," James Monroe replied boisterously. "Nearly took the leg off Private Norris, so the least he can do is provide us with a bit of a change to our bland rations for one night."

The lieutenant looked to David, who shrugged. "Not to worry, sir, I'll not allow the lads go off hunting crocodiles, even if it does turn out to be rather tasty. If you'd like, I'll bring a bite up to you and Mister Martin later."

"Well get rid of it for now," the officer replied impatiently. "Stow your packs and get ready for parade. His lordship wishes to address the garrison."

"Very good, sir." David was grinning. Like his soldiers, he thought this confirmed the GOC's intent to rally their forces to relieve Eshowe.

From all across the camp, hundreds of redcoats and blue-jacketed sailors rushed to the open space of trampled grass that served as their parade ground. Colour sergeants quickly received accountability of their men before turning the companies over to their officers commanding. The entire process took just a couple minutes. As the last company commander took his position, the newly-arrived Lieutenant Colonel Law did a sharp about turn and exchanged salutes with the General Officer Commanding.

Lord Chelmsford sat astride his horse, so that he might be seen and heard by all those present. Never one for grand speeches, it was with equal measures of reluctance and obligation that he decided to personally address the soldiers at Lower Drift.

"Men," he said. "You have no doubt heard rumours abounding about the terrible fate that befell No. 3 Column. It is with deepest regret that I must inform you these rumours are true. Five companies from 1/24th and one company from 2/24th were completely wiped out during a terrible and tragic battle at a mountain called

308

Isandlwana. For those of you in the 3rd Regiment, this will no doubt cause you much grief. I know you were garrisoned with the 24th for some time." He went on to read through a series of notes he'd penned that morning. He detailed as much as he could about the calamity, praising the discipline and gallant heroism of those who fell at Isandlwana, as well as the defenders of Rorke's Drift who, "Repelled the enemy's attempts at invading Natal."

While the assembled soldiers listened intently, they also grew impatient. His lordship seemed to be deliberately avoiding any mention of sending them north to assist their friends at Eshowe. It was only after twenty minutes of detailing the level of misfortune the army had suffered, no doubt in hopes of quelling further rumours or misinformation, that Lord Chelmsford finally addressed the question on everyone's minds.

"I know every man here is anxious to cross the Thukela River and take the fight to the Zulus once more. You won a great victory at Inyezane and no doubt wish to assist the rest of the column at Eshowe. While I will leave the conducting of any preliminary sorties to Colonel Law, understand that we do not have the numbers to launch a renewed invasion of the Zulu Kingdom. As we speak, Cetshwayo is massing his warriors around Eshowe, as well as between the mission station and Lower Drift. There could be as many as 20,000 between here and Eshowe. To put it simply, we must exercise patience. Reinforcements are on their way from England as we speak. We will resume the war against Cetshwayo and his army of heathens once we have additional troops and artillery assembled at Lower Drift. Until then, remain vigilant. You are what stands between the Zulus, Durban, and all of the towns and cities along the coast."

Without further ceremony, Chelmsford nodded to Law, who once more exchanged salutes with the GOC before dismissing the assembled soldiers back to their officers commanding. While he shared in his soldiers' disappointment, David knew their commanding general was correct. Given the terrible defeat already inflicted on one British column, it would be foolhardy to send a few hundred redcoats on a thirty-five-mile trek to Eshowe with potentially thousands of Zulus lying in wait for them.

Chapter XXV: Procuring Rations

Eshowe
19 February 1879

Zulu homesteads, from *The Graphic*, 22 February 1879

While reinforcements from Britain hastily prepared to join the fight in South Africa, the merciless downpours continued unabated, rendering the stronghold at Eshowe a boggy quagmire. The churned-up mud was ankle deep in most places, and the earthworks were left in constant need of repairs. This meant endless work for Captain Warren Wynne and his company of sappers. Improvements continued to be made. One involved filling the empty wooden rations boxes with mud, and then utilising them as a type of brick to stabilise the ramparts.

The use of empty biscuit boxes, however, drew attention to the state of their ration supplies. Colonel Pearson ordered the quartermasters and commissariat to compile a total count of all food stores. Taking into account the drastically reduced size of the garrison, they compiled the following list:

6 weeks breadstuffs, exclusive of whole mealies
2 months coffee
1 month tea
6 weeks sugar

3 months salt

1 month pepper

6 weeks lime juice

1 month preserved vegetables

In addition, there were 200 slaughter oxen kept in the large kraal which provided the column's primary source of meat.

"We can hold strong for a month," Colonel Walker noted.

"After that, the men's health will begin to deteriorate," Surgeon Norbury added. "Unless we can somehow receive supplies of fresh vegetables and either fruit or lime juice, we'll have to deal with scurvy and other ailments, in addition to fevers and dysentery."

Pearson nodded as he scanned the report. Given their already squalid conditions, his soldiers needed every bit of their strength to fight off disease, as well as the Zulus. He knew, in an emergency, the hard mealie used as animal fodder could be ground into bread. Through his hard expression he forced a grim smile.

"At least there's enough coffee to last for two months." With macabre humour, he added, "Once that's gone, we may have a mutiny on our hands. I do, however, feel it prudent that we limit the men to three-quarters rations. Do you think that will adversely affect their health, doctor?"

Surgeon Norbury shook his head. "If they were marching twenty miles in full kit every day, I would say 'yes'. However, other than the occasional improvements and repairs to the defences, the column is relatively sedentary. For the time being, I think three-quarters rations will allow the men to still perform their duties with minimal added discomfort."

It was now the 19th of February, and the column commander's confidence was returning. After learning the full measure of the disaster at Isandlwana, Charles Pearson became overly cautious, lest the same fate befall his men. Despite the numerous skirmishes and alarms over the past few weeks, there had been no definitive signs of the vast Zulu *impi* surrounding them. Satisfied with the report on their ration supplies, he summoned his battalion commanders along with Captains Wynne and Shervinton.

"Gentlemen, it is time we started taking the fight back to the Zulus," the column commander declared. "While there are without doubt numerous enemy warriors lurking in the area, they are not the main *impi*."

He nodded to Captain Shervinton. As one who had spent many years in Southern Africa, and was relatively familiar with Zulu customs, his advice was sought on the matter.

"Most of their warriors have likely returned home for the harvest," the NNC officer explained to the column staff, reiterating his previous assessment to Colonel Pearson.

"And what of the roving bands we've encountered?" Henry Parnell asked. "We do not know with certainty their fighting strength, but surely they number in the thousands."

"Agreed," the captain replied. "These are probably locals from any number of kraals in this region. Unfortunately, as we've conducted very little reconnaissance beyond the mission station, we know almost nothing about the size or disposition of the local population. However, given the loss of our draught oxen and the cutting of all communications with the rest of the army, their numbers are sufficient to keep us holed up."

"We saw numerous mealie fields on the route of march," Colonel Pearson recalled. "According to the intelligence we gathered from the smattering of prisoners we took at Inyezane, Chief Godide had about six thousand warriors under his command. As you said, many of these may have returned to their homes for the harvest. The issue now becomes, if and when they will return reinforced by the main *impi* from Isandlwana."

Henry Parnell spoke up, "If the harvest is what delays their reinforcements, we may have an opportunity, sir."

"I agree." Pearson folded his arms and paused with thought for a few moments. Finally, he said, "I think it is time we quit hiding behind our walls while the Zulus simply wait for disease or starvation to finish us. Captain Shervinton's mounted troops have found a large garden a few miles east of here. Three companies from The Buffs and one company from the 99th will raid it, bringing back anything ripe enough for consumption and destroying the rest. I, myself, will reconnoitre towards the Mlalazi River. Captain Wynne, you will accompany me."

"Very good, sir," Warren replied. He was glad to be escaping from the cramped confines of the fort, even if for only a day. Still a bit weak from his recent bout of stomach problems, he reckoned a few hours out in the open might do his health some good.

The following morning, prior to reveille, the four companies of redcoats stood in parade formation just beyond the eastern drawbridge of the fort. They escorted an empty wagon, drawn by some of the few draught oxen that Colonel Pearson kept at the fort for just such a purpose. Though only one of his companies was taking part, Lieutenant Colonel Welman took it upon himself to lead the expedition.

The faint glow of predawn promised an only moderately cloudy day, though the saturated ground still squished beneath the feet of the marching soldiers and beasts of burden. Thirty minutes after the departure of Welman's detachment, Colonel Pearson, Captain Wynne, and another company of infantry escorts headed north towards the Mlalazi River.

Henry Welman sat astride his horse about thirty yards behind a screen line of skirmishers from The Buffs. There was much anxiety amongst the ranks, particularly from the inexperienced soldiers from the 99th. Prior to departure, Welman had informed the company commanders that, in the event they came upon a large force of Zulus, they were to form a square around the wagon and make their way back to camp. About a mile from the fort they found the remains of a small campfire likely used by Zulu scouts. However, there were no other signs of their adversaries.

As the kraal first came into view, every soldier dropped down to one knee, searching for signs of the Zulus. The company skirmishers on their right had disappeared, scattering into a thick grove of trees in search of the enemy.

Towards the head of the column, Lieutenant Colonel Welman rode up to an NCO from the vanguard, exchanged a few words with him, then summoned all company commanders. "Lead elements have found the Zulu kraal," he explained. "C and G Companies from The Buffs will take the flanks. C Company of the 99th will lead the assault. E Company of The Buffs will be in support."

With drilled precision, the companies quickly reformed from a series of columns into a long skirmish line facing the kraal. They advanced at the slow walk, rifles ready. As C Company of the 99th trampled through a large patch of tall plants and shrubs, they heard loud shouts coming from the direction the kraal. Smaller than the vast complexes belonging to the *amakhosi* and members of the Zulu royal house, this one had perhaps a dozen thatched huts surrounding a modest sized cattle pen.

There was a loud shout from a previously unseen Zulu boy near the entrance, and seven persons emerged frantically from the nearest abode. They were teenage boys and a couple of women. Given that most of the local Zulus had fled further inland after the arrival of the British column, it was likely that they, too, were on a mission to forage food. One of the lads hefted a large, bell-mouthed blunderbuss which he struggled to carry. The British soldiers halted and watched in bemusement as the Zulus tried to load the weapon. It was quickly apparent they were using far too much powder, as copious amounts were poured from a powder horn down the barrel. Handfuls of either crudely-shaped lead balls or stones were dropped down the barrel. A third boy hammered the lot home with a crude ramrod.

"I'll wager ten shillings that sodding thing blows apart," one soldier quipped.

"I'm not taking you up on that," one of his mates said, shaking his head.

The soldiers were still a hundred yards from the kraal and surprised when they saw the two women helping steady the barrel, as the young lad aimed the blunderbuss towards them. Not one redcoat so much as loaded their rifles or even thought about seeking cover. Instead, they stood nonchalantly, pointing and laughing at the absurd spectacle.

Even Lieutenant Colonel Welman found it amusing. "Wait for them to blow themselves up, then advance on the kraal."

Soon there was an audible *snap* as the flint struck the flash pan, immediately followed by a loud boom. The Zulus were flung in all directions, obscured for a moment by the cloud of black powder smoke.

Raucous laughter came from the imperial soldiers, though this was quickly stifled by Welman's next order.

"At the double…advance!"

Running at a quick jog, the force of nearly three hundred men converged on the Zulu homestead. The small band who'd disastrously fired the blunderbuss at them sprinted away. The two women were clutching at their injured arms, while the lad behind the trigger hobbled along while holding onto his dislocated shoulder.

Despite their injuries, they were still much faster than any of the British. Lieutenant Colonel Welman did not wish to pursue them alone on horseback, lest there be enemy warriors lurking about.

Soldiers quickly swept through the compound. Groups of four or five men checked each hut for signs of life or anything worth plundering. Despite the signs of fresh animal waste, the cattle had been taken away, either to graze or simply to be hidden from the redcoats. The huts showed signs of abandonment, the only weapons found being a few rusted and broken assegais.

"Seems the warriors haven't been home for some time," Lieutenant Knight of The Buffs reported to Welman.

The colonel nodded in concurrence. "Burn the kraal," he ordered. "Harvest everything you can onto the wagon, then put the torch to the rest."

While the men from the 99th set about igniting the huts, the companies from The Buffs proceeded to uproot the vast garden which covered several acres. There was plenty of cabbage and other leafy vegetables, as well as carrots and roots that were not quite ripened, but would suffice for their needs.

"Hey look, pumpkins!" one excited soldier shouted, hoisting a medium-sized gourd.

His mates whooped with excitement at the thought of fresh pumpkin pie.

A pair of scythes were wielded by two soldiers who'd been raised on farms, and they cut through the stocks of mealie. While hard on the teeth and mostly used as animal fodder, with enough grinding and some creativity on the part of whoever was cooking, they could be used as a source of food for the garrison.

The columns of smoke from the burning kraal could be seen for miles, yet if it drew the attention of any Zulu warriors, they remained hidden. By late afternoon, the wagon was piled high with grain stalks, mounds of vegetables, and dozens of prized pumpkins. The crops they had seized would scarcely be enough to feed the entire garrison for more than a day, but the raid was still a moral victory for the Southern Column. Not the preferred type of triumph, like that at Inyezane which left hundreds of Zulu warriors dead and dying, but a victory nonetheless.

Lieutenant Colonel Henry Welman led his detachment back to the fort around an hour after Colonel Pearson's return. His scouting of the Mlalazi River had turned up signs of a large Zulu encampment, though it appeared to have been deserted for the past couple weeks. Soldiers of No. 1 Column understood these were just the first of many such raids and patrols, as their column commander became emboldened to extend their reach beyond the immediate confines of Eshowe.

At Lower Drift, the various companies of redcoats were conducting patrols of their own. Sergeant David Fredericks and the men of H Company, 2/3rd Buffs were relieved to be part of one such patrol heading north of Fort Tenedos; if for no other reason than it gave them a chance to knock the mud from their shoes and breathe a bit of fresh air that did not stink of unwashed bodies and animal waste. Even Private Walters, who had become rather gloomy and withdrawn following his court-martial and painful flogging a few weeks earlier, found a certain spring in his step.

"You're looking a might better this morning, Private Walters," Lance Corporal Monroe said, as he walked beside him.

Privates were strictly ordered to maintain their place in the formation, only stepping away to relieve themselves with the expressed permission of their section leaders. The NCOs would often walk up and down the line, checking on their individual soldiers. The company advanced in a staggered column, able to quickly form into battle lines should the enemy show themselves.

"Yesterday was supposed to be my next flogging," the private explained. "Honestly, I got no sleep the night before and wasn't sure if I'd survive another beating. Yet no one came to fetch me. I thought to ask Sergeant Fredericks about it but was afraid to do so."

"Some questions are best not asked," James replied. "There were three other court-martials after yours, mostly for fighting or insubordination. Perhaps that distracted the officers a bit."

"I can only hope," Walters said, biting the inside of his lip. He continued to walk, searching the brush and distant tree groves for any signs of the enemy.

Monroe gave him a reassuring pat on the shoulder and walked up the column to his section leader. The terrain this close to the coast was mostly gently rolling grasslands and only the occasional short hill or ridgeline. Off to their right, he could just make out a few of the company's skirmishers clearing the brush stands.

"Damn it all, I miss being with them," he said, with a nod towards his old mates.

"The needs of the company outweigh yours," David replied reflexively. "And besides, not much chance for you to earn that second stripe dancing through the bush."

"I'm nineteen, sergeant," James said, as a matter of explanation. "I'm in no hurry to be a colour sergeant by the time I'm twenty-one. Although, I admit a corporal's pay would be nice. Anyway, I'm going to check on Peters and Davies. They're both hobbling a bit and might be having issues with their feet."

David nodded in agreement. His assistant section leader bounded back down the column to where two of their soldiers were struggling to keep up despite the rather leisurely pace. Though James Monroe was young and inexperienced as a leader, he was eager and full of the energy brought on by youth. This made him useful when the sergeant needed a runner or someone to check their soldiers during a march.

James' remarks about Privates Peters and Davies concerned the sergeant. Despite being hardened by countless miles of marching during his six years in the ranks, David's own feet were feeling the effects of not being able to keep them dry for any length of time. The skin was raw on the outside of his left foot, as well as both heels. He reckoned when they returned to the fort, he would order his section to, at minimum, wash their feet and socks in the river. There was little else they could do.

"To think, I could have stayed in the fields or the workhouses," he said with a derisive chuckle under his breath.

As he continued to walk, constantly turning back to make certain those behind him were keeping up with the lead elements of the company, his thoughts turned, as they often did, to Lillian and little David. During the weeks of tedium since first arriving at Lower Drift, he'd had little to do but think about his beloved wife and son. Even during times of crisis, they were never far from his thoughts. Thankfully, their home garrison of East London was over 450 miles from the Thukela River, near the southernmost tip of the African continent; far enough away from the war that there was little chance of them being threatened by a possible Zulu counter-invasion. He knew his wife was terribly worried for him and could only imagine

317

her distress upon hearing about the disaster that had befallen the poor lads in the 24th Regiment. But at least she wasn't alone. The Buffs had been in Southern Africa for nearly three years, during which time she had become very close with Rob Anderson's wife, Emma, as well as several of the other spouses.

And while there was a certain measure of guilt at not remaining with the rest of No. 1 Column at Eshowe, H Company's return to Lower Drift had allowed David to send a letter to his beloved, letting her know he was alive and in decent health.

"Zulus!" a voice shouted off to their left.

The company was about four miles north of Lower Drift when a skirmisher spotted a dozen black and brown shields near the crest of a ridge. Lieutenant Martin halted his men. They quickly fanned out on either side of the road, kneeling behind any cover they could find, rifles ready.

Lieutenant Backhouse had ridden over to the skirmishers on their left flank and was scanning the hill with his field glasses. "Bloody fools sky-lined themselves." He pointed towards the handful of warriors who were now clearly visible. The corner of his mouth turned up slightly. He then spotted even more warriors crouching in the grass below the crestline. "But not all of them were foolish."

Robert Martin was also looking intently through his field glasses. He scanned over his shoulder to the right of the road. All he could see was flat grassland, devoid of any enemy presence. "Sergeant Davies, Sergeant Fredericks! Deploy your men in a line thirty yards from the road. Index your sights to 600 yards, fire on my command."

"Sir!"

The NCOs quickly reiterated these instructions to their soldiers who excitedly followed them a short way from the dirt track. They were joined by the company sharp-shooters led by Corporal Knight.

"Load," the two sergeants said, almost simultaneously. They kept their voices calm, lest they scare away their quarry.

Forty-five Martini-Henry breaches clicked open, as soldiers worked the lever actions and chambered rounds. David pointed to a couple of white shields below the crestline.

"I see them," Lance Corporal Monroe confirmed.

"Let us send the Zulus our compliments," Lieutenant Martin said. "At 600 yards! Volley...fire!"

The stillness of the afternoon was shattered by the crashing volley of nearly four dozen heavy calibre rifles. There was very little breeze, and it took a few moments for the smoke to clear. By the time it did, the Zulus had disappeared.

"Think we hit any of them?" Private Peters asked. He squinted his eyes in the lingering wisps of black powder smoke.

Their two officers scanned the ridge for a few moments with their glasses. "Whether we hit any or not, we gave them a fine 'Good Afternoon'," Lieutenant Martin said, with much satisfaction. He ordered Backhouse to ride back and inform the garrison at Fort Tenedos, lest they panic at the noise from their volley.

Following their return to Lower Drift, David and his section sat on the edge of the pont in their shirtsleeves, washing their feet and socks. He grimaced as strips of skin came off the outside edge of his left foot. Thankfully, it didn't hurt. He directed his soldiers to allow their feet to dry in the open air for a couple hours before donning fresh socks. He and Monroe took the time to inspect the feet of their section, sending several of the worst cases to see Surgeon-Major Tarrant.

"Won't be of much help to our friends at Eshowe if we can't even walk there," David remarked.

"When?" James asked.

"When his lordship tells us to," the sergeant conjectured. "I just hope he sends a few more riflemen with us."

Chapter XXVI: A Modest Prize

Captain James Forster
2nd Battalion, 3rd Regiment of Foot (The Buffs)

A week had passed since the last death at Eshowe when tragedy struck once more. The recently promoted Lance Corporal Thomas Taylor, who had assumed James Monroe's position with the battalion sharp-shooters, succumbed to dysentery on 21 February. This coincided with Colonel Pearson leading another patrol out from the fort, this time in search of sufficient grass land that hadn't already been trampled or devoured by their beasts-of-burden.

The 200 cattle and small number of draught oxen remaining at the fort required constant grazing every day. By the third week of February, all grains and grasses within a mile of Eshowe were completely consumed. Many of the black African wagon drivers and voorloopers who'd remained at the fort now acted as cattle drivers, taking the herds to fresh grazing land each day.

On the first such day, the cattle were taken a little over a mile away from the protection of the ramparts. Colonel Pearson accompanied them, along with a single company from The Buffs.

Charles removed his helmet, as did the other officers and men of the escort detachment, when they passed the growing cemetery where Lance Corporal Taylor was being laid to rest by his mates. The late soldier's officer commanding, Captain Forster, read a short eulogy before Reverend Robertson led the company in prayer.

"I fear such funerals might soon become routine," Pearson said quietly to himself. He shook his head. "But, it never will be for those who die or for the friends they leave behind."

The grazing patrol proved uneventful. The infantry escorts sat or lounged in their wide perimeter facing away from the herd. Like his men, Pearson was glad to be away from the fort even if for only a few hours. By mid-afternoon, the cattle finished and the detachment returned to the fort.

Though the British may have felt like they were alone, the eyes of the Zulus were constantly watching them. The *induna*, Phalane, along with Prince Dabulamanzi had maintained a robust presence, watching and waiting for the red-jacketed soldiers to make a mistake. The prince was especially impatient, wishing to take the fight to the enemy. However, with most warriors returned home following the Isandlwana campaign, they simply did not have the numbers to launch a decisive assault.

Dabulamanzi had taken great umbrage when Phalane decided to vacate their camp along the Mlalazi River, after it was discovered by a British patrol several days earlier. Had the *induna* known this band of riders was led by Colonel Pearson and his chief engineer officer, he likely would have been willing to risk an attack against their mounted troops. After all, one prize that had eluded King Cetshwayo's *amabutho* was the capture of enemy officers. The confidence ran high among the Zulus following Isandlwana, and the king wished to spare both his people and the British further needless bloodshed. The capture of important hostages was the surest way to bring a negotiated end of hostilities.

On the afternoon of the 21st of February, a pair of scouts returned to Phalane's new encampment in a forest on a mountain called Mgabhi, about twelve miles northwest of Eshowe. The *induna* had just returned from a hunt with Prince Dabulamanzi and several of the royal escorts. Several wild boars had been taken that day.

"The English cattle have devoured most of their grazing land," one of the scouts reported. "They are sending them further away to feed."

"How many escorts?" Phalane asked. Dabulamanzi's eyes grew wide.

"About a hundred red-jacketed riflemen," the warrior answered.

"Then we shall have a little surprise waiting for them tomorrow," the prince stated. He ordered the scout, "Show me the field."

Phalane had his reservations yet knew he could not overrule a royal prince. Instead, he decided to accompany the men. Dabulamanzi had brought a contingent of a thousand warriors from his own regiment, the uDloko. He selected eighty of his fastest runners in possession of rifles to accompany him. There was a severe shortage of ammunition, as there had been no chance to replenish their stores following the attack on kwaJimu. The war had also seen a complete cessation of powder and musket balls from foreign traders.

The prince carried a percussion musket instead of a flintlock. He had only a smattering of powder, five percussion caps, and no bullets. Despite several protestations, his remaining skirmishers were ordered to share their supplies of powder and musket balls with these selected fighters. As so few of his men carried percussion muskets, Dabulamanzi contented himself with taking five balls and a smattering of powder to refill his horn.

"We shall replenish our bullets when we plunder the British dead," he promised.

The words felt somewhat hollow even to Dabulamanzi. He had made the same pledge prior to the attack on kwaJimu. No one in the uDloko Regiment spoke of the battle, for each shared privately in the shame of their failure. Phalane had only heard rumours about the defeat of the entire Undi Corps at the place the British called Rorke's Drift, and he diplomatically never questioned the prince or any of his warriors.

It was nearly dark by the time the band of warriors reached the meadow. Both the prince and *induna* were pleased to see a mass of trees with a natural earthen berm near the edge closest to the pasture. Large swaths of devoured grass and the divots from hundreds of hooves were evident, but there was still plenty of forage for the enemy's cattle.

"How large was their herd?" Phalane asked one of the scouts, while Dabulamanzi positioned his skirmishers behind the berm.

"I counted 200."

"A fair prize," the *induna* remarked. He then sought out Dabulamanzi, telling the prince, "I leave this to you, highness. May you win cattle and spoils in the name of our king."

The *induna* then departed, making the long trek back to his camp on the slopes of Mgabhi Mountain. Dabulamanzi ordered his men to build up brush shelters to protect them from the pending night-time rains, as well as shield them from unfriendly eyes. His one regret was not taking the time to skin and cook up some of the recently-hunted boar, as he and his men would have to spend the night devoid of supper. The prince had to content himself that they would have a magnificent feast once they returned with the British cattle.

Dabulamanzi awoke the following morning just before dawn. His stomach growled, reminding him that he had not eaten since the previous day's breakfast. As the lands in the Eshowe region belonged to Dabulamanzi, he was more familiar with the terrain than many of his warriors. He knew they were not far from the old mission station. Once they engaged the British, they would need to drive the escorts away quickly so they could escape with the cattle. While he longed to avenge his humiliating defeat at kwaJimu, he and his band of marksmen were in no position to conduct a full-scale battle against the English soldiers.

To his surprise, when the grazers returned about an hour after sunrise, they were joined by only a handful of escorts. The prince counted around twenty red-jackets in addition to the forty black Africans driving the cattle. Much to his chagrin, the drivers halted their herd at a large stand of grass about two hundred paces from the berm. If he'd learned anything from the fight at kwaJimu, it was that their muskets were largely ineffective at ranges beyond fifty to a hundred paces. He decided to wait until midmorning in hopes that as the grasses were consumed, their foes would be compelled to drive the cattle closer to where the Zulus lay waiting.

Before Dabulamanzi could pass the word to his skirmishers, a musket shot shattered the stillness of the morning. The prince cursed under his breath, as a ragged volley was unleashed by the remainder of his warriors. Smoke from eighty muskets clouded their vision, causing many of the marksmen to cough as they breathed in the acrid fumes. As his men started to reload, Dabulamanzi, who had not fired during the initial salvo, took a percussion cap from his pouch and half-cocked his rifle. With only five shots, he wasn't going to waste them shooting blindly. Squinting his eyes, he tried to see through the smoke. He hoped their volley had been enough to drive off the British escorts. As shots continued to echo and his ears now ringing, it was impossible for the prince to tell whether they came from his men or their enemies.

The sounds of musketry alerted the Eshowe garrison, with soldiers upending their mess tins and breakfast as they sprang into action. Two companies from The Buffs hastily grabbed their rifles and rushed out across the north drawbridge. Already waiting for them was Captain Jackson, the officer commanding of C Company. He drew his sword and raised it high, shouting for his men to form a skirmish line towards the sound of the firing.

"Sounds like the Zulus are after our cattle," his colour sergeant said, his voice deadpan and showing a complete lack of surprise. He shook his head. "Shouldn't have sent only a single section from the 99th to escort them."

"Can't be helped now," his officer commanding remarked. The second company was commanded by James Forster. As Jackson held seniority as a captain, he assumed charge of the detachment. Sheathing his sword, he drew his pistol before shouting for the men to advance, *'At the double!'*

The echoes of rifle fire continued as the band of 160 redcoats rushed towards the sounds of battle. They moved at a quick measured pace. Captain Jackson understood the need for expediency, but they needed to maintain a semblance of order while not exhausting themselves before reaching the enemy. The grazing pasture was about a mile-and-a-quarter from the fort, and it took the detachment just under fifteen minutes to reach the fray. When the cattle and their huddling African drivers came into sight, the imperial soldiers instinctively increased their pace.

As soon as they reached the mass of beasts who were contentedly grazing while musket shots slapped the ground around them, Captain Jackson ordered his men to halt. He quickly assessed the situation. All the Zulu fire was coming from a line of trees about 200 yards from the herd. The twenty escorts from the 99th lay prone behind whatever bits of cover they could find and were occasionally returning fire.

"There they are, lads!" the captain called out. "Bound by sections, fire and advance!"

Two of the four sections in each company unleashed a salvo of rifle fire. The remaining two then rushed through the clouds of smoke. At roughly twenty yards, their sergeants shouted their subsequent commands, *'Halt! Present...fire!'* Immediately, the first two companies would bound past them about twenty yards before firing again.

It was a still morning with no breeze to blow away the choking clouds of black powder smoke. This, coupled with their foes lurking in the treeline, made it impossible to see if any had struck their intended targets. For the most part, the redcoats could not see the Zulus; only shadows darting between the trees.

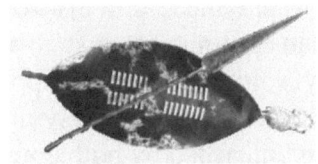

With the smoke obscuring his vision, Dabulamanzi was caught by surprise when he heard crashing volleys to his front. These were not the random shots from his marksmen or the cattle herd's pitiful escorts, but deliberate salvos from a mass of as-yet-unseen imperial soldiers. Martini-Henry bullets smacked into the berm and the trees all around them. He bitterly chastised himself for waiting so long before ordering his men to swarm the small group of redcoats and African drivers. Yet in the din of battle, even during a small skirmish such as this, it was easy for one to lose all sense of time. To the prince, it felt as if only a couple minutes had passed. If British reinforcements were now on the field, it had clearly been much longer.

A scream off to his left alerted the prince, as one of his warriors was knocked back from the berm, a large chunk of flesh torn from his upper right arm. It was then that Dabulamanzi first spotted what looked to be about thirty redcoats emerging from their own clouds of smoke. They were in loose order, advancing both quickly and with sound discipline. He raised his musket to fire. The prince loathed to admit it, but he admired their British adversaries as much as he hated them. With a loud crack from his weapon, a thick waft of smoke masked his vision once more.

"At 100 yards!" Captains Jackson and Forster shouted, ordering their men to adjust their sights.

The officer commanding of C Company, 2/3rd Buffs was pleased with the drill and discipline demonstrated by his soldiers. Anxious as they may have been to get 'stuck in' with the Zulus, even the youngest privates heeded the orders of their section leaders, waiting to rush forward until the lead elements had fired and using the smoke to help shield their movements. One of his soldiers on the left of the formation yelped and slapped as his leg, stating something must have bit him. Despite the tear in his trousers, blood already visible, the young man continued to rush towards their foe.

After each volley, soldiers quickly dropped down to one knee, lest they present a bigger target for enemy marksmen. With the constant salvos being unleashed by both companies, it was difficult to ascertain any return fire from the Zulus. A dull thud as a musket ball kicked up clods of dirt about ten feet from where Captain Jackson stood told the officer their enemies were still in the fight. His men were now within fifty yards of the treeline.

"Companies...online!" he bellowed. The rear sections sprinted forward, dressing off those on either side of them. They kept in loose skirmishing order with six to ten feet between each soldier.

"Fix bayonets!" The voice of the company's colour sergeant boomed.

The sound of horses' hooves behind him alerted the officer commanding. Captain Jackson turned to see Sergeant Lewis and ten 'Uhlans' riding towards him.

"Captain, sir!" the NCO said excitedly, reining his horse in and saluting.

"Sergeant," Jackson acknowledged. "Hold behind our companies until we drive these devils from the woods."

"Understood."

"They're retiring, sir!" a soldier on the line shouted, pointing at about fifty Zulu warriors who were sprinting away over the nearest low hill.

"Right you are," Jackson remarked. He turned to Lewis. "Carry on, then, sergeant."

"Sir!" The mounted NCO waved for his troopers to follow. With a loud shout, they drew their carbines from their scabbards and galloped between the line of redcoats in pursuit of their quarry.

Though the enemy's mounted troops appeared to be few, their arrival, along with the mass of redcoats with bayonets fixed who outnumbered them two-to-one, was enough for the Zulus to know the fight was over. Two of Dabulamanzi's warriors were dead, and another eight were injured. The wounded were helped away by their companions. The slain were, regrettably, left where they fell. Despite the failure of their raid, the Zulu marksmen withdrew in good order with several men protecting those who helped carry their wounded mates.

Maintaining his posture towards the enemy, Dabulamanzi slowly backed away from the tree grove, keeping his withdrawing warriors in his peripheral vision. He spotted one mounted white soldier not fifty feet away. Grinning maliciously as his prey's eyes grew wide, the prince raised his musket and squeezed the trigger. The hammer fell, yet his weapon failed to fire. He swore as he realised he'd forgotten to replace the spent percussion cap. By the time he retrieved a cap from his bag, the rider had sprinted his horse away.

"Patience," Dabulamanzi said under his breath. "I have to learn patience. Let the enemy come to us when we are in a better position to oppose him."

The British mounted troops, realising they could not contend with the Zulus' numbers once deprived of infantry support, veered off to their left in the direction of a small hilltop. From there, Sergeant Lewis hoped to establish a firing position for his men to rain down a few volleys upon their adversaries. Much to his surprise, as they crested the rise they saw a large Zulu homestead occupying the previously unseen ridgetop. There were a dozen huts, a large garden, and cattle kraal.

"Bugger me," the sergeant muttered.

"The Zulus have retired into a forest just to the north," one of his troopers said, as he rode up to the NCO. "Shall we continue to pursue?"

Lewis shook his head and pointed his carbine towards the kraal. "No. We'll see if we can find some fresh carrots and maybe a pumpkin or two for our supper."

The eleven mounted soldiers rode into the homestead, predictably finding it deserted. There were only a few handfuls of vegetables to be found in the garden. It appeared to have already been plundered by the Zulus. They then set fire to the huts, which took some time as the thatch was extremely damp from the recent rains. While most of his men set about finding kindling, Sergeant Lewis dispatched one of his troopers to find Captain Jackson to inform him of the find and that the 'Uhlans' would return to the fort as soon as the kraal was ablaze.

Six African cattle drivers had been injured during the exchange, along with one of Captain Jackson's soldiers, who was grazed in the thigh. The young private had scarcely notice the wound during the battle. As they made their way back to the fort, he said it started to 'hurt like a bastard'.

"Oh, stuff it all," one of his companions chastised. "I've gotten worse from my grand-mum's cat!"

The skirmish, while relatively insignificant, led the British garrison to assume that the enemy, while still a nuisance, was not yet in a position to launch a full-scale attack against them. They presumed this was due to the Zulu harvest. While it was indeed the season for taking in the crops, no one could even guess how long this would take. Would it last a few days? A month? Only when the Zulus returned in greater numbers would they know for sure.

Despite the grains and vegetables taken during the various raids, Colonel Pearson knew it would not be enough to sustain the column's already dwindling ration stores. With communications completely cut, there was no way of knowing when or if Lord Chelmsford would be able to bring reinforcements to them. Intelligence about the Zulus was still severely lacking. As best as the British could determine, the enemy numbered several thousand. Yet they were spread thin, keeping the compound at Eshowe encircled. This, however, gave Pearson little confidence. The fleet-footed Zulus could run great distances in a short time, converging on any emerging threat from the besieged garrison.

Attempts at sending runners with messages for the GOC had thus far been repulsed. They assumed the same could be said of any despatches from Lord Chelmsford. Colonel Pearson feared that if he did attempt to abandon Eshowe, the fast-running Zulus would be able to congregate their scattered forces and ambush him on the road back to Lower Drift. Having already cut the garrison's rations by one-quarter, soldiers were motivated to forage for whatever they could find. They ravaged the surrounding region, but grains and vegetables became even more difficult to find. And while every soldier at Eshowe longed for some fresh meat, it was understood that the 200 head of cattle were an emergency source of food, to be butchered only after their boxes of tinned beef were exhausted.

It was on the morning of 23 February that Pearson, upon the advice of Colonel Walker and his battalion commanders, decided to auction off the personal rations left behind by the mounted Volunteers.

"They left quite the haul of goods behind," Henry Welman observed. "Would be a shame to allow it to go bad."

Though there was a sizeable mountain of foodstuffs collected, there was not enough to go around. Hence, Colonel Pearson decided on the auction. He reckoned that the funds could be used to reimburse the troopers, whose food it was, after the siege was over.

The veritable feast consisted of tins of sardines, lobster, salmon, herrings, cured ham, along with curry powder, jam, condensed milk, pickles, and even tobacco. The men had long become bored with their meagre rations, reduced as they now were. And besides, they had nothing else to spend their pay on. They were rapt with excitement at the thought of acquiring food that in their minds was *'fit for the Queen'*.

That evening the entire garrison paraded outside of Pearson's headquarters. Those on sentry or picquet duty had given whatever money they had to their friends to try to purchase goods on their behalf. As the bidding commenced, men were so anxious for even a scrap of luxury for their taste buds that prices soon reached exorbitant levels. A bottle of pickles went for 25 shillings; more than two-weeks' wages (minus stoppages) for a private soldier. The top bid for a pot of jam came to 24 shillings. 18 shillings won a tin of lobster. Several soldiers pooled their resources, winning a 12-pound ham for the princely sum of £6, 5 shillings; a modest prize for two-and-a-half months' wages. Even some of the officers took part with the 99th's adjutant, Lieutenant Arthur Davison, winning the bid for a bottle of milk and a tin of salmon. After the last item was auctioned off, Colonel Pearson reckoned that £100 had been acquired for £7 worth of items.

As much as the auction had brought excitement to the garrison, particularly for those who scored the winning bids, Captain Warren Wynne found the entire ordeal distasteful. The officer commanding of No. 2 Field Company was more than content with his humble rations. And his fellow engineer officers, who were also his mess-mates, followed his lead. Since the auction had been Colonel Pearson's doing, Warren naturally could not prohibit his sappers from taking part. Still, this did not dissuade him from expressing his displeasure to the one man in his company he felt most comfortable confiding in.

330

"We steal from the Volunteers and extort from our men," he said to Lieutenant Courtney that evening.

"You have to admit it was a morale boost," the subaltern replied. "Besides, we have no idea how long we'll be here. It all could have spoiled by the time we're relieved."

"*If* we get relieved," Warren added darkly. He shook his head. "My apologies, Mister Courtney. I should not express my misgivings to you. Though I confess, I've lately been acting under the assumption that your captaincy has come through. For all we know, you could be my peer by now."

"I have felt overdue for some time," Courtney confessed. "And as I recall, last word from Aldershot was that a vacancy came open before we left. They were simply waiting on confirmation from Horse Guards. On that note, for all we know you could be a major. After all, it is a major's billet that you now occupy."

"Well, we'll never know so long as communication with Natal remains cut," Wynne surmised. "My position is a major's billet, yes, but I'm too far down the seniority list. While I would be honoured to receive a brevet, it does not change my pay or my ability to provide for my family. Let the brevet promotions go to those seeking glory."

"That's very noble of you, sir." Courtney smiled. He noted the tired expression on his officer commanding's face. "You really should turn in. We have a long day ahead of us tomorrow what with the north ramparts in need of repair."

"No, not yet. I still have the caponiers to sketch out. Plus, I have plans for a communications balloon that I need to get to Colonel Pearson as soon as possible."

"You should let one of us handle that, sir," the lieutenant persisted. "I know you're a damned perfectionist, but honestly, you've already fallen once to illness. I'd rather we not lose you *before* you become a major."

Warren gave an appreciative chuckle, but was firm in his resolve to sort out the caponiers himself, as well as begin preliminary sketches for a communications balloon. Knowing there was little else he could do, Lieutenant Courtney decided to try to get some sleep. He and his fellow subalterns shared a space beneath a canvas tarp off one of their equipment wagons. Lieutenant Main was already fast asleep. Willock was not on his bedroll. Courtney surmised the younger lieutenant had to use the latrine. A harsh wind was blowing in from the ocean twenty-five miles to the southeast. A sharp gust ripped directly under their tarp, bringing with it the first hint of the coming storm.

David fell asleep almost as soon as he laid his head down. He woke sometime well after midnight with the rain now coming straight down upon the camp. The drainage trench around their sleeping area was nearly full, and the lieutenant quietly prayed it would not overflow again. His two fellow subalterns were both sleeping soundly. Through the downpour, he could see the light of Captain Wynne's oil lamp at his private sleeping area. Courtney laid back down, pulled his blanket tight over his shoulders, and let out a sigh. He was growing ever more concerned about his officer commanding. Captain Wynne had yet to fully recover from his previous fever, and he desperately needed sleep. If Warren had one flaw, it was that he took on too much rather than delegating to his subordinates. While Courtney loathed talking about his officer commanding behind his back, he decided he would speak with Colour Sergeant Smith on the morrow and get his advice.

Chapter XXVII: We Shall Drink Your Coffee!

Eshowe
24 February 1879

Zulu Warriors

On the night of the 23rd of February, not long after the auctioning of the Volunteers' sundry items, the rains returned with a vengeance. Lieutenant David Courtney awoke to find himself lying in two inches of water. He roused his fellow subalterns. They all donned their greatcoats and hung their bedrolls to dry.

Following morning parade, Courtney sought out Colour Sergeant Smith, who had just finished reviewing the sick list with his section leaders. The company's senior NCO gave a friendly nod. "Top of the morning, sir."

"And to you, colour sergeant." The lieutenant took a quick glance at the list.

"Twenty are down with intestinal problems, four confirmed cases of dysentery," the colour sergeant explained. "Six more have severe fevers with eight more on light duty for the same."

"I hope our captain won't need to add himself to the list," Courtney stated.

"Ah, so you're concerned about him as well," Smith observed.

"To be perfectly candid, colour sergeant, I wanted to ask your advice on the matter."

"There isn't anything I can tell you that you don't already know, sir. I've at least managed to convince Captain Wynne to allow me and Mister Willock to handle all personnel issues within the company. As senior subaltern, who I think the captain views more like a peer than subordinate, it is up to you to compel him to allow you and the other officers to take some of the burden off him."

"He's working on designs for a communications balloon," Courtney recalled.

"I see. Well, if anyone can build one that functions properly, it's our captain. And if you want my advice, sir, seize some of the initiative. We know what tasks need to be done each day. If they get done before Captain Wynne has a chance to address them, so much the better. I will do my part."

"Thank you, colour sergeant," Courtney said. "And I'd appreciate if you kept my concerns for the captain's well-being between us."

"Of course, sir."

While it was true that Colour Sergeant Smith hadn't told him anything that Lieutenant Courtney wasn't already aware of, it was a bit of a relief to know that he could depend on the company's non-commissioned officers to assist both him and Captain Wynne. And with Warren's primary focus of late being on his idea for a communications balloon, it was only natural that his subordinates take over many of the mundane daily tasks. Courtney then decided to go find Sergeant Small. He was supervising repairs on the north ramparts. The lieutenant directed that any reports concerning wear and tear on the defences were to be first run through him. For anything other than structural failure, he could delegate NCOs to take charge of the actual work and save his officer commanding the needless strain.

Following the brief yet harrowing action by the two companies from The Buffs under Captains Jackson and Forster, the garrison learned its lesson about sending the cattle out to graze without proper escort. As they were led further afield to graze, this rather monotonous chore fell to both the redcoats and 'Jack Tars', who at least took some relief from the tedium and squalor of daily life in the fort.

On the morning of the 24th, with the inner compound of the fort rendered into a virtual swamp, Colonel Pearson decided to personally lead a robust patrol to the north to scout the large swaths of forage about a mile or so from the stronghold. Accompanying him was H Company from the 99th Regiment along with twelve of Captain Shervinton's 'Uhlans'. The few black African wagon drivers and voorloopers who'd remained at Eshowe were given the task of driving the cattle. After persuasively compelling his commanding officer, the battalion's adjutant, Lieutenant Arthur Davison was allowed to join H Company, though strictly as an observer.

"A right lovely morning, sir," the young officer said excitedly, as he rode with Colonel Pearson's entourage. He then took a deep breath through his nose. "I am most certainly glad to be able to breathe once more!"

The colonel smiled at the lieutenant's enthusiasm and gaiety, taking a deep breath himself. The air was much 'fresher' once beyond the enclosed confines of the fort.

At just twenty-two years of age, Arthur Davison was quite young for a battalion adjutant. He was assigned the post when the 99th's substantive adjutant, Charlie Harford, volunteered to serve as a staff officer with the Natal Native Contingent and assigned to No. 3 Column. This transpired months before the Regiment was ordered to the Cape. Otherwise, Lieutenant Colonel Welman would have likely denied Harford's request to serve as a volunteer officer with the NNC. Much to the relief of every officer in the 99th's mess, they learned that their battalion adjutant had survived the Isandlwana campaign.

Despite his age and lack of experience, the eager Lieutenant Davison had learned his duties quickly; all the while dealing with the hardships of life under siege with a levity that told of an unbreakable spirit.

In addition to the redcoats and 'Uhlans' were thirty men from the Naval Brigade and a detachment of Native Pioneers tasked with escorting an empty wagon used to carry any plunder back to the fort. As the 'Uhlans' and redcoats skirted the large field of tall grass, they spotted a Zulu homestead at the floor of a long valley. Captain

335

Shervinton rode back to report to Colonel Pearson, who followed him back to where the mounted troops had formed a protective screen, overlooking the Zulu kraal.

"Looks to have been recently occupied, sir," the captain remarked.

Both officers scanned with their field glasses. They could see the smoke from a hastily-doused cooking fire, as well as a pair of goats running loose.

"No doubt they ran off as soon as they saw us," the colonel remarked. He then ordered the officers to him. Pearson checked his watch before addressing them. It was now 9.30 in the morning, and they had ridden about two miles from the fort. "Pioneers and wagon drivers will secure any food stores and other spoils. Infantry will encircle the homestead and provide security with naval detachment in support. Captain Shervinton, your mounted troops will occupy the nearside ridge, ready to support if we run into trouble."

With a few acknowledgments, the officers returned to their men and relayed the orders. The four sections from H Company of the 99th led the way with the Native Pioneers close on their heels. Twice they had to dig out the wagon which, despite being unloaded, easily sank into the saturated earth. By 10.00, the pioneers and wagon drivers were gathering up piles of freshly-harvested mealie stocks along with plenty of cabbage.

Much larger than the one burned by the companies from The Buffs the day prior, this homestead showed signs of having been recently inhabited. Cooking fires still smouldered, and the carcasses of freshly butchered cattle and goats hung from rickety scaffolds. They also discovered a few shields, ten assegais, and a couple of termite-riddled muskets. The assegais were claimed by various soldiers as 'spoils of war'. The rest were tossed into the burning inferno that became the Zulu kraal.

While loading the wagon, a series of shots rang out from the far ridgeline in the distance. The range was too great for the Zulus' archaic firearms. But, in their anxiety, they could not simply watch indignantly as their homes were desecrated.

"You consume our grains, but we shall drink your coffee tomorrow!" a warrior shouted to them in heavily accented English.

"Who knew these black devils drank coffee?" Colonel Pearson remarked, shaking his head.

336

"I'm a bit surprised that any of these kaffirs speak English," Lieutenant Davison mused.

"John Dunn's lands are not far from here," Pearson remarked. "I imagine he did his best to educate a few." He then turned to the officer commanding of H Company. "Captain, be so kind as to take the hill. The 'Uhlans' will ride in support."

"Sir!" the redcoat officer acknowledged with a sharp salute.

"Colonel, permission to join the mounted troops?" Davison requested.

Pearson nodded in concurrence with the understanding that the adjutant was still an observer. He was only to assume command should Corporal Adams fall. So excited was the young officer, he cared not that the cavalrymen would be led by an NCO who was not even a professional soldier, but a civilian volunteer.

The 'Uhlans' rode in a wide arc around the backside of the line of hills. Their immediate concern was to make certain the Zulu skirmishers did not have friends in the area who could surround and ambush H Company.

Advancing up the gentle slope, the imperial redcoats moved in sections, maintaining ten to twelve feet between soldiers. For almost all of them, including the officers and NCOs, this was their first action. Watching from astride his horse near the supply wagon where pioneers and wagon drivers continued in their work, Charles Pearson was pleased with the redcoats' display of discipline. Sections advanced together under the command of their sergeants and corporals, only pausing to fire when enemy warriors showed themselves.

For Lieutenant Arthur Davison, riding with the mounted troops was the greatest thrill he'd experienced in the four years since his passing out from Sandhurst as a newly-commissioned infantry officer. The 'Uhlans' rode in a wedge formation. Davison maintained position behind Corporal Adams in the centre, while keeping enough distance so as not to interfere with their formations and scheme of manoeuvre. They first rode well beyond the rolling hills, away from the fighting, before wheeling their mounts back towards the fray.

"Look alive, lads!" Adams shouted. "Make certain there's no surprises waiting for the redcoats!"

Two of the soldiers riding with him originally came from H Company, 99th Regiment. For them the task of protecting their mates took on a far more personal meaning. They rode parallel to the sounds of firing which were becoming more sporadic. The corporal ordered his men into a gallop. As they reached the crest-line, they saw scores of Zulus fleeing into the tall grass and brush.

"Cease fire!" the officer commanding of H Company shouted as he saw friendly riders approaching.

"It's all deserted back there, sir," Corporal Adams said, with a quick salute.

"Good to hear. Now chase down those bastards!"

As the 'Uhlans' galloped away in pursuit, Lieutenant Davison reined in his horse. He saw a group of soldiers standing over three fallen Zulus. One was dead having, taken a bullet directly through the chest, shattering his sternum, while leaving a pile of shredded lung, bone splinters, and even bits of his heart in a gruesome pile next to him. The others were still alive, yet their spirits would soon be joining their ancestors. One had been struck three times in the chest, stomach, and shoulder. Davison gazed down at the poor man's mutilated body. He was surprised to see his chest still rising and falling in painful gasps. The other warrior had taken a single shot to the upper leg which shattered his femur and tore the artery. His leg lay twisted unnaturally, as torrents of dark crimson flowed from the hideous gash. His eyes were glazing over, and beads of sweat covered his face and body.

"Difficult to take one of these bastards alive," a sergeant noted, shaking his head in amazement at the fearful carnage wrecked by their large-calibre rifles. "Even when injured, they can outrun us. Only way to keep them from escaping is to kill them."

Their best chance at capturing a wounded Zulu was if they managed to graze them in the leg, tearing enough flesh to impede their ability to run, without proving fatal. However, against such a quick-moving foe, this would be a matter of blind luck. The Zulus were difficult to hit at all, and the private soldiers cared little about bringing live enemy warriors back for interrogation. Several could be heard arguing over who scored the killing shot on the warrior shot through the chest.

The sergeant's assessment regarding the fleet-footed speed of their enemies was confirmed when Corporal Adams and the 'Uhlans' returned empty-handed.

"They'd scattered to God-knows-where," the disappointed NCO explained to Colonel Pearson. "Couldn't even get a shot off at them."

Despite this, the colonel was still pleased with the conduct of both H Company and the 'Uhlans'. He was, perhaps, the only one not surprised that only three Zulus had fallen to their musketry, or that the survivors had managed to elude their mounted pursuers.

"The enemy knows this land," he said to his staff officers who had expressed frustration at the lack of prisoners from this skirmish. "And it's not as if I have a regiment of lancers to run them down."

"Perhaps Horse Guards will be kind of enough to send us one," Major Porter mused.

As the patrol pressed beyond the field, they spotted about two hundred Zulus tending to their crops another two miles distant. These quickly dispersed at the sight of nearly a hundred red-jacketed soldiers. Pearson ordered the wagon brought forward and filled with as much mealie as it could hold. Soldiers attempted to burn the rest. Given the recent rains, this proved difficult. Some piles of grass were laid within the field and set alight. The British could only hope the Zulu crops would catch fire before they returned and doused the flames.

The patrol was deemed a success. The men of H Company, 99th Regiment were filled with pride at having fought their first action. Despite his perceived nonchalance at the lack of casualties inflicted by his men, Charles Pearson showed his own frustration that evening as he supped with the column staff. The ridicule the Zulu warrior had shouted, threatening to drink the British coffee, struck a nerve with the colonel. He took it as a personal umbrage following the merciless butchery their mates in No. 3 Column suffered at Isandlwana.

"Whether we starve them to death by burning their crops or slaughter their warriors on the battlefield, I want no quarter given," he stated bluntly. "The sheer barbarism they showed our friends will spell their own destruction. From here on, our rallying cry shall be *'Remember the 24th'*."

"Hear, hear!" the assembled officers shouted in concurrence, beating their fists on the table. For the officers and men of The Buffs, the desire for retribution was particularly fierce, as many had friends from the 24th Regiment who died at Isandlwana.

As if to drive home the impertinence expressed by the Zulus, a small band emerged that evening about 400 yards from the fort. Standing behind the protective mound with just their heads and chests exposed, those who spoke English shouted a series of taunts at the garrison.

"Come out of that hole, you old women!" one warrior chastised. "We thought you English would fight, not burrow and hide in the ground!"

Another held up a tin mug full of cold coffee. "Your coffee and sugar are excellent! Why don't you come out, and we'll share some with you?"

This was a bitter reminder that nearly a dozen wagons from Lieutenant Colonel Ely's convoy had been captured by the Zulus, as was the added taunt, *"Tomorrow we come to take coffee with you!"*

Still another warrior added, "Why don't you take better care of King Cetshwayo's cattle and get them fatter? He will want them soon for the royal herd!"

Seeing some of the sentries loading their rifles, the Zulus quickly dropped behind the reverse slope of the hill which exaggerated their laughter. They shouted a few more insults at the garrison before sprinting away. If the British were becoming bolder, then so too were the Zulus.

Of greater concern to the garrison than the taunts from a handful of Zulus was the fearful toll that disease was beginning to take. The reprieve from death following the passing of Lance Corporal Thomas Taylor lasted just a few days. The evening following Colonel Pearson's raid on the Zulu kraal, Private James Shields of the 99th was found dead in the hospital, having succumbed to dysentery.

His close friend, Private William Knee, was suffering from the same affliction with a fever further addling his mind. "I have to go find Jim," he kept muttering.

With over a hundred patients crammed in and around the hospital tent, it was impossible for Surgeon Norbury and his orderlies to keep track of every man delusional with fever. It was, therefore, with little difficulty that the confused soldier was able to slip away from the hospital in the middle of the night, under the cover of yet another terrible rainstorm. Wearing nothing but his shirtsleeves and trousers, he fumbled his way towards the northern drawbridge.

"Hold!" a sentry shouted. "Where do you think you're off to? The shit trench is off the south gate."

"I have to find Jim," William said, his eyes glassed over.

With the constant downpour, the private on guard duty could scarcely hear him. And in the encompassing darkness, he could not see that the soldier was barefoot and in his shirtsleeves.

"Jim? You mean Jim Williams? Are you his relief or something?"

"I have to find Jim," the addled private persisted.

"Fine, none of my business, I suppose. There's a picquet about 200 yards beyond the drawbridge. Just watch your step out there. If you fall into the stream, you've gone too far."

Private Knee didn't seem to hear him. With his head slightly bowed, he strode with renewed purpose across the drawbridge. "The stream," he said, his mouth turned up in a confused grin. "Yes, the stream. I'll find Jim in the stream…"

The following morning, when it was discovered that William was missing, his own company volunteered to search for him. They did not have to look far, for the body of Private William Knee was found face down in a nearby stream. No wounds or signs of trauma were discovered on his body. Surgeon Norbury and Reverend Robertson were clearly distressed when they went to inform Colonel Pearson and Lieutenant Colonel Welman.

"It breaks my heart to say this, sir, for it is enough of a tragedy every time one of our men dies," the doctor began. "But in my professional opinion, Private Knee took his own life."

"I was told by his company commander that he and Private Shields were close," Welman recalled. "Private Knee even served as best man when Shields received permission to marry last year."

341

"Poor man," Pearson said with genuine sympathy. "It seems he only wanted to be with his mate."

"God have mercy on him," the reverend added sadly.

"Moral qualms aside," the surgeon added. "He was stricken with both typhoid and dysentery, and I don't think he was long for this world. As strange as this may sound—and I hope you'll forgive me for saying this, reverend—but I think it better he departed this life on his own terms."

The Eshowe graveyard, taken during the siege

Chapter XXVIII: Of Cat and Mouse

Royal Kraal of Prince Dabulamanzi
28 February 1879
***

Ever since the failed raid on the British cattle, Prince Dabulamanzi became far more meticulous in his strategy against the invaders. As brother of the king, he held seniority over Phalane and the local *izinduna*, and therefore assumed command of their warriors. With the harvest concluding in various regions throughout the kingdom, they were soon reinforced by the return of several hundred additional local warriors. Led by his uDloko Regiment, the prince re-established his presence at three separate royal homesteads surrounding Eshowe. These gave him a position of strength with which to conduct his operations against the invaders.

He was joined by an *inkosi* named Mavumengwana kaNdlela. The younger brother of Godide kaNdlela, he was one of the architects of the Zulu victory at Isandlwana. Much like Phalane, Mavumengwana tactfully avoided discussing the prince's failed attack on kwaJimu. Privately, the *inkosi* was baffled that King Cetshwayo had not disciplined his disobedient brother more thoroughly. A few years older than his sovereign, he had at least some memories from the reign of King Shaka and knew just how the *Great Elephant* would have dealt with such blatant defiance of his orders.

"Your brother, the king, is enraged that the British have been allowed to settle within our lands," Mavumengwana said plainly.

His words goaded Dabulamanzi, whose ire was even greater than Cetshwayo's. "We cannot attack their stronghold head-on," the prince remarked, recalling the brutally harsh lessons from kwaJimu. "We must draw them out into the open. The hills mask our warriors from their prying eyes, and they have little knowledge as to our total strength."

All told, he now had approximately 5,000 warriors investing the British stronghold at Eshowe. Dabulamanzi knew the enemy's food resources were not unlimited. By the same token, he had no knowledge as to how long they could last. Nearly a quarter of his

343

men were kept to the south, keeping all lines of communication and resupply cut between the redcoats and Lower Drift. And while it was their adversaries who were trapped and starving, keeping his own army fed was a daunting task. He could only hope that his brother would recall the *amabutho* as soon as the harvest was over. By utilising the cover of darkness, Dabulamanzi hoped to surround the fort with 25,000 warriors and lead them to a victory that would far surpass the hard-won struggle at Isandlwana.

Tedium had returned once again to Eshowe with even the senior officers anxious to take the fight to the Zulus. The garrison passed the time as best as they were able when not on sentry duty, rampart repair, or the various patrols within a few miles of the fort. The latter brought with them much frustration. While they came into contact frequently with the Zulus, there was little actual fighting. More often than not they never even saw their adversaries. Usually the Zulus would fire a spattering of musketry in their direction before running off, all the while shouting whatever insults they could best articulate into English.

'Come at us, you old women!'

'Pray the sun shines long today, for you look upon it for the last time!'

'The king comes to claim his cattle and your lives!'

While Colonel Pearson wished as much as any to exact retribution on the Zulus, both to alleviate their own misery as well as avenge the lives of their friends from the 24th Regiment, the coastal regions were vast and the knowledge of the garrison extremely limited. The terrain was also extremely mountainous, meaning numerous enemy kraals and barracks could still be within the near vicinity of the fort that they were unaware of.

It was now the last day of February. Pearson sat on a camp stool, pouring over a crude map of the region which was covered in his own markings. It denoted places where patrols had come into contact with the Zulus, homesteads that they had discovered and destroyed were marked, as well as a large 'X' denoting the place where he'd fought their only decisive battle more than five weeks prior.

"Your pardon, colonel," a voice said.

Pearson looked up and saw Captain Arthur Gelston, the forty-year-old paymaster attached to The Buffs, standing nearby. He and Reverend Robertson carried a large wooden cross between them. Charles knew Arthur had a talent for woodwork, and that he'd spent his free time fashioning a memorial for those killed at Inyezane.

"Ah, I see you've finished," the colonel said appreciatively. He stood and admired the Gelston's work.

"I just hope I spelled their names correctly," Gelston remarked. "I looked over the roll of the NNC officers and NCOs. Whoever scrawled it has terrible handwriting, so I had to do a little guesswork."

Pearson nodded as he looked over the names on the cross:

Lieutenant James Raines
Lieutenant Gustav Plattner
Sergeant Emil Unger
Sergeant Oscar Hydenburg
Corporal Wilhelm Lieper
Corporal Edward Miller
Corporal Carl Goesch
Private John Bough
Private William Dunne
Private James Kelleher

"I would have included the NNC warriors, but I don't know any of their names," Gelston added.

"It's a fitting memorial," Pearson asserted. His eyes wandered in the direction of the growing cemetery outside the fort. "I fear when the time comes to construct a monument to those who've perished here, the list of names will be much longer."

"I've started work on grave markers for those we've lost since the siege began," the captain noted. "Wooden markers will not last long in this climate, I'm afraid. By the time we can do proper stone markers, their names may be lost."

"Then let us hope their souls will be at peace with the words *'Here Rests a Brave British Soldier'* over their final resting place."

A grave from the No. 1 Column, Fort Pearson

While the dead were honoured, some of their more troublesome mates among the living faced a litany of disciplinary measures. The longer an army remained static, especially while under siege, the far greater the lapses in good order. The Buffs' adjutant, Lieutenant Arthur Davison, found himself preoccupied with a trio of court martials. One private was convicted of gross insubordination to a non-commissioned officer and sentenced to flogging. Another faced the same punishment for falling asleep on picquet duty. The third man was accused of abandoning his post; however, when it was found that he was suffering from terrible dysentery and had compelled one of his friends to cover his post while he relieved his bowels, he was acquitted and placed on the sick list. Lieutenant Davison could sympathise with the soldier, for he had been greatly troubled by intestinal issues of his own. He said as much to Colonel Walker, who ratified the proceedings, when the final court marital ended.

"I think that poor lad would rather face a flogging than dysentery," Davison speculated. He placed a hand over his own troubled stomach.

"I'll need to see the compiled sick list for the battalion," Walker replied.

"Yes, sir." The adjutant paused for a moment, his next words fraught with uncertainty. "Colonel, while I understand food supplies are a continuous issue for the column, I am even more concerned about medicines. After all, we cannot exactly forage for those."

"Colonel Ely's convoy brought in an entire wagon of medical supplies," Walker said, trying to reassure his young adjutant.

"And yet our numbers of sick and infirm grow, sir." For being only twenty-two, Arthur Davison was proving to be very astute.

The colonel then decided to be upfront with him. "That is why I need a compiled sick list from you, Mister Davison. We both understand that Surgeon Norbury's remedies aren't infinite, especially if as many as a quarter of the entire garrison has taken ill at any given time."

In addition to the fearful diseases of typhoid and dysentery, the squalid conditions and only marginally clean stream water to drink also brought with it an elevated risk of both cholera and typhus. What medicines the doctor did have available often treated the symptoms yet not the cause. For most, there was little they could do except rely on their natural constitution and hope their bodies could fight off the many illnesses that flourished in such squalid and stagnant conditions.

One man not happy with the results of the court martial was Davison's own commanding officer, Lieutenant Colonel Welman. Arthur sat at his camp stool, compiling his reports for the column staff. He heard the splash of angry feet as Welman stormed over to him.

"A word, Mister Davison," he said, his voice low and laced with anger.

"Of course, sir." Davison laid down his papers and stood, coming to attention.

"Explain to me how Private Williams was acquitted when he clearly left his post without authorisation?"

"The sergeant-of-the-guard was not available, sir," Arthur explained. "Private Williams called a fellow soldier over to cover his post for him, while he sought to relieve his bowels. Surgeon Norbury has attested that Williams should be placed on the sick list before his condition worsens further."

"It is not for a private soldier to decide who should stand in for him," Welman countered.

"Colonel Walker concurred with the findings, sir, as I am certain Colonel Pearson will," Davison replied. He noted the reddening of his commanding officer's complexion and knew he'd overstepped his bounds.

"It seems I was wrong to have placed my trust in you when Mister Harford left us," Welman retorted. "You, sir, are clearly not ready to be battalion adjutant."

"Then I hope you will accept my resignation, sir," Davison replied. Though he felt utterly crushed by this rebuke, he swallowed his pride and maintained his composure.

Welman was caught off-guard by this, yet he was not about to let the young lieutenant know he might have been hasty in his rebuke. Instead, he curtly nodded and informed Davison that he could finish his report to Colonel Walker before penning his resignation. This placed the 99th Regiment in a predicament, as most of their subalterns were very young and inexperienced. Welman begrudgingly admitted to himself that, had Charlie Harford still been adjutant and come to the same conclusion in Private Williams' court martial, he would have thought nothing of it. Instead, he was left with little choice but to accept Arthur Davison's resignation, returning him to his company, and handing responsibilities as adjutant over to an even less-experienced officer.

While Lieutenant Davison finished his last act as battalion adjutant, compiling the various lists given to him each day by the company commanders or subalterns, there was a great commotion near the north gate. The young adjutant rushed over to the ramparts just in time to see a patrol of 'Uhlans' returning with a lone Zulu. But rather than an enemy warrior, Captain Shervinton's troopers had captured a young Zulu lad who'd wandered too far from his homestead while chasing after errant cattle. The terrified boy was likely no older than twelve.

Colonel Pearson, the entire column staff, as well as the battalion commanders and other senior officers crowded into the confined space of the storehouse. Charles Shervinton spoke passable Zulu and offered to translate for the column staff.

"I've already interrogated him some," the captain explained. "He says he is the son of a warrior from the uDloko Regiment, and that he was acting as mat carrier for his father."

"Ask him where his father and their regiment are, and what their total strength is," Pearson demanded.

Shervinton spoke slowly, trying to put the boy's mind at ease, that the redcoats and their African allies weren't going to hurt him. The lad talked quickly, gesticulating wildly with his hands, which were bound in front of him. At one point, several of the officers perked up upon hearing the name 'Dabulamanzi'.

"Why do I know that name?" Henry Parnell asked.

"Prince Dabulamanzi is one of the king's brothers," Shervinton explained. "The uDloko is his regiment." The boy continued to talk, and the captain had to tell him to slow down a few times, so he could translate. "He says they pursued the defeated red-jacketed soldiers as they fled from the slopes of Isandlwana. They chased them all the way to the uMzinyathi River and attacked a place called kwaJimu."

"Where?" Lieutenant Colonel Welman asked, before the captain could answer.

"It's their name for Rorke's Drift," Shervinton answered.

"So, this boy was at Isandlwana and Rorke's Drift," Colonel Walker mused, his arms folded across his chest.

"A distant observer," Henry Parnell clarified.

"That still doesn't tell us anything about where the enemy is now or what their total strength is," Pearson stressed, his voice etched with irritation.

Shervinton spoke again to the young Zulu, asking him repeatedly for more information about the uDloko and where they were. The boy shrugged and spoke quickly. Sweat was forming on his brow; his lack of knowledge evident in the fear in his face.

"He says they've spent the last month taking in the harvest. It was just three days ago that his father received his summons to re-join the regiment. He does not know how many warriors are under the prince's command."

The boy went on to inform them that there was a large kraal several miles to the northeast belonging Prince Dabulamanzi. This name was not unknown to the Natal wagon drivers and voorloopers. They had previously, and rather excitedly, told their British allies that the prince was Cetshwayo's favourite brother, and it was he who lorded over these lands. Upon further questioning, the Zulu boy informed the British that it was Dabulamanzi who led the attack on Rorke's Drift.

"What shall we do with him?" a staff officer asked Pearson.

"I suspect he's told us all he knows," the colonel replied. "We'll keep him here for the time being. Once we sack the prince's kraal, hopefully drawing him into a decisive battle, we'll let the boy go. We don't need an extra mouth to feed. And besides, there is nothing he's seen within the fort that the Zulus aren't already aware of."

He then ordered Captain Shervinton to reassure the lad that he would not be harmed in any way and would be allowed to return home in a few days. As merciless as Pearson was feeling towards the Zulus, he could not bring himself to unleash his wrath on a mere boy.

As he dispatched his few mounted troops to send a patrol to the northeast to ascertain the accounts from the Zulu boy, Colonel Pearson found himself once again regretting sending Captain Percy Barrow and the Imperial Mounted Infantry back to Lower Drift. Still, despite their numbers being so few, Charles Shervinton and the self-styled 'Uhlans' had performed well as the eyes of the column.

In addition to finding the kraal, Shervinton hoped to gather what intelligence he could regarding its size and garrison. On the following morning, the first day of March, Colonel Charles Pearson would lead his men in what he hoped would be the first major battle since Inyezane.

The officer and a dozen troopers set off later that afternoon, riding in a loose wedge, keeping at least thirty feet between each other. There was little doubt in any of their minds that the enemy was watching them, though not once did their adversaries make their presence known. Shervinton suspected this may have been because even fleet-footed Zulu warriors would be hard-pressed to catch men on horseback. The Siege of Eshowe had turned into a waiting game; each side anticipating when their opponents might make a mistake or leave themselves vulnerable.

"Over there, sir!" a trooper said excitedly. He pointed towards a large stand of huts about a mile distant. They had already travelled over six; the furthest they had ventured from the fort.

Captain Shervinton halted his detachment and dismounted. Handing the reins of his horse to one of his men, he pulled his field glasses from his saddlebag and knelt behind a large boulder. "I count at least fifty huts, probably more," he said, as Sergeant Lewis knelt next to him, his own glasses up to his eyes. "Cooking fires, lots of cattle."

"But no women or children," the NCO observed.

"I spoke with that boy we captured just before we left," Shervinton said. He lowered his glasses. "He said there are, in fact, two homesteads in this area. This one is called eSiqwakeni. There is supposedly an even larger one less than another mile from there. *That* is the real prize, as I believe it is the prince's personal kraal."

"I say, there's a bleeding road leading right to it," Sergeant Lewis said, pointing off to their right as he continued to scan.

The captain brought up his glasses once more and grinned. "Well, that will make finding the place in the middle of the night all the easier."

Satisfied that they had accomplished the column commander's intent, they remounted their horses and galloped back to Eshowe. It was nearly suppertime, and the senior staff were anxiously awaiting their return. Captain Shervinton took the time to review some notes he'd made, as well as make a few notations on the battered map he'd been drawing since they first arrived.

"There are two major homesteads, both located to the northeast," the 'Uhlan' commander explained to the column staff and battalion commanders. "Given their size and location, we believe that both belong to the king's brother, Prince Dabulamanzi." He ran his finger over two points on the map where he had sketched a few notes. "The first is about seven miles from here. It's quite large, about fifty or sixty huts from what we could tell. The warriors have sent their women and children further inland from the looks of it, but there is still plenty of life there. We spotted an overgrown trail we can follow. It will take us around a cluster of hills and lead us straight to the kraal."

351

"I thought the Zulus had no use for trails or roads?" Lieutenant Colonel Welman asked.

"Most likely it was used by John Dunn and other European traders, sir," the captain explained.

Welman gritted his teeth, feeling slightly embarrassed. Because the 99th had arrived just prior to the invasion, he had far less knowledge and experience in Southern Africa than any of his fellow officers, most of whom had been in Natal for several years.

The NNC officer continued, "As large as this homestead is, there is another supposedly even greater stronghold about two miles further north. I suspect this may be the prince's royal kraal."

"Any idea as to their fighting strength?" Colonel Pearson asked, his arms folded across his chest, brow furrowed in thought.

"The number of huts at the combined locations is likely in the hundreds, sir. And over the last two mornings, we've seen perhaps five hundred warriors harrying and provoking our patrols. That said, this is only a fraction of their warriors. Judging from the capacity of each hut, and assuming they've received at least some reinforcements from Ulundi, I would hazard that they have at least 5,000 fighting men ready for battle."

"And that's just between those two kraals," Henry Parnell noted. "I suspect they may have more friends lurking about at homesteads we have yet to find."

"A possibility, sir," Shervinton conceded. "However, I believe their greatest concentration of warriors are at these locations. And mind you, Dabulamanzi is a member of the Zulu royal house, so he could conceivably have more kraals or barracks in the region."

The assembled officers conferred quietly in small groups until at last Henry Parnell looked to the column commander. "What do you think, sir?" he asked. "Shall we go and pay a house-call to our gracious hosts?"

"Bastards keep taunting us every day," Welman added. "I wish that 'white Zulu', John Dunn, hadn't taught so many of them to speak English! Only yesterday a couple of their scouts shouted to my lads on the wall that the coffee and sugar they stole from one of our abandoned wagons was delightful, but that we should take better care of 'Cetshwayo's cattle'. Mr Dunn fled to Natal and has yet to fully cooperate with the armed forces of his own country. He could save us a lot of trouble by deciding which side he's truly on."

"Bloody impertinent," Colonel Walker added with scorn.

"Colonel Parnell," Pearson said, after taking a moment to digest all the information given to him. "Ready four of your half-companies. Colonel Welman, select a full one of yours to join the raid. The Uhlans will screen our force, as well as provide a rear guard. Captain Wynne, you will join us with half your company. I suspect we may need them to clear any potential obstacles. We'll also bring a single artillery gun under Lieutenant Lloyd. Natal Pioneers and the 3rd Regiment's bandsmen will act as stretcher-bearers. The Zulus aren't known for being night fighters. If we have a road to follow, then we can attack under the cover of darkness. We will assemble at midnight."

Chapter XXIX: A Prince's Retribution

Eshowe
28 February 1879

Zulu Warrior in battle regalia

"At last, time for a real scrap!" soldiers shouted, as they were briefed by their section leaders. Some attempted to catch a couple hours of sleep prior to the midnight assembly, though most were too anxious at the thought of an actual battle against the Zulus.

Colour Sergeant Michael Smith conducted evening parade for No. 2 Field Company, while Captain Wynne and his subalterns decided which sections to take with them. They chose the most senior and experienced of their sergeants and corporals, who would in turn know which of their sappers were the most level-headed and able to improvise should they run into trouble in the middle of the night.

At midnight, the task force assembled. Between the four half-companies from The Buffs, the full company from the 99th, sixty sappers from No. 2 Field Company, Lieutenant Lloyd's cannon crew, forty Royal Marines from the HMS Active, plus the bandsmen and Natal Pioneers, Colonel Pearson had just over 500 total troops ready to raid the royal kraals of Prince Dabulamanzi. It took some time to assemble and was nearly 2.00 by the time the column departed the fort.

The skies were devoid of clouds and the stars and moon shone bright. It was quite possibly the clearest night they had seen since the start of the war. The South African autumn was nigh, with every British soldier in Zululand praying this meant an end to the ceaseless rains. The mounted troops took the lead, riding in a wide skirmishing formation about fifty yards in front of the column. Several black Africans, who claimed to be at least somewhat familiar with the region, acted as guides leading them to John Dunn's trade path.

Captain Wynne's engineers marched at the head of the dismounted troops with Lieutenant Lloyd's single cannon, along with the escort of marines just behind them. Colonel Pearson rode next to Warren, where he could best direct his forces once battle was engaged. The half-companies from The Buffs followed with the single company from the 99th taking up the rear guard. All moved noiselessly, without so much as a whisper coming from the men in the ranks. Even their horses seemed to understand the need for silence. The only sounds to be heard came from the rattling wheels of the gun carriage.

Though the moon and starlight made it easy to see, the path they sought had not seen much use over the past year while hostilities festered between the Zulu Kingdom and her British neighbours to the south in Natal. As such, tall grasses obscured much of the trail. One of the African guides found the path almost by accident. He tripped over one of the deep ruts that lay completely hidden in the thick, lush grass. With a few wordless signals from Captain Shervinton back to Colonel Pearson and the rest of the column, they veered onto the trail, now able to march at an even quicker stride. They kept a measured pace, averaging just over three miles an hour.

When the 'Uhlans' estimated they were about a mile from eSiqwakeni, they slowed their pace and offered to ride ahead. Colonel Pearson concurred, ordering Captain Wynne to send a section of his sappers with them to act as an advance guard. The engineer officer then passed the word to Sergeant Richard Small who signalled for his section to follow him. Warren also sent one of his subalterns, Lieutenant Main, with this force.

It was now around 4.30, and the first light of the early morning sun cast its glow off to their right. Captain Shervinton halted the advance guard just behind the crest of a gradual rise. He and Lieutenant Main dismounted. Accompanied by Sergeant Small and Sergeant Lewis, they crept forward to take a look at the enemy stronghold. They approached from the south rather than the west, where Shervinton and his mounted troopers had come from the day before.

"There it is," the NNC officer said.

The four men knelt near a brush thicket.

"Not a soul moving down there," Thomas Main observed. He scanned the kraal with his field glasses.

Prince Dabulamanzi's stronghold of eSiqwakeni lay sprawled out about a thousand yards from where they knelt. The smoke from a score of cooking fires from the previous night still smouldered. Off to their left, about 500 yards distant, was a smaller Zulu homestead nestled behind another short rise, which had shielded it from the view of Captain Shervinton's previous patrol.

"Here comes the rest of the column, sir," Sergeant Small said, looking back over his shoulder. The infantry companies were deploying into section lines on either side of the trail, hunkering low as they reached the top of the rise. About 200 yards further back, the Royal Marines struggled to heft Lieutenant Lloyd's gun up the incline; the heavily gouged, rutted trail creating an even greater hindrance than the unspoiled grassland.

"Colonel," Lieutenant Main said quietly, as their commanding officer dismounted his horse and joined them. "They're still fast asleep. If we attack now, we'll catch them with their pants down."

"Not yet," Pearson replied, shaking his head. "I want Mister Lloyd's gun in position first."

"Your pardon, sir, but every minute we wait, the greater the chance of the Zulus spotting us."

"That will do, Mister Main," Captain Wynne said quickly, before Colonel Pearson could chastise his subaltern.

"Yes, sir."

Pearson was clearly irritated, though he understood the lieutenant's desire to launch their attack sooner rather than later. He took a moment to search the large stronghold with his field glasses. There were even more huts than Captain Shervinton had first estimated. The colonel counted at least sixty surrounding the large cattle kraal. Off to their right ran a deep ravine overgrown with brush. Colonel Pearson was scanning this with his glasses when suddenly Captain Shervinton alerted him.

"Over there, sir!"

At the previously unseen Zulu homestead, a lone man emerged from his hut. He walked over to the grassy field behind to relieve himself, oblivious to the swarm of red-jacketed soldiers massing on the ridge behind him. Fearing they would be spotted any moment, the 'Uhlans' commander snapped his fingers and pointed to Sergeant Lewis and three troopers. As they quickly mounted their horses, the Zulu man made his way back towards his hut, when suddenly he halted, his eyes were wide in terror. Just as Sergeant Lewis kicked his horse into a gallop, the man sprinted down the hill towards the royal kraal, shouting a warning at the top of his lungs.

"Damn it all," Pearson swore, now regretting not heeding Lieutenant Main's advice to attack the stronghold sooner. "Captain Wynne, take your men and clear out that ravine then advance on the stronghold. The rest of the column will follow."

"Sir." Warren now stood upright. There was no sense in trying to hide any longer. "Sappers on me!"

The engineer officers left their mounts with a servant and drew their pistols. Wynne followed close behind Sergeant Small's section in the centre while Lieutenants Main and Courtney took the wings. David Courtney pulled a pair of rather large spectacles out of his breast pocket and placed them on his face. This caused Main to laugh out loud.

"Dash it all, Courtney, can you even see through those?"

"Not when they keep fogging up in this damned humidity," his friend replied.

The shouts of alarm woke Prince Dabulamanzi from his deep slumber. He bolted upright, feeling around in the darkness for his musket and ammunition pouch. Though he'd managed to scrounge some more bullets and powder, the lack of percussion caps meant he had to settle for using one of his older and shoddier Tower flintlocks.

Rubbing his eyes feverishly, he emerged from his tent, as scores of warriors began to assemble. The prince had spent the night at his royal *ikhanda*, or barracks, just over a mile further up the road from eSiqwakeni. A pair of warriors who'd risen early to retrieve water had spotted the commotion from the kraal down below. Many of their compatriots were fleeing in all directions.

"My prince, the English are attacking eSiqwakeni!" a warrior shouted anxiously.

The thundering boom of a cannon accented his remark.

Dabulamanzi quickly looked around to assess his fighters. *Izinduna* were rallying their companies, and the prince surmised he had about 400 men ready for battle.

"Skirmishers to the front!" he ordered, raising his musket high. "Follow me; we will take up positions along the crest of the ridge overlooking eSiqwakeni."

"But what of the kraal itself?" an *induna* asked.

Dabulamanzi squinted his eyes as he scanned the valley below. It was difficult to determine how large the British force was, though he guessed they numbered in the hundreds. Redcoats were advancing down the far hill, while a handful of mounted troops were riding towards the lower stronghold. The enemy cannon fired once more, scattering bands of warriors who were driving their cattle away.

"We cannot save it," the prince replied despondently. "But they will not take the royal *ikhanda*."

Dabulamanzi knew he was facing a serious dilemma. He did not have the numbers to deal with the opposing British force, who might well have him outnumbered. And as every warrior who fought at Inyezane, Isandlwana, or kwaJimu could attest, the range and accuracy of the redcoats' rifles was terrifying. Fortunately, unlike much of the regional terrain that was open grassland, there were actually many thickets and brush stands on the slopes of the hill that they could utilise for concealment. The prince ordered his *izinduna* to spread their marksmen out and to fire by volleys in hopes of making the British think their numbers were much larger than they actually were.

Hefting his musket, Dabulamanzi and roughly twenty warriors from his personal escort found a thick brush stand to hide behind. It was very old and gnarled with a thick trunk and branches. He ordered his men to lie prone. Wiping away some of the fallen twigs and leaves, Dabulamanzi proceeded to load his musket. After his humiliating defeat at kwaJimu, he was eager to exact retribution against Queen Victoria's redcoats.

Colonel Pearson had never intended for Warren Wynne's sappers to become the vanguard of his assault force. However, once the column was spotted and any chance at a methodical and deliberate attack evaporated, the men of No. 2 Field Company happened to be those closest and in the best position to support the 'Uhlans'.

Despite the thick undergrowth, Sergeant Small's lead section cleared the ravine very quickly, emerging about half-a-mile from the Zulu *ikhanda*. His pistol still drawn, Captain Wynne glanced back over his shoulder and saw that the long line of redcoats were about 200 yards behind them. Meanwhile, Charles Shervinton's mounted troops had reached eSiqwakeni. Taking brands from the Zulu cook fires, they were setting fire to all the huts and looting what little plunder could be found inside.

"No. 2 Company!" Warren shouted, as the last of his sappers emerged from the ravine. "Skirmishing order, at the quick step...march!"

He and his men rushed towards the fray. The engineer captain could hear the clattering of wheels on the broken-up trail. Having driven the Zulus off with a well-placed shot from his 7-pounder, Lieutenant Lloyd ordered the gun limbered up and brought forward. The weight of the cannon propelled it downhill, compelling the team of horses to sprint the rest of the way to the bottom. The Royal Marine escorts ran as fast as they could in a vain effort to keep up with the runaway gun and its crew. For his part, Lieutenant Lloyd was relieved the cannon made it safely to the bottom of the bowl without tipping over. One crewman was thrown from his seat and landed hard on his bottom near the base of the slope.

"Unlimber and make ready to fire common shot!" the artillery officer ordered, as he rode up on his horse.

While his jarred crewmen unhitched the gun and spun it around to face in the direction of the far hill, Lloyd brought up his field glasses and estimated the range of a large band of Zulus escaping up the hill. Though their quarry had scattered in multiple directions, there were at least fifty or so that he felt were a rich target for his gunners.

"Set for 800 yards!"

"Set for 800 yards!" the sergeant in command of the gun echoed.

A small powder bag and single 7-pound shot were brought forward and shoved into the barrel. A crewman with a large ramrod hammered the charge and shot home. The sergeant and gunner checked the elevation before nodding to their officer.

"Fire!"

The cannon erupted with a loud boom, engulfing the men in a thick cloud of smoke. Through his field glasses and astride his horse, Lieutenant Lloyd could see the shot burst behind the last of the Zulu stragglers. Two of them tumbled to the ground and appeared to have been hit in the legs.

"Swab barrel and reload!"

He then gave the order to increase the elevation a couple degrees. In less than a minute, the well-drilled crew had their gun ready to fire again. With another thunderous report, the 7-pound cannon sent a shot towards their fleeing foe. This time it burst amongst a throng of warriors, sending as many as ten sprawling to the ground. The artillery officer grinned with malicious glee. The shards and round balls of the 'common shot' had likely killed at least half of them. Before the crew could reload the cannon, the last of the Zulus disappeared over the far rise.

"Well done, Mister Lloyd," Colonel Pearson said, as he galloped his horse over to the artillery crew.

"Thank you, sir. I'd hazard we dropped at least ten of the damned kaffirs. I can see several wounded lying on the slope."

"Yes," Pearson concurred, looking through his field glasses. "There's two fellows trying to crawl away. Looks like you got them in the legs."

"That we did, sir," Lloyd concurred.

"Splendid!" Pearson called out to his 'Uhlan' officer. "Captain Shervinton. Take your men and bring me back a prisoner or two. And take the pioneers to support you."

"Very good, sir." Shervinton snapped off a sharp salute before ordering his men to follow him.

The Natal Pioneers were local Africans who, unlike their counterparts in the NNC that were only issued a red head scarf, wore red tunics not dissimilar to those of the professional infantry. Following close behind the 'Uhlans', they started to make their way up the far hill. All the while, the *ikhanda* known as eSiqwakeni was slowly engulfed in flames. Wet thatch hissed as the crackle of flames grew louder. Great plumes of ash whipped up into the air, the pungent smell assailing the nostrils of all within half-a-mile of the *ikhanda*.

No sooner had Captain Shervinton's mounted troopers began their ascent when a barrage of musketry was unleashed from near the crest of the hill. Horses reared, and Warren Wynne swore he could hear the sharp whipping sound of bullets that came uncomfortably close.

Back near Lieutenant Lloyd's cannon, Colonel Pearson watched the skirmish unfold. 'Uhlans', Natal Pioneers, and imperial sappers scattered and sought cover. He could see scores, possibly hundreds, of gouts of black powder smoke coming from well-hidden Zulu marksmen. Though a few of his men were returning fire, it was clear the enemy had re-established himself on high ground with plenty of protective concealment.

"Colonel!" It was Captain Forster from The Buffs, whose companies had at last reached the gun. They were deployed in a long skirmish line with the lone company from the 99th a few yards behind in support. The Buffs' officer took a moment to apprise the situation before giving a confident nod. "Looks like the Zulus are up for a scrap after all. We're ready to advance, sir. Just give the word and we'll drive those bastards from the heights."

Pearson was suddenly filled with doubt. He could not readily tell how many Zulu warriors were on the slopes, or behind the ridge waiting for them. "No," he replied, drawing a perplexed stare from the infantry captain. "We've lost the initiative, and I suspect that every Zulu within ten miles is converging on this place."

He then told his nearby bugler to sound recall. This baffled every soldier in the column, even the 'Uhlans', pioneers, and sappers who were being subjected to the barrage of Zulu musketry. Heeding the bugle call, they rushed back to their colonel, using the growing clouds of smoke from the burning *ikhanda* to mask their retreat.

"We've caused enough havoc for one day," Pearson explained to his assembled officers, nodding towards the enemy stronghold, the heat of the flames causing them great discomfort. "I'll not throw away lives trying to burn another Zulu barracks to the ground. Captain Wynne, you'll proceed back the way you came. Captain Shervinton, divide your men into two elements, one to cover the head of the column, the other the rear. The 99th will provide rear guard for the infantry." The colonel spoke quickly, hastily ordering the confused officers to return to their companies.

Several profane shouts were heard from various enlisted soldiers, particularly amongst the infantry, who were utterly disgusted by this sudden order to retreat.

"We finally got the bloody Zulus into a fight, and now we're running away?" one private asked in exasperation. His subsequent loud complaint of *'Fuck me!'* was met with a sharp slap across the back of the head from his sergeant, along with the promise of ten hours of additional duty for his impertinence.

Colonel Pearson never gave any inclination as to whether he could hear any of the complaints. Though he shared in his soldiers' frustrations, he felt it would be suicide to order his men to launch an attack straight up a slope into the muskets of hundreds of Zulu skirmishers. Had he known he had the enemy outnumbered and that they were bluffing, he might have reconsidered his decision. As it was, he felt it prudent to return to Eshowe, having destroyed an enemy stronghold and killed a few of their warriors.

Near the edge of the ravine his men had cleared earlier, Captain Wynne happened upon a small group of soldiers and a lance corporal from the 99th who were acting as part of the rear guard.

"You'll want to be careful there, sir," the lance corporal said. "We spotted a handful of Zulus lurking about in the brush. Unfortunately, they went to ground before we could pot them."

362

Warren nodded and ordered his men to stay alert. About halfway back to the base of the hill they'd originally came from, several shots rang out from the ravine.

Wynne jolted as he heard a 'snap' not far to his left. "Dash it all," he said under his breath, before calling over his shoulder. "Sergeant Small! Sort out those fellows, if you'd be so kind."

"Right away, sir!" With a subsequent command, twenty sappers formed a hasty firing line beside their NCO. At Sergeant Small's order, they fired a volley into the brush and thickets of the ravine below. With their ears ringing and acrid smoke stinging their noses and mouths, they searched for any signs of life. All was still. "Seems they've hoofed it, sir."

"Very good. Keep your eyes open, sergeant, and pot any Zulu who so much as shows his head."

Small nodded, and the company continued on its way. No other signs of the enemy manifested from the ravine. Captain Wynne checked his watch. It was now 6.45, and the sun was shining brightly down on them. With nary a cloud in the sky, it would be a mercilessly hot day. And of course, they now had seven miles to trek back to Eshowe. He doubted the Zulus would let them retire unhindered.

While pleased that he had driven the enemy away from the royal *ikhanda* and they were now in full retreat, Prince Dabulamanzi was dissatisfied that his skirmishers failed to bring down a single British soldier or their hateful Natal allies.

"Had we allowed them to get much closer, they might have seen how few in number we were," an *induna* explained, as the prince expressed his disappointment at how soon his marksmen had opened fire.

"Pursue the invaders, but keep your distance," Dabulamanzi ordered his senior warriors. "I want them sent cowering back to the walls of their stronghold like whipped beasts."

"Bayade!" an *induna* shouted, raising his musket. This shout of praise was echoed by the surrounding warriors who followed their leaders, as they chased down the fleeing redcoats.

With skill and precision that greatly impressed the British on the few occasions they could see them, bands of Zulu warriors easily kept pace with the retreating column. Utilising drills not unlike those the redcoats practiced, bands of ten to twenty men would fire a volley in the direction of their adversaries, while a similar number bounded towards the next piece of cover or concealment. These warriors, in turn, would unleash salvos of musketry, allowing their friends to subsequently rush past them. Keeping behind any rises they came across and using trees and brush stands to conceal their movements, it was glaringly apparent that the British were struggling to respond with any sort of cohesive return fire.

To their credit, the enemy soldiers were following a different, much longer route, which took them beyond several large groves of forest where the Zulus had hoped to ambush them. The imperial redcoats would later admit that they were extremely lucky the Zulus had no modern firearms among their ranks. Had they been equipped with Martini-Henrys or other similar rifles, the column would have suffered horrendous losses and quite possibly been overrun completely. As it was, they managed to limp back to the safety of the fort at Eshowe without suffering any casualties. In spite of this, as the Zulus halted about two miles from the fort and delivered their parting shots, there was little doubt in anyone's mind on either side who the true victors were that day.

Chapter XXX: Despatches from the Outside World

Eshowe
2 March 1879

Latest News, from *The Graphic*

Frustration at the utter failure of the previous day's attempted raid fouled the mood of the garrison at Eshowe. Though they had destroyed one sizeable kraal and burned several other homesteads, while killing ten or so enemy warriors, the decisive battle they had hoped for never materialised. That the Zulus harassed them the entire way back to their stronghold made them feel utterly vanquished.

For Captain Warren Wynne, who was full of energy the previous day, the hopes that his robust health had been restored were dashed on the 2nd of March. The severe diarrhoea that had plagued him for weeks returned. He spent most of the evening squatting over the latrine trench. Warren later confessed to David Courtney that he felt 'weak and headachy' and did not think he would be fit to lead the company at morning parade. This was doubly disappointing for the devout captain. The 2nd was also Sunday, and his being placed on the sick list meant he would miss Reverend Robertson's church service. Still, it meant he managed to get more than just a couple hours of sleep. And when David Courtney came to check on him at around noon, he found his officer commanding sitting upright on his field bed, penning a letter to his beloved Lucy.

"Ah, Mister Courtney," Warren said, with a tired smile. His face was still pale, yet he appeared in much better condition than when he told his senior subaltern he was going on the sick list the night before. Wynne nodded to the papers in David's hands. "What have you there? Some despatches that need my attention?'

"No," Courtney said, shaking his head and smiling. "Just the notes Reverend Robertson put together for today's church service. Since you were unable to attend, he said I could give them to you."

"Please give my thanks to the good reverend," Warren said earnestly. He took the papers from his subaltern. then remarked, "Though I feel much better, I am going to follow your advice, Mister Courtney, and take it easy today. After all, even the Lord took a day of rest. I do hope to be in better health tomorrow. I would apologise for saddling you with the responsibility of command, though I have full confidence that, should the worst happen to me, No. 2 Field Company would be left in good hands."

"I appreciate your confidence, sir," the subaltern replied, before leaving his captain to finish the letter to his wife in private.

As it was Sunday, the entire garrison was given a day of rest. Only some minor repairs to the north ramparts along with the cattle guarding and occasional mounted vedette continued. The guarding of the herd was becoming an increasingly smaller task, as the number of cattle had thinned considerably. By the first week of March, less than half of the original 200 remained.

It was around 3.00 in the afternoon when one of the mounted patrols led by Corporal Adams of the 'Uhlans' rode with all haste back to the camp. There was no hiding his excitement as the NCO leapt from the saddle, nearly falling onto his backside, while an African groom quickly grabbed the reins of the exhausted beast. Captain Shervinton was out leading a patrol of his own, so Adams sought out the first officer he could find. That happened to be Lieutenant Courtney of the engineers.

"Lieutenant, sir," Adams said, coming to attention.

"Stand easy, corporal," David replied. "Now, what can I do for you?"

"Captain Shervinton is out with a patrol, sir, and I need to get word to Colonel Pearson at once. I believe the garrison at Thukela is trying to signal us."

After Adams explained all that he had seen, Courtney's eyes widened slightly for a moment. He then gave a curt nod and instructed the corporal to follow him. Though not a signals officer, he was well-versed in all forms of communications available to the army. He first found the column staff officer, Captain McGregor, who relayed the message to Colonels Walker and Pearson. Adams was then brought before the column commander.

"Now, corporal, what is it exactly that you saw?"

"A constant flicker of light coming from the direction of Lower Drift, sir. It may not seem like much, but it was the way it flickered; glared, more like."

"Probably just the garrison setting fire to a Zulu homestead," Captain McGregor said dismissively.

"If you wish, sir, I can take you there and you can decide for yourself what it may or may not be," Adams countered.

Pearson folded his arms and contemplated for a few moments. "With no chance of runners reaching us from Lower Drift, the garrison may have indeed resorted to a more improvised means of reaching us."

"It would be a relief to know that all of Natal isn't now overrun with Zulus," Lieutenant Colonel Welman added. "With your permission, sir, I would like to lead the patrol to determine the veracity of the corporal's report."

"See to it, then."

Thirty minutes later, a reinforced patrol led by Henry Welman and consisting mostly of staff officers departed the fort. Despite his promise to relax for the day, Captain Wynne requested to join them, that he might see the possible signal for himself. Captain Shervinton had also returned from his patrol and was cautiously optimistic about what Adams and his troopers had witnessed. As for the corporal, his concern was that the signal would be gone by the time they returned.

It was late afternoon when the officers along with Corporal Adams and half-a-dozen 'Uhlans' reached the rolling ridgeline. The NCO held his breath as they rode up to the highest point. He let out a sigh of relief. The glint of light was still clearly visible in the distance. There was no response from Welman or the staff officers for a few minutes as they sat astride their mounts, taking turns looking through their field glasses at the light.

"What do you make of that?" the colonel asked Wynne. "Do you think it could be a camp fire or trick of sunlight?"

Warren did not answer for a few moments. He tried to determine any distinct features, yet even with his field glasses he could only see the glare of light. "I doubt it's a fire, sir. There's no smoke visible. And the light seems permanently fixed. Given its concentration in one spot, unmoving, it has to be deliberately placed."

"The rest of the army hasn't forgotten about us after all," Lieutenant Davison of the 99th said, with an expression of joy and relief.

"We need to send a return signal," Wynne stated. "There's just one problem. We have no heliograph."

The heliograph was a fairly new innovation which utilised a series of moveable mirrors to reflect the sun's light, allowing the operator to signal using Morse code. It was essentially a solar telegraph, ideally suited for such circumstances. Unfortunately, even though the British Army possessed heliographs in its signals inventory, none had made their way to Southern Africa.

"That's why we have you, Captain Wynne," Henry Welman asserted.

Though Warren appreciated the vote of confidence, and was well-aware of his superior mathematical abilities, he was no miracle worker. It would take the combined efforts of the Eshowe garrison to come up with a viable means of communicating with whatever forces may be gathering at Lower Drift.

By the time this latest patrol returned, word had already spread throughout the fort. This renewed the previously crushed morale of the column. Soldiers talked excitedly, as they went about the drudgery of their daily grind at Eshowe.

The view back towards Lower Drift, where Corporal Adams first saw the signal
The Indian Ocean is just visible on the far horizon

"In the very least, it means that Natal has not been overrun by the Zulus," Sergeant Richard Small of the Royal Engineers said.

He was joined by Colour Sergeant Michael Smith. The two stood atop the barricades that faced southeast. Richard's section was on sentry duty, and Smith was checking the company sappers, particularly their health and morale.

"That is about *all* we know with any certainty," the colour sergeant stressed. "Still, at this point, it is enough."

"How long has it been since we lost all communication?" Small asked. "Two weeks?"

"Nearly three," Smith corrected. "We have to remind the lads not to jump to any conclusions until we know what exactly the state is of our forces in Natal."

"Agreed. We know half of Colonel Glyn's column was destroyed along with all those poor lads from the 24th; God rest their souls. Let us hope Colonel Wood's boys have fared better, and that we can get some damned reinforcements soon."

It was with much surprise that they saw their officer commanding coming towards them. He still moved a bit slowly, given his condition just the day before. Yet, there was great purpose in his step.

"Good afternoon to you, captain," Colour Sergeant Smith said. "I'm surprised to see you up and about."

"I plan on relaxing the rest of the evening," Warren promised. "Meantime, I need Sergeant Small. You took a course on signalling, correct?"

"Yes, sir. I admit I'm a bit out of practice, but I do still have my notes on Morse code in my pack."

"Bring them," the captain ordered. "I've told Lieutenant Main to find a replacement for you as sergeant-of-the-guard. The column has a far more important task for you."

While the elements of No. 1 Column at Eshowe struggled daily with the very real fears regarding their survival, many of those remaining at Lower Drift had allowed their minds to wander. *Why* were the Crown and the Zulus now at war? This was especially true amongst the settler volunteers, who had a more direct stake in the war's outcome than their regular army counterparts. The politics behind the conflict were completely unknown to the men in the ranks. Even most of the officers had no knowledge about the underhanded methods by the High Commissioner that had led to this bitter conflict with the Zulus. All anyone knew was that their nations were locked in a savage struggle, and if the British Empire was to avoid further catastrophe, then Horse Guards needed to send more regiments to the Cape as soon as possible! That, at least, everyone could agree on.

As for the garrison at Lower Drift, there was also a greater sense of urgency to establish communications with the garrison at Eshowe. Despite their own victory at Inyezane on the 22nd of January, news of No. 3 Column's horrifying and bloody defeat at Isandlwana made them ever fearful for their mates who remained trapped under siege. And if they had been wiped out, the roving bands of Zulus weren't feeling inclined to shout it out to them.

The idea for establishing a makeshift heliograph came from the newly-arrived Lieutenant Colonel Francis Law, Royal Artillery. With Law assuming overall command of Lower Drift, Brevet Lieutenant Colonel Coates of the 99th was relegated to taking charge of the companies from his regiment. The orders from Chelmsford were to establish communications, if possible, with the garrison at Eshowe. While the GOC awaited reinforcements from Britain, Law was directed to do what he could to bring some relief to their besieged brethren.

For the soldiers of H Company, 2/3rd Buffs, Lieutenant Colonel Law's arrival brought much anticipation that they would, at last, leave the squalor of their camp at Lower Drift and re-join the fight against the Zulus. On the afternoon of the 2nd of March, both David Fredericks and Robert Anderson watched with wonder as several soldiers adjusted the rather archaic apparatus, from which hung a full-length mirror that Lieutenant Colonel Law brought as part of his baggage.

"Now let us hope the lads at Eshowe can see it," Rob remarked. "Might raise their spirits a bit, knowing we haven't forgotten them."

David nodded in reply and folded his arms across his chest.

"How is Private Rutledge?" he then asked, catching Anderson off guard.

The lance sergeant bit the inside of his cheek before answering. "He's still in rough shape, but the doctor thinks the worst has passed. His fever broke yesterday, and he was able to eat for the first time in over a week. Surgeon-Major Tarrant wants him to rest for a few more days, then return to light duty for about a week. I admit, I am still mortified that I had to learn a hard lesson this way; a lesson that one of my soldiers nearly paid the ultimate price for."

"At least you learned, and Private Rutledge will recover," David said.

"I thought I knew all there was to being a section leader..." Robert's voice trailed off, and he shook his head in frustration.

"Don't think for a minute that I know everything about leading Her Majesty's soldiers," David countered. "Hell, I would say even Colour Sergeant Bennet is still learning. And to be honest, I still blame myself some days for Private Walters' court-martial. I wasn't even sergeant-of-the-guard that night; however, he is one of my men, which makes me responsible."

"As much as we try to beat discipline and obedience into them, they still have minds of their own," Anderson commented. "I'm just glad his punishment ceased after the first flogging."

"Colour Sergeant Bennet had a hand in that," David explained. "He went to the sergeant major, who in turn compelled Lieutenant Colonel Coates to make the subsequent flogging sessions disappear

371

from record. There have been four subsequent court-martials that warranted a flogging sentence. Private Walters' negligence has since been forgotten."

"There have been numerous minor incidents to deal with as well, namely fighting. The daily drudgery and tedium has left the lads bored and frustrated. And with their tempers hot, they inevitably end up taking out their grievances on each other."

Sergeant Fredericks understood. He recalled an incident from the previous day where two of his soldiers—normally the best of friends—had gotten into a rather fearsome brawl. No one could remember why it started, only that both were left with bloody and bruised faces. One soldier's eye was half closed as a result. After giving both men a thorough dressing-down, David awarded them both twenty hours of extra duty. He had then noted with a touch of morbid humour that at least it wasn't the soldier's shooting eye that had swollen shut. He further chastised the men that any further such unbecoming acts would be brought before their officer commanding, which would lead to court martial and a far stiffer penalty than twenty hours extra duty.

"Lance Sergeant Anderson," a voice called from behind them.

They turned to see Lieutenant Martin accompanied by one of Law's staff officers they had not seen before.

"Sir," Robert replied, snapping to attention.

"You took a signalling course once, did you not?"

"I did, sir. It was a two-week class on Morse code that the signals officers gave prior to our departure for the Cape."

"Good. Come with me. Colonel Law has a little task for you."

They did not have to go far. Law had gathered his staff and company commanders near their makeshift heliograph. "Ah, sergeant," he said, acknowledging Rob.

"Sir."

"As you can see," Law explained, "We've managed to fashion a crude means of sending a visual signal to the trapped garrison at Eshowe. I've had my secretary write a despatch which I need you to send to Colonel Pearson. Right now, we're not even sure if they've seen our signal. Starting tomorrow, you will send the message to them every hour."

"Yes, sir."

Lieutenant Colonel Law nodded and then addressed Anderson's officer commanding. "Mister Martin, Sergeant Anderson is exempt from all other duties for the time being. Establishing communications with the Eshowe garrison is now our utmost priority."

The following day dawned wet and misty with thick clouds overhead. This came as a great frustration to the men at Eshowe, since this thwarted their attempts at renewing communication with their forces at Lower Drift. The naval brigade had fired a couple of rockets into the air, though they had gone straight into low-hanging clouds, and their bursts had likely gone unnoticed. Still, soldiers showed resourcefulness, gathering up any mirrors in their possession as well as any flat pieces of scrap metal that could be polished.

Captain Warren Wynne of the Royal Engineers found this challenge to be a means of testing his skills and ingenuity. In his engineering wagon he had stacks of large sheets of tracing paper used for diagramming fortification and other building plans. As he explained to the column commander, he could fashion these into a balloon, using a paraffin lamp as a heat source. It was, in fact, a design he'd been working on even before communications were cut off from Lower Drift.

"I can fashion it out of vegetable parchment tracing paper," he explained to the column commander. "It should be about six-and-a-half feet in height and five feet in diameter. It won't be any bother to construct a simple wire frame to hold a tin box for despatches. A paraffin lamp with a piece of sponge soaked in oil will suffice to heat the air, causing the balloon to rise."

"A simple, yet ingenious design," Pearson said approvingly.

"Thank you, sir. Mind you, this is very much an improvisation, and I cannot say with certainty that it will work. Fashioning the balloon with a heating lamp will be fairly simple. The issue, however, is the weight and inability to steer it once it clears the fort. Tracing paper is quite flimsy and will be easily blown about. Still, I think if we can get this aloft, a gentle wind blowing towards the Thukela River should be able to carry a message to his lordship and the rest of the army."

"I don't care how you do it, just make it happen," the colonel stressed, before leaving Wynne to start on his project.

Warren would be kept quite busy over the next few days. While the innovation surrounding his ideas for a messenger balloon were much appreciated, Colonel Pearson was determined to have a makeshift heliograph constructed as another means of relaying messages to Lower Drift. In addition to his balloon, Captain Wynne designed a frame with a horizontal pivot from which a large 12 by 10-foot tarp could be stretched. Warren's hope was that the tarp could catch the sun's rays and be reflected towards Lower Drift.

Meanwhile, Colonel Forestier Walker's batman discovered a mirror in his master's baggage, measuring 18 by 12 inches. While not as ideal as a full-length mirror, especially when trying to send sun signals across more than twenty miles, it was the most reflective source anyone could find.

The Eshowe Post, from *The Graphic*

On the morning of the 4th, despite the cool, wet weather, Colonel Pearson ordered the 'Uhlans' to escort Sergeant Richard Small to the ridge from where the Thukela signal had first been sighted. The engineer NCO had no experience riding a horse. Lieutenant Willock—whose mount he borrowed—assured him that his was a rather docile beast. He'd found his old, battered, and heavily scribbled notebook from the signals class, which he stuffed into the saddlebag along with a couple of pencils and some writing parchment. With no scabbard for his rifle, he loosened the sling and slung it across his back. With great difficulty and some choice insults from his mates, he managed to pull himself into the saddle.

"Everything alright, sergeant?" a mounted trooper originally from the 99th Regiment asked.

"I think so," Richard replied, gingerly taking the reins in his hands.

"Not to worry. I fell and nearly broke me arse several times on the first day of riding."

"Yes, well, I don't have several days to learn," Small noted curtly.

"Believe me, sergeant, I don't want to see you fall off any more than you do. Especially as Captain Shervinton has ordered me to remain by your side and not let anything happen to you."

"That's very reassuring, private." Richard knew the young soldier meant well. His anxiety at his first horse ride leading him straight into the arms of the Zulus made him rather irritable.

Thankfully the trek to the ridge was uneventful, and Lieutenant Willock's horse proved quite amiable. The Zulus remained hidden, only making their presence known when Sergeant Small and his escorts dismounted. As the 'Uhlans' formed a perimeter, they spotted numerous warriors lurking in the brush a couple hundred yards from where they sat.

The mounted infantryman from the 99th fired a single shot into a thick stand of brush, where he saw a lone warrior spying on them. "Keep back, you bastards!" he shouted.

With the cloudy skies and clinging mist, there was little else for the men to do for the time being. They ate their breakfast of cold coffee and hard biscuits and hoped for a change in the weather. Despite the clinging grey clouds and threats of rain, they knew conditions could change very quickly in the turbulent climate of Southern Africa.

It was just after 11.00. Richard had checked his battered pocket watch when a hard breeze blew in from the east. Carrying the scent of the distant ocean, the assembled soldiers breathed it in with relish.

"Look!" a trooper said excitedly, pointing to a patch of blue skies in the clinging pall.

The winds picked up, nearly whipping the floppy hat from the rider's head. Within fifteen minutes the skies cleared, and the sun shone brightly.

"God himself favours us this day," another horseman remarked.

Small attempted to set up a makeshift signalling device. This consisted of a dozen small mirrors circled around a flat sheet of polished metal. His officers had graciously allowed him to borrow one of their tripods. He tied the device to it with a frayed section of cord. Angling the mirrors in the direction of the Thukela, the light of the midday sun glared brightly. However, they were twenty miles as-the-crow-flies from Lower Drift. It was nearly impossible to pinpoint the light exactly. To the men atop the ridge, it may have appeared that they were shining their light directly at the forts. Yet the beam could have very well been twenty feet above the heads of anyone watching or hitting the side of a nearby hill.

"There we are," the sergeant remarked. "Now to see if anyone at the drift is paying attention."

It wasn't until noon that a return signal was seen in the distance. What no one atop the ridge knew was that twenty miles away, Lance Sergeant Robert Anderson of The Buffs was sending a predetermined message at the top of every hour. Richard flashed the mirror three times, letting them know they were ready to receive messages. The sergeant took out his note pad and pencil. The distant mirror began to flash. He scribbled the short and long signals as quickly as he was able. It had been years since he dealt with Morse code, and their efforts were further frustrated by the return of disrupting intermittent clouds. Finally, the flashes ceased.

Richard wracked his brain, reading through his notebook while trying to discern what the scrawls of dots and dashes meant. "Let's see…*look out for…meet me at…soon as you are aware of my presence*…fuck!"

"His lordship said that?" a soldier asked, with a sarcastic grin.

"I say, first heliograph in Southern Africa, and someone's using it to send rude words," another piped up, using a faux aristocratic accent followed by a boisterous laugh.

Richard shot them a reproving glare, trying to stifle his own urge to laugh, and snapped his notebook closed. Though they had established the first words of communication from the GOC, provided it was he who sent the message, the sporadic clouds rendered the message meaningless.

As for the encroaching Zulus, they knew they would not catch the horsemen before they could remount and ride away. They, therefore, declined to attack and were content to simply watch the British. Solar telegraphs and Morse code were completely foreign to them, and they were curious as to what magic the whites were working.

Though Sergeant Small was noticeably frustrated at not being able to decipher the entire text, the column staff was thrilled at receiving the first words from the outside world in three weeks. Colonel Pearson directed Captain Wynne to have Small relieved of his current duties for the time being, while he acted as the column's signaller. Since the sappers were doing little except local patrols, sentry duty, and supervising maintenance around the fort, Richard was content to leave Corporal Norton in charge of his section, while he rode out each day on a borrowed horse to learn what he could from the forces at Lower Drift.

By Thursday, the 6th of March, the annoying cloud cover had dissipated enough to transcribe the entire message, which they discerned was being re-sent at the top of the hour every day. They garnered enough information to learn that the messages were not actually from Lord Chelmsford, but Lieutenant Colonel Francis Law, Royal Artillery, who'd assumed command at Lower Drift.

Not only did the sun cooperate this day, but the long-forgotten Morse code signals were remembered by Sergeant Small. He was able to scrawl the actual words, rather than dots and dashes, into his notebook. His face beamed with excitement as he flashed a quick return signal, acknowledging that the message had been received. Like before, he could not be certain if the garrison at Lower Drift actually saw it.

Upon returning to Eshowe, Richard found the senior officers at Pearson's headquarters anxiously awaiting his return. This first real day of sunshine since first seeing the signal from Lower Drift had filled them with hope that they would finally have something substantive from the rest of the army. Captain MacGregor took the message and dismissed the sergeant. As Colonel Pearson summoned his staff and other senior officers, noticeably absent was Captain Wynne of the engineers. His seemingly limitless energy had foundered once more, and he'd taken ill the previous day. Standing in his place was his senior subaltern, Lieutenant David Courtney.

"Force of 1,000 men, supported by black auxiliaries, forming at Thukela." Captain MacGregor read aloud as soon as all the officers were assembled. *"Will cross on the 13th. Keep watch for their approach. Take all surplus troops and meet at Inyezane.* It is signed, F.T.A. Law, Lieutenant Colonel."

"Now this is welcome news," Colonel Walker said, with a relieved sigh.

"Indeed," Pearson concurred. "I know Francis Law quite well. We were both subalterns at the Siege of Sevastopol. His battery was posted near my rifle company, and we became friends. Mind you, I have not seen him in many years but am glad to know he is here."

"Getting to Inyezane will be tricky," Lieutenant Colonel Parnell noted. "It's a winding track with plenty of places where the Zulus can spring an ambush."

Pearson nodded and then addressed David Courtney. "Mister Courtney, inform Captain Wynne that we need to look into the possibility of cutting a new track, both more direct and avoiding any possible unpleasantries with the Zulus."

"We'll sort it out, sir," the engineer officer reassured him.

"In the meantime," Pearson stated, "we need to make certain that the rest of the army knows that we're still alive and in the fight. Your non-comm, Sergeant Small, was unable to say with any certainty if his return signals were spotted. We need to rectify this and ensure that both incoming and outgoing communications pass between us and Lower Drift."

It was with an added touch of ingenuity that a detachment led by Captain McGregor returned to the ridge looking back towards Lower Drift. A more stable makeshift heliograph was erected, using Colonel Walker's mirror as a reflective device. The issue regarding whether their return signals could be seen was resolved using a length of gas pipe taken from the church at Eshowe. The pipe was first placed level with the mirror and pointed towards the constant signal coming from the Thukela. A soldier looked down the length to make certain the pipe was pointed directly at the drift then back up the other end, letting the signallers know when they had the mirror properly aligned. This led to the poor fellow being blinded by the intense glare, and it was soon decided to hang a sheet of tracing paper off the end. That way the mirror could be aligned without causing undo eye damage.

And instead of moving the mirror itself, once it was in position, a clapboard strapped to the signaller's hand was used to interrupt the sun's rays and send the signal. Though archaic and dependant on the ever-volatile weather along the southeasternmost coast of Africa, by the second week of March a crude form of communication had been re-established between the British army in Natal and the garrison trapped at Eshowe.

Chapter XXXI: The Long Road Back

Eshowe
5 March 1879

Friends at a Distance, from *The Graphic*
Depicting the signalling efforts from both Eshowe and Lower Drift

Three days after being placed on the sick list, Captain Warren
Wynne returned once more to his duties. David Courtney informed
him of Colonel Pearson's directive, that they reconnoitre to see if a
practicable route could be cut for the relief force, avoiding the
numerous brush stands where Zulus were undoubtedly waiting to
spring an ambush. On the morning of the 5th of March, the four
officers from No. 2 Field Company escorted by three companies of
redcoats under Brevet Lieutenant Colonel Ely departed the fort and
began making their way south. Lieutenant Colonel Ely was given
command of the small force that departed from Eshowe.

"Looks to be a clear morning, sir," Warren said to Ely with a
grin. He finished his coffee and readied to mount his horse.

The 99th officer was not smiling, and indeed seemed more than a
little nervous. He ignored the sappers and shouted rather hoarsely
for the three companies of infantrymen to begin the march. Little
else was said between Ely and Wynne. The three engineer subalterns
talked incessantly amongst themselves, while their officer
commanding halted his horse frequently so that he might scribble
some notes or sketches into his notebook.

"Ah, here we are sir," Warren called to Ely, who halted the
infantry column.

As company officers and NCOs shouted orders for their men to spread out and secure the area, Warren privately wondered if they even needed the jittery senior officer with them. They were several miles from the fort, and Ely kept looking around nervously.

The engineers dismounted and surveyed the terrain that stretched below them. They stood atop a gently-sloping ridge that overlooked a junction of the main road in the distance.

"That bend in the road is where we should begin our work," David Courtney surmised.

Warren tapped his pencil against his lower lip a few times while running some hasty calculations through his head. "Agreed. The slope here is very gradual and will not cause the wagons any undue stress. The ground is also wide open here. If we cut a track from the junction, through here and back to the main road, we'll bypass any potential ambush points the enemy might utilise."

The youngest subaltern, Lieutenant Willock, then spoke up. "Sir, if I'm judging this correctly, it will also cut about five miles off the relief column's journey."

"Yes...yes, I think you are correct, Mister Willock." Warren then walked over to his mount and pulled some marking stakes from the saddlebag. "We'll mark this spot here, so work parties know where to return to. If indeed Colonel Law is sending us a column of reinforcements, departing Lower Drift on the 13th, that gives us a week to get the new path cut and ready for wagon traffic."

The reconnaissance patrol soon returned to Eshowe much to Lieutenant Colonel Ely's relief. Along the way, they spotted a lone rooster walking aimlessly along the road, likely belonging to one of the local homesteads the column had destroyed. Lieutenant Main gave chase after the bird, drawing his pistol and felling the fowl with a single shot.

"Looks like we'll have a bit of celebratory chicken tomorrow!" He held the dead bird up triumphantly.

Upon returning to the fort, Warren compiled his notes and made a sketch on his working map of the region, which he then took to Colonel Pearson. The column commander was pleased and ordered his engineer officer to begin work on the new path with all possible haste.

The following day, the 6th of March, was one of brief celebration for the men of No. 2 Field Company. It was Lieutenant Main's twenty-ninth birthday and, coincidentally, Lieutenant Willock's twenty-fifth. The rooster Main shot the day before was plucked and roasted over the officers' campfire. "A more splendid birthday treat I've yet to have," Main told his fellow officers that evening.

Theirs was about the only reverie to be found at the fort, as the effects of disease and exposure to the elements continued to take its toll on the garrison. During the first week of March, every day was marked with funerals for those who'd succumbed to the plethora of ailments that had stricken so many. And it wasn't just typhoid and dysentery that was claiming lives.

On the 4th of March, Private John Paul, a young man from Lincolnshire who joined the 99th Regiment just two years prior, collapsed while working on rampart repair, subsequently dying from heatstroke. Colonel Pearson soon put out a directive that soldiers were free to walk around in their shirtsleeves while in garrison. Tunics would only be mandatory while on patrol outside the fort. Helmets or other head covering were required any time the sun was beating down on them, though could be removed when beneath shade or on overcast days. Company officers and NCOs were reminded to make certain their soldiers were drinking enough water, as well as eating. Of course, it did not help matters that the garrison had had its rations reduced by a quarter. Still, lack of appetite was one of the signs of heat exhaustion. At one point, Lieutenant David Courtney personally sat with one of their sappers who'd become delirious from the heat and practically force-fed him his supper.

One who'd been suffering greatly as of late was Midshipman Lewis Coker; the fiercely-devoted-to-duty young naval officer whose Gatling Gun helped break the enemy along Wombane Hill during the Battle of Inyezane. Though the detachment from HMS Active had made shelters for themselves, and he was encouraged by his fellow officers to sleep under cover each night, Lewis had insisted on bedding down next to his Gatling. This had left him greatly exposed to the elements, yet never would he abandon the post, not even during the worst downpours. He'd been placed on the sick list on the 2nd of March but had since returned to his post.

Surgeon Norbury went to visit the young officer on the evening of the 6th. As expected, he found Lewis curled up in his blanket, back against the ramparts, just a couple feet from the Gatling.

"Hello, Lewis," the doctor said, kneeling next to him.

"And a fine evening to you, sir," Coker said, forcing a smile. His face was paler than usual. It was clear he was in pain.

"How's the stomach?"

"Not as bad as yesterday." The midshipman then admitted with a nervous grin, "It's my arse that hurts the worst. Still, a bit of stomach problems and a sore bottom aren't going to keep me from performing my duty."

The doctor let out a sigh. Having also come from the HMS Active, Norbury had known Coker since he first attested into the Royal Navy, six years before. He was very fond of the lad, who looked to him like a second father.

"Lewis, listen to me, son. You are of no use if you make yourself sick, or worse. We've lost enough brave lads to all manner of illnesses since this war began. You won't have a chance at becoming the youngest admiral in the Royal Navy should we lose you as well."

Coker gave a tired smile at this. Well-liked by both officers and sailors aboard the HMS Active, Commander Campbell had praised his talents and natural leadership numerous times. The minimum age for taking the lieutenant's exam was twenty, though Campbell felt this could be waived, especially in light of Midshipman Coker's actions during the Zulu War.

"Alright," the young officer at last replied. "I'll make sure I allow myself to get some proper sleep. Can't manage a gun crew if I'm nodding off in battle!"

The surgeon patted the midshipman on the shoulder and made his way back to the hospital tent. A fit of coughing from Lewis made him cringe. He may have convinced the young man to finally look after himself; he only hoped it was not too late.

Soldiers from The Buffs, who'd been in Southern Africa for nearly three years, kept insisting that the onset of autumn would bring with it drier and more pleasant weather. And yet, unstopping rains continued to pummel the garrison at Eshowe. The flood trenches overflowed, and it became impossible for anyone to keep dry. The rains were accompanied by high winds which completely wrecked the large signalling panel Warren Wynne had put so much work into. Though disgruntled by this setback, it did not prevent the engineer officer from continuing to work on his balloon project. Overcast days rendered the makeshift heliographs useless and, like Colonel Pearson, he understood that redundancy was their best way of keeping communications open with the rest of the army.

Meanwhile, work parties were dispatched to begin cutting the supplementary path for the relief column. But rather than simply scraping a dirt track, Captain Wynne took a cue from the engineers of Ancient Rome. He ordered drainage to be cut on either side with the road itself macadamised with a layer of crushed stone that would allow for additional drainage, while also being much sturdier than the wagon-rutted paths they had followed from Lower Drift. This required massive amounts of stone, as well as timber and brush, which meant even larger work parties. The road work, coupled with constant repair and improvements to the fort meant both Warren and his sappers were kept constantly busy.

The morning of the 7th marked the first earnest day of labour on the road. Captain Wynne himself oversaw a detail consisting of Natal Pioneers, as well as a company from Commander Campbell's Naval Brigade. This large force of men alerted the Zulus who, in their curiosity, began to converge on the work detail. They had little time to watch the British labourers, as a renewed rainstorm caused all work to cease around 10.00 in the morning. The rain continued throughout the day, adding to the garrison's ever-present state of misery. Thankfully, it ceased around nightfall.

It was around 10.00 p.m., and Warren lay on his camp bed, reviewing work reports from the day and scribing his orders for the morrow. He was joined by Colour Sergeant Smith, who'd hastily made his way over from the south ramparts.

"Your pardon, sir, but I need you come at once. Picquets are reporting signs of Zulus near the site of our road work detail."

Wynne said nothing but hastily threw on his boots, picked up his oil lamp, and followed the company's senior NCO to the ramparts. Sentries were reinforced by bands of soldiers from The Buffs who were bivouacked closest to the southern face of the fort. Most were in their shirtsleeves, a couple in just their underpants.

"Over there, sir," the corporal on duty said, pointing in the direction of the new scratch of road.

Even in the enclosing night, the starlight gave just enough light to show numerous shadows along a low ridge.

"They're acting rather brazen, not really caring whether or not we can see them," Colour Sergeant Smith observed.

"Inform the column staff and the officer-of-the-watch," Warren ordered.

"Already been done, sir," Smith replied. "I personally spoke with Captain McGregor. He said he would pass the word to Colonel Pearson."

"Good," Wynne acknowledged. "Don't want the entire garrison panicking."

"Does this mean we have permission to send the Zulus our regards, sir?" the corporal asked.

"South rampart only, four volleys," Warren confirmed. He tried scanning with his field glasses, but the darkness impeded his ability to focus on any single target.

"Index 500 yards," Colour Sergeant Smith added. He then nodded to the corporal.

"Right lads," the young NCO said. "At 500 yards, present...fire!"

The stillness of night was shattered with the crashing volley of musketry. The 7-pounder cannon which occupied the southeast corner of the ramparts boomed, as it erupted with a blinding flash.

"Present...fire!"

After four volleys and another thundering boom from the cannon stillness engulfed the fort once more. The smoke cleared, and there were no further signs of movement from nearest the new road.

"Well, that's driven them off," the Buffs corporal said appreciatively.

"It'll be harder to keep them away the further the road work gets from the fort," Colour Sergeant Smith muttered.

Captain Wynne nodded and returned to his bunk to finish his work for the evening.

Unlike the signalling detail and its crude heliograph, which continued to baffle the Zulus, it was plainly obvious what soldiers were trying to accomplish with the new stretch of road.

"They are attempting to link the old traders' path with a shorter route to their stronghold," a scout explained to Prince Dabulamanzi. "It will not only shorten their trail back to the Thukela, but it is out in the open, avoiding our ambush sites."

"They are resourceful," the *inkosi*, Mavumengwana, said with begrudging appreciation. He then looked to Dabulamanzi, "It would be an easy task to disrupt their work. Harass them with skirmishers during the day and destroy their work at night."

The prince nodded in concurrence. "I will see to it, personally."

While Mavumengwana was one of the most respected of the *amakhosi*, Dabulamanzi wondered if his presence was a means of his brother keeping an eye on him. After all, the *inkosi* and King Cetshwayo were close in age, had served with the uThulwana Regiment since its inception, and were lifelong friends. Upon his ascension to the amaZulu throne, Cetshwayo had named Mavumengwana as commander of an entire wing of their beloved regiment. Yet as one of the senior *amakhosi* who orchestrated the attack on Isandlwana, he had not been present with the uThulwana when Dabulamanzi led them and the rest of the Undi Corps across the uMzinyathi and into the disastrous attack on kwaJimu. While the prince believed with absolute certainty that Mavumengwana blamed him for the needless deaths of so many of his childhood friends, the *inkosi* never made mention of it. And though he could have very easily seized control of the Zulu forces in the Eshowe region, he diplomatically deferred to his friend and sovereign's younger brother. Still, his continued presence made the prince nervous. Hence, Dabulamanzi often put as much space between them as possible.

It was just after breakfast when the prince and a few hundred warriors departed the royal *ikhanda*. Dabulamanzi was still feeling quite pleased with both himself and his warriors' for driving the English back to their fort like whipped dogs, even though the red-jacketed soldiers had burned the kraal of eSiqwakeni and slain several of his warriors. Following the scout who'd reported on the British activity, the band of warriors made their way cross-country, keeping to the low ground and utilising tree groves and thickets to shield their movement.

At the edge of a long cluster of hedges, the scout halted and signalled for the prince and his *izinduna* to join him. "Over there, *inkosi*." The man pointed with his assegai towards a large mass of imperial soldiers.

Dabulamanzi knelt next to the scout and surveyed their adversaries. There were at least three or four hundred and they appeared to be evenly divided between labourers and those providing protection. Unfortunately, they occupied a large swath of open grassland about 400 paces away from the protection of the hedges. The prince knew he could not bring his warriors any closer without subjecting them to undo risk, especially as the British outnumbered his force.

"Skirmishers will conduct harassing fire," the prince said. "But use your bullets sparingly. We have little chance of hitting them from this distance."

A few warriors expressed the desire to rush across the open expanse of ground, that they might engage their foes from a more comparable range. Those who'd fought at Inyezane and kwaJimu knew that to leave the protection of the thick hedges was suicidal. Groups of four or five warriors at a time would fire their muskets in the general direction of the enemy work detail. Those who tried to aim were disappointed when they saw their bullets kick up clods of mud less than half the distance to their intended targets. And those who pointed their weapons high never saw where their musket balls landed. It had the intended effect. After the first few shots, swarms of redcoats and blue-jacketed sailors abandoned their work and formed a skirmish line, loosing volleys of their own.

That their shots landed so close, many smashing through the thickets just over their heads, was unnerving. However, the thick brush kept the Zulus concealed, and they used the trunks and any small mounds of earth for protection as they reloaded their muskets.

British return fire was sporadic as they struggled to see their harassers. Content that his ploy was working as planned, Dabulamanzi ordered most of his men to lay low while marksmen continued to frustrate the redcoats' work efforts.

By early evening, the British had finally had enough and began to withdraw back to the fort. However, as they were still within view of the enemy stronghold, Dabulamanzi told his men they would wait until nightfall to proceed forward. They feasted on pre-cooked mealies left over from their breakfast, as they waited for the sun to set.

An hour after dark, the prince summoned the *izinduna* to him.

"Keep low, and do not expose yourselves along the ridgeline," he told his assembled leaders, recalling the mistakes of the previous night's sortie.

The word was passed along to their warriors. Following the prince, they crept out from the protective cover of the thickets. They half-expected to be greeted with a salvo of British musketry. All was silent, except for the signs of activity coming from within the enemy stronghold in the distance.

The prince was quite surprised by the level of work that was going into this new track of road. There were few roads within Zululand, and those mostly consisted of little more than wagon ruts from white traders that had worn their way into the ground over time. The combination of drainage and hard-packed stone gave this path a far more permanent and sturdy appearance.

"Time to cleanse this blight from the land," Dabulamanzi said, grabbing a hold of a long stake used to mark the next section of road.

He and his warriors wrenched these from the ground, using them to chip away and dig great chunks of packed rock out of the road. Within an hour, most of the work done that day was left in ruins.

As he and his warriors ran the seven or so miles back to the royal *ikhanda*, their stomachs grumbling from having eaten sparingly, Prince Dabulamanzi was pleased with their efforts so far against the invaders. The battle at kwaJimu had taught him that victory against Queen Victoria's soldiers would not be achieved in a single decisive battle. Even Isandlwana, which was arguably the greatest triumph ever won by the Zulu *amabutho*, had come at an extremely high cost in lives. Patience was the hardest-learned virtue for the usually aggressive and volatile prince who preferred to face his enemies head-on in open battle. With no signs of fresh British troops crossing the Thukela, and the remnants of the enemy's centre column hiding behind their newly-built walls at Rorke's Drift, Dabulamanzi felt it was just a matter of time before starvation and disease brought this foe at Eshowe to its knees.

He knew he would gain much satisfaction in personally disembowelling the white *inkosi* leading the redcoats cowering at Eshowe. However, the prince knew his honour would be restored, not to mention the praise he would win from his brother the king, should he compel the enemy to surrender and send this man to Cetshwayo as a prisoner of war. The capture of the white men's officers had eluded even the *impi* at Isandlwana, much to the king's chagrin. By taking one of their most senior warriors prisoner, Prince Dabulamanzi could deliver to Cetshwayo the very means of bringing an end to the war.

Chapter XXXII: Spies and Escapes

No. 4 Vedette near Eshowe
7 March 1879

Imperial Mounted Infantryman, possibly from the 99th Lanarkshire Regiment

The day's fighting was not to be over despite the raiding party having returned to Eshowe. The No. 4 vedette post was a favourite target of Zulu skirmishers. Corporal Stephen Carson, a member of the Imperial Mounted Infantry, offered to ride out and relieve the previous shift while his companions were still saddling their horses. One of the few men with the 99th Regiment that had more than a handful of years with the Colours, he'd just completed his fourteenth year in the ranks. And while a competent soldier, he was known to stretch the rules when they didn't suit him. In fact, one reason why he was anxious to ride out immediately was because, contrary to standing regulations, he had chosen to sling his Swinburne-Henry carbine across his back rather than use the regulation scabbard. The leather stitching kept coming undone, and he was tired of nearly losing his weapon.

He'd heard gunfire in the distance, as the Zulus harried the returning labour force. Though the shots had ceased, he found himself constantly glancing over his shoulder as he rode out to his post. Approaching the vedette, he hailed the soldier he was replacing and told him he could head back to the fort. The relieved trooper turned his horse about and started galloping back to Eshowe.

Carson removed his helmet, resting it on the pommel of his saddle, and started to reach for his water bottle when he heard a dozen voices cry out *'Usutu!'*

Twelve Zulu warriors sprang up from the tall grass and rushed towards him, brandishing their assegais. Before the corporal could react, one of the charging men grabbed a hold of the horse's mane. The terrified beast reared up, kicking at the Zulu and nearly throwing its rider off. Holding on for dear life, Carson spurred his horse into a gallop, riding with all speed back towards the fort. A series of shots rang out behind him. What felt like the blow of a hammer struck his left hand. He wasn't even aware of the bullet which passed through the front of his right thigh and through the saddle pommel before embedding itself in his inner left thigh. He felt something akin to a burning lump inside his left leg while nearly being thrown from his mount once more, as a blow struck him in the small of the back. His disobeying of orders and slinging his carbine across his back had, in fact, saved his life. The musket ball smashed into the lock on his weapon rather than burying itself in his spine.

Hearing musketry, several vedettes, both replacements and those coming off duty, rode towards the chaos; their carbines held in their laps. By the time Corporal Carson reached them, the Zulus had scattered into the tall grass.

"Bloody hell, corporal," one trooper said, eyes wide in amazement. "You've been hit."

"Yes, my hand hurts like a bastard," Carson replied, holding the bleeding limb close to his body.

"You've been hit in more than just the hand," the trooper noted, pointing to the blood streaming down both legs.

"Well, there's a spot of bother," Carson remarked, his voice surprisingly calm.

The other picquets assured him they would keep watch over his post while he rode back to the fort to receive medical attention. One of the sentries on the north gate saw the corporal's fearful state and called for men to assist Carson to the hospital.

An hour later, having just heard that one of his men was injured, Captain Shervinton rushed over to the hospital tent.

Corporal Carson was lying on a stretcher in his underpants with a sheet over his torso. He did not appear to be in pain, though his left hand was heavily bandaged, as were both thighs.

"Looks like the Zulus got the drop on me, sir," he said apologetically, holding up his stricken left hand in emphasis.

Shervinton could see the last two fingers had been amputated.

"He's lucky the bullet that struck him in the leg did not sever his femoral artery," Surgeon Norbury explained to the captain, having just washed his hands after performing surgery on the wounded corporal.

"And had it struck a few inches higher, I would have been at risk of sorely disappointing my wife, once I return home," Carson said, with a morbid laugh. He looked at his legs. "The strangest thing is, the right leg doesn't hurt at all. Though I'm sure it will be bastardly sore by tomorrow."

For the corporal, his war was effectively over, as it would be a struggle to walk for some time and his left hand was rendered near-useless. There was also a very real risk of infection, and he was placed on light duty for the remainder of the campaign. Lieutenant Colonel Welman promised to have him sent to the hospital in Stanger once lines of communication were open once more with Lower drift. Carson would from there be sent home to England, where he would have to face a medical review board to determine his fitness for further duty. In all likelihood, he would medically discharged, with a small disability pension. In the meantime, Captain Shervinton needed to find a replacement.

It was now the 8th of March. Much like the previous day, the Zulus returned to harass the British road construction efforts. This time, however, a 7-pounder cannon belonging the Royal Marine detachment accompanied them along with a large force of 700 soldiers. Colonel Pearson was now feeling cautious, the disastrous attempts at destroying Dabulamanzi's royal *ikhanda* having sapped some of his previous assurance. That he'd sent nearly half the entire garrison to protect the road workers was a clear sign of his wariness. However, it also meant there were now far fewer men available to do the actual work.

This work detail was led by Lieutenant David Courtney, as Captain Wynne had finished work on his communications balloon, which he hoped to test that day. He also feared that his officer commanding was slowly taking a turn for the worse, even though Warren assured him almost daily that his health was improving.

"Besides, there's not a man in No. 1 Column who isn't suffering from some form of illness or troubled stomach," the captain had stressed.

On this particular day, for reasons unknown to Courtney, none of the senior officers in the column accompanied them. This felt strange, as nearly half their forces were out on this one detail. An unintended consequence of this was the lack of an appointed commanding officer for the force.

As they approached the work site, it was a section of sappers under Sergeant Richard Small who first came upon the wreckage of the previous day's efforts.

"Son of a perfidious whore!" the sapper NCO snapped.

The men of No. 2 Field Company and the Natal Native Pioneers were equally distraught at seeing their hard work undermined.

Infantrymen from the accompanying companies were ostensibly meant to provide the bulk of their labour force. However, the ringing out of shots in the distance quickly drew them away from their spades and pickaxes to take up their rifles. The Zulus, while keeping their distance, had returned in much greater numbers, no doubt intent on drawing even more of Pearson's forces away from their task of building the road back to the Inyezane River.

"Damn it all," Courtney swore under his breath. The issue with none of the senior officers being present was he had no one to report to that could order the men back to work. In a way, he could not blame the redcoats or their officers for wishing to 'take the fight to the enemy' rather than toil under pickaxe and shovel.

"Bloody hell," Sergeant Small said to his officer. "The Zulus are out there, but they're not coming at us, sir. I'd say we're doing exactly what they want us to."

"I agree, sergeant," Courtney concurred. "But until one of the infantry officers deems the threat subdued enough to detach his men back to us, there is little we can do except carry on."

"Understood, sir." Though Richard did not like the answer his officer gave him, he knew there was little Courtney could do.

A sporadic gunfight continued throughout the morning. While the companies of redcoats only sent the occasional volley towards the Zulus, not one of the company officers commanding had ordered his troops back to assist the engineers on the road work. A pair of cannon had accompanied them, and even these had ceased in most of their efforts as it drew closer to afternoon. Lieutenant Lloyd, commanding the artillery, had noted that his guns had driven the Zulus to ground when an air burst shell exploded well over their heads, sending scores of lead balls into their ranks. Because the shell burst from about fifty yards away, the enemy warriors were confused. To them it seemed as if the British had loosed a salvo of musketry at close range. Like most such skirmishes, it was impossible for the artillery officer to tell how many, if any, of his shells had struck.

"Bloody hell!" a voice shouted, off to Lloyd's right. He turned to see an officer from The Buffs sprawled out on his back, his face covered in blood. Lloyd ran over and was surprised to see the man was still alive.

"All you alright, sir?" a private asked. He and one of his mates helped the officer sit upright.

"I…I think so," the lieutenant said, his eyes glassy and his expression one of confusion.

Lloyd knelt next to him and removed the man's helmet. An enemy musket ball had struck the top of his helmet. Inexplicably, it had deflected downwards, clipping his left temple before sweeping across his forehead. His temple and forehead were bleeding profusely, though it was clear the wounds were superficial. Terrible bruising was already forming around his eyes, as if he'd taken the worst during a boxing match.

"You'd better sit here for a bit," Lloyd said, setting the injured lieutenant's helmet next to him. He then returned to his gun, found a semi-clean rag, and returned to help clean the blood off the officer's face. "We'll tie this around your head, should stop the bleeding."

"Ah, yes, much obliged." The Buffs lieutenant would only learn later just how close to death he'd come. For the moment, he sat in a daze, propped up by a pair of soldiers who were tasked with looking after him, lest his injuries prove worse than they appeared.

As for David Courtney and his sappers, there was a growing sense of frustration and resentment that they were doing all the manual labour alone. At around 1.00, they had only just finished repairing the damage done the night before, when storm clouds blew in from the east.

"Looks like the ocean gods wish to say 'hello' again," he grumbled, before shouting to his men, "Alright lads, let's pack it in before we get soaked!"

The large detachment returned to the fort just as the heavens unleashed yet another torrent of rain onto their heads. Lieutenant Courtney found his officer commanding brooding over the wreckage of his communications balloon.

"Dash it all," the captain said, trying to mask his disappointment.

"I am sorry, sir," David replied earnestly.

"The odds were long, at best," Warren remarked. "It actually flew readily enough, but there simply was not enough weight to keep it steady. And as quickly as the winds change, it's little wonder that it altered course within the first minute, heading in the wrong direction before a large gust smashed it against a stand of trees. Well, that's that, then. I do hope you've had better luck working on the road, Mister Courtney."

"Yes, about that sir..."

Zulu harassment continued throughout the next couple days with bands of warriors breaking and wrecking as much as they could of the new road each night. It was maddening for the garrison at Eshowe. Time was running short, and they needed to get the new stretch of road finished before Lieutenant Colonel Law and his relief forces arrived from Lower Drift.

On the morning of the 10th, with work parties heading out to try to finish the stretch of track needed to reach the Inyezane, a loud cheer came from sentries on the north gate as a black African wearing a red tunic sprinted towards the fort.

His face was dishevelled, and he was sweating profusely. "Message for Pearson," he said breathlessly. He handed a large folded piece of parchment to the corporal at the gate. These were about the only words of English that the man knew. He simply looked at the soldier in confusion when the man tried to question him.

The corporal was feeling a bit suspicious about the messenger. He had him escorted to Colonel Pearson's command post at the storehouse. The message was written in a code used by the Royal Navy. Pearson ordered Commander Campbell to have one of his signallers decipher it.

"It's from Colonel Law, sir," the commander said after one of his men transcribed the message. "It's dated the 24th of February."

Though efforts to maintain signal communications had been haphazard and sporadic, the message did not contain any information the garrison was not already aware of, or was most likely outdated. It was the date, however, that concerned Pearson.

"This 'messenger' left Lower Drift two weeks ago?" he asked incredulously.

"He says his name is Kgabu kaLanga," Captain Shervinton had been summoned to act as an interpreter. "He says he's the groom of Mr Fynney, the Thukela magistrate."

"More likely he killed the messenger and is here as a Zulu spy," Colonel Walker replied incredulously.

Pearson nodded, a sneer creasing his face. "And what of his tunic? Was this a gift from his master?"

"That's the tunic of an 'other ranks' soldier of the 24th," Henry Parnell observed. Though there were no insignia on the jacket, the green collar tabs and cuff facings matched those of the shattered regiment that had met its bloody destiny at Isandlwana and Rorke's Drift. It was also fairly new.

"He could be one of the damned kaffirs who butchered our lads at Isandlwana and then looted one of their jackets," Walker growled, his countenance darkening.

"His body is oiled in the same manner as the Zulus," Shervinton noted.

"Then he'd best start explaining himself," Pearson demanded.

Shervinton question the man. His eyes grew wide in disbelief, and he spoke quickly, gesticulating wildly.

"He says he's part of the iziGqoza," the NNC captain translated. "Which, to be fair, would explain the reason why he's oiled up like their Zulu cousins. And he says the jacket was a gift from Mr Fynney, who acquired it from a quartermaster friend of his. To be honest, sir, that is plausible. The Army only issues new uniforms every April, and the lads of the 24th were in the same state of threadbare tatters that most of ours are. Perhaps Mr Fynney has a friend within the commissariat who gave a tunic meant for the 24th Regiment's eventual uniform resupply?"

"Or the whole story could be a load of bollocks," Pearson countered. "If he's been slinking about the bush for the past fortnight, why does his jacket still look as if it's been freshly issued? Clap him in irons. Tell him if no one at Lower Drift can vouch for his story, then his corpse will swing from the gallows."

The black African protested indignantly, as he was forcibly led away. The words 'iziGqoza' and 'Mr Fynney' clearly audible amongst his otherwise unintelligible rantings.

That evening, as he decided to take the time to pen a letter to his wife, Captain Warren Wynne made mention of the incident.

A 'runner' arrived from the Thukela with a despatch 14 days old. The despatch was in cipher (Navy code). This man was soon suspected, as his story was not satisfactory. He evidently was sent in by the enemy as a spy, with the despatch taken from one of the runners they murdered. It is now, I think, evident that all our runners since the 11th of February have failed, and our letters written to no purpose. I wrote you a note on the 11th, so I hope you will at any rate get that, though there will be a long gap afterwards.

He let out a melancholy sigh, stored his pen away, folded the letter, placed his lips to it, and tucked it away in his satchel. Little did he know, although runners from Lower Drift had failed to reach Eshowe, at least one of the garrison's had made it to the Natal border safely. Wynne's letters, the latest of which was dated 18 February, were in fact bound for England aboard a Royal Mail steamship.

Chapter XXXIII: Sallying Forth

Eshowe
10 March 1879
***

On the evening of the 10th, the same day the messenger accused of
being a spy had arrived at Eshowe, Captain Warren Wynne
requested a private meeting with Colonel Pearson. Weeks of poor
health, constant illness, the failure of his communications balloon,
the destruction of his signalling panels, and now the 'utter fiasco' as
he described their attempts at cutting a new section of road to the
Inyezane, had frayed his usually unbreakable deportment.

"Colonel, sir," Warren said, coming to attention as soon as he
was ushered in to Pearson cramped headquarters within the
storehouse.

"Captain Wynne," Pearson acknowledged. "What can I do for
you, sir?"

"I have been given until the 13th to make the new stretch of road
ready for Colonel Law's reinforcements. However, unless more
vigorous measures are taken to disrupt the Zulus, as well as ensuring
that work details remain at their posts unless under imminent threat,
I cannot be held responsible for the road's completion."

"I see. And what is your recommendation?" Pearson folded his
arms and leaned back slightly in his chair.

"Tomorrow we should go to the furthest point of the new road,
where it meets the wagon trail on this side of the Inyezane River
near our previous battle site. We have to blast some of the rock at
the crossing point anyway. We'll then work backwards towards the
fort. I'll need a robust force of infantry, under the command of a
field officer, that can sustain and defend itself against any potential
threat. And just so there is no question about utilising infantry as
labourers, the actual work will be accomplished by my own sappers,
as well as the Natal Pioneers."

"Very well," Pearson concurred. "That will sort out your work
detail, but what about after you've returned to the fort? How do you
propose to prevent the Zulus from destroying your work each
night?"

"Well, actually, sir, I have some ideas about that. We can use the pioneers' dynamite for more than just blowing up boulders and river rock."

Warren was feeling quite pleased following his meeting with Colonel Pearson. It was reassuring to know he had the column commander's complete confidence, and that he heeded his advice. Of course, Pearson was just as, if not more, anxious for the arrival of reinforcements as the rest of the column. And while the trek back to the battlefield at Inyezane would put a few miles on the boots of the infantry, most would be glad to be away from the squalid fort for a day. They would also only require a pair of wagons to carry the necessary tools and other equipment for the sappers and engineers.

As he crept along through the churned-up mud of the fort, hoping to finish his latest journal entry before turning in for the night, Warren suddenly felt a terrible cramp in his stomach. He placed a hand on his lower abdomen and shook his head.

"Not again," he said, with a tired sigh. He'd eaten only sparingly that day, hoping to finally calm the constant ravaging of his bowels. Hurriedly stumbling his way towards the latrine trench, he knew his efforts had been in vain. It would be another long night for Captain Warren Wynne.

The following morning, while a very large force of seven infantry companies, two cannon, all of No. 2 Field Company, plus the Natal Native Pioneers made their way towards the Inyezane, Captain Charles Shervinton of the 'Uhlans' rode out to check on his picquets. The Zulus were becoming emboldened over the past week. Charles was convinced this meant that the enemy was being slowly reinforced as their harvest season drew to a close. Because the tall grasses offered much concealment even in the otherwise wide-open hills, and since not one white soldier at Eshowe could hope to outrun a Zulu, Colonel Pearson had ordered that the furthest picquets be manned by mounted troops only. This post was held by Corporal Adams and two privates; both young men from the 99th Regiment.

"A fine morning, captain," the NCO said, with a casual salute. He and the two troopers sat astride their mounts, having just finished their breakfast.

Before Shervinton could inquire as to any enemy activity they'd seen the night before, more than two-dozen Zulus suddenly materialised in the tall grass a hundred yards away. The crash of musketry shattered the calm stillness of morning. Though none of their bullets found their mark, the thunderous volley caused the three picquets' horses to bolt away in panic. One of the men, Private Brooks, was flung from his mount, his foot caught up in the stirrup as he was dragged away. His helmet was battered from his head, and his rifle flung loose from his grip.

As Charles and the others tried to rein their horses in, another band of warriors appeared on a steep cliff-face about 300 yards to their right with skirmishers opening fire. Shervinton finally managed to calm his terrified mount and turned to see the first band of Zulus retiring towards the far ridge. He then saw some of the distant men pointing towards the fallen Private Brooks, gesturing wildly, while shouting, *'Isosha liwile!'* which Shervinton knew meant, *'The soldier has fallen!'*

Private Brooks was only half-conscious and unable to pull his foot free from the stirrup. The captain saw five or six enemy warriors now sprinting towards the fallen redcoat, hoping to send another of Queen Victoria's soldiers to the afterlife. Gritting his teeth, he drew his pistol and turned his horse around, galloping towards the stricken man. Two of the approaching Zulus carried muskets. Either they had not had time to reload or simply panicked when they saw the enraged British officer sprinting his horse towards them.

Shervinton only managed to fire off a single shot which nearly caused him to be thrown from his mount. His chances of hitting an enemy warrior with a pistol from atop a mad-dashing horse were practically none, yet it had its intended effect. The small band of Zulus abandoned their prey and scattered. The captain leapt from his mount and pulled Brooks' foot free from the stirrup. Unfortunately, this caused the private's horse to bolt, leaving him without a mount.

"Come on!" Shervinton said, pulling the dazed soldier to his feet. He climbed back into the saddle of his own horse, offering a hand to assist the young private who recovered enough to know the danger he was in, and frantically pulled himself up behind the captain.

Zulus along the cliff-face continued to fire at them. When ten more mounted troops were seen riding towards the fray, they soon departed. All the while, they shouted a plethora of insults towards their adversaries in both English and Zulu.

Having ridden back to where Corporal Adams and the assembling 'Uhlans' were gathered, Charles Shervinton had Private Adams assisted down from his mount before riding back to where the picquet had been attacked. Not far from where they'd had their breakfast that morning, he found the soldier's rifle, as well as his helmet, which was cracked and caved in along the back-cover seam.

"Here, you'll be wanting these," the captain said, as he returned to his men and handed Brooks his helmet and rifle back.

"Much obliged, sir," the private said. "And…thank you for saving my life."

"We don't leave a fallen man behind." Shervinton replied loud enough for all his troopers to hear. He then pointed to Brooks' battered helmet. "Not sure how much good that's going to do you now. You might want to see about getting yourself a wide-brimmed hat, to at least keep the sun off your face and neck."

Since it was nearly time for the sentry change on the picquets, the three troopers designated to replace Corporal Adams and his men were ordered out to the post. Private Brooks was placed on light duty for the remainder of the day and told to rest, after he'd cleaned and function-checked his rifle.

As his men rode out to continue their duties for the day, Captain Charles Shervinton took a moment to gather his thoughts. He breathed in deeply, suddenly aware of the pounding in his chest and thick beads of sweat forming on his brow. He removed his hat and took a handkerchief from his pocket. He quickly wiped over his face and neck. The day had been a harrowing one, and he'd only just finished his coffee and breakfast.

Road work continued under the robust escort of nearly half of the garrison's 1,500 redcoats along with two of Lieutenant Lloyd's cannon. Despite having fallen ill again the previous day, this time with severe diarrhoea, Captain Wynne insisted on supervising the detail. Lieutenant Courtney was growing ever more concerned over the state of his officer commanding's health. Warren Wynne had long been renowned for his superior constitution and physical fitness. He was among the few officers who never smoked and only drank sparingly. The past month, however, had been particularly stressing on the captain. He'd worked endlessly with almost no sleep.

Though the main wagon trail wound its way over the course of about eight miles from the Inyezane crossing to the Eshowe fort, the trek cross-country following the route of the new road was barely three. The sight of such a large force naturally caught the attention of the Zulus, and the bands of warriors were much larger than those seen before, numbering well into the hundreds.

"We've all but sent a telegram to Cetshwayo letting him know what we're doing," David Courtney mused, as he rode alongside one of Lieutenant Lloyd's 7-pounder guns.

"And if they know we're building a road, then they suspect we are either intending to withdraw or are expecting reinforcements," the artillery officer conjectured.

The lingering stench of death assailed their nostrils the closer they came to the river crossing. While some effort had been made by the families of the Zulu dead to conduct proper burials for their loved ones, many of the bodies still lay exposed on the slopes of Wombane or hidden within the thick brush. It was now seven weeks since the Battle of Inyezane. The flies were still thick, as they feasted on the putrid remains of what had once been valiant men.

"Well, at least Colonel Law's lads will know when they're getting close," Sergeant Small of the engineers mused. He marvelled at the profound discomfort of some of his sappers.

Companies of redcoats scattered along the line-of-march in extended order. Lieutenant Lloyd kept his two guns limbered, ready to deploy where needed. While Brevet Lieutenant Colonel Ely of the 99th had led most of the larger patrols outside the fort, on this day the taskforce was commanded by Lieutenant Colonel Henry Parnell of The Buffs. Though no one would say it publicly, many of the enlisted soldiers speculated that this was because Ely was notoriously edgy, and Colonel Pearson felt a steadier hand was needed.

Groups of Zulus soon appeared along the high ridge where they had previously attacked the column. The force of redcoats was even greater than what they had faced before, not to mention ready for an enemy attack. It was with little surprise that the majority of the Zulus had no desire to fight a second Battle of Inyezane. This did not, however, mean that the day was one of complete tedium for the hundreds of infantrymen escorting Captain Wynne's sappers and the NNP. A few shots rang out during the first couple hours while sappers marked and scraped the ground, and indigenous pioneers set dynamite charges to blow large boulders which obstructed the proposed fording site.

Zulu musketry came from distances often 600 yards or greater. Firing away with their antique muskets from such a range was downright absurd. Sections of infantry would periodically return fire with a volley or two; however, at such range, accuracy was difficult even with the Martini-Henry. Lieutenant Colonel Parnell directed his company commanders to allow only sharp-shooters and designated marksmen to engage at such range, the rest only authorised to open fire at 400 yards or less.

Meanwhile, the sappers and pioneers set about their task with great energy. Even the officers removed their tunics and laboured beside the enlisted men. Lieutenants Courtney and Main set about measuring and emplacing the large marking stakes. Willock took up a pickaxe and assisted with one of the drainage trenches. Colour Sergeant Smith, who was taller and more powerfully built than most in No. 2 Field Company, made numerous trips from the river with a large wheelbarrow full of river rock. As for Captain Wynne, he spent much of his time down by the fording site, overseeing the placement of dynamite to blow up the large rocks. As his NNP counterpart, Captain George Beddoes, knew little about actual engineering, Wynne had to keep telling them to not use so much dynamite.

"That is, unless you wish to blow us all to kingdom come," Warren said testily, when he noted that a group of pioneers were emplacing more than twice as much explosives as necessary beneath a large, sharp boulder.

Once satisfied that the dynamite was emplaced correctly, and not going to blow the entire task force back to Blighty, Warren gave his approval to the NNP officer commanding who, rather than being indignant, was glad for the assistance.

Warren had already spoken with Captain Beddoes about procuring some of his dynamite to rig up a booby trap that would, hopefully, prevent the Zulus from disturbing all the work they did throughout the day. The NNP officer set aside a few sticks and tasked one of his NCOs with assisting the engineer officer when the time came.

Mercifully, the day was overcast, yet no rains fell upon the work force; making for quite the pleasant day in sharp contrast to their usual misery. At around 4.00 that afternoon, with nearly a mile of road back to the fort completed, Captain Wynne spoke with Henry Parnell. He concurred that it was time to retire for the day. As the sappers stored their tools, with infantrymen collecting up their kit, Warren, the NNP corporal, and three pioneers set about constructing a trap for the Zulus.

"The enemy keeps pulling up our marking stakes. They are the easiest to disturb," the engineer captain explained.

"But when they do so tonight, we'll have a nasty little surprise waiting for them," the corporal finished, a malicious grin creasing his face.

The explosive trap, or *torpedo*, was a simple device to construct. Buried just beneath the surface were three sticks of dynamite, which was a bit excessive. However, Lieutenant Colonel Parnell wanted to make as much of an impact as possible on the Zulu marauders. Stuck into the dirt just above was a long stake, identical to those marking the road. A string was tied to the stake and the explosive friction tube. As an added precaution, in case the Zulus failed to set off the device, a plank with the word TORPEDO written in large, bold letters was tied to the stake.

"Let us hope none of the Zulus in this region have bothered learning how to read," the NNP corporal said. He tied the warning sign to the stake. They would not have to wait until night to learn if their device worked.

While the massive work detail and infantry escort made its way back to the fort, the rear guard was only about a mile from where the trap was set when a loud explosion echoed off the surrounding hills. This elicited a series of loud whoops and cheers from the redcoats and sappers. One man who was not cheering, however, was the very man who devised the trap. As soon as he heard the fearful boom, Warren Wynne closed his eyes and bowed his head as if ashamed.

"Everything alright, sir?" a voice asked.

He turned to see Colour Sergeant Smith. Like many engineer NCOs, he was mounted.

"It's nothing," the captain said, quickly shaking his head. He then paused and added, "Well, that's not entirely true. I have to confess, colour sergeant, as an earnest Christian it troubles me deeply to know that so much of the science I have learned over the years has been used to inflict death and suffering on my fellow men."

"Religion gives men the motivation to kill each other, science the means," Smith said philosophically.

Wynne shot him a perplexed look. The colour sergeant was concerned that he'd grossly offended his officer commanding. Though he usually kept his personal beliefs private, it was no secret that Michael Smith was an atheist. Science was his deity, and he viewed the very idea of religion as absurd. While Warren Wynne was a devout man of God, he found himself appreciating the candour of his senior non-commissioned officer. In a strange way, that their core beliefs were so drastically different helped strengthen the working bond between them.

Warren, at first, thought to make mention that religion had not played a role in the war between the Crown and the Zulus, but he wasn't entirely convinced of this. After all, King Cetshwayo had reversed the policies of his father and expelled all Christian missionaries a few years before. Warren had little doubt that the slew of European pastors who'd hoped to bring the word of God to the Zulus had expressed their outrage to the High Commissioner. Still, the fervent captain felt it would be an affront to the Lord, had any of the indignant missionaries called upon the British government to use military force against those they wished to convert.

Whatever role the conflicting faiths of the Europeans and Zulus may or may not have played in the causes behind the war, for the first time since passing out from Woolwich as an officer of engineers all those years ago, Warren felt a deep sense of guilt. He'd fired his weapon in anger, while ordering his men to kill during the Battle of Inyezane, but he could justify that as self-defence and the defence of his fellow soldiers. He'd always felt the Almighty understood when men killed each other in battle. But having laid a trap, like one would for a rat, and knowing that the poor souls who'd

405

pulled up the stake were blown to oblivion, was nothing short of murder.

Though not a man of any faith or religion, Colour Sergeant Smith understood his captain's dilemma. He sought to assuage Wynne's sense of guilt the only way he could. "At least we can reasonably assume the Zulus won't be back to disrupt our work again," he said.

Warren looked back at him, and the two shared a moment of understanding. Smith's words did little to ease his guilty conscience; however, he suspected the colour sergeant was correct. Perhaps, in the greater scheme of things, Warren's torpedo trap might end up saving lives. He could only hope.

Booby trap Torpedo, from *The Graphic*

Having returned to his camp bed after giving his reports of the day's work detail to Pearson's staff officer, Captain McGregor, Warren tried to compose his thoughts and took up his journal once more. He was quite proud of this. It was highly detailed with every engineering task he'd undertaken covered in explicit detail. His notes regarding the two forts he'd laid out, coupled with the road-building details were as complete as he could make them. He hoped that perhaps his journal would be of assistance to other engineer officers, that they might learn from his mistakes and improve upon his successes. If nothing else, he hoped to share it with his sons someday, that they might know the reality of campaign life in the Army; the stories of drudgery and sacrifice one rarely read about in the newspapers or official reports.

Warren had started to work on his journal when he halted midsentence to rush to the latrine trench once more. That he'd made it the entire day without any embarrassing incidents had given him hope that the worst was past. But as he clutched at his stomach, not even bothering to throw his boots on before scrambling towards the latrines, he felt worse than ever. More than an hour later, his face flushed and pale, he gingerly sat upon his camp bed and tried to compose himself. Feeling parched, he took a drink from his water bottle which was only about half full.

Wishing to distract himself from his grave discomfort, his head pounding to the point that he did not feel up to making any more technical notes in his journal, he instead decided to write another letter to his beloved Lucy. He was becoming more honest in his letters, regarding the state of his terribly denigrated health. He even told her about the torpedo, confessing his feelings of guilt over its construction. Contemplating the words of Colour Sergeant Smith, he added: *These things are nasty and cruel, but that is just what war is. And if they help to shorten the period of war, they have something in their favour.*

Chapter XXXIV: The Price of Duty

Lower Drift
13 March 1879

Major Hans Garrett Moore, VC

Word had reached Lieutenant Colonel Law that a host of reinforcements were en route from England, with the first waves arriving any day. Lord Chelmsford had, therefore, ordered Law to delay his advance on Eshowe until the 1st of April. Furthermore, his lordship said that he would be arriving before the end of the month and would personally lead the relief expedition. Fearing a Zulu invasion, Colonel Rowlands of the Natal garrison's No. 5 Column began ordering what men he could spare to the northern border, near the Transvaal. The garrison at Fort Tenedos had no desire to attempt to mimic the exploits of B Company, 2/24th at Rorke's Drift and were glad for any reinforcements.

At Lower Drift, the first of these fresh troops to arrive was a single company from the 88th Regiment. Better known as the *Connaught Rangers*, they were an Irish regiment that had developed a fearsome reputation during the Napoleonic Wars. This had continued through the Crimean War. Their collective valour and service was recognised by a pair of cannon presented to their native city of Galway, Ireland. Following thirteen years in India, the Connaught Rangers were despatched to Southern Africa in 1877, where they saw action during the Xhosa War. One of its battalion majors, Hans Garrett Moore, was the lone recipient of the Victoria Cross from the war, for attempting to save the life of a badly injured Frontier Mounted Policeman during which he killed several enemy combatants, while being wounded multiple times.

"Still, we'll need more than a single company of insane Irishmen to break the siege at Eshowe," Lance Sergeant Rob Anderson remarked, as he and David Fredericks watched the new company establish their camp near Fort Tenedos.

"They did break the Siege of Badajoz," David said appreciatively. Referencing the most savage siege of the entire Peninsular Campaign in 1812, which nearly broke the will of the British Army and even that of the Duke of Wellington himself.

"To be fair, that would have been their grandfathers," Rob said. "Although after the Crimea, as well as thirteen years in India, I suspect half this lot aren't even Irish."

"So, no more signalling duty for you?" David asked.

Rob shook his head. "No, they're finished with me. Colonel Law happened to have a signals officer on his staff, so he's taken over duties with the heliograph. I did overhear, though, that at least three fresh battalions are expected to join our little expedition to relieve Eshowe."

The news was confirmed that evening, when Lieutenant Martin briefed all of H Company during evening parade. The 57th West Middlesex, 3/60th Rifles, and 91st Highlanders were expected to land in Durban any day and would be proceeding to Lower Drift with due haste.

"While we had intended for our advance on Eshowe to begin on the 13th, that has been pushed back until the 1st of April," the officer commanding explained to his men. "Also know that his lordship will be personally commanding the relief column. That alone should stress how vital the upcoming phase of the campaign will be for the war effort. For those of us familiar with the road to Eshowe, you'll be pleased to hear that the garrison have constructed a secondary road that bypasses most of the possible ambush points north of the Inyezane. It also cuts about five miles off our trek." He then struck an even more serious tone. "Given the size of the relief column and the possibility that Zulu spies may inform the enemy that Lord

Chelmsford is accompanying us, we can expect to meet with fierce resistance; far greater than what we battled at Inyezane. King Cetshwayo has no doubt become emboldened since the tragic events at Isandlwana. We could very well find ourselves facing the entire Zulu *impi*."

An unspoken discomfort, yet one that had become as much a cause of misery for the Eshowe garrison, was the depleted stocks of tobacco. Coffee was the life's blood of the Army, but for many soldiers, a pinch of shag was their one source of happiness in the otherwise drudging misery. For those who either didn't smoke, or felt they could live without it, there was a fortune to be had in selling their stores of tobacco. At the start of the month, an ounce of shag sold for three shillings. By midmonth, one private managed to talk a fellow soldier out of eighteen shillings and sixpence—nearly two weeks' wages—for a single ounce.

"I get to make a small fortune while salvaging my teeth," the entrepreneurial young private stated rather proudly.

Work continued on the road from the Inyezane crossing. Captain Wynne finally relented to going on the sick list, having come down with a terrible fever in addition to his continued bouts of diarrhoea. Command of the sappers now fell under the charge of Lieutenant David Courtney.

The overall state of health amongst the garrison was becoming rather precarious. Given the constant slew of illnesses and the shortening of rations, every soldier—officer and enlisted alike—had lost at least a stone (14 pounds) of bodyweight. For some, their weight had dropped nearly double that. Trousers and tunics which had once fit snuggly, now hung loose and baggy.

Adding to their plight, Surgeon Norbury's supply of medicines and pain relievers was nearly exhausted. The terrible fevers which wracked most of the sick brought great pain, with men groaning in agony during their more lucid moments. And death was not confined to the enlisted ranks. Captain Henry Williams of The Buffs succumbed to both fever and diarrhoea. And Midshipman Lewis Coker found himself back on the sick list. His superior, Commander

Campbell, feared he'd been too late in sending the young officer to hospital. Coker's fever struck him down with such a fury that he'd been delirious and hot to the touch for the past two days.

Even among those who'd managed to avoid coming down with fever or dysentery, there was a common complaint that they simply referred to as 'Natal sores'. Cuts and scrapes were commonplace, and many had become hideously infected. Soldiers had their fingers or entire hands wrapped in bandages to prevent further exposure of their injuries to the sun. A white disinfecting powder, which thankfully Surgeon Norbury still had an adequate supply of, was used for treating these wounds. For those who developed the sores on their noses or faces, the powder and bandages made them look like something out of a Mary Shelley horror novel.

Despite their collective misery, the improved communications with Lower Drift and the assumption that reinforcements were waiting just beyond the Thukela River buoyed their spirits.

On the morning of the 13th, Colonel Pearson organised a taskforce to link up with the relief column near the Inyezane crossing. He designated three companies from the 99th Regiment, the entire Naval Brigade, thirty sappers from No. 2 Field Company, and fifty from the Natal Native Pioneers; a total of 600 men. In addition to Midshipman Coker's Gatling gun were two mule wagons carrying fifteen rockets, as well as three days' rations. Individual soldiers were ordered to leave their personal belongings behind, allowing them to carry an additional 30 rounds of ammunition in addition to their basic load of 70.

The day dawned cloudy, yet the men of the expeditionary force were filled with excitement and a profound sense of relief. Lieutenant Willock was given charge of the engineer detachment, and the young subaltern was eager for his chance at command. It was now 9.00, and the detachment was waiting for the order to march.

"What the bleeding hell are we waiting for?" one soldier grumbled. "I'd liked to reach the Inyezane before afternoon tea."

The men saw a man from the signal team reviewing a message with Colonel Pearson and Colonel Walker.

After a few minutes, the column commander's expression fell, and he slowly walked over to address the anxious detachment. "Gentlemen, I am afraid there has been a delay in our relief."

He then read the despatch to his despondent soldiers:

Relief delayed until 1 April. Waiting on additional reinforcements. Relief column will consist of 4,000 British and 2,000 African troops. Entire garrison is to be relieved and replaced by the 60th Rifles. An additional 8,000 troops are bound from England.

Few in the column even bothered stifling their groans of disappointment. Many let loose a few choice words of profanity under their collective breaths. Officers ordered their men to store their packs and wait for further orders. Perhaps most dejected of all were the numerous sick crammed into the makeshift hospital.

"I think they were the ones most filled with hope," Surgeon Norbury said quietly to Colonel Pearson.

"I'll talk with them," the column commander replied. He then asked, "Do you have enough medicines and supplies to last another fortnight?"

"Does it matter?" the doctor replied, failing to stifle his despondency. "I have enough medicated powder to deal with the constant sores everyone is dealing with. And since we've had so few battle injuries, bandages aren't an issue. But, I have almost nothing left to treat fevers. The only pain remedy that isn't completely gone is chloroform, and that's just for putting a man under during surgery."

"Do what you can," the colonel stressed.

While Charles Pearson empathised with the plight of his men, if the relief column was being delayed, there was likely a sound reason behind it. He said as much to Colonel Walker as the two reviewed the day's patrol despatches while supping on crushed biscuit and half-a-tin of beef gruel. "The Zulus are becoming ever more brazen," he remarked. "And No. 4 Vedette has been a favourite target of theirs."

"Unfortunately, we don't have scythes available," Walker noted. "Otherwise, we could just send out a dozen men and have them cut down all the tall grasses within a hundred yards of the outpost."

"And given that its location is a blind spot for the fort, we cannot leave it unmanned," Pearson concluded. "While we're waiting on reinforcements, so are the Zulus. We don't know how many the lads at Lower Drift have seen, so they could be in even greater numbers than what we've seen here."

"If Colonel Law only has a thousand men at his disposal, it would be suicide to march from Lower Drift to Inyezane," Walker added.

Charles agreed. "It's about twenty-five miles by the winding wagon track from Lower Drift to the Inyezane ford. Even lightly encumbered, it would take them at least two or three days; plenty of time for the Zulus to spring an ambush."

"The last thing the Army needs is another Isandlwana…" Colonel Walker's words trailed off. He immediately regretted mentioning the hated mountain where so many of their friends from the 24th lay dead and unburied.

Pearson, however, nodded in agreement. Ever since they received word of the disaster, his greatest fear became the same fate befalling No. 1 Column. From a strategic standpoint, he could not fault Lord Chelmsford for waiting another two weeks before launching the relief expedition. He could only hope their sick in hospital could last that long.

Three days of reprieve from the rains brought a renewed sense of hope to the garrison. Perhaps the onset of autumn was near, and the hellish torrential downfalls would soon be over. It was all for naught. On the night of the 16th, the skies unleashed a deluge upon them that once more flooded the fort. It was as if the divines were mocking the bedraggled garrison trapped within the land of the Zulu.

The 16th of March also brought more deaths within No. 1 Column. A soldier from the 99th died of heatstroke, while a marine from the HMS Active lost his battle against pneumonia. Every death at Eshowe was tragic, but one that struck close to home for Surgeon Norbury was Midshipman Lewis Coker. Norbury had been making his early morning rounds when he saw the young officer was deathly still. He'd stopped breathing. His forehead, which had been hot to the touch, was now cold.

413

The doctor, who'd known the lad for years, was visibly heart-broken by his demise. Lieutenant David Courtney arrived at the fort's hospital to check on the sixteen sappers still on the sick list when the doctor emerged, his cheeks stained with tears.

"Poor lad," he said quietly, wiping a handkerchief over his eyes and composing himself.

"Mister Coker?" Courtney asked.

The surgeon wordlessly nodded.

"I am sorry, doctor. I know he was dear to you."

"Like a son," Norbury managed to say before having to wipe his eyes and stifle a sob. He knew it was unbecoming of a doctor and an officer to allow his emotions to get the best of him. And yet, he had known Lewis Coker since he first came to the Royal Navy as a boy of twelve. He and Commander Campbell had both been like surrogate fathers to the lad, who'd showed unlimited promise and an unbreakable sense of duty.

Commander Campbell had said repeatedly that once the siege was over, he intended to help the young midshipman prepare for his lieutenant's exam. A naval lieutenant was the equivalent of an army captain. Such a feat would have been impressive for one of his age, and all the officers saw enormous potential in him. Campbell would later say, "He could have become the youngest admiral in the Royal Navy."

The most significant struggle between the garrisons at Lower Drift and Eshowe continued to be communications. More often than not, their attempts were thwarted by harsh weather. It was decided that the location of their makeshift heliograph was too low to be effective. Lieutenant Colonel Law met with the officers commanding of H and B Companies from The Buffs to discuss the matter.

"According to our mounted troops, the mission station of St Andrew's is just three miles from Fort Tenedos," the colonel explained. "It is located on a high hill with a clear line-of-site to Eshowe. Your men will secure the mission and establish more effective lines of communication with the besieged garrison. Captain Barrow's IMI will act as couriers."

Lieutenant Martin had said little at the meeting. His subaltern, Julius Backhouse, was appalled by the idea. While the two companies packed their kit and loaded ammunition boxes onto a single wagon, he pulled his officer commanding off to the side. "This is madness," he protested. "Two companies, on their own, expected to hold an abandoned church in the middle of Zulu territory?"

"St Andrew's is better located for a signalling post," Martin observed. Though he shared his subaltern's concerns, he understood they had little choice in the matter. "You know as well as I the necessity to improve our communications with the Eshowe garrison. It's a risk we're accepting, but a necessary one." The finality in his tone ended the discussion.

Though he still loathed the idea, Lieutenant Backhouse packed his few personal belongings and saddled his horse without further complaint. While some of the enlisted soldiers shared his concerns, many were glad for a 'change of scenery'.

"Perhaps we'll get another chance to get stuck in with those damned kaffirs," a private said, as he hefted his pack onto his shoulders.

"Be careful what you wish for," Lance Corporal James Monroe cautioned, as he conducted an inspection of the soldiers in the section.

"Oh, come now, corporal," another soldier spoke up. "We haven't scarcely seen a Zulu since we left Eshowe."

"And you think that means they're not out there?" the lance corporal countered incredulously. "You're a sodding fool if you think they don't have eyes on the drift."

Their section leader, Sergeant Fredericks, soon joined them, having been briefed by their officer commanding. "Sergeant Stirling is taking the lead," he said, gathering his soldiers around. "We're on the right flank of the wagon with Sergeant Davies on the left. Lance Sergeant Anderson's section will follow, with the lads from B Company behind him."

It took the better part of two hours to ferry the two companies of redcoats plus the pair of wagons and thirty-two draught oxen across the Thukela. By the time the oxen were spanned and the small column ready to march away from Fort Tenedos, it was nearly noon. Standing in parade formation outside the fort was the penny whistle band from the HMS Shah. Four hundred sailors had arrived the day

415

before, forming a second Naval Brigade. The soldiers from The Buffs would have preferred to see 400 redcoats, but any man who could fire a rifle was appreciated. Many still recalled the tenacity and savage bravery exuded by the 'Jack Tars' at Inyezane.

"Looks like they're going to play us off," Rob Anderson said.

Lieutenant Martin rode up on his horse and addressed his men. "Look smart, H Company! At the quick step…march!"

At the officer commanding's order, the column of redcoats marched past the scores of curious onlookers watching from the ramparts of Fort Tenedos. Much to their surprise, the naval band struck up with *The Buffs* quick march followed by *The British Grenadiers*. Every soldier held his head high, chest outward, as they marched past the fort. Their enthusiasm soon waned about a quarter-mile beyond the defence works. The lead wagon sank into the mud and became stuck.

"Oh, bloody hell," a soldier bickered.

The oxen brayed in protest, while the young African voorlooper kept them in line with his long whip. The driver shouted a few words to the lad, pointing to the left rear wheel which was sunk nearly to the axel.

"Time to get dirty, lads," Sergeant Davies said.

His section stacked their rifles. Several men grabbed a hold of each wheel. David Fredericks' men did the same on the right. Some of Rob Anderson's men pushed. There was little else they could do each time a wagon became stuck, other than attempt to heave it out of the muck.

"Even if the goddamned rains do stop, it'll take a least a month for these fucking roads to dry out," James Monroe said, through gritted teeth as he pulled on a large wooden spoke.

Though it was an ordeal they'd been through innumerable times during the course of the campaign, digging wagons out of the mud never became any easier or less hateful. The men of H Company let out a cheer when the wheels found purchase on solid ground, and the wagon continued on its way. This was followed by a plethora of profanities when the lead wheels along with most of the oxen sank nearly two feet into a pool of sludge. Though it was only three miles to the mission, it took the two companies until nearly dark to arrive, by which time they were completely exhausted and bedraggled.

"We'll leave the oxen spanned for the evening," Lieutenant Martin directed. "Ammunition and rations will be stored inside the church."

Colour Sergeant Bennet then spoke up. "Sir, it will be crowded, but I think we should let the men sleep inside the church as well."

"Agreed," the officer commanding confirmed. He looked west towards the rapidly-setting sun. "The grasses have overgrown this area, so we'll have to sort it out in the morning. Meantime, I think the officers and other ranks can dine together this one night."

The inside of the church was covered in dust with a few spiderwebs clinging to the rafters and roof thatch. A long altar was used as a dining table where hard biscuits and tins of beef were stacked with some canned vegetables and bottles of lime juice. David Fredericks and Rob Anderson found a corner behind the pulpit to have their supper. They were soon joined by their fellow section leaders, Sergeants Stirling and Davies.

"I kept forgetting to ask," Stirling said, "But how was that crocodile your lads bagged the other day?"

"A bit of a disappointment," David replied. "It tasted just like chicken."

It was cramped for the 180 soldiers inside the church. Though with the constant threat of rain, they were grateful to have a roof over their heads. Sentries were placed at the doors and windows, albeit with the suffocating darkness and overgrown grass, it was clear the Zulus could practically walk right up to the front door before they were seen.

He had said nothing since his discussion with Lieutenant Martin earlier that morning, but Julius Backhouse made his feelings clear in his journal, which he penned by the faint glow of a fading oil lamp.

I think it is a most absurd move, and I pity us if the Zulus come down tonight, for none of us will ever leave this alive.

The night passed fitfully for the two companies of imperial soldiers crammed into the musty old building. The floor and doors constantly creaked as numerous men invariably had to step outside to relieve themselves. It was perhaps two hours after midnight when David Fredericks found himself awake with a full bladder. A pair of soldiers sat just inside the back entrance. The sergeant crept past them. He only walked a few feet outside, as the grasses were at least

417

three feet high, and even more the further one stepped away from the building. His eyes half-shut, he relieved himself. He thought he heard movement to his immediate right. Suddenly awake, he stared wide-eyed into the darkness. The moon and stars gave only traces of light to see by, yet there was the unmistakeable rustling of grass just a few feet away. It was too close to the ground, however, to be an enemy warrior. Hurriedly finishing his business, David quickly backed away towards the door to the church.

"Watch out for snakes, lads," he said quietly to the sentries.

Soldiers sorting through stores at Lower Drift

Chapter XXXV: The War Resumes

Port of Durban
16 March 1879
***

Having just received a message from Colonel Pearson that his rations and supplies would run out by the 1st of April, the General Officer Commanding knew he needed to act soon with whatever forces he could scratch together. It was with much relief that Lord Chelmsford received the telegram informing him that reinforcements were en route from Britain.

Despite the strains placed on Her Majesty's forces by the War in Afghanistan, and now this unexpected conflict in South Africa, it was decided that the Zulus had to be quickly and decisively defeated. His lordship had departed Pietermaritzburg to await the arrival of the first troops at the port city of Durban. The mayor offered up his manor house to serve as Chelmsford's headquarters until his departure for Lower Drift.

"At least Horse Guards is finally taking the Zulu threat seriously," said his military secretary, Lieutenant Colonel John Crealock.

The two were breakfasting in the open-air lounge, its balcony overlooking the city.

"The 57th West Middlesex Regiment reached Durban yesterday," Crealock added.

"Before we can deal with Cetshwayo, we must first sort the matter of Colonel Pearson's column at Eshowe," Chelmsford remarked. "I intend to meet personally with the 57th's commanding officer before sending them to Lower Drift."

"The 60th Rifles and 91st Highlanders should not be too far behind them," Crealock observed. "Will you be sending them to Lower Drift as well?"

"Yes," the GOC confirmed. "The 57th has just come from Ceylon, and they're likely understrength. However, I've been assured by Horse Guards that the 60th and 91st have been supplemented with sufficient volunteers."

In addition to the notification regarding his reinforcements, there was a slew of other despatches and telegrams in the stack of papers. These mostly dealt with personnel issues, officer promotions, and orders back to England for recently discharged time-expired soldiers. Seeing nothing else that directly pertained to his pending expedition to relieve No. 1 Column, Chelmsford decided to leave them for the staff officers to sort out.

"Take a note Crealock," he said, standing tall. While pacing back and forth, his hands clasped behind his back, he dictated a message to the Secretary of State for War in London:

Thanks to the prompt dispatch of reinforcements from England, I shall be in three days' time able to advance with a strong column, strength as per margin, to relieve the garrison at Eshowe, which has now been holding that post for upward of ten weeks.

As none of the major generals ordered out have yet arrived, and Colonel Pearson, who at first commanded the column on this line, but is shut-up at Eshowe, and with no other senior officer available, I have decided to assume command myself...

The rest of the despatch covered the logistical matters and avenue-of-approach the relief column would take. The GOC's regarding the necessity of his assuming command was a bit puzzling.

For Colonel Pemberton of the 60th Rifles, expected to arrive soon with his 3rd Battalion, most certainly possessed sufficient rank to lead a force of similar size to Pearson's original No. 1 Column. He was a seasoned veteran who'd held his commission for twenty-six years. Fighting in the Indian Rebellion of 1857, he had been severely wounded, losing two fingers on his left hand during the Siege of Cawnpore.

The truth was, the war had become very personal to Lord Chelmsford. Though he blamed Anthony Durnford for the disaster at Isandlwana, he still regretted his death, as well as those of Henry Pullèine and all the other officers and men whose bodies lay unburied, three months later. He needed a decisive victory; not just as General Officer Commanding, but as the man who was personally leading Her Majesty's forces into battle.

There was also the matter of restoring his personal reputation. After Isandlwana, the past thirty-five years of his career now meant nothing. There were plenty of Durnford's friends, some with considerable influence, who would blame Chelmsford for the disaster. If he did not personally smash the Zulus quickly and decisively, the tragedy of Isandlwana would be how posterity remembered him.

Something that caught the GOC's eye was the names of the four major generals who would be arriving with the various waves of reinforcements. It felt excessive to him, and he could not help but think that these men, who were substantively his peers, were being sent to keep him in line. These four senior officers were men he could not easily bully or manipulate, and it was the name at the top of the list that gave him pause, Major General Henry Hope Crealock.

"I see that Horse Guards is sending your brother to keep a watchful eye on me," he said to Crealock.

Five years the elder brother of John, Henry Hope Crealock was first commissioned with the 90th Light Infantry in 1848. He'd risen through the ranks very quickly, reaching lieutenant colonel at the age of twenty-seven; the same age that Wellington himself had achieved this rank. Having received his promotion to major general in 1870, he held seven years of seniority over Lord Chelmsford, who was promoted to the rank in 1877. Chelmsford's current rank of lieutenant general was by local appointment, rather than being substantive or even a brevet from Horse Guards. This meant that while he was still the General Officer Commanding in Southern Africa, were they any place outside the Cape Colony, he would be the elder Crealock's subordinate

"You're still the GOC, my lord," John stated. "I doubt Henry will attempt to undermine your authority. After all, if Horse Guards did intend to replace you, it would not be with an officer of the same rank, regardless of seniority, but with a substantive lieutenant general or higher."

"When we reorganise the army, he can command a division," Chelmsford decided. "But for now, our first priority is relieving No. 1 Column. And whatever Her Majesty's government decides, I intend to finish this issue with the Zulus. Once Cetshwayo is defeated and clapped in irons, they can replace me with whoever they wish."

421

The 17th of March was a sombre day. Most of the garrison gathered at the funeral service for Midshipman Lewis Coker. One of the most popular officers, both among his peers and the enlisted ranks, his death had struck No. 1 Column harder than any. As a drizzle of rain fell upon them, normally stoic men allowed their tears to fall unashamed.

Warren Wynne and Arthur Davison were still on the sick list; however, both were listed as 'showing improvement' and were therefore granted leave to attend Coker's funeral. There was very little actual ceremony. Reverend Robertson read a few lines of scripture, and Commander Campbell spoke for a few minutes about the young man he'd admired so well. Colonel Pearson decided to suspend the moratorium on firing volleys over the graves of the fallen and he allowed seven men from the HMS Active to form a guard of honour. They fired a single volley as Coker's body was lowered into its final resting place. There was talk amongst the officers and sailors of the HMS Active regarding the erection of a proper headstone for young Lewis Coker. Even the lowest-ranking seamen offered to help pay for the necessary subscription.

Grave of Midshipman Lewis Coker

Among those not able to attend the young midshipman's funeral were those on picquet and vedette duty. While the young officer was laid to rest, three mounted troops took up their positions at the now-infamous No. 4 Vedette. One was Private Walter Kent of the Imperial Mounted Infantry. The other two mounted troopers were on either side of him about thirty yards apart.

"I hate this damned place," the private grumbled.

This was the fourth time he'd had duty at the No. 4 Vedette, and twice he'd been attacked by the enemy. His eyes scanned for any signs of movement. And while the gentle breeze felt pleasant, it also made it more difficult for him to see any Zulus lurking in the blowing grass. Letting out a sigh, he cradled his carbine in his lap. Suddenly, his horse snorted as a single volley of rifle fire sounded from Midshipman Coker's funeral.

"Easy, girl." He patted his mount on the neck.

Five Zulus then leapt up from the grass just ten feet away. With cries of *'Usutu!'* they opened fire on the mounted soldier. His hapless horse was struck in the shoulder by a musket ball. The stricken animal cried out, throwing Kent to the ground, while it sprinted away towards the fort.

"Shit!" the private swore as he staggered to his feet.

His carbine lay just a few feet away. Before he could retrieve it, a Zulu shield smashed him across the face. Kent managed to grab one assailant by the neck, punching several times across the face and mouth before an ungodly pain in his lower side caused him to throw his head back. He cried out in anguish, as he was stabbed nearly twenty times over the course of just a few seconds. His twitching body, covered in blood and hideous wounds, slumped to the ground. The remaining picquets fled towards the safety of the fort, shouting the alarm.

Ten minutes later, half-a-dozen 'Uhlans' and an entire company from the 99th, who Walter had been a part of, swarmed out from the fort. Forming into a skirmish line, sections of redcoats bounded to the site of the ambush. It was one of Kent's old mates who found him. There was no sign of the Zulus who'd slain him.

"Over here!" the private shouted. He choked back his emotion at the hideous sight. Walter's guts were split open down the middle. His eyes were open and lifeless, his head turned to one side and covered in blood.

"Fuck..." Kent's former section leader whispered. Removing his helmet, he stood over the body.

Private Walter Kent was the fifteenth man to die during the Siege of Eshowe, yet he was the first killed by enemy action since the Battle of Inyezane, nearly three months earlier. Death was not finished with the garrison, however. Another young redcoat died of fever later that afternoon.

David Courtney was unaware of the bloody skirmish that claimed the life of another soldier, as he accompanied his officer commanding back to his camp bed. Though he'd handed most of his responsibilities over to his senior subaltern, Warren Wynne preferred to rest on his own bed rather than take up space in the hospital.

"Not much more that Surgeon Norbury can do for me at this point," he said, his voice raspy and strained. "Either my fever breaks or it doesn't. All in God's hands now."

David said nothing, but simply nodded and bit the inside of his cheek as he tried to supress his feelings of helplessness. Though he had not known Midshipman Coker well, he'd been fond of the young man, like pretty much every member of No. 1 Column. And while he'd only gotten to know Warren Wynne over the past three months, since the company assembled at Shorncliffe, he'd become more of a friend to David than his superior officer.

"Has it really only been three months since we left home?" Warren asked, as if reading his subaltern's mind.

"Three months or three lifetimes; I'm no longer certain which, sir." He then helped his officer commanding remove his patrol jacket and sit on his camp bed. Warren had a batman to see to him; however, Courtney had dismissed the man, electing to see to the captain personally. He helped Wynne out of his boots and laid him out on his bed. A canvas tarp provided the only protection from the elements, and a cross breeze blew mists from the morning drizzle over them. Warren's forehead was hot to the touch, and he settled for keeping his blanket just over his legs.

"You're a good man, David," Warren said, licking his parched lips and struggling to keep his eyes open.

Courtney smiled and tried to recall if this was the first time his officer commanding had addressed him by his given name. "Thank you, sir," he managed to say, stifling the emotion in his voice.

Wynne's eyes were closed, his breathing heavy, yet he remained fairly lucid. "I have no plans of leaving this world before I can return home and see my darling Lucy and our boys again. But if the Lord should deem otherwise, I am glad to know that my *other* family will be looked after."

"Excuse me, Mister Courtney." It was Captain Wynne's batman standing at attention. "Your pardon, sir, but Colonel Pearson has asked for you."

David nodded and told the young sapper to look after their captain. He then donned his patrol cap and walked through the stifling muck that was the fort. He scarcely noticed the stench of filth and unwashed bodies anymore. Still, he never ceased to wonder how his own health had remained sound, while so many in No. 2 Field Company had fallen ill. Himself, Colour Sergeant Smith, Sergeant Small, and about four or five sappers were the only ones he could recall who had yet to end up on the sick list. Two of the

425

company's sergeants had spent more time in hospital than out. After Captain Wynne, David was most worried about their health.

He found the column commander talking with Captain McGregor by one of the two orange trees that were spared from destruction when they occupied the old mission. The skies were still grey, adding to the engineer subaltern's gloom. However, the clouds had broken to the south, and the late mid-afternoon sun forced its way through. Were he not in a state of abject misery, David would have found the view of the rolling hills in the distance, beneath the visible rays of the sun, quite beautiful.

"You sent for me, sir?" Courtney asked. He was suddenly exhausted and wished for nothing more than to sleep for a month.

"I did," the colonel replied. He held a scrawled message, transcribed by the signallers, along with what looked like a set of pin-on insignia. Without standing on ceremony, Pearson handed the message to David. "It seems not all of today's news is bleak."

Telegram received with despatches from London. Orders have posted to the London Gazette that Lieutenant Courtney, Royal Engineers, is promoted to captain. Orders will be delivered by relief column.

FTA Law, Lt Col

"Congratulations, Captain Courtney," Pearson said, handing the insignia to David with his left hand, clasping his right at the same time. "We'll have a more formal ceremony, once this troublesome affair is over. In the meantime, I am temporarily relieving Captain Wynne of his command responsibilities. He's done more to preserve the lives of the men in this column than most of us put together. But I do not wish for him to pay the same price for his devotion to duty as poor Mister Coker. I'll let him know, personally, of my decision. I'll also assure him that he can resume his duties as officer commanding of No. 2 Field Company as soon as he's fully recovered."

"Yes, sir."

As he stared at the rank insignia in his hand, the news of his promotion felt very anticlimactic to Captain David Courtney. He knew he should be happy. He'd been waiting for this promotion for several years. Yet the months of hardship and the failing health of his friend and officer commanding left him numb. Without thinking, he removed his tunic, pulled off the old insignia and pinned the new ones to the collar.

At St Andrew's mission, Rob Anderson manned his heliograph post. With B and H Companies now manning the post at St Andrew's, Lieutenant Colonel Law had decided to assign the lance sergeant to communications duties once more. A pair of soldiers were constantly assigned to him, tasked with keeping eyes on the distant Eshowe fort, watching for any signals coming from the garrison.

The previous two days were spent with soldiers pulling up the high grasses in and around the mission. This was quickly disrupted when a slew of snakes were discovered in the undergrowth. One particularly disturbing creature, when stretched out, was over nine feet in length with darker scales and a nasty disposition.

"Stay back, lads!" Lieutenant Backhouse shouted, drawing his pistol. "That's a damned black mamba. If it bites you, you're finished."

Before the officer could shoot the reptile, it slithered away with alarming speed. Indeed, most of the snakes they came across fled from the soldiers. As an added safety measure, the men probed through the grass with their Martini-Henrys, bayonets fixed, before tearing up the grass.

"Wish I had a red meerkat for a pet right about now," James Monroe said, catching his breath as another particularly large black mamba slithered away. Though he'd never considered himself afraid of snakes before, these creatures unnerved him.

"What would you do with a red meerkat?" one of the privates asked.

"Red meerkats, also known as the yellow mongoose, eat black mambas," the lance corporal explained. "When I was learning to read, I acquired several books on South African wildlife."

"We should see if any of the NNC know of a shop where we can purchase a couple," another private said while nervously prodding the grass with his bayonet.

South African red meerkats

The men were labouring not far from where Lance Sergeant Anderson's heliograph was positioned. Also nearby was the HMS Shah's Gatling gun. As an added security measure, Lieutenant Colonel Law had detached the gun and its nine-man crew to the mission.

"Signal's coming, sergeant!" a private shouted to Anderson.

He quickly snatched up his notebook. Positioning the mirror on the awkward apparatus, he signalled back that he was ready to receive messages. From the higher position, it was proving substantially easier for the two garrisons to maintain communications. Rob kept his gaze fixed, copying each letter as the 'dots' and 'dashes' were relayed via flashes of reflected sunlight. It was only after he finished and sent back that the message was received, that he looked down at his notebook and put the letters together into words.

Three more men dead from illness including Midshipman Coker.

"Seems all we hear from them is when someone dies," David Fredericks observed, reading over his friend's shoulder.

"That and when one of the officers has an absurd request. Like when a certain captain asked if someone could forward £10 back to

428

some banker in Durban. About the only message coming directly from Colonel Pearson was asking about his wife."

"What about her?" David asked.

"Apparently, she's great with child and is expecting any day now. Colonel Law sent one of the Volunteers down to Durban with a pile of despatches and asked the man to inquire after Pearson's wife. She's in East London, nearly 500 miles down the coast. I suspect we won't hear anything for a week or so."

David shook his head. "It's just like officers, waiting until they're old men to have children. I mean, I don't know how old Colonel Pearson is, but I suspect by the time I'm his age, my son may very well have made me a grandfather."

"Of course, being mere rankers, no one is going to inquire as to how our wives and families are managing," Rob added.

"So long as my letters reach Lillian, I can manage. I was at least able to tell her that I'm still alive and in good health. Most of the families of those poor bastards trapped at Eshowe have no way of knowing whether their loved ones are still counted amongst the living."

Chapter XXXVI: African Highlanders

Durban, British Colony of Natal
17 March 1879

The 91st Highlanders embarkation at Southampton
From the Regimental archives

It was no small miracle that the 91st Highlanders managed to ready themselves and all their equipment, stores, ammunition, horses, not to mention several hundred newly-arrived volunteers, to begin the long journey to the Cape in just over a week. This sense of haste quickly gave way to intense boredom as the S.S. Pretoria slowly steamed its way first around the Iberian Peninsula, then down the long stretch of the West African coast.

Life aboard steamship from Southampton to Cape Town was tedious and uneventful. Captain Robert Lyttle rightly suspected that much had transpired since they first received their orders to The Cape. He shared his quarters aboard ship with James Sinclair, who'd assumed the duties as one of the battalion majors following Major Bruce's elevation to commanding officer. While the Regiment had received sufficient enlisted volunteers to fill their other ranks vacancies, there was still a shortage of officers. Ostensibly, the eight line companies were commanded by a captain with two lieutenant subalterns. As it was, there were just five captains and thirteen lieutenants in the entire Regiment; three of whom were acting as officers commanding of their respective companies. One was battalion adjutant. This left ten junior officers to fill sixteen subaltern billets. James Sinclair's former G Company had no subalterns, as he'd been compelled to hand command to his lone lieutenant, Geoffrey Collins, when he assumed duties as battalion major.

"Collins is a good man," Sinclair said, one evening as he and Lyttle lay on their bunks. "Still, I can't help but feel the need to check on him and the lads every day or so. And what about you, Robert? How manages A Company?"

"Hmm?" Lyttle asked, not hearing at first. "Oh, they're managing. I was concerned about possible disciplinary issues with the new men, but they've been the least of my problems."

"Most are fresh out of recruit training," Sinclair recalled. "They still shit themselves at the mere sight of a corporal!"

Lyttle winced at his fellow officer's use of profanity. While outwardly a proper gentleman officer, when in private, James Sinclair could be as vulgar as the crudest private soldier from the gutters in Glasgow. Robert made note of this to his friend.

"Bah! Sir Thomas Picton was the most vulgar man in all of Wellington's army. He was likely dropping profanities when a French musket ball ended him at Waterloo."

"Yes, but he was Welsh," Lyttle remarked, as the two shared a laugh.

"You know me, Robert. I am a proper gentleman in front of the ladies. I scarcely say 'damn' around our fellow officers, and I've only said 'fuck' once in the mess."

"I remember that. You had to drink from the common cup afterwards."

"Which didn't improve my speech any," James recalled.

James was reviewing the reports on stores from Quartermaster Gillies for what felt like the hundredth time that week, while Robert tried to pen a letter to his wife. Suddenly feeling board and restless, Sinclair sat up and tossed the stack of papers onto the tiny end table next to his bunk before pulling out his pocket watch.

"Dash it all, it's nearly midnight. What day is tomorrow? The fifteenth?"

"Sixteenth," Lyttle corrected.

431

"Let us hope we reach Natal soon, lest my speech become even coarser over the coming days!"

The following morning the port of Durban came into view, eliciting cheers from the mass of soldiers, anxious to finally be back on dry land after nearly a month at sea. Much to their dismay, only Major Bruce and the adjutant, Lieutenant St Clair, went ashore that morning. By the time they returned later that afternoon, it was clear the regiment would not be departing the ship until the following day. Major Bruce explained to his assembled officers that the harbourmaster had to ready the lighters; small flat-bottomed watercraft that could traverse the submerged sandbar where the water was too shallow for the Pretoria's draft.

On the morning of the 17th, while swarms of the awkward boats ferried men and supplies across the rough surf leading into the port, a deputation of citizens arrived, requesting to meet with Major Bruce and his officers. Leaving his sergeant major to oversee the latest group of men climbing out of the lighters, Alexander Bruce and the officers who'd already come ashore met with the men. The group of citizens were well-dressed, half having donned their ancestral kilts upon hearing news that a Scottish regiment had arrived in Durban.

"Major Bruce," the man leading them said, removing his bowler hat. His speech was softer and more of the upper class 'George Street' Edinburgh accent. He extended his hand. "My name is Mr Jameson. On behalf of the Scottish merchants of Durban, we extend to you a hearty welcome."

He then unrolled a long piece of parchment, which he proceeded to read from:

Sir,

The undersigned Scotchmen, residents of Durban, beg to tender you and your officers, non-commissioned officers, and men, a very hearty welcome to the colony. It affords us the utmost gratification to see among us, for the first time in our history as a colony, the tartans of our Highland soldiers, and to hear the familiar accents of our countrymen once more, reviving as they do associations of our native land, which we cherish as our most precious heritage.

Our little colony yields to none of her Majesty's dependencies in loyalty to our Queen, and we welcome therefore at all times her uniform; but on this auspicious occasion we feel justified in doing more in extending to our countrymen of your regiment a particularly hearty greeting, which we beg you will convey in our name to all ranks. We are confident that if your services are brought into requisition in the field, the traditions of the 91st will be gallantly sustained by the officers and men under your command, and that in Zululand, 1879, another laurel will be added to your Colours.

Stifling a grin, James Sinclair whispered to Captain Lyttle, "I don't suppose we should tell him that half our regiment isn't even Scottish."

"It bears the signatures of over seventy of the leading Scotchmen of Durban," Mr Jameson continued. He rolled up the letter and handed it to Major Bruce, as the two clasped hands.

"You have my thanks," Alexander said. "And that of the entire 91st Argyllshire Highlanders. In the name of Her Majesty, Queen Victoria, I promise you that we will carry the fighting spirit of the Highlands into battle with the Zulus."

There was little time for further pleasantries, as there was a daunting amount of work to be done. The additional commissariat officers and staff ordered to South Africa by London had yet to arrive, meaning chaos and confusion as the overworked supply personnel tried to assist Quartermaster Gillies in requisitioning sufficient wagons and draught animals.

In addition to the logistical nightmare facing the Regiment, there was the matter or reorganising some of their personnel. The musicians of the 91st were ordered disbanded and reassigned to Surgeon-Major Edge. While it was common for bandsmen to act as stretcher-bearers while on campaign, Major Bruce decided to make this a permanent assignment for the duration of the war.

He explained to Bandmaster Kelly, "While I love the sound of Highland pipes and drums as much as any, the Regiment needs grown men capable of carrying the wounded."

"I understand, sir," the senior musician acknowledged.

"We have seventeen 'boys' in the regiment," the commanding officer continued. "They will all be assigned to you. I trust most can at least play basic bugle calls?"

"Yes, sir," Kelly asserted.

Boy was a rank given to members of a regiment who were underage. Often the sons of currently-serving soldiers, they had to be at least fourteen years of age and were most often used as buglers, tailors, or servants. Upon reaching the age of eighteen, if he wished, a boy could enlist onto the rolls of the Regiment as a private. Otherwise, he was granted his discharge from the service.

With wagons and draught oxen yet to be seen, the men of the 91st had to settle for carrying their tents and equipment to the site of their camp about half a mile from the harbour. Ammunition and ration boxes were stacked near the storehouses, covered in tarps, and placed under guard.

As the Highlanders hastened about their work, a harsh breeze blew in from the ocean, carrying with it ominous dark storm clouds. Before the battalion's headquarters tent had even been staked, a crash of thunder heralded the onslaught of a late summer deluge. Soldiers dropped everything they were carrying and hurriedly pulled their greatcoats from their packs. A young lance corporal broke into a fit of laughter. He closed his eyes, turned his face up into the downpour, and shouted, "Welcome to South Africa, lads!"

While his regiment battled against the elements to establish camp in the middle of a horrific rainstorm, Major Alexander Bruce was ordered to meet with Lord Chelmsford at the mayor's house in Durban. He was accompanied by his senior battalion major, William Gurney, having left James Sinclair in command of the camp.

As they were led into the entrance hall of the house, servants took their soaked greatcoats and hats. The entire household staff appeared to be indigenous Africans dressed in European garb.

Only the butler was a white Englishman. He spoke to the other servants in their native tongue before addressing the two officers. "Right this way, gentlemen."

The drawing room was small but comfortable with bookcases of stained oak and expensive portraits on the walls. Only the heat and thick, muggy air gave away that they were not at a gentleman's home in England.

Lord Chelmsford sat on an overstuffed leather chair. His ever-present secretary, Lieutenant Colonel Crealock, sat behind a small writing desk. There were several other officers present who were variously standing or sitting on couches.

"Gentlemen," his lordship said, rising to his feet.

The two officers came to attention.

"My lord," Alexander replied.

"Please, have a seat," Chelmsford said, his expression genial and relaxed. The arrival of two fresh battalions, with a third close behind, gave him the first feelings of relief in nearly two months.

The English butler offered the men brandy, which they gladly accepted. Outside, the rain continued to pummel the house; the winds whipping the spray against the window behind Lord Chelmsford. The GOC appeared not to notice, but Bruce found himself pitying his men, who were feverishly trying to establish their camp in the nightmarish mess. Chelmsford signalled to Crealock, who produced a small stack of papers which he handed to Major Bruce.

"Much has happened since you first received word about this unfortunate conflict we find ourselves in with the Zulus," the GOC began. "The despatches Colonel Crealock just handed you will put you abreast of the current state of affairs." A staff officer then produced a battered map which he laid on the centre table. Chelmsford ran his finger along the Thukela and uMzinyathi Rivers. "Here, gentlemen, is the border between the Natal Colony and the Kingdom of the Zulus. Following Colonel Durnford's mishap at Isandlwana, the remnants of No. 3 Column are holding at Rorke's Drift. To the north, Colonel Wood's No. 4 Column has fortified its stronghold at Khambula, about thirty miles east of the town of Utrecht. I have instructed him to conduct harassment operations in the vicinity of this mountain, known as Hlobane, to disrupt the enemy, as well as draw pressure off Colonel Glyn at Rorke's Drift."

Looking at the map, Alexander Bruce surmised that Utrecht was about 250 miles from Durban. He also saw numerous marks and notations much further south, not far from the ocean, and reckoned that his regiment would not be travelling north to assist Colonel Wood. "Where do you need the 91st, my lord?"

"Here," Chelmsford replied, pointing to the mouth of the Thukela River. "This crossing is aptly called Lower Drift. Colonel Pearson's No. 1 Column crossed into Zululand there two months ago. They won a victory here, at this place marked 'Inyezane'. They have since become trapped at the old mission station of Eshowe. Thankfully, they have a resourceful engineer officer who fortified the mission into a fortress. The Zulus cannot get at them, but neither can they wander far from Eshowe, let alone make the thirty-five-mile trek back to Lower Drift. We've since lost communications with them. This means the Zulus are infesting the region between Eshowe and Lower Drift. We know the column has sufficient rations to last about two months, probably not much longer."

"Highlanders will clear the way, my lord," Alexander reassured the commanding general.

"That is what I like to hear, major," Chelmsford replied. He paused for a moment to compose his thoughts before changing the subject. "I am sorry Colonel Kirk was unable to travel with you. I heard he was ill."

"*Ill* is putting it mildly, sir," Bruce replied frankly. "He has a cancerous growth in his foot, and the doctors will have to amputate soon, if they haven't already."

"I am sorry to hear that," Chelmsford replied earnestly. "A shame that Horse Guards did not at least brevet you to lieutenant colonel before you departed."

"Well, my lord, we were in a bit of a hurry to get here." Bruce forced a smile. "Before we departed Southampton, I saw they brevetted both battalion majors in the 99th. Still, I know my place on the army list compared to Ely and Coates, and I know my substantive promotion will come long before theirs."

The rain continued to resonate off the window with the occasional flash of lightning.

Alexander Bruce was anxious to return to his regiment. Yet, there were several issues he knew he would likely need the GOC's assistance with. "There were no wagons or draught animals waiting for us when we arrived," he said. "My men had to carry their tents to our proposed campsite and are now being drenched as they try to establish camp."

"The weather is something I am afraid they will have to get used to," Chelmsford replied bluntly. "The entire region has been in a perpetual state of near-flooding since January. It is nearly autumn which, along with winter, are the dry seasons in Southern Africa. However, for the moment the late summer rains appear to have no intention of ceasing. Your men are Highlanders, they will make due."

Fortunately for Major Bruce and the 91st, his lordship had ordered many of the wagons from Charles Coates' convoy to Lower Drift be sent back to Durban. This helped alleviate some of the logistical issues the Highlanders and other reinforcements now faced. They were also informed that three train cars had been acquired to take them part of the way to Lower Drift. This was met with much relief from the Scottish battalion, though they quickly learned that the tracks only reached a small rail stop called Saccharine along the Verulam River. This meant they would only get to ride about twenty miles towards their destination. The remaining fifty would have to be made on foot.

It would take two additional days for the 91st Highlanders to have their logistical issues sorted before they were ready to begin the trek to Lower Drift. The entire time they were subjected to relentless showers from the heavens. Despite these hardships, on the morning of the 19th of March, the regiment in tartan trousers boarded the train for the short ride to the Verulam River. By 4.00 that afternoon, the last of their men and stores had reached the tiny depot, and they began the long walk to the Thukela River.

It was also on the 19th of March that a signal from Lower Drift seemed to confirm the story told by Kgabu kaLanga, the poor captive accused of being a Zulu spy. Sergeant Small of the engineers had to stifle a morbid laugh as he transcribed the message from Lieutenant Colonel Law:

What has happened to my messenger of 24 February? He is Mr Fynney's groom. Have you hung him?

"Seems the poor wretch was telling the truth, sir," Small said to Captain McGregor, who oversaw the communications array.

"Tell them he is still our prisoner," the officer directed.

"Who is Mr Fynney, sir?" Richard asked.

"The Natal Border Agent for the Thukela district."

As neither Captain McGregor nor Sergeant Small could recall the name the man had given, it would be another few days before it was confirmed that Kgabu kaLanga of the iziGqoza was, in fact, the name of the border agent's groom. Henry Law, however, seemed content to know the messenger was still alive, and with Colonel Pearson still not convinced the warrior was who he claimed to be, Law let the matter rest.

It was also on this day that another runner arrived at the fort. Rather than being suspected as a spy, this man's arrival was met with cheers by the garrison. The messenger wore the red rag of an NNC warrior on his head and carried a satchel full of despatches and letters. The most important of these was a detailed plan-of-campaign for the relief column. This was also the first news the No. 1 Column had regarding the arrival of fresh troops from around the British Empire. Three full battalions were expected at Lower Drift any time, as well as an additional Naval Brigade from the HMS Shah, bringing with them more artillery rockets and even another Gatling gun.

It was not just a regiment of Highlander infantry that was making its way to the Thukela. At the Verulam River crossing, the 91st was greeted by a large detachment of blue-jacketed sailors.

As the redcoats in tartan trousers departed the train, the naval commanding officer rode his horse over to Major Bruce and saluted. "Lieutenant Carr, HMS Boadicea," he said.

"Ah, good," Bruce replied, returning the salute. "His lordship told me to expect you. How many men did you bring?"

"Two hundred and fifty, sir. We also brought a pair of rocket tubes and a Gatling gun."

"Splendid. Your detachment will take the lead. I have not heard any reports about the Zulu incursions this far south."

"To be honest, sir, I have not heard any sort of reports at all," the naval officer remarked. "We were simply told to make for Lower Drift. Unfortunately, we did not even get this message until after we'd disembarked, and our good ship continued on its way. Otherwise, we could have sailed to the Thukela."

After a few additional pleasantries, the men of the HMS Boadicea took their place at the lead of the column. Poor weather and the previous passage of thousands of men and beasts several months prior had left the dirt track leading to Lower Drift a churned up mess. They reached the town of Stanger, known to the indigenous Africans as KwaDukuza, the following evening. The morning of the 23rd found the Regiment and their naval companions unable to proceed any further, as the camp and road had become an impassable quagmire. Breve Major Sinclair managed to convince a few local farmers and builders to loan the Regiment enough shovels and pickaxes to clear the road leading away from the town and dig their wagons out of the mud.

Each morning, the Highlanders rose well before sunrise, every soldier struggling in the darkness to find his uniform and kit and be ready for morning parade and the long, arduous trek that followed. The 24th was particularly hateful, as there were not only two river crossings plus churned up muddy quagmires for roads, it was a cloudless day and the sun excruciatingly hot. Ten years of Home Service, and only a tiny fraction of its soldiers having ever travelled outside of Britain, left the 91st poorly equipped to handle this sudden and drastic change in climate. The wool uniforms caused men to sweat from the moment they donned their tunics with their packs, weapons, and kit weighing as much as sixty pounds; eight of which came just from their Martini-Henry rifles. Though the river crossings were labour-intensive as they struggled to get their over-laden wagons across, they also served as a reprieve for the men. They were able to soak their over-heated bodies and even bathe during long halts.

By the time the Regiment reached its designated campsite, they were still nine miles from Lower Drift. Soldiers stumbled about in a daze, the effects of heat and utter exhaustion taking their toll. There were no card games under lamplight that night, nor was any man in the mood to tell crude stories or banter. Well before the bugler sounded 'lights out', the vast majority of the 91st Highlanders were fast asleep.

Chapter XXXVII: Return of the White Zulu

Eshowe
23 March 1879

John Dunn

The one man who had a greater history with the Zulus than any, and thus far had made every attempt to remain out of the conflict, was the trader and explorer, John Dunn. The son of Scottish traders and orphaned at the age of fourteen, Dunn's first dealings with the Zulus took place during the civil war which tore the kingdom asunder in 1856. Then just twenty-two years old, John had actually sided with Cetshwayo's brother, Prince Mbuyazi, during the fighting that took place along the banks of the Thukela River. Once they saw all was lost, Dunn and most of the white mercenaries accompanying him had managed to flee by boat, leaving Mbuyazi and his followers to their brutal fate.

Years later, Cetshwayo extended peace offerings to the white trader, offering wives and land in exchange for firearms and other goods. Dunn accepted and, much to the chagrin of his European wife, had over the years taken forty-eight Zulu wives, siring well over a hundred children. His lands and wealth grew, until he was one of the most prominent men in the entire Zulu Kingdom. With

440

nearly 2,000 followers under his care, his was its own private fiefdom. These followers had fled with Dunn before the start of the war and were now struggling to subsist south of the Thukela River. Though Lord Chelmsford had promised to look after Dunn's people, the supplies of food had been appallingly short. Yet, this did not stop his lordship from summoning the 'White Zulu' to press him and some of his fighting men into service of the Crown.

Dunn arrived at Lower Drift accompanied by 150 of his followers and was directed to Lord Chelmsford's headquarters tent. The GOC had just finished meeting with the commanding officer of the newly-arrived 57th Regiment, whom he dismissed so that he and Dunn might speak privately.

"It is good of you to come," his lordship said, offering John a seat. He then produced a cigar, which Dunn accepted.

"It would be even better, my lord, if you'd kept your promise to care for my people. Are we not subjects of the Crown, to be looked after by Her Majesty's representatives now that we've been expelled from our lands?" The words were sharp, though they did not appear to affect Chelmsford.

"As you can well see, Mr Dunn, I am in the middle of fighting a war against the very people who threw you off your lands."

The words seemed hollow. Dunn was among the few completely aware of the shameful ultimatum, the refusal to honour the terms of the land commission, as well as the outright determination by the GOC and high commissioner to start a war against the Zulus.

Still, Chelmsford persisted with the reason for calling this meeting. "And if you want your lands back, then it is time you decided where your loyalties lie."

"King Cetshwayo has been my friend and brother for many years," John answered slowly. "As was his father before him. And yet, I was driven from his royal kraal by zealous warriors who viewed me a threat because of my white skin. I fear that as long as Cetshwayo remains on the amaZulu throne, I can never return home." He took a breath and gave another answer he felt might be more to Chelmsford's liking. "I am also still a subject of the Crown and therefore at Her Majesty's service, provided her representative can promise me that my people will be properly cared for and our lands restored to us."

"Of course," the GOC replied earnestly. "I promise you, once the Zulu king is clapped in irons, you will be one of the richest and most powerful men in all of Africa."

This seemed to satisfy Dunn, though he was still concerned about the current state of his followers.

Chelmsford swore to see to them before continuing. "I think it would be very advantageous if you yourself were to accompany me as far as the Inyezane River. I know you are not a soldier, and therefore I would not ask you to go any further. However, your very presence will ensure better scouting efforts from your men, not to mention I would be obliged for your assistance in sharing your knowledge of Zulu warfare and the country we shall be passing through." The GOC paused and allowed Dunn a moment to think over his words. He then added, "The lands from the Thukela River up to Eshowe were yours; your own private kingdom, as it were. You have a corps of 150 native scouts who not only know the land, but as I hear it are better shots than any of the warriors currently serving in the NNC."

"Personally, I would like to see their skills tested against some of your redcoats," John asserted. "Many are my own sons, and they will serve the Crown well."

Satisfied, the two men concluded the meeting with another handshake, John Dunn placing himself and his scouts at his lordship's disposal. Privately, he felt little to no bond between himself and his ancestral home. Born in Port Elizabeth, he had never even set foot outside of Southern Africa, let alone his late father's native Scotland. His changing of loyalties was more to do with pragmatism, not to mention his own survival. And with his allegiances clearly aligned with the British, he knew there was no going back. That night, alone in his tent, his thoughts turned to his friend and brother, King Cetshwayo. It was a hateful situation he found himself in, and in the darkness, John Dunn wept.

The sun dawned at Eshowe, and for Captain Warren Wynne, there was no more hiding the gravity of his illness. Constant bouts of diarrhoea had left him severely dehydrated, his once robust body severely depleted. When the officer commanding of No. 2 Field

Company failed to turn out for morning parade, Courtney rushed to his side. The captain's eyes were closed, his face pale and covered in sweat. His breathing was ragged, and he was hot to the touch.

"No, not like this!" Courtney lamented. He intended to shout for help but thought better of it, as he did not wish to cause a disturbance. He instead sought out Colour Sergeant Smith, who had taken the initiative to oversee morning parade with Lieutenant Main; Willock having been admitted to the sick list the day before.

"I need four men and a stretcher," Courtney said quietly.

The fear in his eyes told the colour sergeant all he needed to know.

He in turn took it upon himself to fetch a stretcher from Surgeon Norbury's medical staff while tasking three NCOs with helping him carry the captain to the hospital, including the ever-reliable Sergeant Richard Small. Warren clearly had no idea where he was, nor did he so much as wake as his men trampled through the churned-up ground, trying not to drop him in the process. As he was known to all within the camp, many eyes stared in sorrow when he was carried past. The pitiful sight of the man who had kept them alive during the siege brought more than a few tears.

Sergeant Richard Small was particularly shaken. Wiping his hand over his eyes, he quietly said, "Our good captain's war is over."

The presence of thousands of fresh imperial soldiers along the Thukela alarmed both Phalane and Prince Dabulamanzi. What angered Dabulamanzi the most was that he had been unceremoniously replaced as chief *inkosi* of the Zulu southern *impi*. An older warrior named Somopho kaZikhala had been dispatched by his brother to assume overall command. Somopho brought with him several thousand warriors along with the message from the king that, since he was older and more experienced in warfare, he should lead the attack against the British relief column. There was also news that

Cetshwayo had renewed the call to war for his regiments, yet most would not be coming to their aid in the south.

"The king sends our *impi* north, yet our enemy is here!" the *induna* lamented. He then asked, "How many did you say there were?"

"At least 5,000," a scout reported. "And they are mostly white soldiers in red jackets. We believe their great *inkosi*, Chelmsford. is with them."

"Bah!" Dabulamanzi spat. "Not one of us has ever seen Chelmsford or even knows what he looks like."

"All the same," Phalane continued, his voice calm in sharp contrast to his inner frustrations. "Our king has sent more than 20,000 warriors to deal with the red-jacketed soldiers in the north, while we have little over half that number with which to fight this fresh army." The royal *induna* then composed himself. "We must have faith in our sovereign. If he has sent the main *impi* north, he could not have made this decision lightly. With a touch of good fortune, he could bring our abaQulusi kinsmen to our aid."

While Prince Dabulamanzi was still uninspired by his brother's decision, he knew he was not aware of all that was transpiring in the northern reaches of the kingdom. All the same, it was just as likely that King Cetshwayo did not realise that a fresh host of imperial soldiers was now waiting to cross into Zululand from the south. Whatever his personal feelings, including his deep sense of umbrage at having his authority usurped, there was little he could do but continue to fight against the invaders.

It was midday on the 25th of March when the 91st Highlanders reached the fast-growing camp at Lower Drift. The 57th West Middlesex Regiment had arrived three days earlier. Having spent the last six years in Ceylon, they were well understrength; their eight companies having scarcely any more troops than the five companies from the 99th already encamped near Fort Pearson. The two companies from 2/3rd Buffs were still occupying the signalling post at St Andrew's.

Alexander Bruce ordered Majors Gurney and Sinclair to establish their camp near the 57th, while he sought out Lord

Chelmsford's headquarters. The GOC was not in his tent at the moment, and it took some time before Bruce found him standing near the ramparts of Fort Pearson, overlooking the camp. Two officers he did not recognise were with him; one wore an artillery officer's uniform, the other a green tunic from the 60th Rifles.

"Ah, major," Chelmsford said, as he spotted Bruce walking up the path towards him. "Splendid that you have arrived in such short order."

"It was a rough slog, my lord, but we are here and ready to take the fight to the Zulus."

"Soon, major, soon." Chelmsford then addressed the officers with him. "This is Lieutenant Colonel Law, Royal Artillery. He will be commanding your division during the trek to Eshowe."

"Major Bruce," Law said, extending his hand. "It's a pleasure to meet you. I must say, I cannot wait to see your Highlanders in action."

"They won't disappoint, sir," Alexander replied.

"And this is Colonel Pemberton," Chelmsford said, addressing the other officer. "He will be commanding the second division."

"Colonel," Bruce said, clasping his hand.

"I was just telling his lordship that my green-jackets should be here in the next day or so," Pemberton explained. "I've left our 3rd Battalion under the command of Lieutenant Colonel Francis Northey; a splendid and most capital fellow. We were required to fill our vacancies with many young and inexperienced soldiers, as I am certain you were."

"Yes, but my men are ready," Bruce declared. "Regardless of where they came from, they're all Highlanders now, and they will conduct themselves accordingly in battle."

There was a touch of rivalry between the officers which was common, and in fact, encouraged between different regiments. Lord Chelmsford even felt that this would add to the professional pride the young soldiers felt for their regiments, compelling them to fight harder, lest they appear weak or cowardly.

Bruce went on to give his lordship a quick briefing on the state of his battalion and where they were establishing camp. The GOC invited him and the other senior officers to dine with him that evening before he dismissed the major. As Alexander made his way back down the hill, he soon discovered more than just fighting men in and around the large camp. There was a veritable swarm of 'specials'; correspondents from various publications around the British Empire. A couple were known to Alexander, namely Melton Prior of the *Illustrated London News*, as well as Charles Fripp from *The Graphic* who was also an accomplished painter. Correspondents from colonial newspapers, even from as far away as Afghanistan and Australia, had converged to cover this unexpected conflict in a far-flung corner of the globe. Most were young men seeking adventure, Fripp being just twenty-four years of age.

One man who had yet to arrive, and whose return Chelmsford dreaded in many ways, was Charles Norris-Newman of *The Standard*. Going by the rather absurd nickname of 'Noggs', he had been the lone newspaper reporter to accompany his lordship and No. 3 Column during the Isandlwana campaign. A young man with a rather sharp tongue and perhaps too much curiosity than was good for him, he'd been a constant bother to both Chelmsford and Crealock, although the other officers in No. 3 Column had actually taken a liking to him. Perhaps the most uncomfortable question constantly on Norris-Newman's lips, even before the Isandlwana disaster, was *why?* Why were Her Majesty's soldiers engaged in a bloody conflict against a local king who they'd once called 'friend'?

Two days later, the 3rd Battalion of the 60th Rifles marched into camp. Their green uniforms contrasted sharply with the red tunics worn by their counterparts in the other three regiments at Lower Drift. Originally formed in America during the mid-18th century during the Napoleonic Wars, the 60th was originally made up of an astounding seven infantry battalions. The Fifth Battalion wore green instead of red, and like their similarly-clad counterparts in the 95th, they carried Baker Rifles instead of muskets. Now known as the King's Royal Rifle Corps, the 60th had since reduced the three battalions, though all still wore the green jackets made famous during the Peninsular War. The commanding officer of their 3rd Battalion was a forty-two-year-old lieutenant colonel named Francis Northey. A personal friend and protégé of Colonel Pemberton, Northey had served during the Oude Campaign in India in 1858. That, however, had been his last action. He'd spent many of the following years posted to Canada. Indeed, there were very few in the

60th with any sort of campaign service, even among the officers and senior NCOs. And like the 91st Highlanders, around 40% of their ranks were made up of new soldiers straight out of recruit training. The smattering of red jackets throughout their ranks attested to how many of their men were new to both the Regiment and to the Army.

"Not to worry, my lord," Northey said to Chelmsford, when questioned about the state of his battalion. "My men are well-versed in all of their drills. About all there was to do aboard the ship from England was practice rifle and bayonet drill."

Disembarking of the 60th Rifles off the steamship, Dublin Castle
From *The Graphic*

On the same day that the green-jackets marched into camp, so too did the newly reorganised 4th and 5th Battalions of the Natal Native Contingent. Despite having more than double the number of professional infantrymen than any of the original columns, Lord Chelmsford knew he still needed a robust number of indigenous warriors to supplement his army.

The GOC also understood that time was quickly running out for Colonel Pearson and No. 1 Column. By the 26th of March, he had an imposing army of 5,500 men ready to march back into Zululand.

"It will take some time to ferry all troops and baggage across the Thukela," his transportation officer, Captain Molyneux, explained, as his lordship and the senior officers dined in the general's tent.

"Our single pont can only ferry one company or a pair of wagons at a time. Each trip takes roughly half an hour."

"We have an additional 600 sailors in camp," the GOC observed. "Have them assist on the pont, working in two-hour shifts. Also, make certain to have the boat inspected at least twice a day by carpenters. I don't want the bottom falling out with a hundred men on board."

"Yes, my lord."

As soon as the officer left, Chelmsford signalled to Crealock. He produced a sheet detailing the organisation of their newly-assembled flying column. In addition to all the battalion and independent company commanders was John Dunn, whose 150 huntsmen would serve as scouts for the column. Additionally, the bevy of news correspondents circled around behind the GOC, anxiously taking notes.

"Gentlemen," his lordship said. "Once all our men and stores are across, we will march to Eshowe. Tents and all non-essential baggage will be left behind. And yes, that includes my own tent as well. We need to travel light, plus make certain there is room in the laager for wagons, cattle, and men."

"You do intend to laager the wagons each night, my lord?" Lieutenant Colonel Law asked.

"Of course. Colonel Crealock has copies of my updated field force regulations which address this. Speed and caution will be equally important once we cross back into enemy territory."

"We can only hope the weather cooperates, sir," Colonel Pemberton stated.

"The summer has been unusually wet with the last four years of drought coming to a rather abrupt end," Chelmsford recalled. "And for those of you who are new to this southernmost region of Her Majesty's realm, autumn and winter are still very hot. While ostensibly also their dry season, I do not see the rains letting up any time soon."

Lieutenant Colonel Northey was reviewing the orders for the march, his brow furrowed in contemplation. "My lord," he said. "I see that the garrison is to be relieved and replaced by my own battalion."

"That is the plan at this time," Chelmsford confirmed. "The fort at Eshowe was never meant to house as many men as Colonel Pearson has garrisoned there for the past two-and-a-half months.

Lack of food and medicine has depleted their strength greatly, and they are in need of rest. Not to worry, colonel, you will not be left in the middle of enemy territory on your own. With the forces we have here, I intend to maintain a robust presence between Lower Drift and Eshowe. If, by chance, we happen to compel the enemy into a decisive battle before we reach the fort, so much the better. It is time we taught Cetshwayo a hard lesson."

"What of the enemy forces in the area?" Northey asked.

Chelmsford looked to his senior cavalry officer, Captain Percy Barrow, for answers.

"The word we've received from Eshowe is the enemy has increased in numbers over the past few weeks," Barrow stated. "We do not know whether Cetshwayo intends for his main *impi* to engage us, or if he's sent them north to face Colonel Wood's No. 4 Column. As best we can tell, the Zulus have at least 10,000 warriors between here and Eshowe; perhaps as many as thirty."

The assembled officers nodded appreciatively. Even if the conservative estimate proved accurate, it was unlikely that the Zulus would allow Chelmsford to march his army thirty-five miles through their kingdom and relieve the beleaguered garrison at Eshowe without a fight.

For the first time during the meeting, the GOC addressed John Dunn. "Mr Dunn, you and your men know the region better than any. Therefore, you will be the eyes and ears of the flying column."

John nodded and said quietly, "As you wish, my lord."

A large queue formed near the pont. Quartermasters and transportation officers sought to keep order amongst the mass of men, wagons, and beasts getting ready to cross the river. Having first arrived in camp, the 57th Regiment was given priority in the crossing, followed by the 91st Highlanders, and finally the 60th Rifles.

The five companies from the 99th Regiment were already encamped near Fort Tenedos on the Zulu side of the river. They would be joined by the two companies from 2/3rd Buffs that were still guarding the signal station at St Andrew's, thus forming a combined battalion. Some recent personnel issues created a slight dilemma as to who would command them. Under most circumstances, the matter would be left to Colonel Pemberton, as he was their division commander. However, as he was wont to do, Lord Chelmsford elected to resolve the matter personally.

He found Major Bruce down by the pont, observing Captain Lyttle's A Company boarding the flat-bottomed boat for the short journey across the Thukela. Bruce sat upon a camp stool along with his battalion majors and adjutant, a pipe clutched in his teeth. When they saw Chelmsford approaching, the officers quickly stood.

"My lord," Bruce said, rendering a salute. He nodded towards the pont which had lurched its way off the bank with scores of sailors. A petty officer called out the cadence, as they pulled on the heavy ropes. "As you can see, the 91st Highlanders are now crossing into Zululand."

"Splendid, splendid," the GOC replied, almost dismissively. "I'm glad to see your staff officers with you, for I find myself in a situation that you can help me resolve."

"How may we be of service, sir?" Bruce asked.

"As you know, the companies from the 99th and The Buffs are forming their own separate battalion for this campaign. Normally, they would have been led by Brevet Lieutenant Colonel Coates, as he is one of the battalion majors for the 99th. However, it is with much regret that I must say he has instead decided to resign his commission and return home for personal reasons."

"Your pardon, sir," James Sinclair spoke up, "But that's bloody disgraceful."

"Whatever we may think of Major Coates' conduct," Chelmsford stated, now refusing to refer to the resigning officer by his brevet rank, "We still require an officer of sufficient rank to lead this makeshift battalion over the next few weeks."

Alexander Bruce nodded and folded his arms across his chest. He then said over his shoulder, "Major Sinclair, how would you fancy leading a battalion into battle?"

"It would be a privilege, sir," James said, standing tall, looking at Chelmsford.

"I am obliged to you," his lordship responded. "I will inform Colonel Pemberton of the change. Major Sinclair, once you've sorted your personal belongings and baggage, you will join the next available pont across the river."

"Very good, sir!"

"Well, that was a bit odd," Major Gurney said, once his lordship was out of earshot.

By late afternoon on the 28th of March, the last elements of the flying column were across the Thukela. Only Lord Chelmsford and his staff remained on the Natal side of the river. They and the bevy of correspondents would join the column early on the morrow. As the GOC and his staff sat down for supper, a familiar—if rather unwelcome—face showed itself in.

"Glad to see I haven't missed this next adventure!" the man said excitedly.

It was Charles 'Noggs' Norris-Newman; the lone reporter who accompanied Chelmsford during the Isandlwana campaign, and who both his lordship and Lieutenant Colonel Crealock viewed as a sulking viper. Crealock glared at the grinning correspondent.

Chelmsford decided to give a more diplomatic, if somewhat measured, response. "Not had enough of South Africa, Noggs?"

"No, my lord, you need not worry. I shall be ever by your side until the war is over." 'Noggs' continued to stand, his hat held in his hands. He knew there was no chance of Lord Chelmsford inviting him to sit at his table.

"You've missed your chance to scoop the story out from everyone else," Crealock stated, a mocking grin of satisfaction on his face. "A dozen of your peers have been here for more than a week already. Can't imagine what took you so long to join us. You can mess with them. I'm certain Misters Prior and Fripp would be glad for your company."

"And I theirs." 'Noggs' then clicked his heels together and with a 'my lord' to Chelmsford, left the tent.

"A pity he didn't get lost between here and Pietermaritzburg," Crealock grumbled.

"Still," Captain Molyneux spoke up, "Perhaps the Zulus will take him off our hands."

This brought some mild laughter from the assembled staff. Even Lord Chelmsford found the remark a touch amusing. While he did not hold the same level of loathing for Norris-Newman as his

451

military secretary, his good humour had faded considerably over the past three months. Any excuse to laugh was welcome.

After supper, with the sun setting behind the hills to the west, John Crealock was approached by the correspondent, Melton Prior. As both men were accomplished artists, there was a shared respect between them. Prior was arguably the most famous 'special' accompanying the column. Crealock found his company far more preferable than the insufferable 'Noggs' Norris-Newman.

"Your pardon, colonel, but might I have a word with you?"

"Of course," Crealock replied. He gestured for the reporter to take a seat next to him on a pair of camp stools.

"It's rather embarrassing, if one is being honest. You know my credentials. I covered the last Ashanti War, and just last year was in eastern Europe during that beastly conflict between the Turks and the Russians."

"Yes, I recall reading many of your stories," Crealock said appreciatively. "So, what can possibly be embarrassing for you now?"

"I'm no coward," Prior stressed. "It's just that…well, I've had terrible premonitions regarding my own death. I fear that if I cross the river into Zululand tomorrow, I will never return home."

Crealock pondered these words for a moment. He then said, "If it were any other man telling me this, I would call them a coward and send them packing back to Blighty. However, you are perhaps the only correspondent in all of Southern Africa I have any measure of respect for. And so, I will do what I can to help you. Once this beastly affair is over, I'll supply you with all sketches I make during the expedition, along with any notes that would be useful to your readers."

"Much obliged, colonel, much obliged."

Chapter XXXVIII: The Flying Column

Fort Tenedos near the Thukela River
29 March 1879

Lieutenant Colonel Francis Northey
Commanding Officers, 3rd Battalion, 60th Rifles

It took four days to ferry all available troops and supplies across the Thukela River using its single pont. On the final night, Lord Chelmsford slept three or four hours, waking at 3.00 a.m. He'd arranged for the pont to take him and his staff across at 4.00, and they found a detachment of sailors waiting for them. A single wagon accompanied them, carrying the general's personal baggage. Though his tent would be left behind, like all the others.

It was a warm, humid morning. The staff officers led their horses onto the pont, while a light mist rolled in off the Indian Ocean, four miles to the east. There was little talking. The only sounds came from the sloshing of the river current, as the boat was heaved across, along with the occasional snort from their horses. Both Pemberton and Law were waiting for them on the far bank.

"A splendid morning, my lord," Colonel Pemberton said. "Will you join us for breakfast?"

"I'd be delighted, colonel."

Chelmsford's French cook had been killed at Isandlwana, so it fell to the servants of the column staff officers to prepare their meals. On this day, however, his lordship contented himself with the same rations of tinned beef and hard biscuits that were the staple of his soldiers. He had just a few minutes to eat. Reveille would be sounding soon, and there was much work to do this day.

The bugler sounded the notes, rousing the entire camp.

His lordship checked his watch. "Five O'clock," he noted. "Time to bring the war back to the Zulus."

Soldiers emerged into the pale morning light. Heeding the shouted orders from their NCOs, they tore down their tents and made ready to march. Perhaps keenest of all to be underway were the five companies from the 99th Regiment. It was their mates who were trapped at the mission station of Eshowe these past three months. Brevet Major Sinclair had tasked one of the senior captains to assist him as a staff officer, though this consisted of little more than reporting personnel and equipment issues to him.

Despite the order to travel as light as possible, devoid of tents and most of their camping equipment, the flying column still numbered 122 wagons stretching nearly two miles in length. John Dunn's detachment would scout ahead of the column, followed by the vanguard made up of Captain Barrow's mounted troops. Lieutenant Colonel Law's first division would lead the main advance, followed a half hour later by Colonel Pemberton and the second. Lord Chelmsford would accompany Law, that he might keep apprised of any events as they unfolded. Having learned his lesson, not just from the disaster at Isandlwana but from No. 1 Column's initial foray across the Thukela River, his lordship made certain each division advanced with both speed and attentiveness. The organisation of the flying column was thus:

First Division – Lieutenant Colonel Law
2 companies 2/3rd Buffs with 5 companies 99th Regiment
91st Highlanders
No. 2 Squadron, Imperial Mounted Infantry
Mounted Volunteers
5th NNC Battalion
Naval Detachments (HMS Shah and HMS Tenedos)
Two 9-pounder cannon, two 24-pounder rocket tubes, and a Gatling gun.

Second Division – Colonel Pemberton
57th Regiment
3/60th Rifles
Two troops of horsemen; one of European volunteers, the other
African Basutos
4th NNC Battalion
Naval Detachment (HMS Boadicea)
Two 24-pounder rocket tubes and single Gatling gun.

For Sergeant David Fredericks and his mates with H Company, 2/3rd Buffs, there was a profound sense of determination at finally taking the fight to the Zulus. They had roused themselves just before dawn; both companies and the naval Gatling crew parading at just after 5.00.

"Wagons are limbered, and the company is ready to march," Lieutenant Backhouse reported to his officer commanding.

Robert Martin acknowledged, "As I was informed yesterday, we're being merged with the companies from the 99th to form a battalion-sized element."

"Makes sense," his subaltern concurred. "Not that I look forward to having to take orders from that daft fellow, Coates."

"You need not worry about him," Martin explained. "Apparently, he's resigned his commission and is headed back to England."

"That's bloody disgraceful," Backhouse said, his voice dripping with disgust. "So, who's in command?"

"A Brevet Major Sinclair from the 91st Highlanders."

"A Scot? Well, at least we know they like to fight, even if we cannot understand a blind word they say."

It wasn't until around 10.00 that the lead elements of the flying column reached St Andrew's. Lieutenant Martin was met by James Sinclair, who informed him that their battalion was second in the march behind the 91st.

"Not to worry, Mister Martin," the brevet major said, with a grin. "My Highlanders have been ordered not to bite anyone that's not a Zulu."

As the men of H Company found their place along the convoy, Private Peters asked, "What's with the daft trousers those lot are wearing?"

"Scotsmen love their tartans," Sergeant Fredericks remarked.

"Just be glad they're not wearing kilts," James Monroe added with a chuckle.

"Why, think they might scare the Zulus off with what's underneath?" Peters asked.

"Or make them die of laughter," one of his mates said.

"To be fair, whenever we cross one of these freezing rivers, none of us are exactly 'inspiring' in the trouser regions," Monroe added.

The column had halted so the two Buffs companies and naval Gatling could re-join them, and to discuss the next phase of their advance. John Dunn was meeting with one of his scouts, while Chelmsford had called for Captain Barrow to join him and Lieutenant Colonel Law.

"The path north is extremely rugged," Dunn explained. "There are many winding turns, plus any number of tree groves the Zulus could hide behind."

"We checked the route ourselves," Percy Barrow noted. "The road is a churned-up mess from the last time we passed this way."

"What do you propose, Mister Dunn?" the GOC asked.

"The ground to the northeast is more open," Dunn recalled. "There's no real path to follow, but I know the area like the back of my hand. The Nyoni River is much wider there. Provided it's not in flood stage, there are several fording points we can use."

"Captain Barrow," his lordship said. "Take a dozen men and ride with Mister Dunn as far as the Nyoni River. Find us a viable fording point, and we'll establish camp there."

"Sir." Barrow snapped off a quick salute before riding back to his lead troop.

Though it was just a few miles to the Nyoni River, travelling cross-country would hinder further their already ponderously slow pace. And every step of the way the flying column would feel the menacing presence of the Zulus.

A final message had been sent by his lordship to Colonel Pearson, ordering him to ready a force of 500 men to meet them near the site of their previous battle at Inyezane. Pearson, however, was fearful for the defence of the mission. Thousands of Zulus were now converging on them. He was further concerned about the state of his men, weakened by months of food deprivation and disease. A compromise was therefore reached. Chelmsford conceded the colonel's point but directed him to still have this force ready to advance, should the relief column come under attack and find itself getting the worst of the battle with the Zulus.

Listen for the sound of the guns, the final message had said. *Two blasts mean we are on our final approach.*

With field glasses and a naval telescope belonging to the HMS Active, it was possible to watch the relief column as it made its way past St Andrew's mission.

Sergeant Richard Small of the engineers stood atop the southern ramparts, trying to see what he could with his field glasses. "It looks like they're veering east, sir." He called down to Captain David Courtney, who joined him up on the defences.

The acting-officer commanding of No. 2 Field Company pulled his own glasses out of their case and searched the far distance for a few minutes. "They seem to be keeping more towards the coast," he observed.

"That's probably wise, sir," the NCO conjectured. "After all, the road from Lower Drift is full of potential ambush sites. If they cross the Nyoni River and make their way north, back onto the trail, the ground is mostly open until they reach that stretch of road we provided for them at Inyezane."

"Very astute, sergeant," the captain said appreciatively.

"Your pardon, sir," Small then said, his voice hesitant. "But Captain Wynne. How…how is he, truly?"

Courtney swallowed hard, not wishing to answer the question. He was, in a sense, relieved when it was done for him by Colour Sergeant Smith, who was walking up the short steps onto the ramparts.

"If his fever doesn't break soon, he will die," the company's senior NCO said bluntly.

Death had kept its icy grip upon the garrison, with four more dying from disease since they received word of Lord Chelmsford's relief column beginning its crossing of the Thukela. Among these was Lieutenant Arthur Davison, the twenty-two-year-old former adjutant of the 99th Regiment. He and Warren Wynne had taken seriously ill at the same time. If even one so young and fit as Davison could succumb, then so too could their officer commanding, who many of the men viewed as unbreakable.

"I guess all we can do is pray for him," Small said, a sense of defeat in his voice.

"If you think it will help," Smith replied, with a dismissive shrug. He then took a moment to scan the long column of men and wagons in the far distance. "Captain Wynne's only hope is that his lordship arrives soon, within the next couple days, and that we can rush him to a proper hospital. I doubt they brought with them much in the way of medicines that might help his fever."

"We'll do what we can, when the time comes," Captain Courtney added.

By the end of the first day, the flying column had travelled just ten miles, and it would be well after dark by the time the rear guard of the second division arrived in camp. The forming of the laager proved a complete nightmare. None of the African wagon drivers or voorloopers had any experience in laagering. Nor, for that matter, did the British. It was with much aggravation and embarrassment when Captain Molyneux reported to Lord Chelmsford that only a third of their draught oxen could be penned behind the wagons.

"Then the rest will have to be kept in the sleeping areas with the men," the GOC replied, knowing there was little else they could do in the encompassing darkness.

This brought much discomfort and irritation to both men and beasts alike. Over 1,200 oxen were kept tied up within their already cramped sleeping area.

"Should the Zulus attack us, they would likely die from laughter," Lance Corporal James Monroe said. He gave a derisive laugh, as he laid against the outer rampart.

While the Zulus chose not to attack the flying column, they were most certainly watching their every move. Phalane kaMdinwa personally led a force of 300 warriors who followed the column, keeping at least a half-mile between them and their foes. The British had posted picquets beyond their laager which precluded the *induna* and his warriors from getting too close.

What had both hurt and angered Phalane in equal measure was the man he'd seen leading a contingent of warriors armed with rifles. "It's the white *inkosi*, John Dunn," he told some of his warriors that night. "He is leading them away from any place where we can stage an ambush. Dunn is clever, and he knows the land."

"He is a putrid traitor," one of his men spat. "We should take him alive, so he can be properly impaled, like how the divine Shaka punished those who betrayed the kingdom."

Phalane nodded, his heart burning with anger. King Cetshwayo, as well as his father, King Mpande, had treated Dunn not just as a fellow Zulu but a noble *inkosi*. He owed his lands, riches, and numerous wives to the Zulu royal house. Now, he and his half-breed sons had betrayed the king to whom they owed their very existence.

"Once they cross the amaTigulu, they will be most vulnerable," Phalane asserted. "Many warriors now converge on Eshowe, and the king has sent several regiments to our aid. The main *impi* may be headed north to fight the whites occupying Khambula, but we shall destroy those who have infested our lands in the south for far too long."

Chapter XXXIX: The Armies Converge

The amaTigulu River
Ten miles from Gingindlovu
30 March 1879

The Relief Column crossing a river
From the archives of the 91st Highlanders

By the second day, the flying column had reached the near bank of the amaTigulu River. The laager was better organised this time and sufficient to hold all of the column's draught animals. Earthworks were thrown up outside the wagons, and it was behind these that the army slept. It was chaotic, not to mention extremely uncomfortable, for the men crammed behind the defences. Every last man wished he had his tent to sleep under.

A point of frustration for Lord Chelmsford was the complete lack of engineers with the flying column. "A pity Captain Wynne's No. 2 Field Company is trapped at Eshowe," he lamented to his staff that evening. "Still, I suspect that one reason the garrison has held this long is due to their efforts at keeping the mission fortified."

"We'll just have to make due, sir," Colonel Pemberton said. "Though I have little doubt a sapper company could make our travels, especially the river crossings, more tolerable."

His lordship then produced his map, which he set on his camp table, a small oil lamp resting on the top edge. He ran his finger along the route they had covered and made a few marks. "According to Mr Dunn, his scouts have spotted bands of Zulus, at least several hundred, lurking about the hills and in the dense expanses of trees and brush."

"They know we're here, sir," Francis Law said. "So why don't they attack?"

"Likely because the ground is open," Major Bruce stated. "The way we're travelling, with riflemen and cannon able to quickly adjust to any threat, they wouldn't be able to get within 500 yards of the column before they were shot to pieces."

"And, I suspect they are keeping their main fighting force close to Eshowe," Chelmsford speculated.

That night the rains came again. The defensive earthworks only served to channel the pooling water right into the sleeping areas of the thousands of soldiers and warriors in the cramped space between the ramparts and the wagons.

"Some days I wonder if I'll ever feel dry again," David Fredericks muttered.

He sat against a wagon wheel, wrapped in his greatcoat, his thoroughly soaked blanket hanging around his legs. He'd hoped to find shelter beneath one of the wagons, but he'd been too late. Every inch of space was occupied by soldiers crammed together like sardines. As the torrential downpour increased, the shelter offered to those beneath the wagons proved meagre at best. The large bowl created by the earthworks channelled the rains into the cattle laager, turning the ground beneath the wagons into a lake several inches deep.

"I often wonder if the Zulus find this climate to be as insufferable as we do," Lance Sergeant Rob Anderson mused.

"I don't see how they couldn't," David speculated. "Of course, it rains plenty back home. Only difference is, we tend not to sleep out in it every night."

There would be no relief from the incessant feelings of being soaked, for the entire day of the 31st was spent crossing the amaTigulu River. Knowing that it posed a formidable hazard, Lord Chelmsford ordered the column to encamp just two miles beyond its far bank. He had further simplified the laagering process by ordering a standard size of 130 yards which allowed for thirty wagons or carts on each side, with the earthworks erected fifteen yards outside of the wagon line.

The water was waist-deep, and soldiers carried their rifles and ammunition pouches over their heads. Captain Molyneux later in his diary compared the entire column to 'a giant wet sponge'. As he sloshed his way through the current, his shoulders aching from holding his rifle and ammunition pouches overhead, Sergeant Fredericks recalled all the troubles his soldiers had had with their feet during their weeks near Lower Drift. With the constant rains, any attempts to keep the contents of their packs dry proved mostly in vain. They had little choice but to don wet socks every morning. David could only hope that he and his men did not end up with too many blisters, or worse, infections of the feet before they reached Eshowe. Even then, only a change in the weather would bring them any real relief.

As the army made camp two miles from the amaTigulu, John Dunn spotted a lingering haze in the distance perhaps five miles from the camp. Suddenly alarmed, he quickly sought out Lord Chelmsford. "I fear the Zulus are close," he asserted. "That mist, it masks the smoke from campfires. I fear our enemy is closer than expected. I ask your permission to personally scout the area. I know it well and can find my way around even in the dark. All I ask is that you send one other to accompany me."

"I'll go," Captain William Molyneux spoke up.

Chelmsford folded his arms, contemplating what Dunn was suggesting. "How far will you go?"

"Not far, my lord. It's only a few miles to the Inyezane. I suspect the enemy is encamped in the valley just beyond the river."

"Very well," the GOC conceded. "Captain Barrow's mounted troops have seen more bands of Zulus lurking about. It would be good to know how close their army is. You two be careful, and ride back with all speed should you get into trouble."

The hour was growing late, with the sun setting behind the hills, as the two men rode out from the large camp. Molyneux was particularly pleased with the layout. It had a natural glacis on three sides which made building up defences all the easier. The ground was mostly flat and open, allowing for ideal fields-of-fire for the cannon, rockets, and Gatling guns that occupied the four corners of the defences. Each side also had a breach in the wagons, where cattle and horses could be led out to graze. A pair of wagons formed a 'gate' that could be readily shut in the event of an emergency.

"If given the choice, I'd prefer the Zulus attack us here," Molyneux mused.

"Yes, well unfortunately, the enemy has a say in where they attack," Dunn replied.

No sooner had they left the camp than the skies darkened, and a lashing downpour followed. While this made their ride especially miserable, Dunn pointed out that it would likely drive Zulu scouts to ground and help shield them from unfriendly eyes.

"Provided we don't catch hypothermia first," Molyneux said. He clutched his greatcoat close to his body.

It was dark, and under the pummelling sheets of rain, neither man could see more than a few feet in front of them. Despite his extreme discomfort, William reckoned Dunn was correct; unless the Zulus were impervious to the torments of rough weather and able to see in the dark, their ride towards the Inyezane was well concealed. Due to their impeded vision, they rode at a slow trot, and it took a couple of miserable hours to ride the short distance to the river. Dunn found a stand of trees and the two men dismounted. They sought shelter beneath the thick branches and caught their bearings.

"From here, it will be best if I go alone," John stated. He had to nearly shout to be heard over the pouring rain and the roar of the river. "I'll cross the river, while you hold the horses, and see what I can find. I suspect the Zulus are not far."

"That works for me," William replied, trying to find a bit of shelter beneath a wide bough. Even in the dark, the captain could tell that something vexed his companion. "What is it?"

"There is one thing I need; a bit of reassurance. Now you know we are in for a dangerous job. I have never been out with English officers before. I should like to be certain before I start across that our ideals are the same. In Africa, a white man must stand by a fellow while there is still life in him. If his friend is dead, then he may save himself. Do you agree?"

"Of course," Molyneux replied. "You do me great wrong if you think I'll simply ride off back to camp and leave you to the Zulus."

"Thank you, captain. That is all I needed to hear."

Dunn then proceeded to strip naked, leaving only his boots on. He tied his clothes into a bundle, which he handed to Molyneux. Slinging his rifle across his back, he carefully stepped out onto a fallen tree which appeared to span most of the river. It was still fresh, and the green branches held as John pulled his way across. With a final leap at the end, he splashed into the shallow water just before the far bank.

The old explorer's heart pounded in his chest as he crept through the tall grass. It left scores of abrasions upon his naked skin. In spite of the rain, he was able to see what appeared to be numerous glowing spots in the distance. He kept low, his rifle clutched in his grasp. His body shivered from the terrible cold. The glows were much closer than he realised. He flopped onto his stomach, as he caught sight of dancing shadows around what could only be a campfire.

The Zulus had formed half-shell shelters out of brush and branches, to keep the rain off both them and their fires. The grass was trampled flat, and Dunn had to slink his way behind a large Mphafa tree. The long, sharp spines bit into his exposed back and buttocks. He heard a crane screech in the distance. His heart nearly stopped, as this roused several Zulu sentries. One walked Dunn's way, clutching an old musket, his eyes wide as he searched in the darkness. John shouldered his rifle, fearing he would be spotted at any moment. His mind raced. He tried to think of the quickest way back to the river, where he hoped he could make his way across before the sentry's friends caught him. The absolute worst fate for John Dunn was to be captured alive. Captured British soldiers could expect a measure of fair treatment, as Cetshwayo was keen to use them as hostages in negotiations. For the 'white Zulu', there would be no mercy.

John tried to slow his near-panicked breathing, his finger now on the trigger of his rifle. Should he have to kill this man, he would have mere seconds to make good his escape. The Zulu was squinting his eyes, obviously discomforted by the continuing rain. He slowly turned back to his post, shouting a few words to his mates about a crane likely falling victim to a wild cat.

Dunn closed his eyes and shivered violently, his immense relief contrasting with the returned feelings of bitter cold causing his stomach to turn. He then took a moment to scan the far plain and surrounding hills. There were hundreds of fires. Satisfied that he'd seen all he needed to, he slowly crawled out from under the Mphafa tree, fighting the urge to stand up and sprint away.

Upon his return to the river, he was alarmed to see how much it had risen. He'd only been away perhaps an hour. It looked as if the Inyezane had swelled ten feet during his absence. He could just barely see Captain Molyneux waving to him on the far side. Shouldering his rifle once more and gritting his teeth at the thought of returning to the frigid waters, he jumped into the current. His feet caught the submerged fallen tree he'd used to cross before, and he frantically reached beneath the surface, grabbing a hold of a branch. Silently praying the branches would not break, he pulled his way across the teaming current. William crept down to the water's edge, offering his hand and helping John out of the river. Dunn said nothing. He took up his clothes and quickly dressed. As they rode away from the Inyezane, the rains began to lessen.

"The Zulus are there, alright," Dunn said, slapping his hands over his arms and legs, trying to work the circulation back into his frozen limbs.

Unbeknownst to the British scout, the very bivouac that John Dunn had spotted belonged to the Zulu commanding *inkosi*, Somopho kaZikhala. He'd summoned all the *amakhosi*, as well as senior *izinduna* within his army. The king's brother, Prince Dabulamanzi, was growing impatient with Somopho. Many times during the enemy column's advance towards Eshowe, the prince had urged the *inkosi* to converge their forces and attack the British while they were spread out on the march.

"It is time," Somopho said. He and his chief warriors clustered around his campfire, while the rain pounded the brush shelter. "Our armies have converged on this spot, and we will attack the English before they can cross the Inyezane."

"The *ikhanda* of Gingindlovu is near," the royal *induna*, Phalane, added. "It is only right that we destroy the white soldiers so close to a place they burned and desecrated."

"The spirits of the ancestors have driven them to this place," Somopho asserted. He then spoke to the *inkosi*, Mavumengwana kaNdlela. "We shall avenge both the destruction of Gingindlovu, as well as the defeat your brother suffered not far from here at Wombane Hill."

Godide's defeat had been a blight on Mavumengwana, the disgrace to their family lessening his own victory against the English at Isandlwana. Should he, the younger son of Ndlela, succeed in defeating the British so close to where his brother had failed, it would secure his own legacy and ensure that his brother's disgrace was his alone to bear. He kept these thoughts to himself, saying diplomatically, "I wish my brother were here to exact his revenge."

Somopho did not reply but instead spoke to Dabulamanzi. "My prince, you will lead the 'Right Horn' of the attack."

"We should wait until they depart their laager," Dabulamanzi added, the terrible slaughter his regiments faced at kwaJimu still fresh in his mind.

"We will attack during the *horns of the morning*," Somopho asserted. This referred to the hour just before dawn when all was darkest. "If the English are still encamped, then we will butcher them in their beds."

Though the worst of the rains appeared to have passed, there was still a continuous shower as Captain William Molyneux and John Dunn returned to the flying column's laager. The five acres of ground had been churned up by the trampling feet of over 5,000 men, 2,000 draught oxen, and several hundred horses. The field of once-high grass was now rendered into compost which had already begun to stink.

"The smell of our men and beasts likely doesn't help," Molyneux added, as they rode past north entrance.

They soon found the tarp lean-to Lord Chelmsford was using as the column's headquarters. Upon hearing of the scouts' return, he'd immediately summoned all senior officers. They gathered close beneath the stretched tarp. His lordship sat on his camp chair behind a table, the ever-present Crealock standing behind him.

"This is the place where the Zulus will attack us," John Dunn declared without waiting on formalities. "I personally saw hundreds of campfires just north of the Inyezane. And I suspect there may be more such camps both to the west and east."

"The enemy is running out of time," Molyneux added. "If the Eshowe garrison has constructed another road that leads directly from the old battle site at Inyezane to the fort, then it is a straight path for us to take, out in the open, with little chance for the enemy to ambush us."

"I would have to agree," Captain Barrow stated. "Most of the Zulus have remained invested around the fort. However, since our avenue-of-approach must be painfully obvious to them, I suspect they are converging all their forces on us here."

"It would make little sense for them to let us link up with Colonel Pearson," Chelmsford concurred. "They will try to stop us. After which, they can simply wait for the garrison to starve. It would seem if they intend to stop us from reaching Eshowe, it's now or never."

Chelmsford's heart leapt into his throat, and he struggled to supress his excitement. He knew they faced substantial risks against an unknown enemy, for Dunn's report told them little about the Zulu *impi's* size or distribution. They knew not whether this was a scratch force of local warriors or, in fact, their main army. Regardless, his gut instincts told him that he at last would be fighting a real battle against the Zulus. "We'll not make an early start tomorrow," he said. "This is a strong defensive position with entrenchments and earthen ramparts to keep the enemy at bay; not to mention good fields of fire for our rifles and cannon."

"I would like to see those Gatling guns in action as well," Colonel Pemberton added. "I hear the one used at Inyezane performed fine work."

"That it did, colonel," Percy Barrow confirmed. He then asked the GOC, "What are your orders, sir?"

"We will use the NNC to probe the Zulus and draw them into attacking us here. What did you say the name of the local *ikhanda* is?"

"It's called Gingindlovu, my lord," Barrow answered. "Although the lads call it *'gin, gin, I love you'*."

This drew a few chuckles from the assembled officers.

467

"Well, gentlemen, I promise you this," Chelmsford proclaimed, standing to his feet, "I will not make the same mistakes as Colonel Durnford. Nor will Gingindlovu bear the same ignominy as Isandlwana." As he dismissed his senior leaders, his lordship ordered a tot of rum given to each man, 'for a bit of added warmth, and to keep their spirits up'.

Over at the section of line manned by the 99th and 2/3rd Buffs, Sergeant David Fredericks helped Colour Sergeant Bennet break out the rum cask. From their position, they could overhear Brevet Major Sinclair speaking with Lieutenant Martin and the other officers commanding from their scratch battalion.

"Expect a fight soon," the Scottish officer said in his distinctive accent. "The Zulus are converging on the camp, ready to spill our guts. Make certain your section leaders check weapons and ammunition. I imagine they'll get a fair bit of use on the morrow."

Chapter XL: The Sound of the Guns

Gingindlovu
2 April 1879
3.00 a.m.

The 91st Highlanders, Battle of Gingindlovu

A heavy mist hung in the air as Captain Robert Lyttle crawled out from beneath the lean-to he'd made by tying the end of his greatcoat to the hitch of a wagon. As there was two inches of water pooling in the mud, his efforts to keep dry had mostly been in vain. The previous night's rains were unbearably harsh. And with the promise of imminent battle, it was a wonder he or anyone else within the squalid laager managed any sleep. He reckoned he had finally nodded off around midnight. As he fumbled for his pocket watch, he could scarcely see ten feet in front of him, let alone the laager and entrenchments which circled the camp. The gold-plated watch—an anniversary gift from his wife—was damp and streaked with mud. Worse yet, the face was completely fogged up, making it impossible to read.

"It's just after 3.00, sir." It was the reassuring voice of Colour Sergeant Clinton.

The ground was saturated from the rains, and the mud squished beneath the captain's boots. He then saw the adjutant, Lieutenant St Clair, who was quickly walking to each company position. "A fine morning, Mister St Clair." Lyttle gave a friendly nod.

"Compliments of Major Bruce, sir," the lieutenant replied. "He's ordered all companies to 'stand-to'. His lordship has prohibited bugle calls, lest we announce to the Zulus that we know they're coming."

"Very good. Thank you, Mister St Clair." Lyttle then nodded to Stan Clinton. "Colour sergeant, order 'stand-to'."

As soon as Clinton passed the word to the closest section leader, Sergeant Douglas McIntyre, soldiers began stirring all along the company line. Most were likely already awake. Sergeants and corporals conducted a hasty inspection of their soldiers' weapons and kit, paying particular attention to their ammunition pouches. Taking rags from their packs, Martini-Henrys were wiped down as well as any cartridges in their ready pouches that had gotten wet.

While his men inspected their weapons, Captain Lyttle drew his pistol, an American-made 1873 Colt single-action. While most preferred the Adams Mk II or Mk III, so long as it fired .45 calibre ammunition, an officer could carry whatever sidearm he chose.

"Where did you acquire that, sir?" his subaltern, Lieutenant Craufurd, asked.

"An American cavalry officer who visited the Regiment a few years ago. Jane and I offered him a room at our lodgings, and when he left, he gave this to me as a gift. I admit, I laughed when he said, 'may it serve you well in battle'."

"Section leaders are finishing their inspections," Colour Sergeant Clinton reported.

"If the Zulus decide to pay us a visit, we'll form into four ranks. The men can see to their breakfasts now but make certain every section leader knows where to place his soldiers, should the Zulus turn up for tea or breakfast."

The heavy mist hung in the air, obscuring the vision of the numerous picquets posted around the laager. It had been a miserable night, with every man completely drenched and shivering.

"Even our bleeding greatcoats can't keep this shit off us," A private named Richard Marshall grumbled, as he stood and stretched his arms overhead. A volunteer who'd joined the 91st Highlanders just prior to their departure for South Africa, he still wore the tunic and trousers of the 36th Herefordshire Regiment.

"And no sign of the sodding Zulus," one of his companions, also a new volunteer, remarked.

There were six other men on this particular post; two were volunteers, the remaining four original members of the Regiment. The weeks at sea, living in confined quarters, had given the newest members of the 91st ample time to assimilate with their mates. There was still the occasional chiding about the volunteers not being dressed like proper Highlanders.

"At least the Regiment had enough sense not to have us wearing kilts," Marshall observed, as he knelt and pulled off his greatcoat. There was scarcely a cloud in the sky, and the day promised to be as hot and dry as the night was cold and wet.

"True," one of the other soldiers concurred. "Beastly snakes would be crawling up and feasting on your bollocks!"

"To say nothing of all these goddamn ticks," another moaned, as he brushed a mass of the tiny red parasites off his trousers.

Private Marshall fumbled with his water bottle, which he noted was nearly empty. "Bugger me," he grumbled. "I should have just left it open all night and let the rains fill it."

"And you could have had floating ticks for your breakfast," a soldier added.

"The river's a couple hundred yards off," another noted. "Just be careful. Never know what's crawling around at the early hours of the morning."

"Thanks," Marshall replied. "I'll try to keep my bollocks free from snakes and ticks." Slinging his rifle, the young private slowly made his way down to the river. The grasses were tall, roughly four feet in height, and he stepped carefully, lest he come across puff adders or other equally unpleasant creatures of the South African bush. His feet splashed through an inch or two of water the closer he came to the swollen river. The grasses went right up to the edge of the bank, and he had to steady himself to keep from falling in.

As the young private knelt to fill his bottle, he could see the long shadows of clouds in the tall grass. His eyes suddenly grew wide, as he realised there were no clouds in the sky. His heart pounding in his chest, Marshall tried to see through his peripherals without turning his head. He thought he saw the glint off a spearpoint. Slowly grabbing at the buttstock of the rifle still slung over his shoulder, he could now clearly see the unmistakeable outline of a Zulu shield. Dropping his bottle, he spun quickly towards this threat, slinging the weapon off his shoulder and to the ready position. There were six Zulu warriors in front of him. They were crouching low and just as alarmed as the soldier. They flinched back as Marshall brandished his Martini-Henry. It was only when the redcoat fumbled for a cartridge from his ready pouch that they realised the rifle was unloaded. Two of them sprang forward, plunging their spears into the unfortunate soldier's throat and guts. Marshall cried out, partially from the agonising pain, but also to use his last breath to sound the warning to his mates.

As he lay on his stomach, torrents of blood gushing from the hideous wounds, the poor soldier saw dozens of enemy warriors rise up from the grass and start rushing towards the picquet. A pair of rifle shots broke the stillness of morning. They would be the last sounds Private Richard Marshall would hear in this life.

Near the GOC's bivouac, it was 'Noggs' Norris-Newman who first heard the sound of the picquets' shots. As the unfortunate Private Marshall was slain, sentries from the NNC and 60th Rifles' sector had spotted an entire *ibutho* advancing towards them. After firing a pair of salvoes, they abandoned their position, making all haste back to the laager. 'Noggs' was able to see the dark-skinned NNC warriors with their distinctive red rags tied to their heads, running just ahead of numerous green-jackets. Though he could not see the Zulus yet through the last traces of early morning mist, he knew they were not far behind.

"My lord, the enemy approaches!" the reporter shouted excitedly.

Chelmsford closed his eyes as the now-unmistakable crack of musketry echoed; this time from the direction of the 91st's picquets. "And so it begins," he whispered under his breath.

He then nodded to his bugler who took a deep breath and began frantically sounding the notes of *'stand to'*. As company bugles echoed the call along the perimeter, soldiers sprang up from their breakfast and rushed to the defences. Many skidded, with a few falling onto their backsides in the slippery mud.

The GOC pulled himself up into his saddle and called for Captain Molyneux. "Have all battalions stand to their arms; cavalry saddle up. No independent firing! All companies are to fire by volley when the enemy is within 400 yards."

"Sir!" The captain sharply saluted and rode off to inform each of the battalion commanders.

Chelmsford then saw his military secretary, Lieutenant Colonel Crealock, calmly rising up from his camp stool. He took a sketch pad and pencil from his pack, while also taking a moment to make certain his Adams Mk III revolver was loaded.

"Plan on sketching the Zulus this morning, colonel?" the GOC asked.

"Until such time as they get close enough that I have to make use of this," Crealock replied, holding up his pistol before holstering it once more.

"Good man," Chelmsford said. "The world needs to know that we won a great victory against the Zulus this day."

Though he tried to exude confidence, there was an unmistakable tension in his lordship's voice. After all, there had been little in the way of proper reconnaissance, and he still had no idea how many Zulu warriors he now faced. Equally disconcerting was that most of his soldiers were raw and inexperienced. The two companies from The Buffs were the only ones to have seen actual combat when they faced the Zulus at Inyezane, and they amounted to just one-tenth of his infantry. Nearly half the soldiers in the 60th, 91st, and 99th Regiments were fresh recruits still in their late teens to early twenties. Though the 57th had just come from Ceylon, they had seen no fighting; their last action coming fifteen years before during the numerous conflicts against the Maori in New Zealand. And unlike his time spent with the 24th Regiment at the outset of the war, the GOC had had almost no time to interact and get to know the officers and men of this flying column.

"Remember your drills, lads," Chelmsford said quietly under his breath. "And may your officers lead and inspire by their example." Setting the example of cool-headedness under fire was one reason why Chelmsford remained on his horse. And if he was felled by a Zulu musket ball…well, at least it could be said he died well.

Captain Molyneux first reached Major Bruce and the 91st Highlanders. After a brief moment speaking with the staff officer, Alexander quickly reiterated the GOC's orders to his company commanders. The Scotsmen occupied the southern face of the square with the 5th NNC battalion behind them in reserve.

"His lordship has ordered us to fire by volley," Bruce explained. "As there is almost no wind to speak of, do so by section rather than company. I reckon after the first salvo, we won't be able to see or hear a blasted thing anyway."

The officers commanding of the eight line companies quickly acknowledged the directive and rushed back to their men. Captain Robert Lyttle found his subaltern, colour sergeant, and section leaders waiting for him. Corporals and privates were already arrayed into ranks, rifles ready.

"Sections will fire by volley," Captain Lyttle briefed his sergeants. "Watch the range markers, and index sights to 400 yards."

A couple of NCOs winced at this last order. They found it unnerving to allow the Zulus to get within a quarter-mile before opening fire. As unsettling as the idea was, Lyttle concurred with the GOC's reasoning; unless one was a highly-trained marksman or company sharp-shooter, any volleys fired at further ranges would be little more than a waste of ammunition. His volunteer replacements, after all, had yet to complete their basic musketry drills. Thankfully, the Martini-Henry was an overly simple weapon to use. So long as they listened to their NCOs, followed the lead of their more experienced mates, and knew when to adjust their sights, he hoped enough of them would find their targets.

"Mister Craufurd will command the right, Colour Sergeant Clinton the left," the officer commanding continued.

"And where might we find you, sir?" Sergeant McIntyre asked.

"Right here in the centre with the best view of the battle," Lyttle said, slapping his hand against the soggy seat of a wagon that sat just behind the company's position. "I don't much like the idea of my horse getting shot out from under me. If the Zulus wish to use my head for musketry practice, so be it, but I'll not sacrifice that noble beast who's been with me the past ten years."

"You might get some practical use of that American pistol after all," Lieutenant Craufurd noted, with a nod towards his commander's holster.

"If the Zulus get close enough for me to make use of Mister Colt, then the day has not gone in our favour." The captain's reply was deadpan, though the twitching at the corner of his mouth betrayed the macabre humour of his remark.

It was now after 6.00, and the incessant fog was starting to burn off. The air felt thick, and with no clouds to speak of, it promised to be a sweltering day. Firing from the picquets had ceased, as every redcoat, green-jacket, and NNC warrior ran for his life back to the safety of the laager. The rhythmic sound of Zulu war chants created a hum in the air as did the cadence of their weapons drumming against their shields.

Kneeling on the wagon seat, Captain Lyttle wiped the fogging off his field glasses before scanning the enemy force now just over a mile from the laager. The warriors were approaching from the west, making a sweeping arc towards the southern face of the square. Scores of skirmishers carrying muskets, mostly in groups of five or six, bounded ahead of the main regiments, who had deployed into company lines. Lyttle speculated there might be three or four thousand approaching. The hair stood up on the back of his neck, he wondered how many more were behind him.

For the garrison at Eshowe, the mist and dense air had muffled the sounds of musketry coming from the flying column. There was much excitement within the fort, for the forward picquets had spotted the flying column encamped near the Inyezane crossing.

"Nothing to do but wait for the sound of the guns," Colonel Pearson said to Walker.

A few moments later, they heard the boom of a cannon, followed almost immediately by a second.

"Two blasts, that's the signal," Walker said with a relieved sigh.

Pearson was grinning broadly and made ready to give the order for the garrison to prepare to receive their friends. Suddenly, a third blast sounded in the distance followed moments later by a fourth. Pearson's face turned ashen.

"Rally our reserves," he quickly ordered Colonel Walker. "Have them kitted up and ready for battle."

Breaking into a coughing fit as he took his field glasses from a table in his headquarters building, Charles quickly made his way to the south ramparts where dozens of soldiers were gathering.

"Make way!" a sergeant shouted, parting the mob of men.

Pearson stepped up onto the earthworks. The mist was slowly clearing off. The distant sound of rifle volleys echoed in the distance.

"Seems our friends will be slightly delayed, sir," Captain David Courtney remarked, as a cannon thundered once more.

Anchoring the northeast corner of the square was the Gatling gun crew from the HMS Boadicea. To their front, about half-a-mile distant, the regiments of the Zulu 'Left Horn' deployed into company lines. Their rhythmic chants could be clearly heard, like the call of death itself. To the gun's left, the green-jackets of the 60th Rifles were becoming skittish and unnerved at the sight of so many black-skinned warriors ready to disembowel them.

The petty officer commanding the gun was growing frustrated. He turned to see Lord Chelmsford seated astride his horse about ten yards behind him.

The naval NCO quickly stepped over and came to attention. "Your pardon, sir. Last night I stepped the distance to that bush where those blacks are, and it's only 800 yards. This 'no firing' seems like throwing away a chance. I've got her laid true for them; may I give her a turn of the handle?"

"Very well," Chelmsford replied. "You may test the range of your gun. But cease fire as soon as you've done so."

"Thank you, my lord." The petty officer rushed back to his gun. A large drum magazine was loaded, the gunner's hand nervously touching the firing handle.

"At 800 yards!" the petty officer called out.

The crew gave one final adjustment before the gunner nodded they were ready.

The petty officer gave a malicious grin. "Let's send these kaffir cunts Her Majesty's regards."

Captain Molyneux remained close by as Chelmsford's ADC. He was appalled by this coarse choice of words from the gun commander. He jolted as the Gatling erupted, spewing forth a stream of bullets at an alarming speed. Their aim was true. Like a scythe, the fearsome machine gun cut a swath through the ranks of Zulu warriors in the distance. At least a dozen fell, either dead or badly maimed in the swarm of bullets.

"Cease fire!" the petty officer shouted. He then saw the captain near him and turned a slight shade of red. "Your pardon, sir, for my poor choice of words."

Molyneux was impressed by the Gatling's fearsome firepower. "Provided you keep a steady hand, and your gun does not malfunction, you can commit all the vulgar blasphemies you wish."

Despite the brutal effects of the gun, it did nothing to stop the Zulu advance. Warriors were now running much faster, closing the distance at a disturbing pace.

"Steady lads!" Lieutenant Colonel Francis Northey said from atop his horse. He rode down the line behind his nervous soldiers. "Watch the range markers, listen for the orders, adjust your sights, and mark your targets before you fire."

The commanding officer of 3/60th Rifles was concerned with the 'wobbliness' of his men. All were sweating and not just from the growing heat. A few were so pale in the face that the colonel feared they might faint before the fighting started. Still, he was confident that once the shooting began, even the most rattled of his riflemen would instinctively remember his drills and do his part for Queen and Empire this day.

Phalane gasped as he watched a number of warriors fall. Their bodies shattered, as they were struck numerous times. Four were killed outright. Another eight begged for death as they writhed on the ground, their guts split open, arms and legs mangled. The *induna*

had not personally witnessed the fearsome destruction of the Gatling at Inyezane. Yet, he'd heard many of the survivors recount the devastation wrought by a single gun that was worth a score of riflemen.

"Take to ground!" Phalane shouted, hunkering low in the grass.

His men followed suit, raising their shields up by their heads. They crouched down, still able to maintain a steady if somewhat awkward pace. All knew this day would be bloody. Those who'd fought at Isandlwana, particularly those warriors from the iNgobamakhosi Regiment, recalled the horrors suffered at the hands of British musketry. And yet, they also remembered the slaughter they had wrought in turn with their assegais and knobkerries once they closed the distance with their foes. The British redcoat with rifle and bayonet was a fearsome adversary, but at Isandlwana, the Zulus' numbers and resolve had proven too much for them.

Phalane kept low, using his shield and spear to clear the grass in front of his face. He hoped this day would see a return to the glories won at Isandlwana rather than the ignominious defeat suffered at Inyezane.

On the western face of the square, Lieutenant Martin sat astride his horse behind Sergeant David Fredericks' section. In the distance, they could clearly see distinct bands of Zulus as regiments formed into company lines. They kept low with their shields held up near their faces.

"Looks like a swarm of coloured beetles," one private muttered. "Hey sergeant, how close are we supposed to let the bastards get before we pot them?"

"Four hundred yards," their officer commanding spoke up, having heard the young soldier's rather distressed question.

H Company occupied the extreme right of their makeshift battalion's line with David Fredericks' section on the far end. To his immediate right was a company of Royal Marines from the HMS Boadicea. Anchoring the corner was a pair of 24-pounder rocket tubes also from the Boadicea. These were much larger than the 9-pounder rockets utilised by the army. Wildly inaccurate, they were horrifically loud and unleashed such a large jet of flame and explosive power that they tended to terrify both friend and enemy alike.

"I hope those silly buggers don't cock it up and blow us all up in the process," James Monroe said, nodding towards the large boxes of rockets about twenty feet behind the tubes.

"If they do, at least it'll be quick," David replied.

From their position, it was difficult to see much of the approaching Zulus. At the moment, the large force approaching from the west seemed to be veering toward the southern defences. Those coming from the north were attacking the northern face.

"Don't worry, lads," Sergeant Fredericks said. "The Zulus like to envelop their foes. I'm sure there will be plenty for us to shoot at soon enough."

On the southern face of the square, Captain Lyttle raised his field glasses. He watched the regiments of the Zulu 'Left Horn' bounding towards them. They were getting closer; their riflemen opening fire from over 800 yards away. The sounds of enemy musketry occasionally caused the soldiers to twitch uncomfortably. Yet the more the Zulus shot at them, the more confident the Highlanders became. Unless the enemy was within fifty to a hundred yards, their muskets were practically worthless.

Rob Lyttle's A Company was on the extreme right of the battalion line near the southwest corner manned by two companies from the HMS Shah, along with their two 9-pounder cannon. To the left of A Company was Brevet Major Sinclair's G Company, now led by Lieutenant Collins.

The battalion's commanding officer, Major Bruce, was pacing the line on horseback. "Such a splendid display they're putting on," he remarked, as he rode up next to Lyttle's wagon.

Both men scanned the enemy with their field glasses, noting the different coloured shields of each regiment, and how each regiment was arrayed into company lines. The thunder of the Shah's cannon shook them, causing Bruce's horse a great deal of distress.

"We've established range landmarks," Lyttle noted. "We'll commence our volleys once they reach that clump of palms on the right of my sector. I reckon that's about 400 yards."

"Unfortunately, with the tall grass, they'll be difficult for the lads to see until they're within a hundred." Bruce looked up at the captain.

He was grinning genially and shrugged nonchalantly. "Not an issue, sir. I've instructed my section leaders. If their men cannot see a definitive target, aim near the base of the range lines. Unless every last Zulu intends to crawl up to us on his belly, that'll knock a few of them over."

Though he kept his thoughts to himself, the major was deeply stressed by their predicament. The Zulus attacking their face of the square numbered in the thousands. What's more, they resembled nothing of the ill-disciplined hordes he'd always envisioned. Their advance was frighteningly quick yet orderly. The bursting of case shot over their heads did nothing to slow their attack; even as warriors were torn to shreds with each blast. Their skirmishers, clearly visible now as they rushed in small groups well ahead of the main line, opened fire when they were still hundreds of yards out. Most of the bullets flew high over the wagons. A few kicked up gouts of mud well in front of the defences.

And yet, for all that, his captain's words reassured him. True, most of his men were little more than overgrown boys, too young to even grow a proper moustache, and nearly half weren't even Scotsmen. But on that day, every last one was a Highlander!

"Stand firm, 91st!" The major galloped his horse back down the line of his regiment, calling out their motto, *"Ne Obliviscaris!"*

"Never forget!" his soldiers shouted back.

Chapter XLI: Bloody Regards

Gingindlovu
6.15 a.m.

Sailors from the HMS Shah, Battle of Gingindlovu

"At 400 yards!" company commanders from 3/60th Rifles shouted. *"Volley...fire!"*

The crash of musketry was deafening, as the entire battalion unleashed as one. The flash of flame appeared nearly simultaneous to the correspondents watching from atop and behind the wagon laager; a thick cloud of smoke blinding them to the rifles' effects. It was nearly a minute before the acrid smoke cleared enough for them to see again. The Zulus were still coming, and it was impossible to tell how many they had felled with their first volley.

"Fire be sections!" Francis Northey shouted to his company commanders, as he rode down the line. "Make certain you can still see the enemy."

The lack of a breeze made it difficult to keep their eyes on the Zulus. By letting each section control their volleys, the officers commanding were able to somewhat judge the effects of their musketry. While satisfied every time they saw Zulu warriors fall, it seemed for every one they shot, two more sprung up in his place.

To the right of the green-jackets, the HMS Shah's Gatling gun continued to fire with fearsome effect. Twice it had jammed. However, the well-drilled and disciplined crew quickly removed the bolt, extracted the broken or bent cartridge, reset the drum magazine, replaced the bolt, and continued firing in very quick order. The Zulus, viewing this monstrosity as their greatest threat, appeared to be converging the largest number of their warriors on the northeast corner of the laager. Smoke completely socked in the gun crew. Their petty officer directed them to keep firing in a sweeping arc, slowly adjusting the range.

They could now hear the shouts from Zulu *izinduna* imploring their men to press the attack. Some of John Dunn's scouts holding in reserve not far from the Gatling were able to discern the shouts of an induna to his warriors, *"Think what the maidens will say, if they hear the sons of Zulu fled before British dogs!"*

Just then, one particularly large warrior emerged from the smoke. He was bleeding from numerous wounds and in obvious pain. He stumbled forward, grabbing onto one of the smoking barrels of the Gatling. Ignoring the added pain as the flesh on his hand was seared, the warrior gave a loud cry of rage. He raised his assegai. The startled crew had just replaced a spent magazine, and with a shout of *'Fire! Fire!'* from the petty officer, the gunner quickly turned the crank. A burst of ten shots nearly ripping the enraged warrior in half. Blood and viscera sprayed them.

The determined force of Zulus lost in the smoke was now much closer, their musketry becoming more intense. A volley erupted, striking down two of the Gatling's crewmen. Seaman Edward Bird cried out, clutching at his left arm. Seaman John Bulgar was knocked to the ground, having been struck in the right shoulder. The detachment's commanding officer called out for two sailors on the firing line to aid the crew. The petty officer ordered them to man the wheels, helping to traverse the gun while he took over the task of reloading the weapon.

A loud shriek echoed from about thirty feet away. A Zulu sprang up from the grass. He was very young; a boy of just ten or twelve who'd most likely been a mat carrier for either his father or one of his elder brothers. The lad hefted an assegai, likely taken from one of the Zulu fallen.

One of the sailors raised his rifle to fire but stopped himself. "Bugger all, I can't do it. It's just a damned kid."

482

"A kid with a sodding spear!" one of his companions countered.

Feeling the boy posed too little of a threat, the first sailor waited until he was right up to the ramparts before smashing him across the face with the butt of his rifle. He grabbed the dazed Zulu lad by the nape of the neck and pulled him over the defences.

Despite the bloody destruction unleashed by the Gatling gun, the green-jackets were fighting to maintain their composure. The Zulus were now within a hundred yards of the defences. With its gently sloping ground, and with the ramparts being only three feet high, the first two ranks of kneeling soldiers were the only ones with any real protection. The rest were left exposed to the effects of Zulu musketry. This was not lost on any British soldier at Gingindlovu. Had the Zulus received but a small measure of proper musketry training, even their archaic firearms would have created chaos and inflicted scores of casualties. Even from a hundred yards, the vast majority of enemy shots sailed high; either smacking the wagons or flying over them. Still, there were the occasional cries of pain, as soldiers were struck by enemy bullets.

"Fuck!" one soldier shouted. His nearest mate fell to the ground, clutching at his bloody thigh. "Poplett's hit!"

"The colour sergeant's down!" another man in a nearby company called out, as Colour Sergeant Edmund Dallard collapsed into the mud, clutching at his bloody forehead.

"Steady lads!" Lieutenant Colonel Northey called out over the sounds of musketry and cries from the wounded. "Hold your ground! You're giving it to them far worse than they are to us!" The battalion commander scarcely finished the last words. A blow like a sledgehammer struck him in the right shoulder, knocking him from his horse. Francis landed hard on his back, the wind taken from him. His back and neck hurt worse than his shoulder. He did not notice it was bleeding profusely until one of his ADCs helped him up to his feet.

"You're hit, colonel," the officer said.

"Dash it all, so I am," Northey replied, struggling to regain his senses.

"Come, sir, I'll help you to the surgeon," the ADC said. Placing the colonel's non-injured arm around his shoulder, he led him to the battalion's hospital wagon.

483

John Dunn occupied a wagon seat behind the centre of the 60th's line. His ears had been ringing since the first loud crack of his carbine. From his perch, he had a far better view of the battlefield than any of the green-jacketed soldiers to his immediate front. Each time he felt the savage kick of his weapon, it further felt as if he were being stabbed through the heart. Though he could not see their faces, there was little doubt that among the throng of warriors rushing them were many old friends; friends he had known since his youth. Perhaps even men whose sisters were counted among the 'White Zulu's' wives. He took his time and fired carefully. He was further grateful for the billowing cloud of smoke from the end of his carbine each time his weapon erupted. It spared him from having to watch an old friend being brutally killed by his own hand.

Born in Southern Africa, he had never been to his ancestral homeland of Scotland. He was far more familiar with the Zulus than his own people and considered both King Cetshwayo and Prince Dabulamanzi among his dearest friends. The difficult decision to side with the British during this hateful war was more about survival for he and his vast family. As he fired his weapon, he bitterly contemplated that it was fitting if he should die this day. Would God judge him like Judas; a betrayer of his spiritual brethren who he loved most of all?

As his weapon becoming fouled, and cartridges more difficult to feed and extract, John paused for a moment. He fumbled through his haversack for a wire brush to scrub some of the scorched residue from the breach. He then chanced a glance across the field. The Zulus were within about 200 yards of the laager; even closer over by the Gatling gun. They kept low, utilising the tall grass for concealment as they surged forward. It seemed as if the volleys from the 3/60th Rifles were failing to strike their targets at all. He watched as one section unleashed a deafening barrage, only to have nearly every bullet kick up clods of dirt well behind the rear ranks of enemy warriors. Another section fired and the same occurred. The young and inexperienced soldiers on the line were starting to panic. Dunn saw a lot of fidgeting, as many struggled to maintain their resolve. Squinting his eyes, John swore he could see the sights on one private's weapon still set to the 400-yard line.

"My lord!" he shouted to Lord Chelmsford, who was pacing the line from atop his horse in front of Dunn's wagon. The GOC turned to look up at him.

Dunn frantically pointed towards the green-jackets, whose volleys were failing to make any sort of impact. "Your men are firing over the Zulus!"

The smoke obscured much of his vision. Chelmsford struggled to see beyond the ramparts. What's more, he was utterly embarrassed by Mr Dunn's assertion that his soldiers were firing over the heads of the enemy. Raw and inexperienced as the average private in 3/60th may have been, their officers and NCOs should have known better!

"Captain Hutton!" He called out to the nearest company commander. "Be a good man and have your men adjust their sights. You're shooting too high." His words were spoken calmly, yet firmly.

The nerves of the young soldiers in the 60th were already frayed, made worse by the felling of Lieutenant Colonel Northey. However, there was nowhere for them to go, and each man knew they had no other option but to fight or die. Sights were adjusted, and as subsequent barrages were unleashed, his lordship was pleased to see they were having the intended effect once more. In the distance, it appeared a large force of warriors was pressing to the British left, heading towards the western face of the square. Chelmsford deduced that the force attacking the green-jackets were the 'Chest' of the amabutho. Those concentrating their efforts on the northeast corner near the Gatling gun were the 'Left Horn'. He decided he'd best check the southern defences. He'd yet to see them but assumed that was where the Zulu 'Right Horn' was heading.

It was Dabulamanzi who led the attack of the 'Right Horn'; his personal pride still deeply wounded by his defeat at Rorke's Drift nearly ten weeks earlier. What's more, he was personally insulted that Somopho usurped his command of the southern *impi*. Not only was it a terrible slight to the king's brother, but he felt the *inkosi* had missed many opportunities to ambush the English and was now attacking them when they were at their strongest.

Dabulamanzi had learned the painful lessons of his attack on kwaJimu, and now Somopho was making the same mistakes. The prince had urged him to wait until the British left their camp, then attack them as they crossed the Inyezane. Dabulamanzi viewed the southern *impi's* previous defeat to be more a lack of leadership on the part of Godide than an error in tactics. Somopho, however, had stressed, 'We've waited long cnough'. Stating he wished to snare the English, who he viewed as vermin in a trap of their own making.

That the British were so well entrenched was deeply troubling, and he could not help but think the *amabutho* was doing exactly what the white soldiers wanted them to. What incensed the prince even more, as well as every warrior under his charge, were the metallic glints from behind the barricades.

Thinking these were the spearpoints of traitorous warriors from the Natal Native Contingent, he growled in rage. "Our treasonous kinsmen, the iziGqoza, hide behind their white masters!" he shouted to his warriors. "Today we must finish what our king started. Slaughter the traitors, leave none alive!"

"Usutu!" his men shouted in unison, brandishing their weapons.

A hundred paces in front of the nearest companies, groups of skirmishers sprinted towards the enemy ramparts. The prince had admonished them not to open fire until they were within one to two hundred paces from the enemy. His own experiences engaging the redcoats, from the plateau along Shiyane Mountain during the attack on kwaJimu, had demonstrated how ineffective their muskets were at longer ranges.

His riflemen crouched low, bounding twenty or so paces before falling onto their stomachs. The tall grass concealed them, though it also blinded them. Every warrior's heart pounded in his chest, as he waited for the inevitable crashing volleys from the imperial soldiers. Every time they rose up from their bellies, keeping as low as possible, many gritted their teeth. They sprinted another few dozen feet. Around the fifth such bound, some of the skirmishers began to feel more confident. Perhaps their use of concealment was working, and the English could not see them. They'd reached a stand of palms and knew they were getting close. A few of their less-disciplined companions had started firing at the enemy laager, despite their

486

prince's command that they get much closer before engaging. After a few breaths to steel their nerves, the stalwart band of riflemen stood to rush forward.

From his wagon perch, Captain Lyttle could see the enemy skirmishers were nearly to the palm cluster. While the Zulu main line was at least 200 yards behind them, the captain thought it was time to answer their adversaries' annoying pops of musketry. *"Enemy skirmishers, at 400 yards!"* he called down to his company. "Sergeant McIntyre, send them our regards."

The NCO grinned. "Front rank, up! Present...fire!"

With the echo of twenty-five rifles pounding in their ears, the sergeant behind him shouted, "Second rank, up! Present...fire!"

A noticeable pause followed the second volley. A Company's front was now completely socked in with black powder smoke. Soldiers coughed and waved their hands frantically in front of their faces. After a few moments, the men in the third and fourth ranks rose up and fired towards their foe.

The corner of Lyttle's mouth turned up in a partial grin. He watched the tall grasses ripple from their initial salvos. It was impossible to tell if any had struck their mark; however, it pleased him to see how well his soldiers were executing their drills. Moreover, the Zulu skirmishers had completely disappeared.

"Looks like they've gone to ground, lads," the captain stated, his voice carrying along the line. He called out to his subaltern. "Mister Craufurd, kindly ask the naval guns to send a few shots into those palms."

The lieutenant saluted quickly and galloped his horse to the pair of cannon, still firing case shots towards the main Zulu body. It took the better part of a minute for the gun crews to adjust. Still scanning for any signs of movement, the captain suspected there was either a ditch or embankment near the palm. His suspicions were confirmed, as the guns fired once more; one solid shot, the other explosive 'common' shot. One palm splintered down the centre as the metal cannon ball smashed through it. The second shot shredded much of the surrounding foliage. About twenty Zulus were seen scrambling away from the palms, leading Sergeant McIntyre's section to fire another volley towards them. In synch, as if conducting a drill-and-ceremony presentation, soldiers would simultaneously reach into their pouches, draw out a cartridge, load their weapons, close the breach with an audible snap of the lever and, as one, shoulder their rifles to fire once more.

"Splendid work, captain," Major Bruce said, riding over to A Company's place on the line. "Our lads are holding a lot steadier than those rattled boys from the 60th."

"Any man who claims to not be terrified when going into battle is either a liar or a fool," Lyttle observed, continuing to scan for enemy movements through his glasses. He then shouted down to his company, *"Enemy advancing to our left-front, at 300 yards!"*

"We can't even see them, sir," one sergeant called back.

"Aim for the base of the range marker!" Colour Sergeant Clinton shouted, from the left end of the line.

"I'll leave you to it, captain," Bruce said with a smile and nod, appearing to not even notice the pair of musket shots which smashed into the side of the wagon Robert Lyttle was using as his observation post.

The lines of Zulu warriors were bounding towards them, trying to use the tall grass for concealment, while their skirmishers engaged with their muskets. Privately, the captain felt the relentless discipline of both armies was a credit to British and Zulu alike. Soldiers and warriors acted instinctively. For Robert Lyttle, it was a privilege to watch his sections of riflemen work their craft with steadfast precision.

The noise of constant rifle fire, coupled with nearby cannon, left Lyttle's ears ringing. He scarcely heard the cries of Sergeant McIntyre, as he fell screaming to the ground, his hands clutching at his face. A nearby private was struck in the side, as he tried to help his section leader.

"Stretcher bearers!" Captain Lyttle shouted over his shoulder.

The Regiment's bandsmen were clustered behind one of the wagons. The sergeant major would direct them to where injured soldiers had fallen. Four of these men rushed to the stricken sergeant, keeping their heads low. Zulu bullets continued to whiz over their heads or slap the ground around them. Douglas McIntyre was groaning in agony, blood seeped through his fingers as he clutched the shattered skull around his left eye. He was lifted onto the stretcher and hastened away. Another bandsman offered his shoulder to the injured private. Though in terrible pain, he was still able to walk. McIntyre's assistant, Corporal Wallace, took charge of the section. The battle continued unabated.

Something Prince Dabulamanzi could never have prepared himself or his warriors for was the enemy's use of cannon. The Zulus were certainly familiar with the white soldiers' iron logs that spat great flames and destruction; however, they had little experience fighting against such terrible weaponry. It was apparent the redcoats were using the palm cluster as a range marker. One poor warrior had his arm torn off at the shoulder by the bouncing solid shot that split one of the trees. Three others had their flesh and bones shattered by the explosive shot that burst over their heads. Another was dead, a lead ball from the shell embedded in the top of his skull. He had no other injuries. From a distance, one would think he was suffering from a seizure rather than the throes of death.

From his horse, Dabulamanzi could see the ripples through the grass, as the redcoats fired in the direction of his regiments. Only a handful of bullets found their marks, telling the prince that the English had great difficulty seeing them and were simply guessing where the Zulus were. The volume of musketry from these concentrated volleys was having a psychological impact on his warriors, given that any attempts to return fire were only minimally effective.

"We must close the distance, quickly!" he bellowed. He rode along the ranks of his main regiments. "Bound by companies; twenty paces, then drop! Close with them and show that they cannot hide behind a few feet of dirt!"

In the distance, the prince saw the attack from the 'Left Horn' appearing to stall as it attacked the northeast corner of the square. He could see nothing of the main assault from the 'Chest' on the northern ramparts, though one of the regiments was manoeuvring around, attempting to engage the English on the western side at closer range. The eastern defences were, as yet, not being attacked.

Dabulamanzi spurred his horse towards the *ibutho* on his right flank. "Take your men and swing in a wide arc to the right," he ordered their *inkosi*. "We need to envelop the entire laager, forcing every last warrior they have into battle."

Speed and manoeuvre became crucial. His men were now within range of the redcoat's musketry as well as their cannon. The last hundred paces or so would be the most precarious, for the grasses there were trampled flat. And while the prince felt Somopho's plan to attack the English while they were still laagered was foolish, if they could breach the defences, the redcoats would break. The only question now was, did the southern *impi* have enough warriors to create such a breach?

Chapter XLII: Who Will Break First?

Gingindlovu
6.40 a.m.

Zulu Attack, from *The Illustrated London News*

The fresh attack along the western defences that Dabulamanzi had spotted was now manifesting itself to the defenders. Approximately 2,000 warriors from the Zulu 'Chest' were bounding by companies towards the 99th Regiment and 2/3rd Buffs. Trusting in the two Buffs companies, who had already seen action in the war, Brevet Major Sinclair focused his attention on the as-yet untested companies from the 99th.

Among their few veterans was twenty-seven-year-old Lieutenant George Johnson. His youthful looks led Lord Chelmsford to question whether he was even old enough to hold the Queen's Commission. The GOC was surprised not only to learn Johnson's real age, but that he was a veteran of Inyezane as well as the 99th's senior instructor of musketry. Julius Backhouse, of similar age and experience, was one of Johnson's closest friends.

Much like the green-jackets on the north face, the young soldiers from the 99th Regiment had to fight to calm their nerves, as the Zulu war chants echoed over the din of rifle fire.

Johnson took the opportunity to walk the line, reminding both officers and other ranks alike to, "Watch the markers, adjust your sights!"

The Zulus were able to get within a couple hundred yards before being subjected to Martini-Henry volleys from the western flank. The large rockets on the northwest corner, while terrifying, were only marginally effective when compared to the 9-pounder cannon or Gatling gun. The Zulus were therefore able to unleash their own salvoes of musketry at a much closer range. As the two forces exchanged rifle fire, one private from the 99th fell dead, his throat torn away by a Zulu musket ball. Several others were wounded. Each time a man was struck down, it rattled his mates all around him. Not only fearful that they might be next, they felt helpless that they could not save their friends. Even the 'veterans' from The Buffs were unnerved. The Zulus were both closer and much greater in number than those they'd fought at Inyezane.

Lieutenant Backhouse found himself standing near George Johnson, who appeared to be fretting a bit as the 99th's companies came into action.

"Something wrong, old friend?" Julius asked, over the deafening crash of the first volleys.

"The lads are a bit rattled and seem to be pulling their shots," the musketry officer noted. "A Zulu can be twenty feet away, but you won't hit him if you jerk the trigger and send your bullet ten feet past his head!"

Johnson thought to inform Brevet Major Sinclair, as well as the company commanders, that their men needed to take their time and quit pulling their shots. But then, he decided to take matters into his own hands and set the example. He saw a dead soldier, who'd been dragged about ten feet behind the line of companies. Adjusting his helmet, the lieutenant confidently strolled over and took the man's rifle and ammunition pouch.

"I'm sorry, son, but right now we need every rifle we can muster," George said apologetically to the dead private. He then walked to the gap left in one of the companies left by a wounded soldier who'd been carried off to the hospital wagon.

Lieutenant George Johnson
Instructor of Musketry, 99th Regiment

"Take a breath before you fire and calm down!" the musketry officer shouted. He then chambered a round and shouldered the rifle. Following his own directive, he took a breath, focusing his gaze on the front sight post and what appeared to be a Zulu warrior about 200 yards beyond. He exhaled partially and squeezed the trigger. The brutal kick of the Martini-Henry startled him, as he knew it should. The cloud of smoke obscured his vision for a few moments, the acrid taste causing him to cough violently.

Lieutenant Johnson then walked the line, shouting encouragement to soldiers and NCOs, as well as informing their officers commanding that they needed to keep an eye on how their men were shooting. Twice more he took a moment to send a shot towards the rampaging Zulus. A gentle gust of wind blew the black powder smoke away after his second shot. He grinned with satisfaction, as he watched his quarry double over, clutching at his guts.

"You see, lads?" he called out. "Keep calm and remember your drills…" His words were cut off. He felt a horrific pain burst through his chest. Dropping the rifle, he managed to say, "By God, I've been shot!" before collapsing onto his knees.

Julius Backhouse was immediately at his side, as were two other soldiers near Johnson. There was nothing to be done. Backhouse leaned his friend back, cradling him in his arms. George was shot through the heart. His eyes had already clouded over; his soul departing for whatever lay beyond this life.

As Lieutenant Johnson' bloody and lifeless body was carried away from the ramparts, 'Noggs' Norris-Newman grimaced and ceased in his frantic scribblings. He could see clearly where the shots had come from. There were three or four Zulus crouched behind a thick bush about a hundred yards to his front. His gaze ever fixed on the brush, Noggs hefted his carbine and chambered a round.

"Over there," he said, pointing out the position to his friend and fellow correspondent, Christopher Palmer. "Those are the bastards who got poor Mister Johnson."

"I see them," Palmer asserted.

Despite the cover offered by the bush, from their elevated position the two civilians could clearly discern two of the Zulu marksmen.

"I'll take the one on the left," the reporter stated. 'Noggs' checked the sights on his weapon, setting the range to 100 yards. Taking a slow breath, he placed his front sight on the chest of the Zulu, who was partially obscured by the thicket. The crack of Palmer's rifle startled him, causing him to twitch as he fired.

Both men struck their targets. While 'Noggs' had grazed his in the shoulder, Palmer's bullet smashed through the forehead of his victim, sending the man flying backwards. The injured Zulu and another previously unseen skirmisher quickly rushed from the brush stand, trying to find better cover. They only managed to travel a few yards before a burst of rifle fire from the 99th tore them to pieces. Bits of flesh, bone, and mists of blood sprayed from the shattered bodies.

"At 200 yards!" Captain Lyttle shouted down to his company.

The smoke was thick despite the measured volleys from his various sections. Every man's ears were pounding from the barrage, and the officer commanding of A Company, 91st Highlanders was concerned that none of his sergeants could hear him. He jumped down from his wagon perch, only then noticing the bench and backrest were riddled with bullet holes. "Lucky I didn't get a nasty splinter," the Scottish captain said with deadpan humour.

The drop of just a few feet gave him a different perspective, and he realised how impeded his soldiers' vision was. *"Index 200 yards!"* he shouted to Lieutenant Craufurd, grabbing him by the shoulder. He then ran to the other end of his company line, echoing the order to Colour Sergeant Clinton.

"Can't bloody well see them," the senior NCO commented, his face taught though his voice remained calm.

A scream from their left told them that another of Lieutenant Collins' soldiers had been hit.

"Still, they're making their presence felt."

"Have the lads maintain the same elevation," Lyttle directed. "Fire low and keep adjusting their sights. I imagine once they clear the grasses at around 100 yards, we'll see them well enough."

'Usutu!'

The battle cry to their immediate front alerted the men. A force of Zulus, either previously unseen or simply fast sprinters, emerged from the edge of the tall grass.

"Bugger all, they're in a bit of a hurry," Stan Clinton remarked. He then shouted, his voice booming, *"At 100 yards!"*

There was no pause now between volleys. The Highlanders reloaded and unleashed as fast as they were able. The other seven companies in the 91st, having seen the Zulus emerge at the same time, were following A Company's lead, quickly adjusting their sights and firing with incredible speed. With the enemy so close, Captain Lyttle was relieved to see that weapons malfunctions were minimal. Though he saw the occasional soldier down on one knee, attempting to clear a jam or stuck cartridge. There were others who were struck down by Zulu return fire, but Lyttle knew their enemies were suffering far greater than they were. He also knew the Zulu penchant for extreme bravery was well-founded and could only hope they would break first.

The GOC had spent most of the battle behind the northern defences manned by 3/60th Rifles. The 57th Regiment, along the eastern face, was now being engaged yet appeared to be holding well. Along with The Buffs, they were the only troops in the flying column with a measure of experience. Chelmsford had only taken a cursory ride on the southern and western ramparts before they were attacked in earnest. His greatest concern was the green-jackets. Not only were they untested and appeared ready to falter at one point, they were taking the brunt of the Zulu's attack. The rocket tubes on the northwest corner had created a lot of noise yet were inflicting few, if any, casualties. Conversely, the Gatling gun on the northeast corner had been utterly terrifying in its savage effectiveness.

About thirty minutes after the attack commenced, the men of the Rifles had steadied their nerves, despite the felling of their commanding officer and a handful of their mates. Their concentrated volleys, along with those of the Royal Marines on their extreme right, appeared to be driving the Zulus back.

Chelmsford held up his field glasses, trying to scan through the smoke. He saw groups of men turning and running, and it appeared the 60th had broken the Zulu 'Chest'.

"Captain Barrow!" He shouted over his right shoulder.

The officer commanding of the Imperial Mounted Infantry sat atop his horse nearby, his troopers forming the reserve behind the north wall. He'd watched the early assaults from one of the wagons, having suffered a gunshot wound to the left leg. Stating that the injury was not serious, the bullet having gone clean through part of his outer though, Barrow tied a rag around the wound and carried on as if nothing had happened.

"Sir!" the hussar now called back, riding over and snapping off a salute.

At that moment, a low-flying rocket flew through the grass to their left, scattering the Zulus and leaving a trail of burning grass in its wake.

"The enemy appears to be retiring. Take your men and finish the lot."

"My lord."

Barrow saluted once more and rode back to his men. He then called out the commands for a series of pre-planned orders. The companies of riflemen in front of them halted in their firing. The entire 2nd Squadron, Imperial Mounted Infantry, and the Natal Volunteers galloped their horses over the defences and in pursuit of the fleeing Zulus.

Once beyond the choking smoke surrounding the laager, it was much easier for the mounted troops to see. Bands of Zulus did appear to be in retreat, and Barrow ordered his men to ride as far as the edge of the flattened grass. As they fired a pair of volleys, the hussar officer saw a large force, consisting of at least five or six companies of warriors, emerging from their left.

"They're not broken yet, lads!" he called out, before ordering half his squadron to bring their mounts about to form a right angle off their front, in order to engage this threat.

"Percy!"

Barrow looked over his right shoulder and saw his fellow captain, William Molyneux, shouting his name while sprinting his horse towards him.

"Come to join us for a bit of fun, William?"

"The enemy is reforming," Molyneux explained, pointing off to Barrow's right.

"So they are," Barrow noticed before turning to his bugler. "Sound recall."

The young mounted bandsman's eyes grew wide. He saw hundreds of warriors rushing towards them. Licking his lips, he placed the battered bugle to his mouth, fervently sounding the notes which ordered the IMI to retreat.

Captain Molyneux drew his pistol, as an enemy warrior sprang up from the grass a few feet from him. The man had his assegai drawn back, ready to plunge it into the officer's side, when William shot him through the forehead. So close was the warrior, that blood and bone sprayed Molyneux. The bullet smashed through the Zulu's forehead before exploded it out the back.

Sections of infantrymen from the various Rifle companies opened fire, hoping to suppress the enemy enough for the IMI troopers to return safely. Several horses and troopers were injured by Zulu musketry, and as William Molyneux's horse reached the barricades, it was struck beneath the saddle, sending the captain spilling head-over-heels into the muck behind the ramparts. William

497

shook his head, slowly recovering his senses. He saw the poor beast was mortally wounded. There was little to do but take his pistol and put the loyal creature out of its misery.

Percy Barrow and the IMI had withdrawn back to the ramparts; however, they remained outside them near the Royal Marines and the Gatling gun.

"Fuck it, sir," one of his sergeants said. "There's no point in us returning back to the laager now; not when they'll need us to come right back out again."

Barrow concurred and ordered his men to fan out and dismount their horses. They kept low, relying on the murderous fire of the Gatling to protect them from wayward bands of relentless Zulus.

Satisfied with how the northern battle was progressing, despite the setback by the mounted troops, his lordship decided to see how the eastern defences were holding. Contrasting sharply with their mates in green-jackets, the redcoats of the 57th Regiment were conducting themselves as if they were practicing musketry at an Aldershot range. The enemy return fire was particularly intense, and Chelmsford felt it prudent to dismount his horse.

The truth was, there was little for the GOC to do. This was not a battle of manoeuvre, at least not from the British perspective. He had chosen the ground and was rightfully pleased that it was the most defensible piece of terrain within five miles of the Inyezane crossing. Yet once the infantry stood to their arms, there was nothing left for Chelmsford, except to watch the battle unfold. There was little even for the company officers commanding, except to perhaps call out the occasional adjusting of ranges. Few above the rank of sergeant played an active role in the Battle of Gingindlovu. Still, the mistakes of the Isandlwana campaign had been avoided, and for Lord Chelmsford that was enough.

Scanning through a large break in the smoke as a breeze blew in from the east, the GOC could clearly see the lines of warriors from the Zulu 'Right Horn' attacking the southern and eastern defences. While they still numbered in the thousands, their strength was much less than what he'd anticipated.

"It would seem this is not the main *impi* we are facing," he said to Colonel Pemberton, who was also taking a few moments to see how the 57th Regiment was holding.

"That means Cetshwayo has sent them after Wood," the colonel conjectured. He then shrugged. "Nothing for it, sir. We still have a battle to win here. Even if this is the smaller of the Zulu armies, they are fighting with a lot of pluck."

"That they are, colonel, that they are."

It was then that Chelmsford saw John Crealock, still seated astride his horse, tying a rag around his upper right arm.

"By God, colonel, you're hit," Chelmsford noted, nodding to Crealock's bleeding appendage.

"It's just a scratch," his military secretary said reassuringly.

Behind the officers, all was chaos within the wagon laager. The thousands of draught oxen and donkeys brayed in terror at the ear-splitting roar of musketry and cannon fire; all the while, hundreds of Zulu bullets struck the wagons or snapped over their heads. Casualties were not just confined to the imperial soldiers, either. One of the voorloopers, a boy of about twelve, was shot through the head while he lay on his stomach beneath one of the wagons. The lad's father, one of the wagon drivers, knelt over him, sobbing in sorrow.

"My lord!"

Chelmsford turned to see it was Lieutenant Colonel Law, who'd spent most of the battle on the southern and western flanks of the laager. "The attacks to the west and south have stalled, sir," the colonel reported. "The Zulus are keeping to the grass and seem content to exchange fire with our lads. Those indefatigable Highlanders halted the enemy's attacks within thirty feet of the laager! Request permission to send the NNC out to finish this. They're getting awfully restless. A few have accidentally fired their weapons, despite orders to hold their fire. I'd rather we send them into the fight, rather than leave them lurking behind our lads, while their non-comms keep putting the boots to any of the ill-disciplined."

Chelmsford gave an affirmative nod. "It is, indeed, time to end this. Captain Molyneux, give my compliments to Captain Barrow and order his squadron to attack the enemy's right flank. Tell him it is time for cold steel to win the day."

Chapter XLIII: Time to End This

Gingindlovu
7.00 a.m.

British mounted troops from the Imperial Mounted Infantry (IMI) pursuing
the fleeing Zulus, Battle of Gingindlovu

For the first time in his twelve years of holding the Queen's
Commission, Captain Percy Barrow of the 19th Hussars was at last
leading a charge of 'flashing steel', like his regimental ancestors of
old. While Horse Guards in London had yet to dispatch the cavalry
reinforcements that his lordship requested, they had sent crates
containing several hundred sabres. The mounted troops already in
southern Africa were at least equipped like proper cavalrymen!

His men scabbarded their carbines and drew their swords; the
entire squadron forming into two ranks. Barrow shouldered his
blade, riding his horse to the very centre of the front line of troopers.
He then held his weapon high.

"Second IMI!" he shouted. "It is time we gave the Zulus a taste
of British steel! For Queen and Empire; for England and Saint
George! With me!"

His troopers gave a loud battle cry, spurring their horses as they followed their officer commanding towards the enemy. The Gatling gun fired one last suppressive burst before it was silenced, lest it become a threat to the Imperial Mounted Infantrymen.

The Zulus of the 'Left' and 'Right Horns' had nearly converged, keeping to the tall grass as they exchanged fire with the 57th Regiment. Scores of dead and dying warriors lay strewn about, the earth saturated with the blood and gore. Most of those remaining kept low on their stomachs. It was impossible, at first, for Percy and his men to differentiate the living from the dead. It also meant the grasses the Zulus used for concealment had left them blind to this unexpected attack on their right flank.

"Sound the charge!" Barrow called to his bugler.

The lad, who less than thirty minutes prior had been terrified for his life when the squadron withdrew to the laager, was now filled with exhilaration as he played the rapid notes. This was followed by a loud roar from the mounted troopers. They spurred their mounts into a dead sprint. Though most of the troopers were infantrymen who had only basic practice with sword drill, their sudden presence was enough to drive in the Zulu flank. While the Zulus had them overwhelmingly outnumbered, the brazenness of this assault, following more than an hour of fruitless and bloody charges towards the British defences, utterly shattered their morale.

Soldiers hacked and stabbed at their fleeing quarry. Barrow gave an appreciative grin, as one of his sergeants brought his blade down in a hard chop, cleaving off the back of a warrior's skull.

A few hundred yards behind them, mounted troopers from the Natal Light Horse assisted as best as they were able with their carbines. They swept south along the western face of the square. In the distance, they could see hundreds of dark-skinned warriors from the Natal Native Contingent spilling forth from the southwest defences. These were followed by John Dunn's scouts, who wielded both rifle and spear. The NNC were especially ruthless, driving their spears into any Zulu they found, living or dead. Just as no quarter was given to the iziGqoza twenty-two years prior, neither did they show any mercy to their injured or fleeing kinsmen. War cries changed to shrieks of terror and pain, as Zulu and iziGqoza battled with renewed fury. Yet with the IMI bearing down on their flank, and renewed volleys of musketry coming from the British redcoats in the laager, the Zulus could no longer stand.

Dabulamanzi closed his eyes in sorrow and rage, as both 'Horns' of the *impi* collapsed. Had they engaged the British in open battle outside of their defences, he had little doubt that his warriors would have carried the day. However, as bloodied and beaten down as they were, following numerous attacks against their well-entrenched positions, their spirits were simply crushed.

The prince kicked his horse into a gallop and was riding towards one band of fleeing warriors, when a sharp pain struck his right thigh. He looked down to see a bleeding gash running from the front along the side. The retreating warriors were being subjected to British musketry, some of which was now being directed towards Dabulamanzi. Shaking his head in frustration, he turned his horse about and began riding away. There was an *ikhanda* not far from the battlefield, and he hoped to perhaps rally his men there. His darkest feelings were not towards his white enemies, but against the *inkosi* who he now blamed for this grim defeat.

"Somopho bears the shame of Gingindlovu, not Dabulamanzi."

For Captain Percy Barrow, this was no longer a battle but an execution. His men tore through the fleeing Zulus, killing without mercy. There was no order to be had amongst their foes. Yet if a single *induna* had managed to rally his warriors to him, they could have easily surrounded and cut Barrow's mounted troops to pieces. It was not to be. Order and discipline, the very hallmarks of the Zulu *amabutho*, had evaporated under the onslaught of imperial firepower, followed by the flashes of charging blades.

As one band of mounted redcoats chased down a small group of Zulus, they cornered three injured warriors at the edge of a spruit. All bore terrible injuries, two having been shot through various limbs, while the third's right arm was mangled and scorched from the flames of a low-flying rocket.

Among the pursuing soldiers was a private named Edward Powis. Originally from G Company, 2/24th, his mates had all perished at Isandlwana, and he was anxious to exact retribution. "Well, what do we have here?" he asked with malicious glee.

The warriors were exhausted and in much pain. Having thrown away their weapons, they made no attempt to fight. Powis and three companions dismounted. The Zulus thought perhaps they were being taken prisoner, until one of the redcoats smashed the pommel of his sword into a warrior's head, dropping him to his knees. Another grabbed the badly burned man by his charred arm, chunks of scorched flesh coming off in his hands. The warrior screamed in agony.

"I've waited a long time for this," Powis said, his face red with fury. He briefly recalled the day he'd been selected to join the IMI. His section leader had, at first, spoken against it; however, their commander, Lieutenant Charlie Pope, had consented. Now both the officer and sergeant were dead. Their mutilated bodies left to lie, exposed to flies and wild beasts these past three months.

"Come on, Edward," one of his mates said, punching a warrior in the stomach and doubling him over. "Remember what you said you would do if we ever caught the bastards who butchered your mates."

"I said I'd cut every last one of their fucking heads off."

His eyes narrowed as a Zulu looked up at him. Their gazes locked. The warrior seemed to accept his fate and bowed his head. With a shriek of fury, Powis swung his sword down in a hard slash, burying the blade deep into the back of the man's neck. He struggled to wrench his weapon free, as his fellow soldier held the convulsing body upright, blood gushing all over him. With two more vicious chops, the vengeful redcoat cleaved the warrior's head from his body. One of the remaining Zulus cried out in sorrow and anger, spewing curses towards the imperial soldiers. The other, the man with the seared arm, seemed more compliant and simply nodded in acceptance. It was savage butchery. As the cavalry sword was fairly lightweight and not meant for severing limbs, it took the vengeful soldier numerous strikes to decapitate each of his victims. By the time it was done, both Powis and his companions were covered in blood.

503

"You should go work in an abattoir when you're done with the Army, mate," one of the soldiers said, laughing at the macabre sight of his friend.

"Not exactly a story you'll read in the papers back home," another remarked. "They tend to omit the more unpleasant bits."

"I have a lady-friend back home who will enjoy hearing about this," Edward asserted. "Her brother was with my old company, and she'll be glad to hear I avenged him."

"Who would have thought cutting the head off a damned kaffir would help get you into a lady's frock?" the first soldier asked with a grin.

Despite the savagery exhibited by vengeful soldiers like Private Edward Powis, even more fearsome were the hate-filled warriors of the Natal Native Contingent. Many were iziGqoza, the cousins and hated enemies of the Zulus. At last, with their bloodlust beyond control, they were able to avenge the fallen fathers, brothers, and other loved ones that Cetshwayo's army slaughtered twenty-two years before on the banks of the Thukela. Many a warrior cried out the names of slain kinsmen as they fell upon the fleeing Zulus, 'washing their spears' in the bloody bodies of their foes, bashing brains in with knobkerrie clubs, and splitting the guts of any who failed to flee from their wrath.

Rifle and cannon fire had ceased, leaving a pall of acrid stench lingering in the air, with the ears and heads of the survivors within the British laager pounding. Rifle barrels were hot to the touch, and wisps of smoke came from the naval Gatling gun. A pair of spent drum magazines lay nearby, with shell casings littering the ground around the entire perimeter. Though the butchery of Zulu wounded by the NNC continued, for all intents, the Battle of Gingindlovu had ended.

Lord Chelmsford checked his watch and saw that it was now 7.25 in the morning. The entire battle had lasted about an hour-and-a-half. "The Zulus have been sorted out just in time for breakfast," he said with a grin and a sigh.

In spite of these feelings of relief and satisfaction, the GOC was devoid of any feelings of triumph. He knew this had not been the main Zulu *impi*, but a scratch force less than half that size. Searches of the field would later reveal that many of the enemy dead were grey-haired men, too old for the king's muster.

Zulu weapons were already being collected, as soldiers longed for evidence that they had killed the warriors who were responsible for the slaughter at Isandlwana. Unbeknownst to the British, while there were a few Zulus who'd fought against the centre column, these were men who lived in the coastal regions. Given the threat of Chelmsford's reinforcements, they had been exempted from the king's second muster.

All along the perimeter, as well as the trail of death leading to the Inyezane, spears, knobkerries, and shields were collected. In all, 435 firearms were also found strewn throughout the field. It was with a measure of disappointment when the British discovered that only five of these were Martini-Henrys, the rest being archaic muskets. One Martini-Henry had no markings at all and could have been a black-market trade to some *inkosi* before the war. Three were stamped *24th Regiment*, while one was marked *32nd Regiment*.

"Curious," John Crealock said as he hefted this particular weapon. "I didn't know anyone from the 32nd was in Natal."

"That most likely belongs to Lieutenant William Cochrane, who came to us from the 32nd," Chelmsford replied, recalling the young transportation officer attached to Anthony Durnford's mounted column. "He was one of the few to survive Isandlwana."

"He would have most likely been carrying a pistol while mounted," Captain Molyneux conjectured. "Some kaffir probably stole this from his tent when they looted the camp."

"I'll have this put in my baggage," Crealock decided. "Once we return to Pietermaritzburg, we can inform Mister Cochrane that we retrieved his rifle."

"My lord, we found this as well," a sergeant from the 57th Regiment said, holding an officer's sword in his hands.

"By God, I recognise that blade," a young officer, who served as Crealock's clerk, spoke up. "I was assisting in the headquarters tent of 1/24th, prior to our leaving for Mangeni on the 22nd of January. That sword belonged to Lieutenant Porteous." He then added sadly, "Last week would have been his thirty-second birthday."

Francis Porteous was officer commanding of A Company, 1/24th, who died along with all his men at Isandlwana. Crealock told his clerk to take the sword and place it in his baggage, along with

Cochrane's rifle. As far as he could remember, Porteous had been unmarried, his next-of-kin unknown. He therefore decided to eventually return the sword to the surviving officers of the 24th Regiment, who would know the proper place to send it.

Though every last man at Gingindlovu was anxious to scour the field for spoils, the GOC was keen to maintain discipline within the column, especially since he could not be entirely certain that the Zulus were utterly beaten. He therefore only allowed one section per company to take part in the looting and collection of enemy weapons. The men in Sergeant Fredericks' section were ecstatic when Lieutenant Martin directed them to search the area to their immediate front.

With bayonets fixed, David and his men walked slowly through the tall grass, searching for any signs of life amongst the enemy fallen. The IMI and NNC had conducted their slaughter mostly to the north and east, so the likelihood of finding broken Zulus still among the living was much greater along the western defences manned by the 99th and The Buffs. Few of the attacking warriors had gotten any closer than a hundred yards from the ramparts, and most of these were torn apart by concentrated volleys of musketry.

"The Martini-Henry would fell an elephant," Private Peters thought aloud as he gazed upon the mangled corpses. "These poor bastards have been nearly cut in half."

"Good God, what the fuck did they eat?" another soldier said, trying not to wretch at the terrible smells coming from the ruptured entrails of a nearby slain warrior.

"They faced their death with exceptional courage," Lance Corporal James Monroe said with an appreciative nod. "None of these men were shot in the back."

"Can't say I would have conducted myself nearly as well in the face of the Martini-Henry," Private Peters confessed.

Most of the Zulus they found this close to the defences were dead; the wounded who were able to move or be carried away by their friends long gone. The few wounded they did come across were either missing limbs or had been completely disembowelled by heavy calibre bullets that tore their guts through the exit wounds in their backs and sides.

"Not long for this world," Private Walters said quietly. He then added rather unconvincingly, "At least they will die well."

"Try telling him that," Peters countered, nodding to one poor man whose intestines lay split open on the ground next to him. He was devoid of any other injuries, meaning his inevitable death would be both slow and extremely painful. "Hey sergeant, mind if I finish this one? Not right that such a brave man should suffer so."

"Just use your bayonet," David said.

As Private Peters plunged the long triangular spike into the side of the Zulu's neck, his feelings of remorse and respect for his enemy contrasted entirely to the vengeful bloodlust from Private Powis of the IMI. Sergeant Fredericks knew that every man in the flying column would handle the matter of the Zulu dead differently. While he personally bore no hatred towards their enemy, he could not blame those who were either attached from or had friends in the 24th for their fury and desire to avenge Isandlwana's slain.

They soon came upon an officer from the 60th Rifles. The man was kneeling before half-a-dozen bodies lying sprawled within the tall grass. The ground was black and sticky with blood.

"Everything alright, sir?" David asked as he approached the officer.

"A veritable slaughterhouse," the man said, though he remained kneeling and did even glance back at the sergeant.

It was indeed a horrific sight. One Zulu lay contorted on his side, his face caved in near the right eye, while the back of his head was completely blown away. Another had been hit in the side, with his guts ripped from his body through the saucer-sized exit wound near the opposite kidney. Torn intestines and half-digested grains from the man's stomach created a putrid stench. Still another warrior was missing part of his leg and had either bled to death or died from shock.

"Alright lads, enough gawking," David said to his section. "Lance Corporal Monroe, take ten men and see if anyone is still alive in this butcher's yard. The rest will start gathering up enemy weapons."

About fifty yards from where the tall grasses began, James Monroe and his half-section found a trio of Zulus lurking behind a shredded palm stand. Before the lance corporal could raise his rifle, the men quickly came out from behind the palm, their hands raised, one speaking quickly.

"Surrender, surrender," the man said. James suspected it was one of the few English words the warrior knew.

"Come on, we won't hurt you," the lance corporal replied, nodding his head towards the camp. Though he knew the men could not understand him, he hoped the inflection in his voice would let them know he meant them no harm.

As he led the three prisoners over towards the laager, there were a few things that surprised Monroe about his charges. Firstly, was their age. Two were quite old, one of whom had a thick, grey beard. The third was very young, likely in his late teens. James could not be certain if this youth was a warrior or a mat carrier for one of the older men, who may have been his father.

"Excuse me, lance corporal!" a man called out to Monroe.

In addition to the correspondents, such as 'Noggs' Norris-Newman, there was a photographer, hauling his heavy camera over his shoulder on its long tripod.

"Can we help you, sir?" James asked.

"I have not seen many living Zulus and was wondering if I might take a photograph of yours."

"By all means."

While the photographer set up his camera, James turned the three Zulus to face the man. "*Hlala phansi*," he said to the warriors, ordering them to sit down. The youngest of the three had seen a camera before and knew what was being demanded of them. He quietly explained to the old warriors what was happening. Though disgusted that they were to be displayed as trophies of the British, they simply sat and glared at the photographer. Lance Corporal Monroe and several of his soldiers stood behind them. All came to attention, with rifle butts resting on the ground, bayonets fixed.

Only a small handful of prisoners were taken this day. Among these was the youth captured near the Gatling gun. He sat by himself, utterly despondent, his arms wrapped around his knees. An interpreter learned that his father had died long before the war. He'd been acting as mat carrier to one of his brothers, who was killed during the battle. As he was little more than a boy, he was offered his freedom.

He refused dejectedly, "Once you English are finished with the Zulus, I will have no home to return to."

The men of the HMS Boadicea took charge of him, some saying he'd make a fine mascot. Over the next few years, the lad eventually learned to speak English. He even took on a British name, and once he came of age, attested into the Royal Navy. He rarely, if ever, spoke to his mates about his previous life as a son of Zulu.

Zulu Prisoners, guarded by soldiers from The Buffs, following the Battle of Gingindlovu

There was little found in the way of loot amongst the Zulu dead. The only warriors wearing any sort of regalia lay to the south of the 91st Highlanders' position. This was collected up, and Major Bruce stated it would make a fine trophy for the Regiment. While very few Martini-Henrys were taken from the fallen warriors, among some of the pouches belonging to dead marksmen were letters and stationary taken from the camp at Isandlwana, now used as wadding for their muskets.

After allowing his men time for a hasty breakfast, his lordship ordered details sent forth to bury the Zulu dead. He further directed that the laager be reduced in size. He intended to only take about half his force the rest of the way to Eshowe. Chelmsford also made a decision regarding the fort. He knew it would be unpopular, yet necessary.

"We managed to decipher a message from Colonel Pearson," Captain Molyneux explained. Since the two forces were about fifteen miles from each other, it was now easier for the Eshowe garrison to send messages from their makeshift heliograph to the approaching relief force. "They send their compliments, stating they could see the Zulus scattering in every direction."

"Have my thanks sent back to Colonel Pearson," Chelmsford replied. He then dictated the following the message, to be signalled to the garrison:

Eshowe will be evacuated after relief and an entrenched post put near Inyezane. Three battalions will leave here for you tomorrow. You will bring all you can and destroy the rest.

"If I may speak plain, my lord," Colonel Pemberton said, "your decision will not sit well with the garrison after all this time."

"It is my decision to make," Chelmsford retorted. "And as you know, colonel, the roads between here and the Thukela are in far worse condition than when Colonel Pearson came this way in January." He then addressed all the senior officers. "With our current plans in need of revision, the fort at Eshowe is now redundant. We will leave a robust force at a more defensible position closer to Lower Drift. The rest of our army will regroup beyond the Thukela River, in preparation for a renewed invasion."

For the assembled officers, even the ever-loyal Crealock, the GOC's words could not have been clearer. They may have won a decisive victory at Gingindlovu, but in the larger strategic scheme the entire invasion was now in shambles. The centre No. 3 Column Chelmsford had thought to lead into the royal kraal at Ulundi months before was completely shattered, and the Zulu *impi* was now threatening Colonel Wood's northern column. They had won this battle, but unless fortunes turned drastically in their favour in the long-term, there was the very real possibility of losing the war.

Chapter XLIV: An Anticlimactic Return

Gingindlovu
2 April 1879

The 91st Highlanders marching through Zululand

By nightfall the laager had been reduced. The exhausted men of the flying column were at last able to appreciate their victory over supper. Nearly 500 slain warriors had been buried, though it was widely speculated that twice as many had actually fallen. They would continue to find evidence of this over the coming days. However, they felt little relief. They knew that most of the Zulu *impi* remained intact despite their horrific losses. As decisive a victory as the Battle of Gingindlovu was, it did little to assuage the persistent fear most of the men had regarding the Zulus. After all, the tales of murderous destruction and slaughter following Isandlwana were fresh in their minds. Once the euphoria of triumph subsided, not to mention relief at still being alive, there remained the incessant terror that the Zulus would return.

These thoughts consumed the men of David Fredericks' section, as they established their position for the night about 200 yards from the laager. Tasked with picquet duty, his men were more unnerved now than they'd been during the nights leading up to the battle.

"For all we know, they're lurking about the brush, waiting for us to march out again," Private Walters said.

"As I understand it, the GOC is leaving us and the 99th here," James Monroe mused.

"And that's supposed to make us feel better?" Private Peters countered. "One battalion's worth of soldiers left behind a few feet of earth with a thousand whining beasts corralled behind us."

"Quit your bickering," Sergeant Fredericks said, as he made his rounds of his guard posts. "A single company from the 24th withstood the Zulu onslaught at Rorke's Drift. And besides, we gave them a sound thrashing today. You lot are sounding like a bunch of scared old women."

"It's not just fear, sergeant," Monroe explained. "It's respect. We may have butchered the Zulus today, but by God they showed indominable pluck."

The feelings of profound admiration for their enemies' courage were not confined to the officers and men.

Having first cleaned his carbine, 'Noggs' Norris-Newman retrieved his notebook and wrote his thoughts regarding the Zulus:

No praise can be too great for the wonderful pluck displayed by these splendid savages, in making an attack in daylight on a laager entrenched and defended by European troops with modern weapons and war appliances. This fully confirmed the opinion I had never failed to express, that they would fight us again and again, no matter how often they were beaten, as soon as any trusted chief could assemble some thousands of them.

None within the British flying column were able to grasp just how soundly the Zulus had been defeated. An *ikhanda* was located in the Mhlatuze valley several miles from Eshowe, and thus far remained undetected by the English. It was here Prince Dabulamanzi returned to, hoping to rally the survivors of the southern *impi* into renewing the fight against the invaders. Though they had suffered a grievous defeat with perhaps one in every ten warriors slain, this was far less catastrophic than the disaster at kwaJimu, where upwards of a third of the Undi Corps had been left dead or maimed.

And yet, there were only a few hundred gathered in and around the kraal. Somopho was nowhere to be found, nor were most of the *izinduna*. Of those gathered around the *ikhanda*, many bowed their heads in the presence of Dabulamanzi; whether out of respect for their prince or shame at their defeat, he could not say. He found a lone *induna* seated near a campfire. The man was very young, likely in his early twenties.

"*Bayade, inkosi,*" the man said, raising his hands up to his face.

"It would seem the southern *impi* has abandoned the defence of the kingdom," the prince replied bitterly. "Where is Somopho? Where is Mavumengwana? Cowering like his brother?"

"They have gone home, *inkosi,*" the *induna* answered. "The royal *induna*, Phalane, has taken it upon himself to inform the king of the battle."

"The very survival of the Zulu Kingdom is at stake," Dabulamanzi stressed. "How can so many retire to their homes, knowing the whites will destroy them, should they win this war?"

"Not all of us have run, *inkosi*. I am of the iNgobamakhosi Regiment. We destroyed the whites at Isandlwana, at the loss of many brothers. When the king proclaimed the next royal muster, we were anxious to join our regiment in smashing the English once more. But in his wisdom, Cetshwayo ordered those of us living in the coastal regions to aid the royal prince in destroying this column of white soldiers." Unspoken by the *induna* was the king's subsequent directive, placing Somopho in command of the southern *impi*, superseding Prince Dabulamanzi.

"And you remain to aid your prince," Dabulamanzi said appreciatively. "Then we shall make the English continue to bleed until we drive them from these lands. I'll not fight in the company of cowards and old women."

Having witnessed the triumphant victory of the flying column, Captain David Courtney spent much of the following morning at the hospital tent, checking on the score of men from No. 2 Field Company who were down with various illnesses. The worst of these was their officer commanding, Captain Warren Wynne. Courtney found him sleeping, his hands clutching at the sheet covering him. He was shivering violently.

David placed a hand on his forehead, and it was extremely hot to the touch. "Has he spoken at all?" the officer asked a passing orderly.

"Very little, sir. When he does stir, his eyes usually remain closed, and he calls out to his wife and children. I have two boys of similar age as his sons. It's heart-breaking to hear him mumble such things as, *'I am sorry I won't be coming home'*."

Hearing these words made Courtney feel as if he'd been punched in the stomach. Though he knew Warren's condition was grave, it saddened him deeply to hear that his friend and officer commanding had given up on life. He hoped it was simply his fits of delirium, and that Warren would find that inner strength which had carried him through so much hardship.

It was not only Captain Wynne who required medical attention. Twenty men from No. 2 Field Company were now on the sick list, with nearly 200 from the entire garrison crammed beneath what little shelter Surgeon Norbury was able to provide. One who appeared to be improving was Lieutenant Thomas Main. He was seated on the edge of a hospital cot, shirtless and pulling on his socks. His face was sweaty, but his complexion had improved significantly.

"Glad to see you looking well, Mister Main," David said.

"I seem to have been sorted out. Once I quit having to spend most of the night at the latrine trench and was finally able to get a full night's sleep."

"Will you be able to ride your horse?" Courtney asked. "It looks like we'll be leaving within the next day or so."

"Leaving?" the lieutenant asked. "I heard his lordship won a great victory but did not realise we were leaving Eshowe. Surely, he hasn't decided to abandon this place after all we've been through."

"That's not our decision to make," the captain stressed. "I suspect the entire invasion force is being withdrawn so that we might regroup once the remaining reinforcements arrive from Britain."

While Thomas concurred with the officer's assessment, there was a shared sense of defeat throughout the garrison. It seemed the months of living in absolute squalor, with many of their friends dying from any number of horrible diseases, was for nothing.

Lord Chelmsford decided to take only the minimal amount of men and equipment with him for the remaining journey to Eshowe. They left all the wagons at Gingindlovu, instead taking fifty-eight donkey carts. His lordship was determined to reach the mission in a single day. This would prove a daunting task. The trails were still in terrible condition, plus it was a fifteen-mile trek, much of it going up a series of steep hills. It also promised to be a blistering day, as the sun rose on the morning of the 3rd of April.

The makeshift battalion of companies from the 99th Regiment and 2/3rd Buffs remained at the laager as did the two NNC battalions. The rest began their journey at 7.30 in the morning. The sun was already beating down on them. The men were soaked in sweat beneath their wool tunics before they'd taken a single step. There was much trepidation by the departing forces, as well as those left behind. Soldiers making the trek worried that they might not be able to withstand another sustained attack, should they end up facing the Zulus out in the open. Whereas those left at Gingindlovu were concerned that, even with its reduced size, the laager was too big to man with their small garrison.

Less than two miles from the battlefield, a previously unseen Zulu homestead was spotted by Percy Barrow's vanguard of mounted troops. They found it completely deserted, though there were signs of it being recently occupied. Without waiting for orders, the captain had his men put the cluster of huts to the torch. This was met with cheers by the column of imperial redcoats, as they marched past the kraal.

Riding at the head of A Company, 91st Highlanders, Captain Robert Lyttle's hand kept inadvertently brushing against his pistol holster. He'd fired a pair of shots from his American Colt revolver during the battle, when a hoard of Zulus came within thirty yards of the barricade. He had just thirty loose cartridges in his pouch. He felt he would need them all should the Zulus return.

The trail leading to the Inyezane fording site was lined with all sorts of debris from shields, assegais, knobkerries, bits of regalia, even the occasional firearm.

One Highlander picked up an old musket as the battalion waited to cross the river. "Broken flint, stock's all termite eaten." The soldier turned the weapon over in his hands. "Barrel and hammer are almost completely rusted. I'd be surprised if this sodding thing fired at all." He threw it into the brush, his face etched in disgust.

"And what in the bleeding fuck is that stench?" another private added, his nose scrunched.

"You know very well what it is," Colour Sergeant Clinton said coldly, as he walked down the line of soldiers.

"Filthy dead kaffirs stink," one private grumbled.

"And a dead Scot smells even worse," an English soldier within the company retorted.

Meanwhile, the company's senior NCO walked over to their officer commanding who, along with Lieutenant Craufurd, had dismounted and was watching the crossing. The subaltern was scanning the far bank with his field glasses, while the trail companies of the 57th Regiment waded across the gently flowing current.

"Any signs of the enemy, Mister Craufurd?" Clinton asked.

"No live ones," the officer replied. "I count at least eight trails of drag marks through the far grass." He then noted how much of the flattened grass was held together by black swaths of congealed blood. "Looks like those poor fellows were in sad shape."

"I suspect we'll find some of them after we cross," Clinton observed grimly.

There would be a long wait once the flying column reached the far bank. Signallers at Eshowe had sent a message from Colonel Pearson, asking the GOC to bring any spare oxen they had so he would not be compelled to abandon his wagons to the Zulus. Recalling the nightmarish shortage of wagons and carts in Natal, and the exorbitant prices the Army paid for what few had procured from local settlers, Chelmsford was wary to lose any more. The column was therefore ordered to halt and set up a defensive perimeter, while a pair of riders from Captain Barrow's IMI were sent back to Gingindlovu. They were still close to the old laager, but it would be another two hours before a band of NNC warriors was spotted escorting over 200 draught oxen. They were then spanned to the carts. Being only lightly loaded, they were able to move with much greater speed than during the past few days.

All the while, Charles 'Noggs' Norris-Newman and the bevy of correspondents took notes and scribbled sketches for their respective publications. "I bet old Melton is regretting he missed out on this," Noggs said to his friend, Christopher Palmer of the *Cape Argus*.

"Poor fellow was having premonitions about his own death," Palmer recollected. "Apparently, he's convinced his lordship's military secretary to bring back some sketches and paintings for him."

"Yes, well sadly for me, Colonel Crealock despises me to no end," Noggs said with a mischievous grin. "Were I to ask him the same, he'd likely tell me where I could stuff my pencils." He glanced at Lord Chelmsford and his staff officers who were watching the slew of oxen being spanned with the carts. Crealock was nearby and looked their way. 'Noggs' shot him a grin and tipped his hat. The colonel pretended not to see him.

"See what I mean?"

"Yes," Palmer remarked. "I guess you won't be giving him any favourable write-ups in the *Standard*."

"I wouldn't waste my reader's valuable newspaper space with mentions of that cretin," Charles spat. "My candid accounts of the Isandlwana disaster were enough to earn me his ire."

"Yes, I read some of those. I'm surprised his lordship didn't have you clapped in irons when you showed your face again."

"He lets Crealock be his wasp," 'Noggs' explained. "Most of his fellow officers despise him for being little more than Chelmsford's lapdog, yet I think he relishes it. But even he is not daft enough to have a reporter arrested. God knows they have enough of a public relations headache to deal with back home."

Once the spare oxen were spanned to the carts, the column began its march again. Norris-Newman became rather excited when they reached the site of the old battlefield at Inyezane. Though he had not personally seen it before, he explained to Palmer that it was described to him in detail by several soldiers from The Buffs.

That the column had reached the battlefield was confirmed when the lead elements came upon the large wooden cross erected over the graves of the British dead. It was barely visible. Over the months since the battle, the ground had become overgrown in tall grass and scrub brush.

"At least the Zulus did not desecrate our fallen brave," Chelmsford noted appreciatively.

"Besides gutting them at Isandlwana," Crealock added bitterly.

The GOC did not reply to this. They understood the Zulu practice of disembowelling slain enemy warriors was to 'release their spirits', but that did not make it any less barbaric to the British officers. It was uncertain if the Zulus leaving the British dead undisturbed was out of respect or fear they would be haunted by the troubled spirits.

Sailors from the HMS Shah crossing the Inyezane River

The next leg of the trek to Eshowe proved hateful for the men of the relief force. The climb past the Inyezane battlefield was extremely steep. The two-hour delay while draught oxen were brought up meant it was now midday. The heat was nearly unbearable. Sweat stains saturated the tunics and trousers of the miserable soldiers. Some had unbuttoned their jackets. Their NCOs were in the same state of extreme discomfort and did not bother berating their men for this transgression.

During the steepest climbs, it seemed the column only advanced a mile every hour. It was, therefore, late afternoon by the time they reached the new stretch of road cut by Captain Warren Wynne's engineers. Much to Chelmsford's relief, they spotted a force of about 500 soldiers marching towards them from the direction of Eshowe. Riding well ahead of them was Colonel Pearson and a bevy of staff officers.

"Ah, here's Pearson," Chelmsford said, allowing a trace of excitement in his voice.

The colonel looked much changed from the last time the GOC saw him. He now had a thick beard which was almost completely grey, despite Pearson being only forty-four years of age. His eyes were tired, his face pale and gaunt. The blue patrol jacket he wore appeared loose and baggy. Still, he managed a broad grin and sharp salute as he rode over to his commanding general. "My lord."

Chelmsford returned the salute then extended his hand. "How are you?"

"Splendid, sir, just splendid. As directed, I have brought five hundred men to assist, in case you come under attack during the final stretch of your journey."

"Much appreciated, colonel, but they won't be necessary. It would seem Cetshwayo's warriors have had enough of dying for the next day or so. Have your men return to Eshowe. You and your officers can ride with me. I want to hear all that's transpired since we first lost communications with you."

"Of course, my lord."

Captain McGregor was sent back to the detachment from Eshowe. Colonels Pearson and Walker, along with a few aids, rode with the GOC and his staff. They were still a few miles from the fort, and it would be a race if the exhausted flying column was to arrive before nightfall.

In a strange turn of events, the first to arrive at Eshowe would not be a member of the relief force but the reporter, Charles Norris-Newman. Having spurred some of his fellow correspondents into racing him to the fort, he'd found a shortcut cross-country and arrived about five minutes before his nearest competitor.

"Just like how I was the first to cross into Zululand at Rorke's Drift," he recalled, smugly thinking back to the dark, foggy morning, when he'd forded the uMzinyathi River before the lead elements of Colonel Glyn's No. 3 Column on the morning of 12 January.

It was now 5.00 in the evening, and there was much confusion as 'Noggs' rode into the fort. Soldiers gathered around, not certain what to make of the man who wore a large, floppy hat, an old faded officer's patrol jacket, with a sword hanging loosely from his belt.

"Who the bleeding piss is that?" one soldier asked, perplexed.

"First to Eshowe!" 'Noggs' called out with a grin of self-satisfaction. He ceremoniously dismounted and started shaking hands with the nearest soldiers who'd gathered to hear news from the relief column.

"You're three months late," one private said with condescension.

A few minutes later the next wave of correspondents arrived, anxious to 'scoop' the story of the heroic stand by the outnumbered and beleaguered garrison at Eshowe. Despite a few ribs and insults from a handful of soldiers, most of the garrison greeted the reporters warmly, anxiously asking for any sort of news from the outside world. Another round of cheers came from the sentries as Captain Percy Barrow's vanguard approached the fort. While most of the IMI soldiers veered their horses to the designated campsite for the flying column, their officer commanding rode into the fort, anxious to see his old comrades.

Hunger, fatigue, and exhaustion from the intense heat had badly worn the men of the flying column. Many felt it was nothing short of a miracle that they hadn't all succumbed to sunstroke. As the sun set with the fort just a mile or so in the distance, a sense of relief came over the column, accompanied by a quick spring in their collective steps. It was still well after dark by the time the lead elements reach Eshowe. As a means of announcing their approach, the pipers from the 91st Highlanders struck up with *'The Campbells Are Coming'*. This elicited a voracious ovation from both the garrison and the column.

Many soldiers came out from the mission to meet their relief. They clasped hands with tartaned Highlanders, green-jacketed Riflemen, and West Middlesex redcoats alike.

"I say, I expected you lot to be in far worse condition," one NCO from 3/60th remarked as he clasped hands with Sergeant Richard Small of the engineers. "Thought perhaps you'd all be wasted away by now."

"Thankfully, most of us are little worse for wear," Small replied. He decided not to mention the terrible havoc disease had had on the garrison, or that it felt as if his stomach had not stopped rumbling since Colonel Pearson first ordered the rations reduction.

In a rather bizarre paradox, it was the men of the flying column who were now in desperate need of subsistence. In what was perhaps the greatest showing of foresight, Colonel Pearson had ordered some of the short rations to be stockpiled into an emergency stash should Chelmsford's relief efforts fail. In all, there were enough tins of beef, biscuit boxes, crushed mealies, and canned vegetables to last the garrison for three days. Since the entire force would be leaving Eshowe the following morning, his lordship directed the garrison and flying column to enjoy one last hearty meal.

One man who made the most of this magnificent feast was 'Noggs' Norris-Newman, who was invited to dine with the officers of the Naval Brigade.

"I say, this is the finest feast I've had since before we departed from Lower Drift!" the reporter said boisterously, as he was handed a tin bowl filled with beef broth and pumpkin slices.

"You should try some of the roast beef next," the petty officer who now commanded the fort's Gatling gun said. "It's kind of dry, but if you soak it in the broth, it's quite good."

"Well, it's quite the change from tinned beef and hard biscuits," 'Noggs' said. He raised his mug in salute to the Naval Brigade's commanding officer. "And I must thank you, Commander Campbell, for your fine hospitality."

"Don't thank me until you've tried the pumpkin tarts." The senior officer grinned "That our ship's cook volunteered for this expedition has been a godsend to us."

At the flying column's camp, sentries took up their posts while men wandered to and from the fort. Bedrolls were laid out. The skies were clear and filled with stars. It promised to be a pleasant night for both the relievers and the relieved. Many of the men who made the arduous journey from Gingindlovu had been mad with hunger and spent from exhaustion when they reached Eshowe. Having eaten their fill, and the sun long since set, the collective soldiers found themselves both wide awake and in good spirits.

Sitting on his campstool, a pipe clutched between his teeth, Captain Robert Lyttle ran a bore brush through the barrel and cylinders of his Colt revolver. He then ran a rag over the pistol, buffing out any errant smudges.

The voice of Brevet Major Sinclair called out, "A fair evening, Robert!"

"That it be," Lyttle replied, with a nod towards his old friend. "I take it the lads from the 99th and The Buffs fought well yesterday?"

"Well enough." Sinclair shrugged. "I mean, they're not Highlanders, but we're still here. Lost a few lads from the 99th, including their senior musketry instructor, Lieutenant Johnson. But they kept to their drills, and never once let the Zulus within a hundred yards of the camp. So, there's something to be said for that. Mister Collins informed me that two lads from my company were wounded. How fared your lot?"

"Four wounded, only one serious," Robert answered. "Poor Sergeant McIntyre is in terrible shape. Took a musket ball to the left eye. He needs a proper hospital and doctors who can perform the necessary reconstructive surgery on his face. Colonel Law says the military hospital at Stanger might be able to help him. In the meantime, the battalion surgeon has made him as comfortable as he can. He said the biggest danger between now and when he can be evacuated to Stanger is infection."

"I suppose it's the same for a number of the wounded," Sinclair reasoned. "Just so you know, I'll be returning to the Regiment soon. His lordship has said that only the 99th and The Buffs will return to Lower Drift. The rest of us from the flying column will be establishing another more permanent fort somewhere between Gingindlovu and Lower Drift."

"Strategically, that makes more sense than leaving this place garrisoned. I do feel for the poor souls who suffered through the last seventy-two days under siege. They now feel their efforts were in vain. But, I also understand Lord Chelmsford's reasoning. It's simply too far, and the terrain too rough between here and Lower Drift to keep this place supplied."

"Yes, well, this was only meant to be one stop along the way to Ulundi," Sinclair remarked. "Had the entire invasion not fallen into tatters, we would still be in Aldershot."

"I keep hearing rumours that the Regiment will soon be merged with the 93rd Sutherland Highlanders," Lyttle said, recalling conversations he'd heard before they left Britain.

"Oh, it's no rumour," Sinclair confirmed. "This will likely be the last campaign for the 91st as its own Regiment. Major Bruce confirmed to me while we were aboard ship that a number of reforms are coming down from Horse Guards. One of which is merging all the single-battalion regiments into pairs. That way every regiment has a standard of two battalions. Now, what they'll do with three-battalion regiments like the 60th Rifles, I know not." He paused and let out a sigh. "Still, I suppose it is good that the 91st has added one last battle honour to its Colours."

"I suppose it is," Lyttle concurred. He thought about poor Sergeant Douglas McIntyre and the others who'd lost their lives or were gravely wounded. Every streamer and every battle honour stitched to a regiment's colours was paid for in lives and bloodshed.

Chapter XLV: One Last Sortie

Eshowe
4 April 1879
***

Reveille sounded at exactly 5.00 the following morning. Officers and senior NCOs had already been awake for some time. Despite only getting four or five hours of sleep, the soldiers of the garrison and flying column emerged from their slumber refreshed and full of energy. Though the men who'd defended Eshowe for the better part of three months were disgruntled at having all their arduous work handed over to the Zulus, few complained about leaving the squalid and cramped conditions behind. At Pearson's headquarters, the GOC met with the senior officers of both columns.

"Colonel Pearson and No. 1 Column will depart Eshowe and make straight for Lower Drift," Chelmsford ordered. "I, myself, will lead a sortie in the direction of a hill called eNtumeni, a few miles west of here. Some of the prisoners informed us that Cetshwayo's brother, Dabulamanzi, has a homestead in the area. Hopefully, Mr Dunn can help us find it."

"We destroyed one of his royal kraals as well, my lord," Pearson spoke up.

"There's something else, sir," Francis Law added. "A pair of older warriors among the prisoners told us it was Dabulamanzi who led the attack on a place called kwaJimu."

"It's their name for Rorke's Drift," Chelmsford explained. He then sneered. "So, this brother of Cetshwayo's seems to get around. Gentlemen, I plan on personally ending his war against the Crown."

As he gazed upon the humble cemetery just outside the old mission, Colonel Pearson's thoughts turned to those who perished since the war began in January. Forty-two redcoats, sailors, and allied warriors from No. 1 Column had given their lives, yet only fifteen had died in battle. The rest succumbed to fever or dysentery

524

during the hellish months under siege. He said as much to Colonel Walker.

"And I fear that number will soon rise to forty-three," his fellow colonel speculated.

"Yes, poor Captain Wynne." Charles shook his head sadly. "If not for him, I don't think any of us would have survived. We owe him our lives. Sadly, we cannot save his."

"Surgeon Norbury made certain he and the rest of the sick were made as comfortable as possible in the hospital wagons," Walker stated. "The flying column's sick and wounded will be joining us as well."

"I know," Pearson said. "Once we finally return to Lower Drift, we'll have the wounded and sick dispatched down to Stanger. I suspect those requiring more urgent care will be sent on to Pietermaritzburg. It's all in God's hands after that."

While the officers discussed the transportation of the sick and wounded, soldiers walked through the cemetery paying their respects to friends who had perished in their absence. Most had no actual grave markers, just simple wooden crosses that were already starting to rot from the incessant rains and inclement weather that plagued the entire region.

"I wonder which of these is Tommy Taylor?" one asked. He referred to the lance corporal who'd been named a company sharp-shooter shortly before his death.

"At least he's in good company," the man's section leader reasoned, glancing at some of the other graves. Eleven soldiers from 2/3rd Buffs had died during the siege.

"In the middle of nowhere on this far-flung corner of the Empire," the soldier added.

"And in this remote place, it is England," his section leader stated.

He gazed around at the desolate landscape. The cemetery sat on a gradual slope, and while the ground was normally covered in tall grasses, they had been decimated by the constant grazing of the cattle maintained at Eshowe during the siege. "You don't suppose the Zulus will desecrate them, do you?"

"They left the graves and markers at Inyezane alone," another man recalled. "I think they have enough common decency to allow our lads to rest in peace."

Other soldiers from the garrison were walking past the graves, taking a moment to say goodbye to fallen friends before beginning the long journey back to the Thukela. There was much work to do and a little time to make both columns ready for departure. The 200 oxen that Lord Chelmsford had ferried up from Gingindlovu meant they could retrieve most of the wagons. There were 116 in all, and they were loaded with supplies, what remained of their rations, ammunition boxes, and the tents they had been unable to use since arriving at Eshowe. Many were utilised by Surgeon Norbury to transport the 200 sick and injured soldiers.

"Well, that's it then," Colour Sergeant Michael Smith said to Captain Courtney. "All section leaders have inspected their men's kit. Every man on the sick list is accounted for and in the hospital wagons."

"Thank you, colour sergeant," Courtney replied. "Did you see Captain Wynne?"

"I did, sir. He's still the same. Perhaps a wagon ride in the fresh air will help him."

"Can't be any worse than breathing in the squalid filth here," the captain remarked. "A shame we're leaving this place to the Zulus, though I can't say I'll be sad to see the back of it."

The sun was high overhead when the lead elements of No. 1 Column departed the fort. Captain Courtney and No. 2 Field Company took the lead, escorting Lieutenant Lloyd and his cannon. They were closely followed by 2/3rd Buffs and the 99th Regiment who acted as escorts to the wagons and baggage. Forming the rear guard was Commander Campbell's Naval Brigade along with their Gatling gun and assorted artillery.

As the first two sections of No. 2 Field Company formed a vanguard for the column, one of the corporals walked over to Colour Sergeant Smith. "It's the strangest thing, colour sergeant. I feel like I can breathe again. To be honest, my mind is full of many different things, like I've been released from a prison of our own making."

"That's not so strange," Smith replied. "In many ways we were prisoners, with the Zulus our gaolers."

"Fearful hard times…" the corporal said, as he walked back to his section, his voice trailing off.

"Fearful hard times, indeed," Smith echoed.

The sortie was led by Captain Percy Barrow's Imperial Mounted Infantry, supplemented by the mounted troops under Captain Charles Shervinton, as well as John Dunn's scouts. The intent was to catch Dabulamanzi and his followers off-guard. And while Chelmsford had given no specific orders as to whether the prince was to be taken alive or dead, if he were captured, he would make for a valuable hostage.

Dabulamanzi, however, had no intention of being dragged away in chains. He had anticipated this very action by Lord Chelmsford and posted scouts between Eshowe and his kraal near eNtumeni Hill. Wordlessly, they returned to their prince when they first saw the approaching band of imperial soldiers.

"The kraal is in sight, my lord," Barrow reported. He'd ridden back to where Chelmsford and the mounted volunteers followed his imperial regulars.

"Splendid," his lordship replied. "Send your men forward, captain, and let us see if we can catch us a Zulu prince!"

The IMI soldiers rode in a large wedge formation, keeping both sword and carbine close. While pursuing their fleeing foes at Gingindlovu had been exhilarating, every mounted redcoat preferred to keep some distance between himself and the Zulu spears.

"Over there, sir!" a private shouted, pointing to the right of the large kraal.

Scores of Zulus could be seen racing up the steep hill where the prince's royal homestead lay. Many had already reached the top and were calling out war chants, beating their weapons against their shields. A single shot rang out from atop the ridge about 1,300 yards from the kraal.

"What bloody fool is trying to engage us from such a range?" Barrow asked incredulously.

"I think I know," John Dunn replied, riding up behind him. The trader was calm, even as another musket shot was fired from above. He dismounted and handed the reins to one of his servants.

Meanwhile, a score of Barrow's troopers were pursuing a small group of Zulus near the base of the hill. Forming into a hasty line, the sergeant leading them gave the order to fire a volley at their fleeing quarry. This startled several of the horses, leading to one poor soldier being thrown from his mount.

"Son of a bleeding whore!" the private bellowed, as he staggered back to his feet.

The sergeant and remaining troopers spurred their horses forward through the cloud of smoke. They found a pair of dead Zulus and a third raising his hands in surrender. The man had apparently been frightened by the spate of gunfire and, at first, thought to hide from the redcoats. He was much older than the two slain men and might have been their father or grandfather. The IMI sergeant ordered the old man's hands bound and a rope tied around his neck.

"Have some of the volunteers take him back to the fort," Captain Barrow ordered. He jolted when he heard another rifle shot from behind him.

Percy turned to see John Dunn kneeling next to a Zulu clay oven, reloading his rifle. A return shot echoed from the hill above. Curious, Lord Chelmsford rode towards the 'white Zulu', seemingly unperturbed by the rifle fire coming from the ridge. He casually pulled out his field glasses and scanned the ridge. There was a lone Zulu with a percussion rifle; the rest had disappeared from view. The man was very large and wore the regalia of an *inkosi*.

"Having a bit of sport, Mr Dunn?" the GOC asked.

"It's Dabulamanzi," John explained. He checked his sights, shouldered his rifle, and fired once more.

Through his field glasses, Chelmsford saw the bullet smash into the rocky ledge about ten feet below where their enemy stood.

"I don't think even our best marksmen could take down a man at this range," Captain Molyneux mused. "And that damned kaffir certainly isn't going to hit a thing with his old musket."

Lord Chelmsford took a few moments to take in the surrounding terrain. Dunn fired another shot at his old friend—now enemy. The ground leading up eNtumeni was steep and covered in brush stands. He suspected there were Zulus lurking behind the thickets, waiting for careless riders to come past. And while the hill could be climbed by their horses, the prince would see them coming and be long gone before they reached the top.

"Thank you, Mr Dunn, but I think we've done enough shooting for one day," the GOC emphasised. He then noticed the large piles of mealies, freshly cut from the recent harvest. "Well, if nothing else

528

we can make certain his royal highness goes hungry for the time being."

One of Barrow's soldiers had already lit a dry branch with the smouldering coals from the Zulus' morning campfires and was setting the nearest hut alight. Several others followed suit. A few more piled dry grasses in and around the mound of mealies before setting them on fire.

"Alright lads," the captain called out, once satisfied that the grain stores were sufficiently burning. "Time to go home."

"What? Back to Blighty, sir?" one soldier asked with a mischievous grin.

From atop the ridge, Prince Dabulamanzi watched as another of his royal homesteads was consumed in fire and smoke. He rested the butt of his rifle on the ground, his hands clutching the hot barrel through a rag. He seethed in fury at this latest indignity, made worse by his complete impotence to exact any sort of retribution against the invaders. The English were acting recklessly, but with the warriors from the southern *impi* having mostly scattered back to their homes, Dabulamanzi simply did not have an army with which to fight them.

"My prince," a voice said behind him.

He turned to see a young warrior.

His face was flushed and sweaty, having run a great distance. "The English are abandoning Eshowe."

Though elated by this news, Dabulamanzi supressed his feelings. "Then we will finish what our king started when he expelled those cursed missionaries. Let us destroy any last remnants of their god in the land of the Zulu!"

It took the entire morning for No. 1 Column to make ready to depart. They did not even leave Eshowe until almost noon. Lord

Chelmsford and the flying column followed about an hour after the trail wagon of Pearson's force disappeared from view. His lordship had directed the columns to first make for Gingindlovu; however, when the lead elements of the flying column came across the rear guard of Pearson's force trying to deal with a wagon that had overturned and was now blocking the road, the general ordered No. 1 Column to instead head straight for Lower Drift. This led to some consternation amongst the 99th and Buffs companies, not being able to reunite with their mates. Pearson reassured Colonels Parnell and Welman that their errant troops would be sent back to Lower Drift once the flying column relieved them at Gingindlovu.

As the relief force made its way around the wrecked wagon, one of Chelmsford's staff officers pointed behind him. "My lord, smoke rises from Eshowe."

"Dash it all, we should have booby-trapped the place," Colonel Pemberton grumbled.

His lordship said nothing. It was no surprise the Zulus would descend upon the fort once it was abandoned. They were doubtless burning everything that remained of the old mission station as a means of retribution against the invaders. This was the second time Lord Chelmsford had crossed the border into Zululand with an army. And for the second time, he was retreating back to Natal.

Chapter XLVI: We Have Achieved Nothing

Fort Pearson, Lower Drift
7 April 1879
***

The return to Gingindlovu had been, at times, a chaotic mess. When they finally reached the site of their victory over the Zulus, the stench was appalling; a pungent concoction of rotted grass and mealies from the laager, coupled with the rotting bodies of numerous enemy warriors scattered about the area, hidden in the grass, and behind thickets of brush. With the excitement of battle now just a memory, the heat and utter tedium of the strenuous march took its toll on the long column of imperial soldiers. Many collapsed from heat exhaustion. Those who could still walk did so in a mental fog of delirium.

On the second day of their journey, they reached the old battle site at Inyezane. Though just under eleven weeks had passed, it felt like a lifetime ago for those who'd fought the Zulus on the morning of the 22nd of January 1879. Captain Arthur Gelston, the paymaster from 2/3rd Buffs who carved an ornate wooden cross with the names of the fallen, was at last able to erect his memorial to those who gave their lives during the opening battle of the coastal campaign.

The sight of Fort Tenedos and the Thukela River was greeted with much excitement by the men of No. 1 Column. They were, at last, re-joined by the companies from the 99th and 2/3rd Buffs who'd been left at Gingindlovu.

On the morning of the 8th of April, H Company, 2/3rd Buffs stood in parade formation before their officer commanding. It was another cloudless day, and the gathered redcoats dared hope that perhaps the torrential rainfalls were finally over for the year. They still had the South African heat to contend with, however. During the middle of winter, it was as hot as a July day back home in Britain. Even after three years in Natal, most of the men had yet to truly adjust to the heat, and especially the extreme humidity, from being so close to the Indian Ocean.

On this particular morning, Lieutenant Martin ordered the company to remain on parade after the section leaders finished morning inspection.

"Company, 'shun'!" Colour Sergeant Bennet bellowed, as nearly ninety pairs of boots came together. He then turned and saluted his officer commanding before stepping off and standing next to Lieutenant Backhouse, who stood a step behind Martin and two paces to his left.

"Lance Sergeant Robert Anderson, come forward," the officer commanding said.

Rob briskly made his way over to the lieutenant and stood before him at attention. Lieutenant Backhouse handed Martin a trio of gold chevrons.

Colour Sergeant Bennet read from a parchment he pulled from his breast pocket. *"By order of Lieutenant Colonel Parnell, commanding officer, 2nd Battalion of the 3rd Regiment of Foot; for exemplary conduct and cool-headed leadership in the face of the enemy, and having proven himself worthy of greater responsibility, Lance Sergeant Robert James Anderson is hereby promoted to the rank of sergeant."*

Lieutenant Martin then handed the chevrons to Anderson and clasped his hand, stating a few quiet words of congratulations. Both men then came to attention and exchanged salutes. As Rob quick-stepped back to his place in formation, the officer commanding led H Company in a round of applause. Perhaps proudest of all was David Fredericks. Anderson had served as his assistant after the battalion's arrival in South Africa. He'd watched the young soldier grow as both a man and a leader. It was truly fitting that Rob was now his peer rather than his subordinate.

That evening, David sat along the grassy slope nearest the ponts. Most of his men were having their supper, while he penned a despatch he needed to submit to Lieutenant Martin. As he finished and signed his name, he was joined by Lance Corporal James Monroe.

"You sent for me, sergeant?"

David said nothing but signalled for his acting assistant to sit next to him. He handed the young man a single sheet of parchment. "I wanted you to see this, before I submit it to our officer commanding."

James' expression beamed as he read the despatch.

To Lieutenant Martin, Officer Commanding, H Company, 2/3ʳᵈ Regiment

Sir,

It is with distinct pleasure that I offer my recommendation that Lance Corporal James Monroe be advanced to full Corporal. Since coming to H Company, he has served as one of the battalion's highest skilled marksmen, as well as the company's primary musketry instructor. Following Corporal Anderson's advancement to section leader, Lance Corporal Monroe took over the duties of assistant section leader without hesitation or complaint. His commitment to the morale, as well as discipline of his soldiers has been exemplary. He is ready to assume these responsibilities on a permanent basis, and I therefore request your endorsement of this recommendation.

David Fredericks, Sergeant

"I am honoured that you think me ready," Monroe said, practically stammering.

David gave a wry grin. "Well, there isn't anyone else in the section that I could think of to replace Anderson, now that his promotion has been made permanent."

"How exactly did that happen?" James asked. "I thought Sergeant Milne still held the billet, even though he's running ponts up at Rorke's Drift."

"It's not Milne that Anderson is replacing, it's Sergeant Davies," David explained. "Did you not notice him packing up all his kit after morning parade? He's headed back to Blighty; decided to call it a day and retire after twenty-two years with the Colours."

"Blimey, I thought for certain he'd want to stay and finish the war out," James speculated.

"Oh, it crossed his mind. But having a Zulu musket ball clip the side of his helmet at Gingindlovu gave him second thoughts. With Anderson already acting as a section leader, Mister Martin saw fit to promote him to full sergeant and make his position permanent. Funny thing, he was fresh out of his mum's womb when Davies first joined the ranks."

"Yes, I often forget that Rob is only three years older than me."

David then said, "And I often forget that he is four years *younger* than I am." The two men shared a laugh before the sergeant added, "Won't surprise me if he's our sergeant major by the time he's thirty."

The dying was not yet over for the No. 1 Column and their relief. On the night before the flying column reached Gingindlovu, anxious sentries opened fire on returning scouts from John Dunn's detachment. A brawl ensued with several soldiers from the 60th Rifles bayoneting their own men. Five green-jackets and eight of Dunn's scouts were injured during the chaos, with one of the African's dying soon after. Enraged and embarrassed, Lord Chelmsford ordered that the sergeant who gave the order to open fire be court-martialled.

An even greater tragedy struck on the morning of 7 April. Lieutenant Colonel Francis Northey breathed his last. Though his wound had not at first appeared too serious, internal bleeding took its toll with the surgeons unable to stop it. Northey had been very popular, both within the officers' mess, as well as with the men in the ranks. His death struck the men of 3/60th Rifles hard, many unashamedly shedding tears as his eulogy was read. And yet, it would be another week before the last casualty from the Battle of Gingindlovu departed this life. Sergeant Douglas McIntyre of the 91st Highlanders, who'd been shot in the left eye, died while in a hospital tent at Stanger on the 15th of April. Captain Robert Lyttle would receive word of his sergeant's demise two weeks later. For the men of the relief column, the tedium of garrison life at their cramped camp, which they established between Gingindlovu and Lower Drift, continued. They watched for Zulu incursions and waited for Lord Chelmsford to despatch new orders to commence hostilities against the Zulus once more.

Having at last reached the Thukela, Lord Chelmsford left orders for Colonel Pearson. He held seniority over Pemberton and, therefore, remained in overall command. There were no feelings of triumph, however. Despite having saved No. 1 Column and routed the Zulu force at Gingindlovu, Lord Chelmsford was in anything but a celebratory mood. Nearly three months had passed since the initial invasion. Given his experiences in fighting the Xhosa the previous year, he fully expected to have routed the Zulus, clapped King Cetshwayo in chains, and been back in London celebrating his triumph by this time. Instead, he and the High Commissioner, Sir Henry Bartle-Frere, still had recriminations to face for having started an unsanctioned war. Nearly 1,500 British soldiers, settler volunteers, and African allies had died so far. The stronghold at Eshowe, a marvel of engineering genius designed by the ailing Captain Warren Wynne, had to be abandoned. A squalid camp that now housed the three regular battalions from the relief column was all that remained of the British presence in Zululand. In short, the entire invasion had been a catastrophic failure, and Lord Chelmsford had nothing to show for the loss of men, material, and treasure.

Regardless of whatever reproaches awaited him, his lordship turned his attention to the greater strategic picture. The majority of reinforcements sent so far from London were currently gathered around Lower Drift. Rorke's Drift was held only by the shattered remnants of No. 3 Column and Middle Drift defended by a single battalion of NNC warriors. And as autumn slowly turned into winter, the lands would dry up and the rivers fall. This meant the Thukela and uMzinyathi Rivers would become far less of a natural barrier than they currently were. What's more, given the state of the few dirt roads that existed, the distance between each of the major focal points became even more pronounced. Simply put, Chelmsford's forces could not be everywhere at once.

"Had Durnford not cost me the centre column at Isandlwana, Cetshwayo would be in chains, and we'd be on our way back to London in triumph," he lamented candidly to Crealock. The GOC then scowled and shook his head. "How did it come to this? We are now back to where we started...worse, in fact. With Colonel Glyn's column shattered and Durnford's consigned to oblivion, much of the border between the Zulu Kingdom and Natal is essentially undefended. And while we've been slogging our way along the coast to extricate Pearson, Colonel Wood has been left on his own."

"Yes, and his No. 4 Column is two hundred miles from here," Crealock noted.

Both men knew that Gingindlovu had proved nothing. The enemy he faced had not been the same as the ones who routed Durnford and Pulleine. Nor did they have any real numerical advantage over the relief column. As best as anyone could guess, there had been, at most, 10,000 Zulu warriors at Gingindlovu against 5,500 British soldiers and allied Africans. The main *impi* was still out there, and he would have to face them sooner or later.

There was little the GOC could do now but return to Pietermaritzburg and wait for the remaining reinforcements to arrive. So long as Colonel Wood managed to keep the Zulus distracted near Khambula, and provided the remnants of Colonel Glyn's column held onto Rorke's Drift, that would give Chelmsford enough time to reorganise and launch a second invasion of the Zulu Kingdom. He was more determined than ever to finish this war before another senior general could replace him.

With the decisive victory at Gingindlovu, the Siege of Eshowe came to an end. For David Courtney of the Royal Engineers, there was little cause for celebration. The journey back to Lower Drift had taken its toll on men and beasts alike. No sooner had they reached the Natal bank than a plethora of tasks required his attention. There was the matter of rations and ammunition resupplies to request, as well as inventory of all of No. 2 Field Company's wagons, engineering tools, and soldiers' kit. Courtney was thankful to have Lieutenant Willock and Colour Sergeant Smith to assist him. Lord Chelmsford had ordered his other subaltern, Thomas Main, down to Durban to await the arrival of additional engineer assets.

There was also the daily sick list to review. Each morning and evening he made his way to the hospital tent. Surgeon-Major Tarrant and Surgeon Norbury worked tirelessly to care for the numerous invalids in the column. Courtney could only hope that the score of sappers still stricken with fever and dysentery would eventually recover. There was one, however, he feared would never leave South Africa.

David removed his helmet, as he stepped into the hospital tent Surgeon Norbury had erected outside Fort Pearson. The sides were rolled up, a breeze blowing in off the river. His hope was that a bit of fresh air would help those still lingering from illness and infirmity.

Courtney did his best to stay out of the way of the doctor and his orderlies. He made his way over to where his friend and officer commanding lay. Warren Wynne had scarcely opened his eyes in nearly a week, and David knew he would never recover. His body had wasted away, and his fever refused to break. It made the despatch the officer clutched in his hand even more heart-breaking.

"Well, the fighting's over," he said, unsure if Warren could hear or understand him. "The general and the redcoats gave the Zulus a sound thrashing. The garrison has been relieved, and we're now back at Lower Drift, where it all began." He paused and took a few breaths to compose himself. He then held up the sheaf of papers. "I was summoned by one of the GOC's staff officers. He gave me this. It's my orders, promoting me to captain. There's a despatch from Colonel Pearson, as well, which his lordship has endorsed. I'll read it to you. *For exemplary service and superior conduct in the discharging of his duties, it is recommended that Captain Warren Richard Colvin Wynne be brevetted to the rank of major.* I thought you might like that."

His eyes wet with emotion, Captain David Courtney was not sure if his mind was playing tricks on him. He thought he saw Warren smile for the briefest of moments. There was a change in his breathing, and he gasped a lungful of air for the first time in weeks before relapsing into raspy, laboured breathing once more. What David had not the heart to say, was that Chelmsford made him acting officer commanding of No. 2 Field Company, with the understanding that this position would likely become permanent in the near future.

He then heard *'Captain Courtney!'* called from outside the tent. Letting out a sigh, he donned his helmet once more. Swallowing his emotions, he came to attention and saluted.

"Sleep well, sir."

Appendix A: The Legacy of Warren Wynne and the No. 1 Column

Captain Warren Wynne died on his thirty-sixth birthday, 9 April 1879. With no chaplain available, Captain David Courtney took it upon himself to oversee the funeral service. So great was his grief, he struggled to finish the eulogy without breaking down in tears. Wynne was buried at Euphorbia Hill near Fort Pearson. A large stone cross was erected over his grave. Sadly it was dismantled in recent years, and the grave is in a terrible state of disrepair.

Warren's exemplary service, as well as his brevet to major, was posthumously acknowledged a year later in *The London Gazette*, dated 5 May 1880:

Captain Warren Richard Colvin Wynne, Royal Engineers, to be Major, in recognition of his distinguished services during the Zulu campaign of 1878-1879. Dated 2nd April 1879. Since deceased.

His father, John, undoubtedly heartbroken by the loss of his son, died four years later at the age of eighty-five. Lucy Wynne never remarried, living an extremely long life as a widow before passing away in 1946 at the age of ninety-four. All three of their sons lived very long lives, well into their eighties or nineties. The middle son, Harry, followed Warren into the Army. He served during the Great War, rising to the rank of lieutenant colonel in the Royal Artillery.

Of all the officers and men of the No. 1 Column, it was Warren Wynne who Colonel Pearson singled out for praise, following the relief at Eshowe:

'I have been given credit for my skill in rendering our fort at Eshowe impregnable, but it was made so by Captain Wynne, my Commanding Engineer, and his brother officers, under whose directions we all worked. Captain Wynne died of an illness brought on by exposure, and by unflinchingly remaining at his duty when almost incapable of performing it.'

Securing Wynne's legacy was the detailed diary he kept, as well as all the letters he sent to his wife and family. The last of these spoke candidly of the fever that had wracked his body and ruined his previously robust health. In 1880, Lucy Wynne had the diary and letters compiled into a book. Just a few copies were published for private circulation amongst family. In the introduction, she wrote an emotional tribute to her late husband, dedicating the compiled work to their sons. In 1988, editor Howard Whitehouse, at the request of Paddy Griffith Associates, compiled the diary, as well as all of Wynne's letters, into a book which he called *The Widow-Making War: The Life and Death of a British Officer in Zululand, 1879*. The dedication from Lucy Wynne served as the preface, while Whitehouse added many of his own clarifying notes in between the diary entries and letters. Warren Wynne's extreme attention to detail is evident in the pages, and *Widow-Making War* is easily the most comprehensive first-hand look at the harrowing feats of the No. 1 Column, and quite possibly of the entire war.

The grave of Captain Warren Wynne
Left image was taken in the early 1990s by Ian Knight, the right photograph by
the author in 2017

Aside from Colonel Charles Pearson, Captain Warren Wynne is among the few whose name is remembered from the Siege of Eshowe. Most of the rest are simply overlooked, even in circles where historians and enthusiasts still discuss and analyse the Anglo-Zulu War. Following the siege, No. 1 Column was almost immediately forgotten. There would be no awards for valour; the survivors having to content themselves with the eventual awarding of the South African Campaign Medal for their heroism and sacrifice.

Appendix B: Historical Requiem – The Survivors of Eshowe

Colonel Charles Pearson was relegated to a brigade command during the reorganisation for the second invasion, having been superseded by the recently arrived Major General Henry Crealock. This was just as well, as Pearson's health had suffered greatly during the Siege of Eshowe, and he was invalided home in June. He was given a hero's welcome, being presented with an ornate sword by the citizens of his native Yeovil in Somerset, England. He was personally knighted by Her Majesty, who appointed him as a *Knight Commander of the Most Distinguished Order of Saint Michael and Saint George* (KCMG). He was further named a Companion of the Bath.

From 1880 to 1884 he served as Commander of the Royal Victoria Hospital at Netley, where many of the Zulu War's wounded veterans were treated, including Private Frederick Hitch, VC. During this tenure he was promoted to major general. In 1885, he was dispatched to the West Indies as commander of all British Forces in the Caribbean, where he remained for the next six years.

Upon his return to England he was promoted to lieutenant general, retiring four years later in 1895. In December 1899, he travelled to Southampton to see off his former battalion, 2/3rd Buffs, as they departed once more for South Africa; this time to fight the Boers. Lieutenant General Sir Charles Knight Pearson, KCMG, CB, died in London on 2 October 1909 at the age of seventy-five.

Lieutenant Colonel Henry Parnell became the 4th Baron Congleton in 1883 following the death of his elder brother, John, the 3rd Baron Congleton, who died without male issue. He eventually rose to the rank of major general, and in 1895 assumed command of the Malta Infantry Brigade. He would hold this post of seven years until his retirement in 1902.

Major General Henry Parnell, Baron Congleton died in 1906 at the age of sixty-seven. His eldest son, Harry, was just sixteen when he succeeded his father as the 5th Baron. Harry was killed eight years later during the opening weeks of the Great War, with the barony passing to his younger brother, John. Most recently, John Patrick Christian Parnell became the 9th Baron Congleton in 2015. He is the great-great grandson of Major General Henry Parnell.

Captain Percy Barrow was given command of all mounted troops in the First Division during the second invasion of the Zulu Kingdom, while also appointed Assistant Adjutant General. In 1880, he was named aide-de-camp for the Aldershot Division, though he did briefly return to Southern Africa the following year.

Following his return to Aldershot in 1882, he was assigned to General Sir Garnet Wolseley's Egypt expedition, where he was once again given commanded of mounted infantry troops. The following year he was promoted to lieutenant colonel and assumed command of his 19th Hussars.

On 29 February 1884, Lieutenant Colonel Barrow was badly wounded at the Battle of El Teb, Sudan, when his horse was shot out from under him and he was surrounded by Mahdist warriors. He was only saved from certain death by a senior non-commissioned officer, Quartermaster Sergeant William Marshall, who earned the Victoria Cross for saving Barrow's life, was later commissioned, and eventually retired as a lieutenant colonel.

Percy Barrow was soon after named Colonel of the 19th Hussars. However, his injuries would continue to plague him. Two years later, after being injured during a sporting contest, he fell ill, having reopened his old wounds. Colonel Percy Barrow, CB died on 13 January 1886 at the age of thirty-seven.

Captain Arthur Fitzroy Hart was appointed brigade major for the 2nd Brigade of the 1st Division during the army's reorganisation, in preparation for the renewed invasion of Zululand. In 1881, he served as Deputy Acting Adjutant and Quartermaster General under Brigadier General Wood during the First Boer War. The following year, he was appointed to the Intelligence Department during General Wolseley's Egyptian campaign. He was wounded at Kassassin, yet still took part in the Battle of Tel-el-Kebir. He was subsequently promoted to lieutenant colonel.

From 1891 to 1895, Lieutenant Colonel Hart commanded the 1st Battalion, East Surreys in India, during which time he was promoted to full colonel. He spent the next four years on Home Service in both Aldershot and Belfast, Ireland. He returned to South Africa in 1899 as a major general in command of the Irish Brigade during the Second Boer War. While noted for his personal bravery, Major General Hart's tactics and strategy were terribly outdated, with the advent of smokeless powder and magazine-fed rifles. He was lambasted by his own troops and blamed for excessive casualties during the Battle of Colenso. He did, however, redeem himself when sent to the Orange Free State, where he decisively defeated the Boers laying siege to Wepener.

Following the British Empire's final victory over the Boers, Major General Hart returned to Britain in 1902. In an interesting turn, having been married since 1868 and the father of four now-grown children, he added his wife's maiden name of Synnot to his own, becoming Arthur Fitzroy Hart-Synnot by Royal License. Two years later, he retired from the Army. Major General Arthur Fitzroy Hart-Synnot died on 20 April 1910 at the age of sixty-six.

Captain Charles Shervinton served with the First Division during the second invasion of the Zulu Kingdom. For his daring rescue of Private Brooks, he was recommended for the Victoria Cross. However, as neither Lord Chelmsford nor his eventual replacement, Sir Garnet Wolseley, would endorse the recommendation, Shervinton's gallantry was left unrecognised.

Following the war, his younger brother, Tom, who had served with him, died of disease in February 1880 at the age of twenty-one. Charles would remain in Southern Africa for a time, leading a troop with the Cape Mounted Rifles during the Basuto Gun War. He later made his way to Madagascar, where the Merina Kingdom was in constant struggle against French colonial forces. Shervinton served as a volunteer officer with the Malagasy forces, though they were eventually defeated. The French confiscated all his lands, leaving him impoverished.

By the time he returned to England in 1895, having spent nearly twenty years abroad, he was in very poor health and disillusioned after his experiences in Madagascar. Captain Charles Shervinton took his own life in April 1898 at the age of forty-five. He'd sent a rather cryptic telegram to his father, saying 'It's all up.' His father rushed to the hotel he was staying at, only to find him dead with a gunshot wound to the temple, and the pistol still in his hand. Though Charles had married in 1884, it is unknown if he ever had children.

Surgeon Henry Frederick Norbury was *mentioned in despatches* for his efforts in saving the lives of many sick and wounded during the Siege of Eshowe. He was subsequently promoted to fleet surgeon and named a Companion of the Bath (CB). Rather than returning to the HMS Active, his promotion to fleet surgeon saw him placed in charge of the Royal Naval Hospital at the Cape of Good Hope; a post he would hold for three years. He subsequently returned to England and was placed in charge of the Royal Naval Hospital, Stonehouse in Plymouth. He held various postings over the next twenty years, mostly in Plymouth. In 1898, he was appointed Director-General of the Medical Department of the Royal Navy.

Highly respected for his skills in medicine, Henry Norbury received numerous awards and honours during his lifetime, including Knight of Grace of the Order of St John of Jerusalem, and was elevated to Knight Commander of the Batch (KCB) during Queen Victoria's Diamond Jubilee in 1897. His wife, Juliet, died in 1909 after thirty-seven years of marriage. Eight years later, he married Edith Mary Burke. Fleet Surgeon Sir Henry Frederick Norbury, KCB died in Southeast London on 10 December 1925 at the age of eighty-six.

Reverend Robert Robertson returned to his old mission at kwaMagwaza, only to find it had been burned to the ground by the Zulus. While the ending of the war had allowed him to expand his missionary work, the Zulu civil war between Dinuzulu and Zibhebhu in 1884 forced Robertson to flee the region. He later assisted in the building of various churches throughout the region, notably at eThalaneni and Nhlwati near the Lebombo Mountains. He died on 9 November 1897 at the age of sixty-seven. He never married nor had children. In his will, Reverend Robertson asked that he be buried wearing his pastoral vestments, with his body wrapped in the British Union Flag.

Appendix C: List of Casualties, the Eshowe Campaign

The following gave their lives during the Battles of Inyezane and Gingindlovu, as well as the Siege of Eshowe

The Battle of Inyezane:

Lieutenant James Raines
Lieutenant Gustav Plattner
Sergeant Emil Unger
Sergeant Oscar Hydenburg (died of wounds)
Corporal Wilhelm Lieper
Corporal Edward Miller
Corporal Carl Goesch
Private John Bough
Private William Dunne (died of wounds)
Private James Kelleher
Five unnamed warriors of the 1/2nd NNC

The Siege of Eshowe:

Captain Warren Wynne (died after the relief, posthumously brevetted to major)
Captain Henry Williams
Lieutenant Arthur Davison
Lieutenant George Evelyn
Midshipman Lewis Coker
Lance Corporal Thomas Taylor
Private William Barber
Private Charles Coombes
Private William Dunne
Private Walter Kent
Private William Knee
Private Arthur Kingston
Private Brian Lewis
Private William McLeod
Private James Monk (died after the relief)
Private Edward Oakley

Private John Paul
Private Phillip Roden
Private James Shields
Private James Stack
Private Alex Tarrant
Private William Tubb
Private Thomas Venn
Artificer James Moore
Leading Seaman James Radford
Able Seaman Alex Smith
Marine William Stagg
Drummer Arthur Mortimer

*Note: Most of those who died during the Siege of Eshowe succumbed to disease rather than enemy action

The Battle of Gingindlovu:

Lieutenant Colonel Francis Northey (died of wounds)
Lieutenant George Johnson
Sergeant Douglas McIntyre (died of wounds)
Private Patrick Armstrong (died of wounds)
Private George Baker (died of wounds)
Private John Lawrence
Private Richard Marshall
Private Thomas Perkins (died of wounds)
Private James Pratt
Private John Smith
Five unnamed warriors from No. 4 and No. 5 Battalion, NNC
One unnamed warrior from John Dunn's detachment

In addition to those killed, died of wounds, or succumbed to disease, an additional 73 soldiers were wounded during the campaign.

Estimates of Zulu losses are roughly 350 killed at Inyezane, with at least another 1000 slain during the Battle of Gingindlovu. As fighting was minimal and sporadic during the Siege of Eshowe, Zulu losses are not known with any certainty.

The cemeteries at Eshowe and Fort Pearson today

Appendix D: A Fictional Character's Historical Story

When writing about actual historical events, I try to include as many historical characters as possible, basing their personalities on what we know about them. But in order to fill in the gaps of a novel, I am compelled to include many fictitious characters, based around actions and traits that would have been common during the Victorian Era. Sergeant David Fredericks is one such character. He was 'born' through research conducted into who the majority of men were that chose a life in Queen Victoria's Army. While officers came from the landed gentry, the enlisted ranks were overwhelmingly born into the poorest classes of society.

An interesting story is no doubt waiting to be told about the further exploits of 2nd Battalion, 3rd Regiment of Foot (The Buffs). In my story, David hopes to return to Britain after the war is over, that he might find his brother and sister again. However, if he chose to make the Army a career, he would not see England again for another twelve years. In 1880, after four years in Southern Africa, 2/3rd Buffs was sent first to Singapore, then Hong Kong where they remained until 1891 when the battalion was finally rotated home to Aldershot, before being posted to Ireland.

During this time, David would have continued through his career; if ambitious and talented enough, progressing up through the NCO ranks, perhaps even becoming the battalion's sergeant major. The chance of his earning a commission, however, was negligible at best. Despite the abolition of commission purchase in 1871, one still required a certain level of wealth, education, and social class to become an officer. Frank Bourne, the colour sergeant of B Company, 2/24th at Rorke's Drift, was the rare exception of an enlisted soldier eventually commissioning. Even then, Bourne came from the middle-class and was well educated before joining the Army. Though offered a direct commission after Rorke's Drift, he needed to wait another eleven years until he sorted the 'wealth' issue and could afford to become an officer.

Another interesting thought is David's son, who by 1891 would be a grown man, roughly nineteen years of age. Perhaps by this time he would have a few younger siblings; though the number of children in soldier families varied considerably. Officers tended to marry much later in life, averaging fewer children and, in many cases, none. Having spent his youth with his parents abroad, young David would have no memory of Britain and only the faintest ones of Southern Africa. It's entirely possible that he would follow his father into the Army, as was common among soldier-sons. All three of Garrison Sergeant Major Henry Gallagher's sons served careers in Her Majesty's Armed Forces, as did four sons of Colour Sergeant Anthony Booth, VC. However, if the red jacket did not suit young David, the British Empire was at the height of its power, covering nearly one-third of the globe. This meant there was certainly no lack of possibilities of adventure for ambitious young men, especially those already living in the Far East.

It should be noted that life expectancy was relatively short during the late 19th century, especially by modern standards. Diseases contracted on Foreign Service claimed infinitely more British soldiers than any enemy weapons of war. Major Gonville Bromhead, VC, the famous commander of B Company, 2/24th at Rorke's Drift, immortalised by Sir Michael Caine in the film, *Zulu*, was just forty-five when he died of typhoid fever while stationed in India. While many like David Fredericks joined the Colours to escape poverty and the factories, life on campaign was extremely harsh. It was difficult for anyone, soldier or civilian outside of the gentry class, to maintain proper nutrition. Hence, people in Victorian times tended to be shorter than today. Water was unfiltered, and one can only guess what sort of micro-organisms lived in the rivers and lakes where redcoats filled their water bottles. Another factor that drastically affected life expectancy was widespread tobacco use. In Victorian times, and even through much of the 20th century, it seemed like almost everyone smoked. Soldiers who abstained, trying to salvage their teeth and lungs, were still subjected to its ill effects. Barracks blocks, crowded tents on campaign, and public buildings back home were filled with people lighting up their cigars and pipes. Tuberculosis ran rampant, killing young and old alike. Retired Sergeant Joseph Windridge, a survivor of Rorke's Drift, lost six of his children over the course of two weeks due to acute tuberculosis. Many of the most famous Anglo-Zulu War veterans—the defenders of Rorke's Drift—died in their late forties to mid-fifties, often from lung or heart issues. There were exceptions, of course. Sergeant George Smith lived to eighty-five, Brigade-Surgeon James Reynolds, VC, eighty-eight, while Lieutenant Colonel Frank Bourne reached ninety-one.

As for David Fredericks, he would be close to retirement eligibility by the time he and Lillian returned to England. So long as he remained injury and illness-free, he could remain with the Colours for a few more years. Albeit, it seems most career NCOs chose to leave the Army at between twenty and twenty-five years of service. Where a soldier retired varied, and it wasn't always near where they'd been raised. GSM Henry Gallagher was born and raised in Tipperary and maintained a strong connection to his native Ireland. Yet when he retired, he and his wife settled near Portsmouth Harbour. David and Lillian Fredericks could have returned to Kent and might even have found David's younger siblings, provided they had not succumbed to injury or disease and still lived in the county. How well David and Lillian lived was firstly dependent on his pension from the Army. If he'd reached quartermaster sergeant or sergeant major, he could expect to live quite comfortably. Yet even if he never rose above sergeant, they would still fair far better than during their impoverished youth. If he continued his education, as some soldiers managed during their careers, he could find a decent middle-class job after leaving the Colours. Sergeant George Smith, another Rorke's Drift veteran, earned a second-class education certificate during his career and made a fine living working for an estate agent after his retirement.

Sergeant David Fredericks is essentially a composite of many different persons who lived, or could have lived, during the Victorian Era. Whether he died of illness in the aftermath of the Anglo-Zulu War or retired a sergeant major and lived a long and happy life well into old age, he represents an era of young men who joined the Colours to escape poverty and who made their mark on the world, for better or worse, as redcoats of the British Empire.

Appendix E: Glossary of Terms

Note: All terms from the isiZulu language will appear in italics

Assegai – Term used to describe a Zulu spear, though it does not appear in the isiZulu language. Their actual name for the short stabbing spear is *iklwa*. Assegais usually referred to the throwing spears, though it was often used to describe all spears carried by the Zulus.

Battalion – British Army unit designation, consisting of eight line companies plus battalion staff officers. Commanded by a lieutenant colonel, with the sergeant major as the senior non-commissioned officer.

Boer – From the Dutch term meaning 'farmer', refers to all Dutch-speaking settlers in South Africa.

Bombardier – An artilleryman, roughly equivalent to an infantry lance corporal, except a bombardier was rated as a full non-commissioned officer, while a lance corporal was not. They wore a single gold chevron on their right shoulder.

Boy – British army rank given to those who were underage. The minimum age was fourteen, and they served as buglers, bandsmen, and officers' servants. Upon reaching the age of eighteen, they were given the option of enlisting onto the roles as a private. Contrary to the myths depicted in both art and film, the youngest boy at Isandlwana was sixteen.

Brevet – A temporary promotion given to officers who were filling a billet above their substantive rank, as well a reward to those who performed exceptional service. Though they would wear the insignia and be addressed by their brevet rank, they were still paid at their substantive grade and were always subordinate to substantive officers of the same rank. Example: Henry Pulleine was a brevet lieutenant colonel. Yet he was still paid as a major and was subordinate to Antony Durnford, who was a substantive lieutenant colonel.

Captain – Commissioned officer, just above lieutenant and below major. Most often given command of line companies, and in some cases used as battalion staff officers.

Colonel – A senior commissioned officer, just above lieutenant colonel and below brigadier general. Most often used as staff officers at the highest levels or in command of columns consisting of multiple battalions.

Colour Sergeant – The senior non-commissioned officer within a company, responsible for day-to-day training, drill, discipline, and logistics. He was the equivalent to a modern Company Sergeant Major (British Army) or First Sergeant (U.S. Army). He wore an insignia of three gold chevrons, with two crossed flags and a crown above, on his right shoulder.

Company – British Army unit consisting of up to a hundred soldiers including officers and other ranks. Commanded by a captain with a colour sergeant as the senior non-commissioned officer. Note: Companies on overseas service were notoriously understrength, with seventy to eighty total soldiers being the norm.

Corporal – First of the non-commissioned officer ranks in the British Army. They acted as assistants to the sergeants and were sometimes given command of their own sections or specialty units, such as company sharp-shooters. They wore two white chevrons on their right shoulder.

Drift – A natural river crossing, more commonly known as a 'ford' in modern times.

Hlomula – Literally meaning 'beautify', it was the ritual where Zulus would repeatedly stab a fallen enemy even after they were dead. Differing in meaning from the process of disembowelling, which was meant to free the trapped spirits, *hlomula* was viewed as a sign of respect towards a dangerous and worthy foe.

Ibutho **(plural *amabutho*)** – A term used to describe a Zulu regiment. Each *ibutho* was age-based, with the king raising new regiments around the time young Zulu males turned seventeen to twenty, based on the needs of the kingdom. They served as the chief labour force at the king's pleasure, in addition to their military responsibilities in defence of the kingdom. Zulu men were considered youths until they could marry, usually around the age of thirty. At which time, and with the king's permission, they would take wives-often marrying en mass together-and be allowed to take charge of their own households. Married regiments were exempt from labour and menial details and were only assembled during times of war or national emergency.

Impi – The name given to a large Zulu army consisting of numerous *amabutho*.

Induna (plural *izinduna*) – An officer within the ibutho selected by his peers. Most often given charge of roughly a hundred warriors, they were roughly the equivalent to a captain in the British Army.

Inkosi (plural *amakhosi*) – A Zulu chieftain, sometimes referred to as a 'baron' by the British, for their titles came by birth right rather than appointment. In war, they commanded the *amabutho*, with the older and more experienced *amakhosi* placed in charge of the younger regiments.

Inyanga (plural *izinyanga*) – Diviners, also derogatorily referred to by Europeans as 'witchdoctors'. They oversaw all spiritual ceremonies for the Zulu *impi*, as well as serving as herbalists and healers.

Iqawe (plural *abaqawe*) – Zulu warriors of great renown who had shown extreme bravery and prowess in battle. Those elevated to the *abaqawe* were regarded as the most valiant heroes of the Zulu Kingdom.

Koppie – Comes from the Dutch term, 'kop', which literally means 'head'. It is used to describe a small, stony hill that stands out on an otherwise flat landscape.

Kraal – Though not a Zulu term, it came to describe local African homesteads. Typically, they consisted of several huts surrounding a central cattle pen. Kraals that belonged to the nobles of the *amakhosi* could hold dozens or even hundreds of huts, with thousands of residents. The Royal Kraal at Ulundi is said to have had several thousand huts with numerous cattle pens and arena pits.

Laager – A term used by the Dutch to describe encircling wagons as a means of defence. Can also be used to describe temporary wood or stone fortifications.

Lance Corporal – An uncommon British Army rank just above private. Though not officially a non-commissioned officer (a status which changed in 1961), they are often given leadership responsibilities and used to assist the sergeants and corporals. They wore a single white chevron on their right shoulder.

Lance Sergeant – Another uncommon British Army rank, lance sergeants were corporals who were either temporarily appointed to a sergeant's billet, or who had displayed great leadership potential and were waiting for promotion to full sergeant. They wore three white chevrons on the right shoulder.

Lieutenant – Junior commissioned officer, most often used as a subaltern within a company or staff officer at the battalion. Because promotions were so painfully slow during most of the Victorian Era, they tended to vary considerably in age, with older lieutenants often given command of companies while waiting for an eventual promotion to captain. *Note: While the U.S. Armed Forces pronounce the rank as it is spelled "lew-tenant", in British and Commonwealth Forces it is pronounced "left-tenant".*

Lieutenant Colonel – A commissioned officer above major and below colonel, it is the rank used by commanding officers at the battalion level.

Major – A commissioned officer above captain and below lieutenant colonel. Most often used as staff officers, there are two per battalion, each of whom can assume overall command if needed.

Ndabazitha – A Zulu term of reverence to their king, equivalent to 'your majesty'.

Nek – Refers to the lower ground between two high points. In modern times, this has been mostly replaced by the term 'saddle'.

Private – Most common rank in the British Army, outnumbering all other combined ranks approximately eight-to-one, and given to all other ranks upon their enlistment and completion of basic recruit training. In a company, between seventy and ninety of the soldiers will be privates. They wear no rank insignia.

Quartermaster – A commissioned officer, tasked with overseeing all supply and logistics for the battalion. Though the equivalent of a major, because they are in the Support Arms (i.e. Commissariat / Transport / Medical) they technically cannot give orders to combat soldiers (i.e. infantry, cavalry, artillery). They are, however, given the respect of their rank and referred to as 'sir' by subordinates.

Quartermaster Sergeant – A senior non-commissioned officer acting as chief assistant to the battalion quartermaster. Though nominally equivalent to a colour sergeant in terms of rank, they were senior due to their position being a regimental appointment. They wore four gold chevrons on the right sleeve.

Second Corporal – A junior non-commissioned officer within the Royal Engineers and Army Service Corps. They wore a single chevron on the right shoulder similar to infantry lance corporals. The difference being second corporals were billeted as NCOs, whereas lance corporals were not.

Sergeant – A non-commissioned officer given command of a section consisting of up to twenty soldiers. They answered directly to the colour sergeant and oversaw the daily drill, discipline, and welfare of their soldiers. Each sergeant usually had at least one corporal or lance corporal to assist him. They wore three gold chevrons on the right shoulder.

Sergeant Major – The senior non-commissioned officer within the battalion, he is responsible for the overall training, standards, and discipline. He also acts as a mentor to the younger lieutenants, even though they technically outrank him.

Subaltern – Term to describe the junior commissioned officers of a company, usually lieutenants, who were tasked with aiding the officer commanding. The senior subaltern would assume command in the captain's absence.

***Usuthu* (sometimes spelled *uSuthu* or *uZulu*)** – Refers to the uSuthu faction who fought for Cetshwayo during the Zulu civil war of 1856. Following Cetshwayo's victory, it became the battle cry of all Zulus who fought for the king.

Voorlooper – An African boy used to guide the teams of oxen and draught animals.

A Note of Thanks from the Author

Thank you for taking the time to read **Lost Souls: The Forgotten Heroes of Eshowe**. This is the first book in my series on the Anglo-Zulu War to take the reader beyond what we saw in the films, *Zulu* and *Zulu Dawn*. I have long felt that the heroism wrought by both British and Zulu alike in the southern theatre of the war deserved to be told with the same respect and admiration as the more famous battles at Isandlwana and Rorke's Drift. My intent with this series is to cover all theatres of the war, not just those that we know from film. The fourth volume of this series, titled, **Cruelty of Fate: The Battle for Khambula**, will therefore chronicle the story of the war in the north, whose events happened simultaneously as those depicted in **Lost Souls**.

Please know that I enjoy hearing from fans and readers, and can be found on the following social media sites:
Facebook: www.facebook.com/legionarybooks
Twitter: https://twitter.com/LegionaryBooks
Official website: Legionary Books.net

If you enjoyed **Lost Souls**, I would also be most grateful if you could post a review on Amazon.

To find more of my books, please visit my author's pages on Amazon and Amazon U.K.

Thank you again for taking the time to read **Lost Souls**. Until our next adventure!

Cheers!

James

For up-to-date information about upcoming books, as well as important people and dates in history, please subscribe to my monthly Mailing List (hosted through Mail Chimp), either through my website, or go to http://eepurl.com/dr8bgr

Further Reading / Bibliography:

Bibliography

Castle, Ian, and Ian Knight. 1992. *Zulu War 1879, Twilight of a Warrior Nation.* Oxford: Osprey.

Greaves, Adrian. 2005. *Crossing the Buffalo: The Zulu War of 1879.* London: Weidenfeld Military.

Guy, Jeff. 2002. *The View across the River: Harriette Colenso and the Zulu Struggle against Imperialism.* Charlottesville: University of Virginia Press.

Harford, Henry Charles. 2015 (first edition 1881). *The Zulu War Journal.* Barnsley: Pen and Sword Books.

Knight, Ian. 1990. *Brave Men's Blood: The Epic of the Zulu War, 1879.* London: Greenhill Books.

Knight, Ian. 2005. *British Fortifications in Zululand 1879.* Oxford: Osprey.

Knight, Ian, and Ian Castle. 1994. *Fearful Hard Times: The Siege and Relief of Eshowe, 1879.* London: Greenhill Books.

Laband, John. 1992. *Kingdom in Crisis: The Zulu Response to the British Invasion of 1879.* Barnsley: Pen and Sword.

Office, Horse Guards War. 1873. *Queen's Regulations and Orders for the Army - 1873.* London: Her Majesty's Stationary Office.

Wynne, Warren. 1995 (first published for private circulation, 1880, by Lucy Wynne). *A Widow-Making War: The Letters and Diaries of Major Warren Wynne, RE.* Edited by Howard Whitehouse. Nuneaton: Paddy Griffith Associates.

The story of the Anglo-Zulu War now follows the war the north, as the British No. 4 Column faces the very warriors who triumphed at Isandlwana

Cruelty of Fate: The Fight for Khambula

Made in United States
Troutdale, OR
06/26/2023

10803853R00343